BOEING 737

THE WORLD'S JETLINER

Captain Dan Dornseif

4880 Lower Valley Road • Atglen, PA 19310

Other Schiffer Books on Related Subjects:
The Boeing 787 Dreamliner, Claude G. Luisada and Steven D. Kimmell,
ISBN: 978-0-7643-4637-8
Jet City Rewind: Aviation History of Seattle and the Pacific Northwest, Timothy A. Nelson,
ISBN: 978-0-7643-5106-8

Designed by Justin Watkinson
Cover design by Molly Shields
Type set in BaseTwelveSerifBI/Akzidenz Grotesk/Minion Pro/Univers LT Std

ISBN: 978-0-7643-5325-3
Printed in China

Published by Schiffer Publishing, Ltd.
4880 Lower Valley Road
Atglen, PA 19310
Phone: (610) 593-1777; Fax: (610) 593-2002
E-mail: Info@schifferbooks.com
Web: www.schifferbooks.com

For our complete selection of fine books on this and related subjects,
please visit our website at www.schifferbooks.com. You may also write for a free catalog.

Schiffer Publishing's titles are available at special discounts for bulk purchases for sales
promotions or premiums. Special editions, including personalized covers, corporate imprints,
and excerpts, can be created in large quantities for special needs. For more information,
contact the publisher.

We are always looking for people to write books on new and related subjects.
If you have an idea for a book, please contact us at proposals@schifferbooks.com.

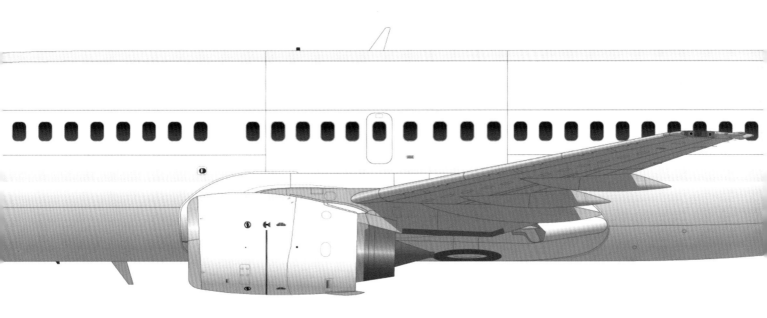

Dedicated to Brenda, the love of my life.

CONTENTS

FOREWORD

Boeing launched the 737 airplane type into a crowded marketplace in 1968, with little expectation of dominance in the emerging short to medium range jet transport market serving small communities. Boeing's 727 was already providing such services, albeit with three engines where two might do. Several competing twin-jet designs were already in service, being tested for certification, or well into the initial design stage.

Boeing's motives were mixed. Some in the company cited a "family plan" to have an entry into every sector of the marketplace to stimulate customer loyalty, even if at a loss at the bottom of the family. Some cited a need to "move down" from the 727 to serve even smaller communities and airports. Most saw the 737 as a loss leader to achieve both of these objectives and held out little hope for profit, either near term or long term.

Indeed, several years into production the program was nearly canceled, surviving by the sale of a military derivative and financial analysis that each unit was finally paying for its costs, but only if credited with the lifetime sale of spare parts attributable to each aircraft.

What is surprising is the Boeing Company invested substantially into improvements in the airplane configuration at that bleak moment in its history, creating the "737-200 Advanced," an airplane with enhanced short field performance, range, and speed. It also certified an unimproved airfield option to attract customers who would fly into gravel runways, and applied sophisticated fluid flow technology to prevent engine damage from rocks. The 737 became the test bed for higher thrust engines, restoring its reputation (and that of all twin jets) for successful operations at high altitude airfields.

The 737 was a subject of controversy during its United States introduction. Although it was the first jet transport certified for operation by a two-person crew through stringent new FAA rules, its initial operations produced contention with pilot unions. Later on the 737 became a platform, adopting and in some cases pioneering technological innovations. Case in point: it was first to incorporate performance-based navigation capability, a feature of the FAA's Next Generation airspace that opens airspace capacity, increases operational efficiency, and de-conflicts flights from other traffic and terrain.

With a fuselage designed for six-abreast economy seating just like the 707 and 727, the initial 737-100 design was a pretty stubby airplane, with a wingspan nearly the same as its body length, acquiring the nicknames "Fat Albert" and "Fat Little Ugly Feller (FLUF)" among pilots and air traffic controllers: "…follow the company FLUF to RWY 31…." The 737 was the first commercial twin jet with wing-mounted engines, rather than the tail-mounted configuration of its European and US rivals. These early configuration decisions produced a resilient design that would be stretched and re-engined three times, each with concomitant aerodynamic improvements, producing the most durable and long lasting jet transport platform in the history of the business.

Many historical achievements by individuals and organizations speak for themselves, with their stories told boldly across the historical horizon by the accomplishments. Some, however, creep up on the populations served until consciousness emerges, and we wonder why it took so long to realize we were witness to a seminal change in the way things are done, thought of, and appreciated. The Boeing 737 is one such aeronautical achievement.

Why did Boeing invest so much in a "loss leader?" Why did the airplane have such staying power in an industry notorious for blind alley designs? How can it be that the last 737 flying will likely have a pedigree of over one hundred years? Why is the remarkable story of this aircraft just being told for the first time almost fifty years from its conception?

Captain Dan Dornseif flies the 737 for a major US airline, is equally happy at the control stick of his Piper J-5 Cub, and has an abiding love for aviation and an insatiable curiosity about history and the "story behind the story." He first attacked the Boeing archives in late 2014, and immersed himself into the 737 program through interviews and research at Boeing, the Seattle Museum of Flight, and sources around the world. I became aware of Dan when Boeing historian and archivist Michael Lombardi called me and told me, "You have to meet this man."

I retired from Boeing in 2000, after forty-two years of service, and have been involved with the 737 since it was conceived in 1968, on many occasions in my career and in many different ways. More important, I know the Boeing engineers, pilots, managers, and technicians whose creativity and leadership have shaped the 737 program from the beginning and do so to this day. So many times I have said to myself, "When are we going to write the definitive history of this airplane and celebrate what it has done for the Boeing Company, the airlines who operate it, and the millions of travelers who have used it as part of their business and recreational lives?" The reason Mike introduced me to Dan is he knew I had half an inclination to write a book myself; hugely underestimating what it takes to accomplish such a task.

My first correspondence with Dan in February 2015 convinced me he was the person to do a responsible job of celebrating one of my favorite airplanes, and since then my job has been to connect Dan with my 737 associates at Boeing, both retired and currently employed. The journey we have shared since then has been extraordinary: old memories awakened, new ones discovered, and relationships renewed. As you read this book, you too will discover and become a member of the 737 family and appreciate the amazing factors that evolved Fat Albert into the swan she has become in the latest version (737 MAX) that first flew on January 29, 2016.

Enjoy!

Peter Morton, March 2017

ACKNOWLEDGMENTS

This writing would not have been possible without the help of many exceptional people who have contributed to this history of the Boeing 737. Several of these people spent years designing, marketing, and flying this fine aircraft. Numerous key players in this story spent time with me to help tell the story. Others shared their artistic abilities and photograph collections, bringing this book to life. I would also like to give special thanks to those who spent many hours editing this work, and ensuring the highest level of accuracy possible. Organizations such as Boeing, Delta Air Lines, Lufthansa, The Museum of Flight, Rockwell-Collins, and Southwest Airlines have kindly contributed significantly to this work. I owe a debt of gratitude to these organizations and the following people: Bill Ahl, Chadi Akkari, Wayne Aleshire, Ardell Anderson, Josh Baynes, Doug Bodah, Bob Bogash, Chris Brady, Mike Conklin, Rob Costello, Ray Craig, Chris Davis, Rex Douglas, Greg Drawbaugh, Tom Edmonds, Delmar Fadden, Jay Ferrell, William T. "Buddy" Fincher, Marie Force, John Fredrickson, Steve Fulton, Ernie Gee, Sabra Gertsch, Roger Guay, Jeffery "Gus" Gustafson, Dan Hagedorn, Lee Hall, Mike Hannon, Amy Heidrick, Jennings Heilig, Mike Hewett, Larry Howard, Mike Hutto, Thomas Imrich, Al Jones, Jessica Jones, Andrew Klamka, Kurt Lehmann, Keith Leverkuhn, John Little, Mike Lombardi, Dina Lorraine, Tom Lubbesmeyer, Joe Marott, Glen Marshall, Paul McElroy, Cindy Messey, Leslie Miller, Fred Mitchell, Peter Morton, Chester "Chet" Nelson, Gary Oakes, Joe Ozimek, Vic Page, Bob Patterson, Lauren Penning, Petr Popelar, John Quinlivan, Ian Robertson, John Roundhill, Alexandre Sanz Bech, Michael Sanz, Christina Semmel, Vickie Shuler, Patrick Stephens, Fredrick C. Strand, Joe Sutter, Dick Taylor, Steve Taylor, Michael Teal, Patrick Thomas, Larry Timmons, Lon Volberding, John Warner, Richard West, Carlton Wilkerson, Dave Wilson, Mark Wilson, Jack Wimpress, and Brien Wygle

Editors
D. Paul Angel, Pamela Cookingham, Brenda Fernandez, Kimberly Fincher, Sherri Latimer, Peter Morton, and Cory Von Pinnon.

Interviews
Anderson, Ardell (Boeing, retired): Museum of Flight, Seattle, Washington, May 12, 2015

Bogash, Bob (Boeing, retired): Museum of Flight, Seattle, Washington, May 12, 2015

Craig, Ray (Boeing): Museum of Flight, Seattle, Washington, July 7, 2015

Fadden, Delmar (Boeing, retired): Museum of Flight, Seattle, Washington, December 13, 2015

Ferrell, Jay (Boeing, retired): via teleconference, May 12, 2015

Fulton, Steve (Alaska Airlines): Museum of Flight, Seattle, Washington, December 13, 2015

Hannon, Mike (Virgin America): via teleconference, August 28, 2015

Hewett, Mike (Boeing, retired): via teleconference, July 7, 2015

Imrich, Thomas (Boeing, retired): Museum of Flight, Seattle, Washington, December 13, 2015, and Mercer Island, Washington, December 14, 2015

Jones, Al (Boeing, retired): Dupont, Washington, October 5, 2015

Lauber, John (NASA, retired): Museum of Flight, Seattle, Washington, July 7, 2015

Leverkuhn, Keith (Boeing): Renton, Washington, October 5, 2015

Mitchell, Fred (Boeing retired): Seattle, Washington, July 7, 2015

Morton, Peter (Boeing, retired): Museum of Flight, Seattle, Washington, May 12, 2015; March 21, 2015; October 5, 2015; and December 13, 2015

Oakes, Gary (Boeing): Museum of Flight, Seattle, Washington, October 5, 2015

Ozimek, Joe (Boeing): Renton, Washington, October 5, 2015

Page, Vic (Boeing, retired): Museum of Flight, Seattle, Washington, May 12, 2015

Quinlivan, John (Boeing): Museum of Flight, Seattle, Washington, October 5, 2015

Roundhill, John (Boeing): Dupont, Washington, October 5, 2015

Sutter, Joe (Boeing, retired): Renton, Washington, October 5, 2015

Taylor, Dick (Boeing, retired): Museum of Flight, Seattle, Washington, May 12, 2015

Taylor, Steve (Boeing): Museum of Flight, Seattle, Washington, July 7, 2015

Teal, Michael (Boeing): Renton, Washington, October 5, 2015

West, Richard (Southwest Airlines): Dallas, Texas, October 21, 2015

Wilson, Dave (Boeing): Museum of Flight, Seattle, Washington, October 5, 2015

Wygle, Brien (Boeing retired): Museum of Flight, Seattle, Washington, May 12, 2015

INTRODUCTION

This book began with a desire to write a definitive volume about my favorite aircraft, the Boeing 737, which I have been fortunate enough to pilot for the last fifteen years. When a pilot spends that much time interacting with an aircraft that proves itself to be incredibly reliable, responsive, and a true "pilot's airplane," that person cannot help but hold the machine in high esteem. It is from this vantage point that I began to write. Beginning the research on the Boeing 737 had me pouring through my collection of books and files, looking for as much information as possible. Once these resources were exhausted, my journey took me to the Boeing Archives, where I met corporate historians Mike Lombardi and Tom Lubbesmeyer, who have spent countless hours with me on this quest. Their helpfulness and desire to see an up-to-date and complete book on the Boeing 737 led to my introduction to Peter Morton. Peter's career at Boeing has been intertwined with the 737 through the years, and he shared my desire to see such a book published. Through his participation, I was introduced to many people who all had a significant hand in making this fine aircraft a success. This is where this project took on a new life.

Meeting these people brought the human element into the story. I was able to hear of the trials and tribulations of building an airplane first hand. It was in this way that this book was not only a piece about an airplane, but also became about the fine people at Boeing that made the 737 possible. I have come to know that Boeing is not just an ordinary company. There is something special about each of these people and their unwavering pursuit to make the best airplanes in the world. I have heard of it being referred to as the "Boeing DNA," and it truly exists. For Boeing people it is not a job, it is a crusade, and this special airplane is the result of this mind-set.

Each chapter in this book will look at the Boeing 737 from different perspectives during its history, including the aircraft that existed in the short range jetliner markets before the 737 was developed. The process that designers Joe Sutter and Jack Steiner went through to develop the "original" series of the 737 will also be looked at from both men's perspectives. The story of each generation of the 737 is told, as well as technical information which will give the reader an in depth look at the aircraft systems from a "big picture" perspective. Systems and external differences that make each version of the aircraft unique are presented with diagrams, photos, and descriptions.

The Boeing 737 has become a wildly successful airplane, but there were several times in history when this jetliner program was almost canceled. These challenges are being told in the following pages, many times with firsthand accounts that are in print for the first time. We will go deep inside Boeing and hear from the managers, engineers, aerodynamicists, and test pilots that made the Boeing 737 the fine jetliner it has become. From the flight line at Renton to grass runways in the Congo, and pre-GPS operations to icy runways in the Arctic circle, you will experience the amazing story of the Boeing 737.

SAS, with its fleet of Caravelles, serves more cities with pure jets than any other airline. No jet surcharge

FROM SAS TO THE WORLD...

Happiest Combination in jet age travel

On *SAS,* one good thing leads to another. You speed to Europe aboard the magnificent *SAS* Global Express with hospitality non-stop. Then you whisk through Europe, the Middle East or Africa on the *SAS* Caravelle Pure Jet, quietest airliner in the sky. You exchange distance for a smiling song, a wink of time, a specially-planned "Jetline" meal! . . . Happy thought for your next trip — the Global Express and the Caravelle Pure Jet, exclusive *SAS* combination. Plan with your *SAS* agent, or *SAS,* 638 Fifth Avenue, New York 20, N. Y.

SAS Caravelle Pure Jet flights link 8 Middle East cities

ROME is one of 19 extra cities at no extra fare on SAS. See London and Paris, too

SERVICE with the Scandinavian touch

EXOTIC INDIA . . . Japan and all the Orient . . . on SAS

FLY SAS TO EUROPE transatlantic or transpolar . . . or go one way, return the other

COPENHAGEN . . . jet crossroads of Europe

Fly with travel's Happiest Combination...

FIRST OVER THE POLE

SAS

SCANDINAVIAN AIRLINES SYSTEM

The Caravelle introduced the glamor of jet travel to short range routes. *Author's Collection*

CHAPTER 1

EARLY SHORT RANGE JETLINER HISTORY

Prior to the late 1950s, short range airliner operations were relegated to propeller driven aircraft. Although most were good, safe designs, there was much room for improvement. Their piston engines and propellers generated a great deal of noise that was transmitted into the passenger cabin, so travelers were frequently annoyed, uncomfortable, and complaints were common. Additionally, these airplanes were slow enough to partially negate the advantages of flying over ground-based transportation. This was especially true on shorter flights, considering the time spent getting to the airport, checking one's luggage, and retrieving it at the destination. More often than not, people chose ground-based transportation over flying on short haul trips. Aircraft manufacturers realized that to increase passenger revenue (and thus aircraft sales), it was imperative that future aircraft not only be designed with a top priority on safety, but also on passenger comfort and speed. Jet engines were an incredible advancement, with their smooth, vibration-free operation. The comfort and speed which could be offered by such aircraft had outstanding potential for increasing the numbers of passengers traveling on airlines around the globe.

Boeing would eventually dominate the market for jetliners that could fly for short distances and be economically successful. However, several aircraft designers jumped into the short range design arena well before Boeing, who was, at the time, concentrating on larger, longer range aircraft. Sud Aviation of France, the British Aircraft Corporation (BAC), Douglas of the United States, and Tupolev of the Soviet Union designed and sold jet aircraft with these short range goals in mind. Although these manufacturers produced competent aircraft, faster jetliners with better performance were desired. As technology advanced, these priorities were incorporated into the newer aircraft under development.

The Players in the Short Range Arena
The Sud Aviation SE-210 Caravelle

The Sud Aviation SE-210 Caravelle's history began nearly seventeen years before the Boeing 737's emergence and demonstrated the need for advanced jet aircraft in the short range market. Due in part to the forward-thinking requirements of the French Comite du Materiel Civil, the need for a short range jet was identified and acted upon early by European countries. The specifications brought forth on November 6, 1951, led to the development of France's Sud Caravelle, the world's first successful short haul jetliner. Sud Aviation and de Havilland developed a partnership to design the Caravelle with improved features for international use. Together, they incorporated the knowledge and lessons learned from the Comet 1 disasters into the overall design, ultimately creating a trend-setting aircraft. The Caravelle, which first flew on May 27, 1955, was sleek and modern, featuring a large wing swept at a modest twenty degrees. This allowed the airplane to meet cruise speed requirements using a relatively simple wing flap design while simultaneously demonstrating

The Sud Aviation Caravelle VI-R prototype (c/n 62, l/n 59) wearing United Airlines colors for promotional purposes and test registration F-WJAP. This aircraft was never delivered to United, but was instead delivered to Cruziero do Sul in February 1961. *Courtesy of The Museum of Flight*

This aircraft (c/n 42, l/n 44), named *The Santa Maria* in keeping with the Caravelle theme, was the demonstrator aircraft for the ill-fated Sud-Douglas cooperative effort before becoming the testbed for the General Electric CJ805-23C engine. This aircraft and engine combination never saw production. *Courtesy of The Museum of Flight*

acceptable takeoff and landing speeds. The Caravelle's tail was a "cruciform" configuration, with horizontal stabilizers mounted high above the fuselage, midway up the vertical stabilizer. This arrangement enabled the Caravelle's twin Rolls-Royce Avon Mk.

The later Caravelles used the proven Pratt & Whitney JT8D engine. This -10B3 model (OH-LSC, c/n 185, l/n 174) was delivered to Finnair on August 27, 1964. *Courtesy of P. Popelar*

This Tu-104A (c/n 76600602) was operated by Czechoslovakian carrier CSA and is currently on display in Petrovice, Czech Republic. *Courtesy of P. Popelar*

527 turbojet engines to be mounted on the rear fuselage. A major advantage of this design was that much of the engine noise was generated behind the passenger cabin, resulting in a quieter ride and increasing traveler comfort.

Attached to the front of the Caravelle's long fuselage was a bullet-shaped nose and cockpit section adapted from the British de Havilland Comet. The main landing gears were also similar in design to those used on the Comet and shared the same wheels and brake assemblies. Although it was an admirable design, the Caravelle added some complexity for maintenance crews because of the use of metric hardware throughout. Many airlines had Caravelles in mixed fleets, combined with Douglas and Lockheed aircraft, which used IAE standard hardware. This required the use of additional tool kits specifically for the Caravelle, increasing work time for mechanics. Through this experience, the companies from Toulouse and Hatfield learned that the use of standard IAE hardware was advantageous for future designs.

From the advent of the rear-engined aircraft configuration to the pioneering of airliner construction through international cooperation, the Caravelle was centric. A total of 282 Caravelles were built over their long production history (1958–1972), and even saw orders and deliveries of a modified version (VI-R) to United Airlines in the United States. The tremendous success of Sud Aviation and de Havilland's partnership set a precedent for similar ventures in the future.

The Tupolev Jetliners
In the early 1950s, the Soviet Union also realized the benefits of designing a short range jet. Many cities in Eastern Bloc countries were situated fairly close together, much like in the United States and Western Europe. Airlines such as Aeroflot and Interflug were interested in procuring optimized jet aircraft for these shorter routes, and Andrei Tupolev's design bureau created the first aircraft types to fill this niche. The Tupolev Tu-104, which first flew in June 1955, was designed to have capabilities similar to the Comet and the later Boeing 707. The Tu-104 was a competent machine, but lacked the creature comforts and good air conditioning of the 707. When the Comet 1s were grounded in 1956, the Tu-104 remained the only operational jetliner in service anywhere in the world until 1958.

In an effort to perfect his aircraft, Andrei Tupolev focused on designing a slightly smaller jetliner and constructed the Tu-124. The Tu-124 was a scaled-down version of the Tu-104, designed for smaller loads on shorter flight segments. This was the first jetliner in history to enter service with fuel efficient turbofan engines. It had a passenger capacity of fifty-six and a range of 1,304 statute miles. The Tupolev 104 and 124 shared some of the same design features as the de Havilland Comet, chief among them the location of its jet engines nested in the wing root. Although mounting the engines in this location had the advantage of being aerodynamically clean, it transmitted a lot of noise to the cabin. There were safety issues as well: if there was an "uncontained failure" of one of the engines, the adjacent fuselage and fuel tanks might be prone to shrapnel damage. Also, as with the Comet, the engine exhaust noise itself caused structural wear and tear on the airframe over time due to their proximity to the fuselage. De Havilland mitigated this in the Comet 4 by canting the engines' exhaust slightly outward, away from the fuselage, while future jetliner designs would sport pod-mounted engines, eliminating these comfort and safety concerns.

In total, 164 Tu-124s were completed when production began on its new and improved replacement, the Tu-134. Despite its slightly smaller size, the Tu-134 would have been a fairly direct competitor to the 737-100 and DC-9-10, had a free market existed between the East and the West. Because of the Cold War this was not the case. The Tu-124 was still a relatively new design, but the impetus for a new type was said to have originated with Soviet leader Nikita

The Tu-124 was smaller than the earlier Tu-104. This example was the first prototype (CCCP-45000, c/n 0350101), which first flew on March 24, 1960. *Courtesy of The Museum of Flight*

The sleek lines of the Tupolev Tu-134 are evident with the aircraft climbing out with the landing gear in transit. *Courtesy of P. Popelar*

European Airways (BEA) and British Overseas Airways Corporation (BOAC). The fledgling BAC decided to look globally for the need of a short range jet aircraft. The original design parameters are said to have been heavily influenced by Sir Freddie Laker, who wanted a new aircraft to fit the needs of his British United Airways (BUA) operation. At the time, there was a widespread desire to replace the Vickers Viscount turboprop with an economical, short range jet. The resultant design featured the rear engine concept "borrowed" from the Caravelle, but with a full T-tailed design. Unfortunately, the implications of the T-tail design were not yet completely understood. The BAC One-Eleven manifested a "locked-in stall" (sometimes referred to as a "deep stall"). This condition, if allowed to progress, was often unrecoverable.

Khrushchev. In March 1960, he flew to France for a meeting with Charles de Gaulle on a Tu-104. While he was in Paris, Khrushchev had the opportunity to fly aboard a Caravelle. Reportedly, he was so impressed with the quiet comfort of the aircraft that he ordered changes to be made to the Tu-124. These modifications ultimately led to the creation of the Tu-134. It utilized the same nose and fuselage structure as the Tu-124, but featured a podded, rear engine format with a T-tail configuration. The wings of the Tu-134 were highly swept and bore similarities to Tupolev's earlier jet designs. The main landing gears retracted directly into pods on the trailing edge of each wing.

The Tu-134 prototype (the sole Tu-124A) first flew on July 29, 1963, well ahead of American designs. Although the new Tupolev certainly looked the part of a sleek jetliner, it lacked leading edge slats for good short field performance. Even so, it was a solid aircraft and proved very successful throughout the years. In total 852 were produced, and several are still in service today with private operators. Having first entered revenue service in 1967, the Tu-134 has been in continuous service for over forty-nine years. This is remarkable, and a testament to the solid design and economics of the Tu-134.

The BAC One-Eleven

The British were not wasting time in the short haul race, either. In 1960, the British Aircraft Company (BAC) had just recently formed from a merger of English Electric, Bristol, and Vickers-Armstrong, bringing vast design experience to the table. Until then, British airliners were largely built to the specifications of Britain's state operated airlines: British

The T-tail Design and the Deep Stall Phenomenon

In the 1960s, the "T-tail" became very popular with aircraft manufacturers, and during this era most of the 737's major competitors featured this configuration. The T-tail had been implemented with the BAC One-Eleven and the Tu-134. Meanwhile, Douglas was incorporating it into their DC-9, which was still in the planning phase. As with any aircraft composition, the T-tail had advantageous strengths, yet included necessary compromises made by the engineering teams. Developers were eager to make their aircraft conform to their potential customers' wish lists. A relaxed environment in the cabin, conservative fuel consumption, and the ability to use short

The BAC One-Eleven prototype (G-ASHG, c/n 004) doing a low pass during early flight testing prior to its fatal crash on October 22, 1963, due to the deep stall phenomenon. *Courtesy of The Museum of Flight*

runway lengths were among the manufacturers' top priorities for future sales success. The T-tail's configuration allowed the engines to be pod mounted on the rear fuselage, so most of the engines' noise was generated behind the aircraft, resulting in decreased sound levels inside the cabin during flight. This created a much more comfortable environment for passengers. In addition, the T-tail's horizontal stabilizer rode high on top of the vertical stabilizer in relatively undisturbed airflow, clear of interference from the rest of the aircraft. The designers were then able to use a smaller aerodynamic surface for the horizontal stabilizer/elevator, reducing aerodynamic drag and fuel consumption. Additionally, since there were no podded engines attached to the wings they could be a smaller, more efficient design. The result was a very clean airflow around the wing. Since the wings of all jetliners are designed to be efficient at cruising speeds, provisions have to be made to allow the aircraft to have acceptably slow landing speeds. This was accomplished by adding trailing edge flaps and sometimes slats or "Krueger flaps" to the leading edge of the wing. A slat is a curved panel that extends forward and down from the top of the leading edge of the wing. Krueger flaps serve the same purpose, but extend from a compartment under the leading edge of the wing to create more camber (curvature) over the wing surface. If an aircraft's engines are not mounted on the wings, these flaps and slats can be continuous, which make them more efficient and lend to a simpler

design. Conversely, with a wing-mounted engine design, provisions have to be built into them allowing room for the engine pylons on the front of the wing, as well as space for the engines' thrust to pass through when the trailing edge flaps are extended. This causes the flap design to be more complicated to be effective at reducing takeoff and landing speeds, thus requiring less runway length.

The T-tail satisfied the main desires of many airlines, but came with a set of compromises that manufacturers felt were necessary and acceptable. Since the horizontal stabilizer was mounted to the top of the vertical stabilizer, additional structure was required to make the entire assembly rigid and strong, adding a significant amount of weight. Longer fuel and hydraulic lines, as well as additional bleed air ducting and wiring, were required with the rear-mounted engines. This was because the engines were much farther away from the aircraft's major systems, to which the engines and their accessories supplied power. These features added weight, limiting the aircraft's ultimate weight lifting ability and fuel range. This performance penalty, to some extent, canceled out the aerodynamic benefits. Even so, the T-tail design appeared to be a success until a phenomenon known as "deep stall" (also known as "locked-in stall" or "super stall") was discovered during flight testing of the BAC One-Eleven prototype.

On October 22, 1963, the BAC One-Eleven prototype crashed in a field near Chicklade, England, during flight testing. The

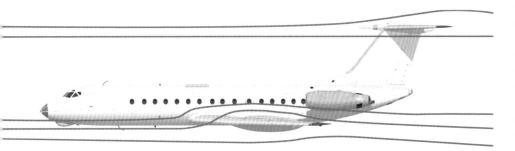

aircraft was being put through many tests in the low airspeed range of the aircraft's operational "envelope." During one test the flaps were set to the eight degree (intermediate takeoff) position and the aircraft was loaded to an aft (tail heavy) center of gravity. During the stall test the aircraft began pitching up uncontrollably, quite contrary to the pilot's control inputs. Even with its nose angled up much higher than normal, the aircraft descended into the ground with an unfortunate loss of all on board. An intensive investigation ensued and discovered the fatal flaw known today as the deep stall. When pilots or engineers speak of stalling an aircraft, this has to do with the aircraft's wing reaching a "critical angle of attack." This occurs when the angle between the chord line of the wing and the wind that is striking it becomes excessive. For the wing to produce enough lift to support the weight of the aircraft, the air flowing over the top of the wing must remain attached and adhere to the top of the wing. When the critical angle of attack is exceeded, the air flowing over the wing can no longer make the corner and separates from the top of the wing, causing a very significant loss of total lift. Generally, when an aircraft is stalled it is easily controllable by the pilot. The stall can be broken by lowering the nose, decreasing the wing's angle of attack, and the wing begins to fly again. In most aircraft this maneuver is not inherently dangerous, provided there is plenty of altitude to recover. With a T-tail design, a stall can cause greater instability if safety features have

This diagram shows how the T-tail can be affected by the wake of the stalled wing, rendering pitch control ineffective. *Courtesy of Jennings Heilig*

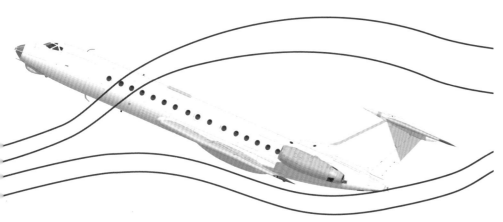

not been designed into the aircraft to prevent a normal stall from developing into a deep stall (see diagram opposite).

As the aircraft's angle of attack increases past the normal stall angle and allows the horizontal stabilizer and elevator to fly into the wake of the stalled wing, things turn bad very quickly. Since the tail of the aircraft is flying completely in the turbulent air produced by the stalled wing, the elevators become ineffective and the pilot cannot lower the nose to recover. On the BAC One-Eleven, this phenomenon was exacerbated by the fact that its elevator system was not hydraulic, instead operated with servo tabs, requiring a stable airflow to effectively move the elevators. The pilots simply had no way to regain control of the aircraft. This was not the only aircraft to experience this problem: a Hawker Siddeley (de Havilland) Trident also crashed near the Staines River in 1966 because of the same phenomenon. This situation was also experienced by a Boeing 727 in late 1963, with test pilot Lew Wallick at the controls. Fortunately, due to the 727's hydraulically controlled elevator system, combined with Capt. Wallick's excellent stick and rudder skills, the aircraft was recovered from the deep stall.

With their newly found knowledge of how the deep stall could occur, engineers on both sides of the Iron Curtain set to work making the T-tail design safe and easy to fly. Engineers at BAC and Boeing prevented the problem by installing a device called a "stick pusher" on their T-tailed aircraft, which is designed to do exactly what its name implies. As the stall warning system detects that the aircraft is approaching the stalling angle of attack a small device physically forces the pilot's control yoke forward, lowering the nose well before elevator authority is lost to the wake of the wings. This was found to be a very straightforward way to mitigate deep stall risk.

As the deep stall issue was identified and corrected the BAC One-Eleven trumped Caravelle sales in the United States, gaining significant orders from American Airlines, Braniff, and several other airlines. Its success was due in part to BAC's early aircraft delivery slots. Incredibly, the aircraft was completed and ready for revenue service a full nineteen months ahead of the Douglas DC-9. Although BAC had a significant advantage in timing and sales, the aircraft had its performance limitations. Notably, the BAC One-Eleven's takeoff and climb performance was only suitable for near-sea-level airports with fairly long runways, due in part to its thrust limited engines and lack of high lift, leading edge devices. This issue alone made a purchase from United Airlines or Western Airlines unlikely due to their mountainous route structures. Additionally, the cabin had a diameter of 134 in., making it quite cramped by comparison to the DC-9. There were also many reported reliability issues with the electrical generating systems on the early aircraft. Eventually the American market became more sluggish for BAC, as Douglas and Boeing developed competing designs. Furthermore, BAC's struggle was compounded when the Civil Aeronautics Board (CAB) began to reject order requests for the British jet from smaller American carriers. A few airlines like American, Braniff, and Mohawk persevered against CAB and succeeded in purchasing a limited number of One-Elevens, while many others were deterred. CAB's opposition was based on the belief that airlines would have required government subsidies to operate the One-Eleven profitably. These complications, combined with the BAC One-Eleven's lack of carrying capability in challenging environments, helped Douglas' new DC-9 (and later the Boeing 737) eventually take the upper hand.

Enter the DC-9

In the early 1960s, the Douglas Aircraft Corporation faced a dilemma. Its DC-8 was in direct competition with Boeing's 707, and the Boeing product was well in the lead sales-wise. The expense of the DC-8 program left Douglas struggling financially. This placed the Long Beach manufacturer in a predicament. How could it develop a new jet without much capital investment? In its quest for an answer Douglas took a serious look at the Sud Caravelle. A deal was considered between Sud and Douglas to produce a version of the French jet which would have General Electric turbofan engines and would be produced under license by Douglas. However, due to a lack of interest from the airlines this idea was abandoned on December 31, 1961.

As the negotiations with Sud fell through, Douglas turned its focus to a new design, Concept 2067. This design was to be built as a scaled-down DC-8, with four underwing mounted jet engines. As time went on, it became clear that Rolls-Royce and Pratt & Whitney were developing engines that could allow the new design to be a twin-jet. This would be ideal, making the aircraft less expensive to maintain and simultaneously reducing operating costs. For these reasons Douglas proposed Design Concept 2086, which included two different configurations for

The Douglas DC-8 Prototype (N8008D, c/n 45252, l/n 1) in flight during testing. This aircraft was fitted with a speed brake on the rear fuselage, directly behind each wing. These were not installed on production DC-8s. *Courtesy of The Boeing Company*

the design study known as the "Compact Jet." The first design study looked similar to the eventual 737, with twin, underwing mounted engines. The second looked akin to the BAC One-Eleven, with its T-tailed, rear-mounted engine design. After much research on the part of his engineers and aerodynamicists, Douglas founder Donald Douglas Sr. became convinced that the rear engine configuration would be best because of passenger comfort and aerodynamic efficiency. This may very well have been influenced by Mr. Douglas' exposure to the Caravelle, an aircraft with which he was undoubtedly impressed. In this way the Compact Jet study evolved into a new aircraft called the DC-9.

The DC-9 had goals to achieve. It had to be simple and easy to maintain, durable enough to deal with short sector operations, and it had to have good short-field performance.

The primary competitor to the DC-8 was Boeing's first jetliner, the Boeing 707. The aircraft pictured is a later 707-321B "Intercontinental" model (c/n 18337, l/n 276). For a period of time Pan American World Airways operated the Boeing 707 in its fleet with the Douglas DC-8. *Courtesy of The Boeing Company*

Douglas Concept 2067 shows the early proposed Douglas DC-9 design circa June 1959. *Courtesy of The Boeing Company*

The Douglas DC-9 Prototype as seen during the rollout ceremony. N9DC (c/n 45695, l/n 1) was the first of 2,439 DC-9s (and later variants) produced at the Long Beach facility. *Courtesy of The Boeing Company*

Also, it was designed from the outset to be offered in varying fuselage lengths to meet a wide range of airline requirements. The powerplant chosen was the new Pratt & Whitney JT8D turbofan, which also powered the Boeing 727-100. History has shown this engine to have been an excellent choice because of its incredible reliability and longevity. Simplicity was achieved by using ailerons and elevators manually controlled by the pilot through the use of control cables and servo tabs. This system was effective and easy to maintain. The rudder system was hydraulically boosted on some versions to help augment control in case of an engine failure.

The initial DC-9 prototype and -10 series production aircraft did not have leading edge slats, only having the double slotted trailing edge flap design feature. This worked well for the lighter, early aircraft, but slats were added to the DC-20 and higher series airframes to enhance short field performance. The aircraft came standard with an auxiliary power unit (APU) to provide independent electrical power and pressurized air for engine start and air conditioning. Offered equipment included an air stair that deployed under the rear fuselage to allow passenger boarding similar to the 727. A forward integral air stair was also an available option. The DC-9's low sitting stance on the ground made the baggage compartments in the lower fuselage easily accessible for ramp crews. The result was an aircraft that could be operated in and out of airports without any ground equipment. In fact, it used to be common practice to use the aircraft's thrust reversers to "power back" from the gate without a tug! The DC-9 was a cutting edge aircraft with its many cost effective features and its fuel efficient, durable airframe. Boeing was quick to notice the DC-9's development and responded with studies to create a competing aircraft.

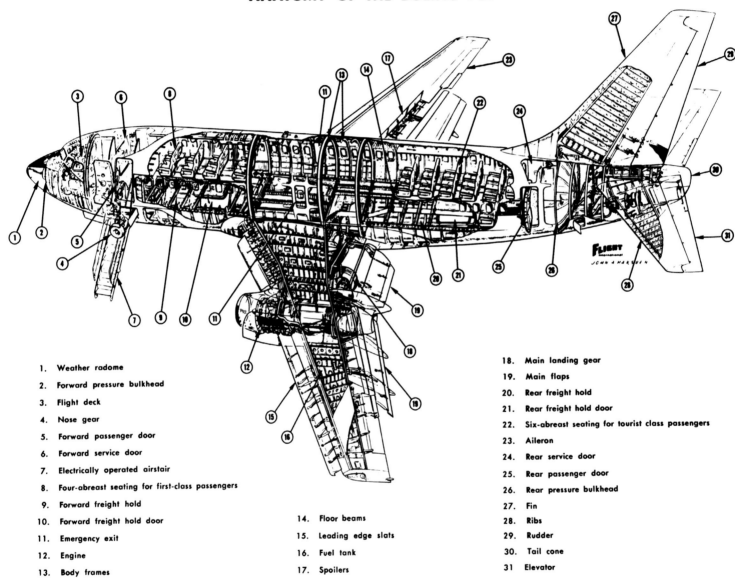

ANATOMY OF THE BOEING 737

1. Weather radome
2. Forward pressure bulkhead
3. Flight deck
4. Nose gear
5. Forward passenger door
6. Forward service door
7. Electrically operated airstair
8. Four-abreast seating for first-class passengers
9. Forward freight hold
10. Forward freight hold door
11. Emergency exit
12. Engine
13. Body frames

14. Floor beams
15. Leading edge slats
16. Fuel tank
17. Spoilers

18. Main landing gear
19. Main flaps
20. Rear freight hold
21. Rear freight hold door
22. Six-abreast seating for tourist class passengers
23. Aileron
24. Rear service door
25. Rear passenger door
26. Rear pressure bulkhead
27. Fin
28. Ribs
29. Rudder
30. Tail cone
31 Elevator

A cutaway drawing of the Boeing 737-100 with the early thrust reverser configuration. *Courtesy of The Boeing Company*

CHAPTER 2

THE GENESIS

As early as 1958, Boeing conducted studies to create a twin-jet aircraft that would provide economical jet transportation on short flight segments. The goal was to have a jetliner smaller than the 707, 720 (a 707 derivative), and the 727 concept studies which could operate profitably even on stage lengths as short as one hundred miles. The aircraft would have to fly efficiently at typical cruising altitudes of 20,000 to 30,000 feet. Having literally bet the company on the 707 project, many among the ranks at Boeing were hesitant to pour resources into this venture, especially since a third jetliner (727) was also being developed.

The "stretched" 727-200 series was a very popular jetliner, with 1,260 aircraft sold to airlines around the world. *Courtesy of The Boeing Company*

The second production Boeing 727-100 (c/n 18368, effectivity E2) photographed while in flight. *Courtesy of The Boeing Company*

This photo shows a full scale mockup of the proposed Boeing 2707 Supersonic Transport (SST). Although this aircraft was never built, it and the 747 were occupying most of Boeing's resources when the 737 was being designed. Many technologies developed from the SST program went on to benefit future aircraft designs.
Courtesy of The Boeing Company

Joseph F. Sutter played a key role in the final design configuration of the Boeing 737. Sutter is also widely recognized as the "Father of the 747."

John E. "Jack" Steiner was a leader in the design of the 737. Steiner began his long career at Boeing as a hydrodynamicist on the Boeing 314 Flying Boat and was the program manager for the Boeing 727.

It was not until 1964 that Boeing began to revisit the concept of a short range, twin-engined jetliner. Since most of Boeing's engineering resources were being used on a multitude of other projects (including the 747 and Supersonic Transport), the design of the 737 was handled unconventionally. At Boeing, new aircraft designs were normally created in the Design Department, but this new jet would be designed and built by the 6-7000 Production Department. Charged with the oversight of the project were Joe Sutter, who later gained fame as the "Father of the 747," and Jack Steiner, reputed to be "one of the best airplane designers in history." In 1964, these men were considering an initial design with wing-mounted engines and a low mounted horizontal stabilizer. Their aircraft was coming to the ball much later than several competing designs and would have to be significantly better to gain a sales foothold in the long run. Many designs were considered, including the rear engine platform that was fast becoming a standard configuration for short range jet transports. Another interesting design had podded engines mounted high on the fuselage, but had the horizontal stabilizer mounted behind and below the engines. Additionally, a very DC-9-esque design was also on the table. All of these ideas had different strengths and weaknesses, and the engineers had many decisions to make. Two teams were formed to explore the 737 concept. At the time, Boeing had two organizations that could develop new technology and designs. There was the "Staff" group, run by Joe Sutter, and the "Project" group, led by Jack Steiner. These two men were asked by higher management to independently find the best possible design.

Joe Sutter, chief of technology on the 727 at the time, recalled how the 737 began:

I was told one day that Boeing management wanted to have a meeting about a new, short range airplane, but I could not attend for some reason. Jack Steiner went by himself. Steiner reported that they agreed that we could do a study to build a new small airplane. I told my guys that Steiner was doing a study, we know… that we are going to launch something, so get to work and start designing an airplane. So then the next thing that happened, Steiner called me in and said, "We can't just copy the DC-9. We have to do something new. The new thing is that we are going to go to a six

abreast [seating] body." "Well," I said, "that is going to make a short, fat, dumpy little airplane," and we sort of inferred that you can't put the engines back there [on the tail] and use a T-tail unless you put a span on it that's twice as big because of the locked-in stall. After a lot of discussion he agreed that his gang would be the Red Team and I could do a Blue Team. We got permission to look at how we would do the airplane. With a 100 seat airplane, with a six abreast body, it was a flying football. We decided that we couldn't put the tail back there…or you would have locked-in stall. So we figured why not put the engines underneath the wings. It's a lower Mach number airplane, so we could take some penalties on Mach number, drag, and whatnot. I actually cut out a 727-200 nacelle [out of paper] and slid it around on a drawing and decided that we could put it under the wing. It wouldn't stick so far [forward] that you couldn't open the passenger door…. Also, we could locate the engines so that the turbines were aft of the rear wing spar, so that an un-contained failure would not penetrate the wing fuel tank…. It looked like it might work, so I put my guys to work on that and then we were supposed to have two months to study it. In two weeks we decided that we could get six more passengers with the same engines. We took that to Steiner and he agreed that we would look at doing the airplane that way. That's how the 737 got started.

In July 1964, Steiner and others from Boeing visited the Hamburger Flugzeugbau (HFB) company in Hamburg, Germany. The company operated out of the old Blohm & Voss facility, where it was testing and preparing to produce the HFB 320 "Hansa Jet." This aircraft was much smaller than the 737, but had an advanced design. It was essentially a ten-seat business jet featuring engines mounted high on the rear fuselage and a T-tail. A discussion with HFB representatives Mr. Pohlmann (general manager of engineering), Werner Blohm (manager of sales), Dr. Studer (project manager for the HFB 320), and Capt. William "Swede" Davis (chief pilot for the HFB 320) ensued. The primary topics were the wind tunnel data on the T-tail configuration and the "deep stall" phenomenon,

One early concept for the 737 had high-mounted engines with a conventional tail structure. *Courtesy of The Museum of Flight*

The Boeing design teams led by Joe Sutter and Jack Steiner left no stone unturned to find the best configuration for the 737. *Courtesy of The Museum of Flight*

Enjoy a dynamic, long-range career with the world leader in jet transportation

Boeing Supersonic Transport Design

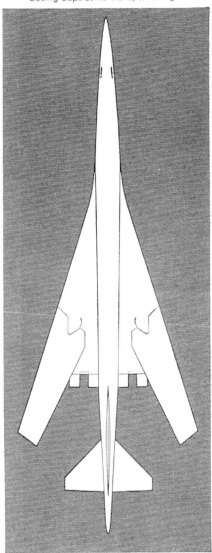

Boeing 727 Short-to-Medium Range Jetliner

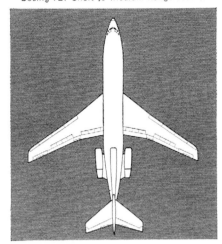

(Drawings show relative size of three airplanes)

New Boeing 737 Short-Range Jetliner

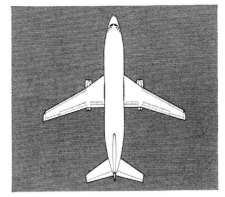

The Boeing Company, today's world leader in the field of jet transportation, is already at work on the next generation of jets — including the country's newest short-range jetliner, a variable-sweep wing supersonic passenger liner and other manned aircraft systems. To maintain its leadership, Boeing continues to pioneer evolutionary advances in research, design, development, manufacturing techniques.

Experienced engineers and scientists interested in expanding the scope of their careers in this dynamic field will find professional challenge and unique advancement opportunities with Boeing's Airplane Group. Immediate openings are available at both Renton (near Seattle), Washington, and Wichita, Kansas, for qualified graduates in engineering, physics, mathematics, business administration, operations research and production management. Specific areas of assignment are listed at the right.

Salaries are competitively commensurate with your experience and educational background. Moving and travel allowances are paid to newly hired personnel. Boeing is an equal opportunity employer.

Send your resume, today, to:
Mr. Thomas Sheppard, The Boeing Company, P.O. Box 707-BGN, Renton, Washington 98055; or Mr. Gerald Caywood, The Boeing Company, Dept. BGN, Wichita, Kansas 67210.

DESIGN ENGINEERING
Structural
Hydraulic
Air Conditioning & Pneumatic Systems
Aircraft Control
Power Plant
Fuel Systems

MANUFACTURING ENGINEERING
Tool Design
Tool Coordination
Tool & Production Planning

DEVELOPMENT ENGINEERING
Structural Dynamics
Stability & Control
Fatigue Analysis
Loads Analysis
Stress Analysis
Hydraulic & Electrical Systems
Weights
Metallurgy
Non-Metallic Materials
Support Equipment/Facilities
  (Electronics)
Propulsion
Navigation & Guidance Systems
Military Operations Analysis
Flight Test Operations
Flight Test Instrumentation
Structural Test
Propulsion Test
Mechanical Test
Electro-Optical Systems
Environmental Control
Antenna Systems
Radar Systems
Weapons Delivery Systems
Electronic Countermeasures

COMPUTER TECHNOLOGY
Programming & Systems Analysis
  Commercial Applications
  Manufacturing Support Applications
  Engineering & Scientific
Operations Research Analysis
Systems Research Analysis
Mathematical Statistics & Research
Analog & Hybrid Flight Simulation

BOEING
AIRPLANE GROUP

Commercial Airplane Division • Military Airplane Division
Other divisions: Missile • Space • Turbine • Vertol • Also, Boeing Scientific Research Laboratories

This is a 1965 ad illustrating Boeing's need for engineers during this very busy and technologically demanding era. *Author's Collection*

The second HFB-320 Hansa Jet (c/n 0002) photographed in flight. The first prototype was lost during flight testing to a deep stall. *Courtesy of The Museum of Flight*

since the Hansa Jet was known to have an undesirable sharp, pitch-up tendency during stalls. Steiner and his staff acquired valuable information from the meeting. It is noteworthy that on May 12, 1965, after a year of certification testing, the Hansa Jet prototype was lost during stall testing. The aircraft configuration was a flaps 20 (intermediate setting) stall that eventually went into a flat spin. The aircraft had a parachute installed to help in recovery from such a situation, which the pilots deployed, but the plane still remained in the spin until impact. Both pilots left the aircraft in an attempt to bail out, but only the pilot in the right seat was able to get clear of the aircraft. Capt. Swede Davis became entangled with the aircraft's deployed spin chute and his body was found with the aircraft's wreckage.

Joe Sutter remembered considering the aft-engine, T-tail configuration and other considerations for adopting the eventual 737 configuration:

If you remember the BAC One-Eleven and the Trident, both of them had a problem with a locked-in stall. The engines, at a high angle of attack, would blank out the aerodynamic effects of the horizontal tail. So the horizontal tail became ineffective, and so when the wing stalled, it just pitched up. The BAC One-Eleven started at well over 13,000 feet and it just came straight down into the ground in a locked-in [nose high] attitude. When we were working on the 727, we had heard about that and the 727 horizontal tail was increased [in

size] a little bit, because we could see in our wind tunnel tests that we were not too bad off. That was fine until one day when Lew Wallick was the pilot. The airplane was doing fine with stalls and whatnot, but one day he had flaps full down and it went right into locked-in stall and it wouldn't come out, but he pulled in the speed brakes and she came out…. So we knew all about this locked-in stall business when the 737 came along, with bigger engines and a wide body. Steiner, who wanted to do that [use a T-tail design], acquiesced with the aerodynamicists and stability control guys. The horizontal tail kept getting bigger and bigger…. More span to get it outside of the wake of the engines. That was one reason why we wanted to get rid of the aft engines, but the other was that when you hang these engines on the back of a short body, that's weight. If you take the engines and put them underneath the wing, the engines are pulling down while the wing is lifting, so you can take a lot of weight out of the airplane. When we were all done with our quick studies we could carry six more passengers with the same size engine. I convinced them that even with problems this is the way to go. So that is how it came about. (Author's note: Distributing an airplane's weight across the wing by locating the engines on pylons under or ahead of the wing provides "wing-bending moment relief," thus allowing a lighter wing structure. This has become the

A Hansa Jet demonstrator is shown during passenger boarding. After solving the deep stall issue forty-seven were produced. *Courtesy of The Museum of Flight*

A scale model of the 727-100 compared to the early small 737 concept. *Courtesy of The Museum of Flight*

de facto design standard for large commercial transport aircraft today.)

On November 9, 1964, Boeing designers Jack Steiner, George Sanborn, and John Yeasting presented the 737 concept to Boeing's board of directors. After much deliberation, the designers were allowed to take the next step and test the market for the aircraft by getting information from airlines around the world. This would present a major challenge to the design team, because each airline had its own ideas as to what attributes the "ideal" aircraft would possess.

Working with the Airlines

During 1964 and 1965, Boeing sought the input of many airlines regarding the 737. Initially, the major contributors were United Airlines, Lufthansa, Western Airlines, and Eastern Airlines. Since Boeing's designers had already committed to building a twin-engined aircraft suitable for a two-pilot crew, the biggest decision remaining was size. Solid arguments were made for a larger and a smaller airframe. This put the Boeing design team in the challenging position of determining the ideal size of the new jetliner while catering to the needs of each airline.

Western Airlines was a hot target for Boeing's sales team. Terrell "Terry" Drinkwater was president of the Los Angeles-based airline and was actively looking for a new aircraft to add to its fleet. In 1964, Boeing representatives met with Drinkwater at his company's headquarters in an attempt to sell him the 737, but Boeing had yet to commit to producing the 737. According to Jack Steiner's memoirs the meeting was awkward at best. Even though Drinkwater had called the meeting with Boeing to discuss the aircraft, he kept the sales team waiting in a dark conference room for quite a long time. When Drinkwater finally did arrive, he brought with him a small television set and tuned it to the World Series game that was in progress. As the Boeing sales team started making their pitch for the 737, Drinkwater remained distracted by his television, constantly adjusting its antennas in a futile attempt to improve reception. Western's message came across loud and clear: if Boeing was not willing to "go firm" and commit to building the 737 they were not interested.

An artist's rendition of the nearly final configuration 737-100. *Courtesy of The Museum of Flight*

The Case for a Smaller Design

At Boeing, there was concern that the 737 design was becoming too large, rapidly approaching the size of the 727-100 already in production. The sales department at Boeing was advocating for a much smaller aircraft for two main reasons. First, there was a very real concern that the 737 would interfere with the sales of its slightly larger sister, the 727. With one less engine to feed and care for, as well as a two-pilot cockpit, the economics of the 737 were a big consideration. Second, they felt an aircraft smaller than the DC-9 would be ideal from a sales standpoint. If the DC-9 could be squeezed out of the market by the larger 727 and a smaller 737 design, Boeing could reap the profits. This tactic has been coined the "pincher effect" and is still in play in today's market.

Deutsche Lufthansa of Germany had been looking for a new aircraft since 1962; its study was referred to as "Type X." In the end, this project identified a need for an aircraft that could carry eighty-two passengers with a baggage allowance of forty-four pounds each and 1,000 pounds of freight. The new aircraft would have to be able to accomplish this economically, with a stage length of up to 500 miles. Gerhard Hoeltje, chief engineer of Deutsche Lufthansa, personally visited Seattle and made the wishes of his company clear. Lufthansa wanted a smaller aircraft, and was taking a hard look at the Douglas and BAC machines. Eastern Airlines had similar concerns. Eastern was already entrenched with a large number of 727s and was looking for a much smaller aircraft to compliment its existing fleet.

The Case for a Larger Design

Dave Olsen, one of Boeing's marketing analysts, had different ideas and strongly believed in the benefits of the wider 727 type fuselage. His viewpoint was in alignment with the opinions of those in management at United Airlines. United was not worried about the aircraft being too large, as its main desire was to have a wider fuselage. If this would require a larger aircraft then so be it. United had requested that the tail section be redesigned to allow the installation of another row of passenger seats. To accommodate this request, Boeing's engineering department

moved the horizontal and vertical stabilizers farther aft. Aerodynamicists were pleased by the new configuration, since the stabilizers' location farther back on the fuselage gave the elevators and rudder more control authority. This location increased their leverage, allowing the surfaces to be made slightly smaller and resulting in reduced parasitic drag.

The airline market at the time had a large bearing on the size debate with the 737. In the mid-1960s, short range passenger travel was increasing at an average of eighteen percent per year according to Jack Steiner's piece titled "Short Range Jetliner Notes." This signaled a large expansion in the airlines' short haul route structures. United and Boeing noticed this as the larger 737 configuration was finalized. This meteoric rise in passenger

This artist's conception depicts the final 737-200 configuration. *Courtesy of The Museum of Flight*

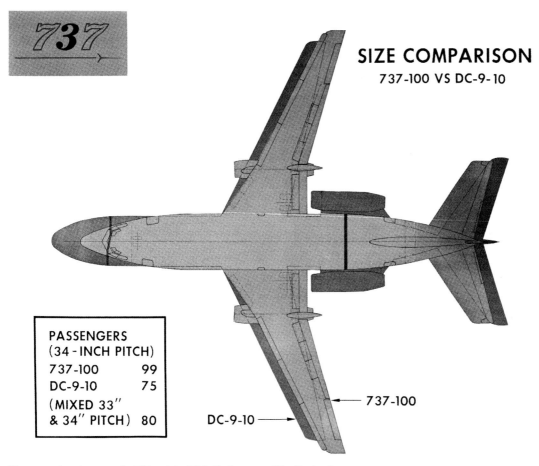

SIZE COMPARISON
737-100 VS DC-9-10

PASSENGERS (34-INCH PITCH)	
737-100	99
DC-9-10	75
(MIXED 33" & 34" PITCH)	80

DC-9-10 ⟶   737-100

Size comparison between the 737 and the DC-9-10. *Courtesy of The Boeing Company*

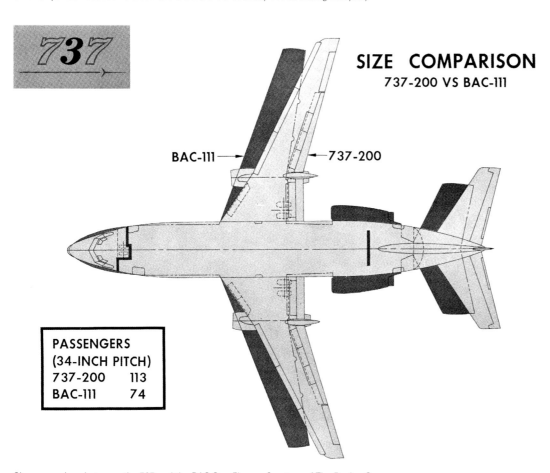

SIZE COMPARISON
737-200 VS BAC-111

BAC-111 ⟶   ⟵ 737-200

PASSENGERS (34-INCH PITCH)	
737-200	113
BAC-111	74

Size comparison between the 737 and the BAC One-Eleven. *Courtesy of The Boeing Company*

volume, combined with the quality of the 737, would eventually allow the aircraft to be tremendously successful, despite its late arrival to the marketplace.

By April 1965, the final basic configuration for the 737 was decided upon, which happened to be markedly similar to the original 1964 configuration. The design team actively resisted the T-tail arrangement for the 737. With the BAC One-Eleven prototype lost to the deep stall characteristic and the particularly harrowing incident during stall trials on the 727, it seemed Boeing was looking more for a conventional tail configuration. There were many benefits to this design helping offset some of the aerodynamic disadvantages. Importantly, there was a significant weight savings. The T-tail design requires a lot of additional structural weight to strengthen the vertical stabilizer to withstand additional stresses in flight. As the studies progressed, the design team moved gradually to a wing-mounted engine configuration. This yielded more weight savings, simply because the engines were much closer to the fuel, hydraulic, and air conditioning systems, meaning the bleed air ducts, fuel lines, and hydraulic lines could be much shorter, and therefore lighter. It was believed that the total weight difference was approximately 1,200 pounds, allowing six more people to be carried, or an additional 182 gallons of fuel could be loaded. Because of the lighter structure, the designers had the latitude to make other improvements to the basic design. The heavier, yet more powerful Pratt & Whitney JT8D engine could easily be used in lieu of the JTF-10 engine, which was initially considered. This would give the airframe greater flexibility and more parts commonality with the 727.

In many ways a wider fuselage was advantageous, since it greatly increased passenger comfort with a roomier cabin than any major competing aircraft at the time. This design change also facilitated the adaptation of the 727 forward fuselage and cockpit structures for the 737. This allowed further enhancement of parts commonality, reducing maintenance and production expenses. Aircraft performance could also be improved through the reduction of weight with wing-mounted engines. Using some of this weight savings to enhance the structure of the 737 enabled higher cruise speeds at lower altitudes. Other major benefits of the wider fuselage were a better aircraft to passenger weight ratio, a smaller overall footprint, and the need for less gate space. A cargo carrying version was also planned, and this wider fuselage allowed the use of standard cargo containers, unlike Douglas' narrower DC-9. There was a small price to pay for the wider fuselage, as it would increase the aircraft's fuel consumption by 3.7%. Even so, the accumulation of benefits gave the 737 design, with its wider fuselage, a distinct marketing advantage over the competition.

There were other significant gains in using the wing-mounted engine design for the 737. Every airplane must have a weight and balance calculation before each flight. The takeoff weight is calculated and the location of the aircraft's balance point (front to rear) is determined. There is always an acceptable range for the balance point. If preflight calculations show the loaded aircraft's balance point to be outside this range people, baggage, and/or cargo must be removed or shifted. Moving weight around at the last minute costs time and on-time performance for an airline. The 737 design put most of the aircraft's mass very close to its ideal center of gravity. The passenger cabin was centered over the wing, along with the aircraft's fuel. The cockpit and the electronics compartments were quite heavy. Putting these in the very front

of the aircraft counterbalanced the weight of the aircraft's tail, which made the 737 nearly perfect in this respect. Baggage compartments (one in front and one behind the wing) could also be evenly loaded, simplifying the weight and balance scenario. Because of the foresight of its designers, the 737 was very simple to load and tended to inherently stay within its balance limits. In fact, many airlines had no need to (and still do not on certain 737 models) account for where the passengers physically sat in the aircraft. If passengers all sat in the front or in the back, the aircraft would still be within its wide center of gravity limits. As a result, airlines used average balance numbers that made the weight and balance calculations simple and easily allowed for "open seating." With tail-mounted engines, the fuselage and passenger cabin needed to be extended farther in front of the wing and made the location where people sat much more critical, complicating the loading scenario. It is interesting to note that an empty 727 (especially the stretched 727-200 models, which had a long fuselage forward of the wing) was particularly susceptible to this problem. Because of this, some fuel or ballast was required to be on board the empty aircraft, or it would likely have been a tail-sitter! For that reason, from the initial design of the 727-100 the ventral airstairs on all 727s were made robust enough to prevent this problem.

With the engines mounted under the wings the passenger cabin could be longer, with seating farther back toward the tail. It has been a long standing requirement not to have passenger seats in very close proximity to a jet engine's core in case of a catastrophic, un-contained engine failure. On aircraft like the 727 with fuselage-mounted engines, these areas were used for lavatories and galleys. Other aircraft like the Caravelle used this area for additional baggage space. This effect gave the 737, with wing-mounted engines, an enormous efficiency advantage. When compared to the 727-100, the eventual 737 design was much smaller at sixty percent of its footprint, but could carry eighty percent of the passenger load of the larger jet.

Operationally, the low tail, wing-mounted engine format benefitted airlines by making maintenance in these areas far simpler and safer, limiting the use of very tall stands and cherry pickers. Removal of ice and snow from the aircraft on the ground was vastly simplified, allowing the deicing crew a clear view of the tops of the horizontal stabilizers without the use of an excessively tall platform.

When taking into account all of the advantages of the wing-mounted engine and conventional tail design, it was decided that this configuration was markedly superior to the T-tail design very popular at the time. The design difficulties, handling characteristics, and added weight simply overshadowed the minor aerodynamic advantages of the T-tail. The 737 would ultimately become the trendsetter in this regard, as nearly all of the larger airliners produced today have a conventional tail design. History shows that the 737 engineers made a sensible choice.

The Flexible Competitor

Meanwhile at Douglas, the Boeing threat was on the radar and their sales and design people were aggressive in their efforts to secure orders for their aircraft. They could also see that every airline wanted something different. Instead of making one aircraft fit all of the airlines' needs they were willing to engineer the DC-9 into whatever size and configuration necessary to meet the individual airlines' requirements and ensure the sale. The narrow fuselage had the advantage of allowing the aircraft to be short and small or long with a higher capacity. Their use of the Pratt & Whitney JT8D powerplant was also very wise. This engine was eventually offered in many different thrust ratings to meet the needs of each airframe size. If the five-abreast fuselage was a lemon, it would seem Douglas was determined to make as much lemonade as possible.

The Launch of the 737 Program

"If the 737 proves to be a successful program, it may be the only time in history that a manufacturer entered a field as late with respect to its competitors as we did this one and made a success of it." –Jack Steiner

Lufthansa was squarely in Boeing's sights as a potential customer for the 737. The airline had been a loyal customer so far and was operating a large number of Boeing 707s and 727-100s. Maintaining this relationship with Lufthansa was paramount for Boeing's sales team. However, it rapidly became apparent that it would be a hard sale. During this time Lufthansa had leased a sole DC-8 (the prototype N8008D, c/n 45252, l/n 1), which was being used in revenue service. According to Jack Steiner, it soon became apparent that a pro-Douglas movement was afoot within Lufthansa's management. This was fueled by the airline's desire for a smaller aircraft than what the 737 was developing into. Also political pressures were pushing the purchase of a European product, namely the BAC One-Eleven.

In late 1964, Gerhard Hoeltje, the technical executive of Lufthansa, met in Seattle with Boeing's Joe Sutter. Sutter remembers: "Over at Lufthansa, the guy running the airline was Gerhard Hoeltje. He was a very strong-willed guy. He ran the Berlin Airlift for the US Air Force. He was well-respected and he was running the brand new Lufthansa…Hoeltje was the boss and he was a real general." When Hoeltje visited Seattle, he was presented with a 1:40 scale model of the final configuration 737 in the airline's colors. This meeting was conducted entirely in his hotel room. He made his concerns very clear to Boeing's staff. It would appear he was in favor of the 737 purchase, despite the opposing forces of others in Lufthansa management. In essence, he was willing to stick his neck out and order the 737 if Boeing would commit to making the 737 project "firm." Finances were tight in Seattle, with the Supersonic Transport (Boeing 2707) and the 747 projects taking the lion's share of available funds. After the meeting with Hoeltje, Boeing executives deliberated at length about the 737, because none of the other airlines were ready to place an order. But Hoeltje was becoming impatient and was not willing to delay any longer. By February 1965, Boeing would have to promise to produce the 737 or Lufthansa would have no choice but to order the DC-9.

Boeing's board of directors met in New Orleans to deliberate the future of the 737 program. At the conclusion of the meeting, president of Boeing William Allen announced the decision to "go firm" and produce the 737. Shortly thereafter, on February 19, 1965, Lufthansa ordered twenty-one 737-130 aircraft. This was a two-fold historic event. Not only did this order launch the world's best-selling jetliner into production, but it was also the first time a foreign airline had been a launch customer for Boeing. Although the Lufthansa order was larger than expected, the 737 program was still on shaky ground. More orders would need to be procured

quickly to keep the program alive. Chief Test Pilot Al Jones recalls another such meeting:

One thing about Dick Taylor and the 737, I think he's the one guy who saved that program. They were about to cancel the whole thing because it wasn't selling and we had lots of problems. I think Lufthansa was our only customer, and they bought the first [737s]. It wasn't selling well. I sat in on a meeting where I was in the background. I wasn't doing anything except listening. Dick spoke up about the fact that we could solve the problems that the airplane had and the board of directors said, "OK, we'll keep it going." He was the main reason that airplane continued on, I think.

Eastern Airlines had also been a loyal Boeing customer in the past, but a new management team was at the helm. The airline's president, Floyd Hall, generally liked the 737, but others on his team had different ideas. Eastern's Vice President of Planning William Crilly was previously an engineer for Douglas and still had a strong allegiance to the company and the DC-9. Vice President of Finance Todd Cole had come to Eastern from Delta Air Lines, which was also a company that historically purchased Douglas aircraft.

Aside from the preferences of key management, Boeing faced other obstacles persuading Eastern to order the 737. Eastern had identified the need for new aircraft early on. Boeing's jet was at least a couple years from service, while Douglas offered much earlier delivery slots for its DC-9. As an added incentive, Douglas offered Eastern a lease agreement for other aircraft until its order could be filled. It would appear Douglas wanted to make the Eastern deal with a "whatever it takes" approach. Eastern wanted an aircraft a bit smaller than the 737 concept, but a bit larger than the DC-9-10. In response, Douglas designed the DC-9-30, which was 14 ft. 11 in. longer than the -10, to further attract Eastern as a customer. This new aircraft featured substantial changes to the wings, with the addition of leading edge slats to enhance the aircraft's takeoff and landing performance. As a result, the -30 series aircraft had little parts commonality with the earlier version. Despite Boeing's best efforts, on February 25, 1965, Eastern Airlines announced its order for twenty-four stretched DC-9Bs (later re-designated the DC-9-30) with an additional lease of fifteen DC-9-10 aircraft. This was a major setback for the 737 program at Boeing, and once again placed the 737 program in jeopardy. It was imperative that more orders come in for the program to survive.

Over the years, Boeing had developed and maintained a strong working relationship with United Airlines' President William A. "Pat" Patterson. United had been on Boeing's wish list as a customer from the very beginning of the 737 concept. United had already identified a need for an aircraft of slightly higher capacity than the 737-100. Boeing offered a slightly larger version of the aircraft which added an additional six feet of fuselage using two three-foot extensions: one in front of the wing and one immediately behind it. This new version became known as the 737-200 series. To accommodate United's needs, Boeing used a wider cabin on the 737 similar to the 707 and 727. The wider fuselage proved to be one of the 737's greatest strengths. The lengthening of the cabin and the aerodynamic improvements to

Western Airlines President Terrell Croft "Terry" Drinkwater with one of his company's Boeing 720-047Bs (N93146, c/n 18452, l/n 310). *Courtesy of Delta Air Lines*

the tail section were also born from Boeing's proactive efforts to fulfill United's desires. This flexibility ultimately paid off on April 5, 1965, when United placed what was (at the time) the largest airliner order in history. United agreed to purchase forty Boeing 737-222 aircraft with options for another thirty. In addition to this, United also ordered twenty-six Boeing 727 jetliners. Boeing had achieved a great victory. With this order, the 737 program was now on a much more solid foundation.

Meanwhile, at Western Airlines, Terry Drinkwater had become interested in the now-firm 737 and was very insistent with his board of directors that Western place an order for the aircraft. However, there were other opinions within the management ranks at Western. One of the managers, Dick Ault, was very supportive of purchasing the DC-9. The company had been a long time operator of the Boeing 720 (a short-range 707 derivative) and was not content with the aircraft's reliability statistics. Additionally, it appeared, at the time, that the DC-9 design would provide better lifting performance out of high-altitude Denver Stapleton Airport, where Western had many flights. Western's Vice President Stanley Shatto joined others in top management

and mandated that if Western was going to purchase the 737 it had to meet standard FAA rules, with additional stipulations. The FAA requires that any transport category airliner must meet certain performance requirements on every flight. According to the rules, an airliner has to be able to have an engine failure just prior to liftoff and still have satisfactory climb performance to clear terrain and obstacles on departure within specified altitude margins. Shatto insisted that the 737 be able to accomplish this single-engine climb, but with the additional weight requirement to accommodate a full passenger cabin and plenty of fuel. This "hot and high" airport performance requirement forced Boeing's engineers to try to match the DC-9's single-engine climb performance. The fix was to increase the 737's wingspan from 87 ft. to 93 ft. This would increase lift, but also had the negative effect of increasing weight. The change proved to be a good move, because it ultimately won the sale for Boeing and made the 737 a much more versatile aircraft in the process. Western's order for sixteen 737-200s was announced on August 6, 1965. Western later told officials at Boeing that if the wing had not been changed they would have bought the DC-9. By November 1965, orders

Before cutting metal for the first aircraft, Boeing built the "737 Class 11 Mockup Vehicle," a full scale replica to check the fit of all components. At this stage interference problems could be addressed and solved. An earlier 727 mockup is visible behind the 737. *Courtesy of The Boeing Company*

for the 737 had already exceeded those of the BAC One-Eleven. According to Jack Steiner, it became apparent at this point that the real challenger to the 737 would be the DC-9.

Designing the 737
Keep it Simple

Boeing designed the 737 to take advantage of cutting edge technology, but kept the aircraft as simple as possible to build, fly, and maintain. Each system was designed with this in mind. One case in point was the aircraft's flight control system. Most jetliners at the time, including the 727, had an inboard and outboard aileron on each wing. All four ailerons functioned together at low speeds (flaps extended), augmented by the flight spoiler system, to have responsive roll control from side to side. Conversely, when the flaps were retracted, the outboard ailerons were locked out in a neutral position. The use of outboard ailerons at high speed had a tendency to cause torsional twisting forces

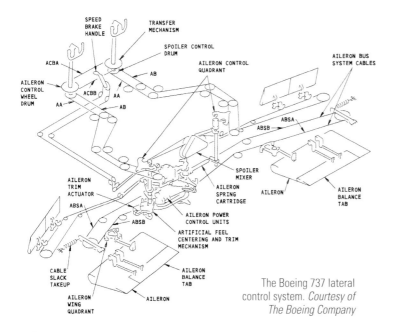

The Boeing 737 lateral control system. *Courtesy of The Boeing Company*

to the wing, hence they were deactivated at higher speeds. One major disadvantage to the inboard and outboard aileron configuration was that it added significant complexity to the aircraft systems. The designers of the 737 realized that their aircraft was going to cruise at slightly lower speeds than its predecessors and also had a much shorter wing. These two factors eliminated the need for inboard ailerons, allowing the aircraft to use outboard ailerons full time without ill effect.

Even though simplicity was built into the 737's flight control system, it still utilized state-of-the-art technology. All primary flight controls were hydraulically powered (unlike those on the DC-9 and BAC One-Eleven) through redundant systems. The ailerons and elevators were powered by two independent hydraulic systems. Each hydraulic system could easily handle the entire load by itself, although under normal circumstances they worked together. As an additional safety measure, a backup, cable-driven system was added in case of complete hydraulic failure. This backup system in the 737 was similar to the primary system on the DC-9. The rudder also had an alternate control mode in case normal hydraulic power failed. The third, standby hydraulic system would actuate the rudder in an emergency. The entire system was robust and extremely redundant.

The landing gear system is another example of simplicity built into the 737 design. Using forty percent fewer moving parts than the 727's landing gear system, a cost effective, straightforward design was achieved. For example, the 727 had a landing gear door system that required complex hydraulics and valve sequencing to operate. Prior to the landing gear's extension, doors covering each landing gear leg had to be opened in sequence. Once the landing gears were down and locked the gear doors would close, once again in sequence. Gear retraction followed the same operation in reverse order. Each of these doors required numerous hydraulic lines and valves to function. In contrast, the landing gear for the 737 used the geometric movement of the landing gear legs themselves to move their doors into position mechanically. Where the 727 used a separate door to cover the main gear wheels while retracted, the 737 used the outboard wheel itself, which was flush with the lower fuselage to achieve drag

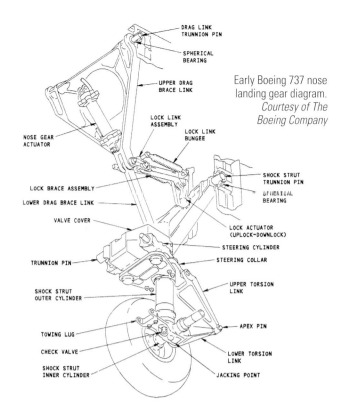

Early Boeing 737 nose landing gear diagram. *Courtesy of The Boeing Company*

DRAG LINK TRUNNION PIN
SPHERICAL BEARING
UPPER DRAG BRACE LINK
NOSE GEAR ACTUATOR
LOCK LINK ASSEMBLY
LOCK LINK BUNGEE
SHOCK STRUT TRUNNION PIN
SPHERICAL BEARING
LOCK BRACE ASSEMBLY
LOWER DRAG BRACE LINK
VALVE COVER
LOCK ACTUATOR (UPLOCK-DOWNLOCK)
STEERING CYLINDER
STEERING COLLAR
TRUNNION PIN
UPPER TORSION LINK
SHOCK STRUT OUTER CYLINDER
APEX PIN
TOWING LUG
CHECK VALVE
LOWER TORSION LINK
SHOCK STRUT INNER CYLINDER
JACKING POINT

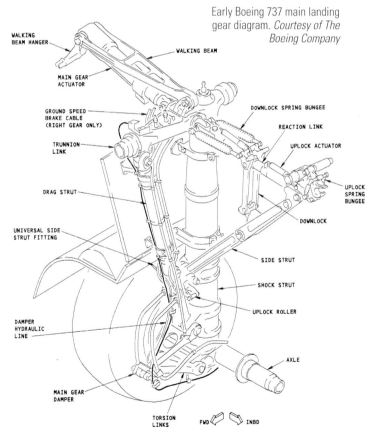

Early Boeing 737 main landing gear diagram. *Courtesy of The Boeing Company*

WALKING BEAM HANGER
WALKING BEAM
MAIN GEAR ACTUATOR
DOWNLOCK SPRING BUNGEE
GROUND SPEED BRAKE CABLE (RIGHT GEAR ONLY)
REACTION LINK
TRUNNION LINK
UPLOCK ACTUATOR
UPLOCK SPRING BUNGEE
DRAG STRUT
DOWNLOCK
UNIVERSAL SIDE STRUT FITTING
SIDE STRUT
SHOCK STRUT
UPLOCK ROLLER
DAMPER HYDRAULIC LINE
AXLE
MAIN GEAR DAMPER
TORSION LINKS
FWD   INBD

reduction. A specially designed hub cap was installed on each outboard wheel for this purpose. This also streamlined the alternate landing gear extension system and provided simple free fall operation, which used gravity to lock each gear leg into position. Therefore, no provision had to be made on the 737 to move the doors out of the way prior to landing gear extension.

When comparing the 737's electrical system to that of the earlier 727, it is apparent that the former is less complex. Both aircraft use a 115 volt, 400 cycle alternating current (AC) system as their basis, but their execution is a bit different. The 727 was designed to have more than one generator powering portions of the electrical system simultaneously. In this type of system, the alternating frequencies of each generator may vary slightly. Since this was not good for the electrical system and could cause damage to the generators, the synchronizing of cycle frequencies was required, either manually (as on the 727) or automatically (as on the DC-9). This required additional equipment or controls to accomplish. The 737 was simpler, since the electrical system was not set up to parallel AC power under any circumstances. Only one generator could power a bus at a time, but redundancy was retained by allowing automatic switching of power sources for most of the system. This concept eventually became typical of all subsequent Boeing twin-engine aircraft models.

The 737's systems were simplified for several reasons. As a general rule, systems with fewer moving parts require less maintenance and boost an aircraft's reliability. In addition, a smaller number of components made the 737 more cost effective to produce and shortened production time. Some simplification was also required for the aircraft to be certified for and effectively flown by a two-pilot crew. In short, simplicity generated operational economy and reliability for the airlines. This became an important element of the 737's appeal.

From a production and operating cost perspective, total parts count was also very important to the 737 program. Jack Steiner recorded the following comparison between the 727 and 737 in his notes (courtesy of the Boeing Archives):

	727	737	Percentage of 727 Parts Count
Main Landing Gear	1,076	438	40%
Wheel Well Parts	679	94	14%
Total Structure	73,780	47,570	64%
Hydraulics	251	126	50%
Cockpit Instruments	92	54	59%

The benefit quantified by Steiner's chart was twofold. A smaller parts count meant the machine was simpler to produce. Therefore, it required less labor and had fewer parts-related expenses. Also, since the 737 had fewer parts, it followed that there was less likelihood of line maintenance costs and flight cancellations due to mechanical issues. This design concept was beneficial for Boeing and the airlines.

Even with all of the refinements and changes to the design of the 737, the 737 and 727 are more similar than different. This is not surprising, since having as much parts commonality as possible with the 727 was a high priority. This was advantageous from a production cost standpoint, and also reduced training requirements for pilots and mechanics transitioning to the 737 from other Boeing products. To that end, the final production "original" series 737 had sixty percent parts commonality with its older sister, the 727.

Redefining the Art of Cockpit Design

The designers of the 737 had another challenge to conquer; one that was not only difficult, but could not be solved by traditional engineering alone. The required cockpit crew complement was a very hot topic, and in 1965, Federal Aviation Regulation (FAR) Part 25 was enacted. This new set of specifications governed the certification of commercial aircraft weighing more than 75,000 pounds. One of the provisions of FAR Part 25 was the requirement for the aircraft's cockpit and crew complement to be certified based on workload studies as a "quantitative" assessment. This new requirement pushed Boeing's engineers to completely rethink the art of cockpit design and produce an aircraft with a markedly superior cockpit configuration.

It is noteworthy that the Douglas DC-9 and the BAC One-Eleven were certified under the older rules (CAR 4b), which established more of a "qualitative" set of parameters. Neither of these aircraft were required to meet the strict cockpit design requirements that the 737 met and exceeded. According to the DC-9 Type Certificate Data Sheet, all of the follow-on aircraft up through the -51 series were grandfathered in under CAR 4b. Not until the certification of the DC-9 Super 80 in 1981 was this requirement mandated, as the new version was certified under FAR Part 25.

When airlines search for an aircraft to purchase economics dominate the decision-making process. The expense of employing and training a third crew member was significant, and had the potential to swing sales over to the DC-9, in particular. Douglas would have an important advantage unless the requirements of FAR Part 25 could be altered to allow a larger jet to have a two-crew cockpit. This was of paramount importance and a gargantuan undertaking for Boeing. It was necessary to apply for the change, even though Douglas protested for very strategic reasons.

Douglas was not the only obstacle. The Air Line Pilot's Association (ALPA) quickly acted to block any change of the federal regulation. Its reasoning was simple: three crewmembers in the cockpit would be safer than two. This was a strong argument, and required Boeing to produce significant empirical evidence to the contrary. Additionally, a significantly advanced cockpit design was required to prevail in certifying a two-pilot cockpit for the 737.

Marketing manager Peter Morton, who was later instrumental in the design of the Boeing 757 cockpit, recalled how the art of cockpit design made a pivotal change with the 737 program:

When I went to Boeing in 1958, there was not a flight deck group. It was called the "Installations" Group. That was its name, and its sole purpose was to install whatever the airplane systems designer would conceive of: the necessary indicators and controls, the hydraulics designer, air conditioning designer, the fuel designer, and so on. Installation's job was to install it. They did not have a defined responsibility to consider human factors, such as it was in those days. Each systems designer would specify how they wanted their system to be operated, not as part of an integrated concept. It wasn't until the 737 that Boeing created their first "Flight Deck Group," and established a person in charge of it, Harty Stoll, and had him report at a high level, where there was interest and responsibility for the entire airplane operation. That was James Copenhaver, the 737 Chief Project Engineer. At this point, Mr. Copenhaver was getting a fair amount of help from Dick Taylor, who was the Director of Engineering for the 737 and a qualified Boeing test pilot. On the 757, we developed this concept into a formal document called the Crew Interface document, which became source material for the Operations Manual and Quick Reference Handbook, as well as the Minimum Equipment List. This document formalized the practices that Harty Stoll created in the initial 737 flight deck design.

There were places where the systems on the 737 were rethought, and these design alterations went far beyond the instrument panels and their presentation to the pilots. A lot of thought was given to the autopilot system as a tool which could be used by the pilot to reduce his or her workload. The Sperry SP-77 autopilot was developed with this goal in mind. Superior to the earlier SP-50 design used in the early 727s, it had a feature called "Control Wheel Steering" (CWS). When the autopilot was engaged in CWS mode, the pilot was able to "set" the aircraft manually to a pitch (nose up or down) or roll (banking from side to side) angle and then let go. The autopilot maintained that condition until it was either disengaged, or the pilot made a modification to the aircraft's flight altitude. This allowed the pilot to have manual control over the aircraft, and then, in essence, let go of the controls to attend to other tasks. The 737 was the first commercial aircraft to employ this system and it is still a feature on every 737 delivered today.

The alternate landing gear extension was another system that was designed specifically with pilot workload in mind. In earlier designs, if the normal system that extended the landing gear failed (hydraulic system A for all 737s) a rather involved procedure would ensue. It was not only distracting for at least one of the pilots, but it could even be physically tiring. For example, on the 727, to use the alternate gear extension one of the crew members (normally the flight engineer) had to open up three doors in the floor of the rear portion of the cockpit. A manual extension cranking tool was mounted near the cockpit door. This tool would be inserted into the labeled socket for each landing gear leg and manually turned until the respective gear down indication was observed. This not only took time, but also required a crew member to leave his station to complete the task. Since the 737 would have to demonstrate non-normal procedures with one pilot incapacitated this had to be simplified. The 737's alternate gear system was designed with the "set it and forget it" mindset. Within arm's reach of either pilot, a small door on the cockpit floor would be opened to expose three red handles. These handles were connected via a cable system to the mechanical locks that held each individual landing gear leg in the retracted position. Provided the normal landing gear control handle was not selected to the "UP" position, pulling these handles caused the respective landing gear leg to free fall into the "down and locked" position. Verification could be made by simply looking for the green annunciator light, indicating the extension was complete.

On earlier aircraft, the pressurization control system required human input prior to takeoff, at the beginning of the descent, and in case of an emergency return to the departure airport. All of these times are busy, and a new design was required to meet

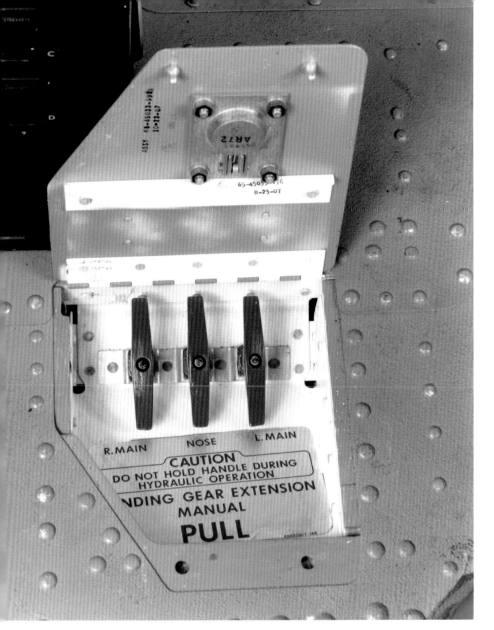

The emergency landing gear extension handles are in easy reach of both pilots under a hatch on the cockpit floor. Pulling these handles causes the landing gears to free fall into the extended position. *Courtesy of The Boeing Company*

The early analog pressurization control panel. *Author's Collection*

top left corner of the overhead panel. If a non-normal condition was sensed on this panel the corresponding "FLT CONT" light would illuminate on the top left corner of the annunciator panel. This made it easy for the pilot to locate the system. On the flight control panel the pilot could see the specific warning light. The non-normal checklist (often referred to as a Quick Reference Handbook or "QRH") was organized into systems so the appropriate checklist could be found quickly and efficiently.

Dealing with an in-flight engine fire and subsequent engine shutdown needed to be accomplished easily with one pilot incapacitated. If the warning system sensed an engine fire, a red fire handle illuminated and an alarm bell sounded. These handles were labeled to identify the engine in question: #1 for the left engine and #2 for the right. The proper procedure for a pilot faced with an engine fire required the pilot to manipulate the affected engine's thrust lever, start lever, and fire handle. All of these items were positioned in order of operation (forward to aft) between the pilots. This allowed the crew to deal with the issue easily and with a very high degree of "efficiency of movement." The central location of these controls made it convenient for the other pilot to confirm these critical actions were executed properly.

737 flight deck designer Hartwell "Harty" Stoll also recognized that there were certain systems panels that were looked at more frequently than others: fuel, electrical, hydraulic, pressurization, and engine instrumentation. The cockpit was painted dark grey except for these panels, which were painted light grey, allowing rapid visual identification of these high reference systems.

There were times when the aircraft's warning system was designed to not alert the pilot to a minor problem and it was automatically handled by a backup. These "two channel" systems, such as mach trim, speed trim, and auto-slats, had a second, fully functional channel to manage the task. A single channel fault on these systems would not alert the pilot unless the second channel failed, or the pilot specifically tested the warning system by pressing the annunciator panel on the glare shield. If there was

the "set it and forget it" criterion. The 737 employed a fully automatic pressurization system which under normal circumstances only needed to be set with the planned cruise altitude and field elevation of the destination airport. Once airborne no changes needed to be made if the flight went as planned. The best feature of this system was that it would be completely hands off in the event of an emergency return to the departure airport. If the system sensed it had not reached the cruise altitude set during the preflight, cabin pressure changes would be scheduled for an arrival back at the departure airport. The crew would be alerted with an "OFF SCHED DESCENT" light, but would not need to intervene. This system worked so well that by 1982, many 727s had been modified with the 737 style system.

One of the most important systems designed to help the pilot quickly assess a malfunction (or "non-normal" condition, as it is referred to by Boeing) was the master caution system, which was made to reflect the position of a particular system's panel in the cockpit. For example, the flight control system panel was on the

The order of systems listed on the left and right master caution panels emulate the order in which they are installed on the 737 overhead panel shown (737-700 pictured). *Author's Collection*

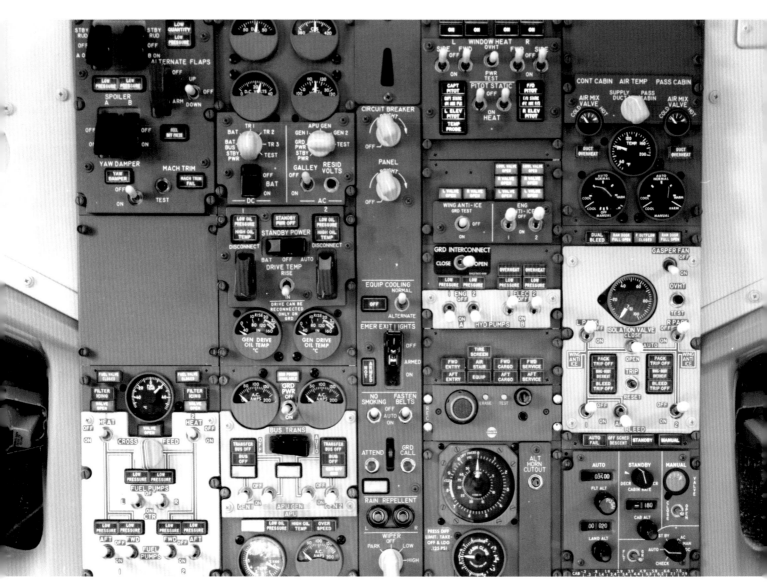

The layout of the 737-200 overhead panel corresponds to the master caution annunciators shown. *Courtesy of The Boeing Company*

a single channel fault it would make itself apparent only during this pilot-initiated test.

The warning system on the 737 was designed to provide important systems information to the pilots while not overloading the crew with too much information. This was a very important concept, as NASA (and later NTSB) Human Factors Specialist Dr. John Lauber recalled:

> Some accidents and incidents that had occurred involved overwhelming the crew with warning information, flashing lights, sounding buzzers, warning horns, and this and that. It was an issue that was of concern…the plethora of warning information was something that was cited in one accident that comes to mind, which was the British accident involving the Trident *Papa India* that crashed near the Staines Reservoir. It was a situation involving some crew human factors. The captain…was not communicating effectively with the crew. As they departed Heathrow [London], one of them retracted the leading edges [slats] early and basically they stalled the airplane. As that scenario unfolded there were all kinds warning lights, bells, buzzers, and stick shakers. One of the factors noted in the accident report was this overwhelming flow of information that was not well managed, putting people in a situation where it was almost impossible under the pressure of real-time operations to be able to sort out what all of that meant. That was an issue that was being addressed.

Boeing engineers also sought input from their highly respected test pilot staff, an important element in designing a truly efficient cockpit. Test Pilot Brien Wygle remembered:

> We had to consider the incapacitation of a pilot or the distraction of one of the pilots…The [Control Wheel Steering] system came from Wichita, where it had been used on the B-52; of course that was not a certified system, but it was a useful way of flying the autopilot without taking your hands off the controls. I asked for the pre-takeoff checklist to be on the [control] column and they did that. I also asked for the little notepad on the sliding window so it was easy for either pilot to take a note. These sound like small things, but they added up enormously when [it] came to time and motion studies. The landing gear alternate extension system was a big deal; it was tremendous. Not only was it simple, but it worked like a charm. Most pilots have had experiences [in other airplanes] trying to get the gear down, struggling away. The 737 had a quick release system that worked perfectly: the gear just popped out. Another place I put effort was the checklist. I took the 727 checklist and wanted to cut it way down. It was not too popular among some of my fellow pilots, who felt that every item had a place on the 727. I wanted a checklist that would be brief, but would be totally safe. As an example, the 727 had "No Smoking" signs and "Seatbelt" signs on the checklist, and on the 737 we automated them, so that when the gear came up

the "No Smoking" [sign] went off. When the flaps came up the "Seatbelt" sign [would turn off]. That was automated, so you didn't have to do it anymore. The pilot could, of course, override it. I didn't see any point of having it on the checklist. We had developed an early "panel scan" or "flow" system going from aft to forward, left to right, forward to down, putting all of the switches where they were supposed to be before you would start the checklist. So I wanted the checklist to make sure that the flaps were right and everything you needed for a safe takeoff, but not every comfort item. Our challenge was to get a two-man crew out of this. So we wanted to be sure. We were blessed with an excellent flight deck design staff and together we came up with a pretty good cockpit.

When Boeing redesigned the cockpit, everything down to the smallest detail was addressed. Even the pilots' seatbelt systems were attended to. Since the FAA had determined that the 737 needed to be flown easily with one pilot incapacitated, an unconscious pilot would have to be kept from interfering with the aircraft's flight controls. With the old seat belts, the pilots' shoulder harnesses had a built-in inertia reel similar to a modern automotive seatbelt. It allowed movement unless rapid deceleration was sensed by the system, which would cause it to lock. This system, which allowed a pilot freedom of movement to access all of the controls in the cockpit, would not prevent a disabled pilot from slumping over the controls. To prevent this from occurring a small lever was installed on the inboard side of each pilot's seat. Being placed within easy reach of the other pilot, the shoulder harnesses could be locked, keeping an unconscious pilot upright and away from the flight controls.

It's All in the Wing

The wings of the new 737 had to be quite unique to meet the design's speed and efficiency goals. First and foremost, consideration had to be given to the nature of the aircraft's mission. Short stage lengths meant the aircraft would spend a large percentage of its flying time at lower altitudes compared to longer range aircraft like the 707 and 727. For low altitude operations (20,000 to 30,000 ft.), the wings had to be smaller to allow moderate speed with acceptable fuel efficiency and to provide a smooth ride through turbulence. On the other hand, it would have to be large enough to carry enough fuel to meet its range requirements. Although this sounds easy enough, one must also look at the rest of the mission.

The 737 was designed to replace older aircraft operating from short runways with a variety of temperatures and field elevations. In general, a designer wanted to install a large wing to meet this requirement. But the engineers at Boeing realized they had an aircraft that needed a small wing for cruise and a large wing for takeoff and landing performance. The question was how could they meet both requirements.

The answer lied in the wing flap system originally developed for the 727. The 727 was designed for a different mission than the 737, but shared a similar problem. The 727 was designed to have a larger but highly swept wing optimized for high altitude and high speed flight. Its highly swept wing design had a similar effect on takeoff and landing to the 737's smaller wing. To meet the needs of the 737, lift would have to be greatly increased to bring the aircraft's takeoff and landing speeds down low enough to allow operations on shorter runways, and to improve climb performance at higher weights. The use of high lift devices that could be deployed at lower speeds transformed the aircraft's wing, optimized for cruising efficiency, into a low speed, high lift wing to meet all of its design goals.

The Wing Flap System

The 737 borrowed many design features from its big sister, the 727. The trailing edges of the wing employed a system of Fowler-type flaps that were nothing short of beautiful to see in action. As the flaps extended, they moved out from the trailing edge of the wing and increased the total area of the wing. As they extended farther they began to move downward, increasing the curvature of the top of the wing and greatly enhancing lift. This curvature developed a strong low pressure area on the top of the wing, generating high lift. The faster the air flowed over this curved surface the more lift was generated. Realizing this increased curve was not quite enough, the designers decided to put three "slots" in each flap panel. This allowed a small amount of high pressure air to transition from the bottom of the wing to the top of the flap assembly. This high pressure air accelerated quickly once it passed to the top and created additional lift without an increase in the speed of the aircraft. The use of three slots allowed the effect to compound upon itself and resulted in a system that was pure genius!

Despite these huge gains in performance more low speed performance still needed to be milked out of the 737's small wing. For this, the engineers focused on the leading edge of the wing. By allowing the leading edge of the wing to slide down on track assemblies, the same effect that was generated at the back of the wing could be put to use on the leading edge. These sliding panels

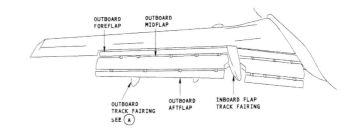

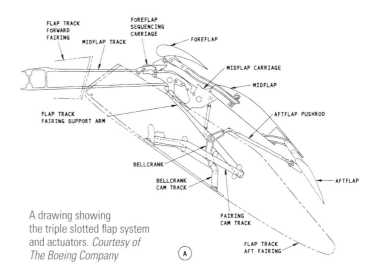

A drawing showing the triple slotted flap system and actuators. *Courtesy of The Boeing Company*

One of the 737-222 test aircraft shows the leading edge slat configuration. The outboard slat extended farther than the inboard panels, exposing the gap between the slat and the wing. Note the early 727-type thrust reverser. *Courtesy of The Boeing Company*

were called "slats," and also increased the curvature of the top of the wing. Boeing Aerodynamics Engineer Vic Page recounted:

Because the 737 was an airplane that would be going into small fields we needed a very high lift system, so that we could come in at low approach speeds and takeoff easily. So we not only put on the three position [triple slotted] trailing edge flaps we had developed for the 727, but we also put on a three position leading edge. This was the first airplane that ever had a three position leading edge: one position being retracted, the next position being part way down with no gap, and the third position where we would gap the slat [away from the wing].

The three slats on each wing were positioned outboard of the engine nacelles. As the trailing edge flaps extended the slats automatically deployed part way to enhance takeoff performance. As the trailing edge flaps were extended farther toward a fully extended landing setting the slats continued movement to a fully extended position, exposing a small slot behind them. The same concept applied, as it allowed high pressure air from the bottom of the wing to energize the airflow over the top of the wing, creating even more lift.

Additionally, the leading edge inboard of the engines needed some augmentation for low speed flight. Since this section of the inboard wing was thicker compared to the outboard section, a device called a "Krueger flap" was designed into the wing. A Krueger flap was normally faired into a compartment in the bottom of the forward section of the wing. As the pilot deployed the trailing edge flaps, the slats automatically moved to their intermediate position

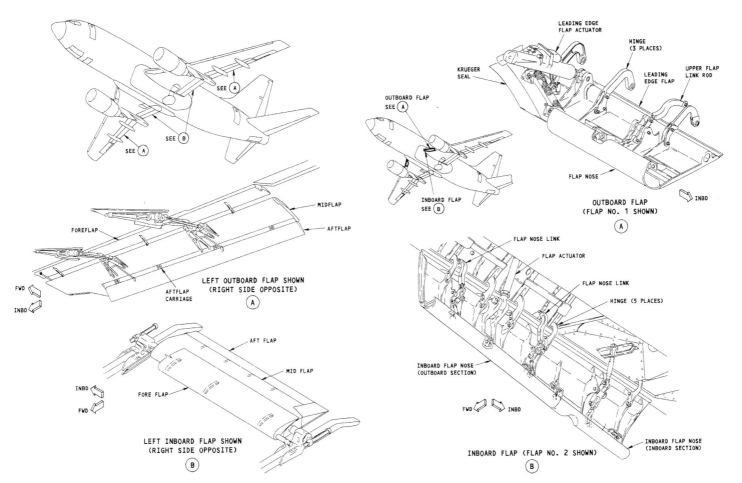

The position of the flap panels shown in a drawing of the 737-300. The flap system of the early 737 is similar. *Courtesy of The Boeing Company*

A drawing showing the position of the inboard Krueger flaps on the 737-300. The early 737s are similar. *Courtesy of The Boeing Company*

and the Krueger flaps unstowed from the bottom of the wing, deploying forward and down, under the leading edge of the wing. They served a similar purpose to the slats and created a more curved upper surface of the inboard section of the wing. When extended, these devices were designed to snug up to the engine pylon, avoiding air spillage around the flap.

The 737 was designed for a unique set of specifications and was the result of creative thinking. Many of the obstacles the designers faced ultimately resulted in a much better aircraft. The two-pilot cockpit, the Western Airlines takeoff performance requirements, and United's desire for greater capacity were examples of influences that changed the final product for the better. Meeting these challenges resulted in a special, unique, and successful jetliner.

The Pratt & Whitney JT8D Powerplant

Choosing an engine can easily make or break even the best airframe designs. This selection was particularly important because the original series 737s were to be offered with just one basic engine option. Initially, the 737 was to be powered by the Pratt & Whitney JTF-10. This engine was essentially a scaled down version of their JT8D engine, which was powering the 727. This smaller engine was considered to be the right size for the early, smaller proposed 737. The JTF-10 design went on to be successful as the basis for the powerplant of the General Dynamics F-111 Aardvark and Grumman F-14A Tomcat. As the 737 concept

evolved into a larger, heavier airplane, more power was required. Boeing already had extensive experience with the more powerful JT8D, used exclusively on the 727. It had been known for reliable operation, and had just become the engine of choice for the Douglas DC-9.

The JT8D was a derivative of Pratt & Whitney's military J52 turbojet engine, which was originally designed to power the USAF's AGM-28 Hound Dog missile. As time went on it proved itself, powering the later A-4 Skyhawk and A-6 Intruder naval aircraft. As the Boeing 727 came to fruition, the modification of the J52 engine saw an additional compressor stage added which was also larger and considered the "fan stage." Roughly fifty percent of the air that was moved through this first stage bypassed the core of the engine. It flowed around the core or "hot section," where this cool, high-velocity air remixed with the engine's hot exhaust at the engine's tailpipe. These engines, often referred to as "turbofan" engines, tended to be much more fuel efficient and quieter than pure turbojet engines. The air that flowed into the hot section of the JT8D was compressed by counter-rotating low and high speed compressor spools consisting of thirteen sets of compressor blades. As the air flowed through these compressor stages it was compressed 14.6 times the outside air pressure. Next, it was fed into the burner section, where fuel was introduced into the very hot, pressurized air, where it ignited. There were nine combustors controlling the atomization of fuel and were designed to feed extremely high pressure exhaust through the two turbine

A cutaway model of the Pratt & Whitney JT8D used on the Original 737 series. *Courtesy of Chadi Akkari*

stages, which turned their associated compressor stages with incredible power and force. In this way, the JT8D (like other jet engines) sustained the compression, combustion, and exhaust cycle. The hot exhaust mixed with the bypassed fan air was finally ejected out of the back of the engine and produced thrust for the aircraft. A comparison between the air pressure in the engine's intake and the higher pressure of the exhaust was a direct way to measure engine power, referred to as engine pressure ratio (EPR). EPR was usually referred to as "eeper" by flight crews and quantified the power setting for this type of engine.

By choosing the larger engine and designing the 737 around its lowest thrust version, Boeing managed to avoid the pitfalls of the BAC One-Eleven. The One-Eleven was committed to the smaller, less powerful Rolls-Royce Spey engine, which stunted the growth of the airframe for much of the aircraft's production run. The JT8D eventually grew from 14,000 to 17,400 pounds of thrust over its lifespan. The major differences between the -1 and -9 variants of the engine involved a parameter known as "thermal limits." As altitudes or temperatures increase, an engine has to create more heat to produce the engine's rated thrust, which in this case was 14,000 pounds. The -1 engine could not create maximum power under hot and high conditions because it would reach its maximum temperature limits fairly early on. Later models, like the -7, could hold their power ratings under much more extreme conditions. The final -17A engine used on the 737 was optimized to produce up to 16,000 pounds of thrust for limited periods of time. Some later 737-200s were fitted with the -17A and exhibited excellent takeoff and climb performance.

The JT8D series of engines became the workhorse of the jet airliner fleets in the 1970s and '80s because of their excellent performance and reliability. They were also much quieter and more fuel efficient than their turbojet counterparts at the time. As time passed, even these excellent engines were eventually outclassed by newer high-bypass turbofan engines, such as the SNECMA's CFM56, which went on to power future generations of the 737.

707 727 720

It comes from a fine family.

The Boeing 737 Twinjet is the newest—and smallest—member of the world's most famous family of jetliners.

It's also the world's most advanced short-range jet. Even though it will fly shorter routes (100 to 1300 miles) and serve smaller cities, the 737 will delight you with a cabin as wide as that of the biggest Boeing jet in service.

The 737's interior spaciousness is unmatched by any other short-haul airliner. It has more height above the aisle. More head room over the seats. More shoulder and elbow room along the windows.

The 737 also inherits the benefits of Boeing's unequalled jet flight experience. Boeing 707s, 720s and 727s have flown more miles, carried far more passengers than any other jets. They are, in fact, the world's most popular jetliner family.

Watch for the superb new Boeing 737 Twinjet. It has already been ordered by: Avianca, Braathens, Britannia, Canadian Pacific, Frontier, Irish, Lake Central, Lufthansa, Malaysia-Singapore, Mexicana, NAC-New Zealand, Nordair, Northern Consolidated, PSA, Pacific, Pacific Western, Piedmont, South African, United, Western, Wien Air Alaska.

BOEING 737

Author's Collection

A National Airways of New Zealand Boeing 737-219 prior to delivery posing with The Museum of Flight's replica of a Boeing B&W, the first aircraft designed and assembled by Boeing in 1916. *Courtesy of The Boeing Company*

CHAPTER 3

THE "ORIGINAL" SERIES: 737-100 AND 737-200

The 737 came into existence due to the skill, knowledge, and dedication of a group of people who were willing to "paint outside the lines" to create an incredibly capable airplane. Dick Taylor, director of engineering for the 737 program, expressed his thoughts on what made the 737 an amazing success:

I would like to tell what we accomplished. For instance, we certified two airplanes at the same time: the 737-100 and the 737-200. We got the certificates in December 1967, and that was after the shortest time period from first flight to certification of any of the Boeing airplanes: eight and three quarter months. A lot of it was on the basis of such a terrific crew of people. Jim Copenhaver was one of the best project engineers that Boeing ever had. He had a way of getting drawings out to the shop on a schedule they could achieve. On every program I had been on there was always some sort of tension between engineering and manufacturing. And some engineers would make a drawing, throw it over the fence, and say, "you build it." Not Copenhaver; he was working the problems for the manufacturing people. He was elegant in that regard. This permeated Copenhaver's team, all the way down through the hydraulics guy, the flight control guy, and Harty Stoll, the cockpit designer. Harty and I had a relationship all the way through. It was a story of people, and I think that is why the 737 was the airplane it was. The other reason I think was that we were seventeen months behind Douglas. They had built an airplane. They had a group of airlines operating the DC-9. Boeing had two airlines: Lufthansa and United. We developed our market from that. We did it by carefully using our time to produce an airplane that had a low weight per passenger. It had the highest lift coefficient in the configuration for landing that we had ever built. When we certified it and compared it to our competition, we could carry more passengers from a shorter field, fly a longer distance, land in a shorter field than the DC-9, and were technically better. We beat the competition and created our own market. How many airplanes have we sold today...over 12,000 and delivered over 8,000, and we are building forty-two a month. We have a backlog that won't quit!

Plant Two

Boeing management elected to use Plant 2, at Boeing Field (KBFI), to conduct the assembly of the first eight 737 airframes. This facility had a vibrant and interesting history. Just prior to WWII, the need arose for a large production hall to support the looming war effort and the facility was increased in size to 1,776,000 square

feet. Officials were well aware that during the war this building would be a prime target for enemy attack, so extraordinary measures to protect it were taken by the US government. Strategists devised a plan to hide the massive structure from aerial visibility by building a full scale replica of a neighborhood on the roof. The plan was implemented, with houses made of real wood and

B-17 Flying Fortress production at Plant 2 during WWII; 6,981 of these bombers were produced here during the course of the war. *Courtesy of The Boeing Company*

Boeing's Plant 2 had a colorful history, including being used to produce B-17 bombers during WWII. A replica of a civilian neighborhood was built on the roof to disguise the factory in case of an enemy attack. *Courtesy of The Boeing Company*

fabric, trees made from thousands of feet of baling wire, and painted streets to complete the illusion. Once operational, Plant 2 was a powerful workhorse for Boeing's military aircraft production. In fact, 6,981 Boeing B-17s rolled out of this building at a peak rate of sixteen per day.

Many other fine aircraft were also assembled at Plant 2, including the Boeing B-307 Stratoliner, B-29, B-50, B-377 Stratocruiser, and the B-52 Stratofortress. Most notably Boeing's first jet, the sleek B-47 strategic bomber, was the genesis of the rich ancestral line of Boeing jets. In late 1965, the 737 became part of this facility's colorful history, albeit briefly. Among the first 737s built were the prototype 737-130, six production aircraft, and the Structural Test Airframe. The facility featured an expansive assembly hall, but suffered from having a very low roof structure. The restricted vertical space available created distinct challenges, such as forcing the builders to assemble the aircraft without their vertical stabilizers and rudders. These were added last, outdoors in a parking lot that was later converted into Taxiway B at Boeing Field. The next 263 Boeing 737s were assembled from start to finish at the Thompson site, approximately one-half mile south of the Plant 2 complex, on East Marginal Way South. In the early 1970s, Boeing's 737 production was moved to Renton, Washington, a community proudly designated the "Jet Transport Capital of the World" by local newspaper *The Record Chronicle*. The City of Renton also posted a sign to declare this and made it highly visible to motorists driving into the community.

Construction of prototype aircraft N73700 (Boeing 737-130, c/n 19437, Effectivity Number PA099) began with these first fuselages assembled on site at Plant 2, unlike subsequent 737 fuselages, which were built in Wichita, Kansas, and transported to Seattle by rail. The assembly of the major airframe components began in June 1966. On January 18, 1967, N73700 was nearly ready for its first flight. A large number of representatives from the airlines and Boeing gathered at the Thompson site to witness its christening by stewardesses from each of the aircraft's airline customers. After 737 production was moved to Renton, the Thompson site was used for a variety of Boeing programs over the decades, until being semi-mothballed and offered for sale. When no sale was consummated, Boeing converted the building into the completion center for the Navy's P-8A Poseidon anti-submarine warfare aircraft—a derivative of the 737-800. So after fifty years, the Thompson site was once again full of new build 737s!

Ship One's mid-fuselage assembly viewed from the rear, with the overwing exit visible toward the front of the section. *Courtesy of The Boeing Company*

The assembly of the rear fuselage pressure bulkhead for Ship One in Plant 2 at Boeing Field. After the first eight airframes 737 fuselage assemblies were constructed in Wichita, Kansas, and transported to Seattle by rail, a tradition that still exists today. *Courtesy of The Boeing Company*

Ship One at the Thompson plant after leaving Plant 2. The vertical stabilizer was added outdoors due to the lack of vertical space at Plant 2. *Courtesy of The Boeing Company*

Adorned with the attractive demonstrator paint scheme, Ship One is shown shortly prior to rollout. *Courtesy of The Boeing Company*

One of the eight 737s built at Plant 2 was the static test airframe, which was not intended for flight. Using hydraulic jacks to simulate maximum loads, the airframe was tested to destruction to determine maximum loads. Note the sensors and test wiring attached to the bottom of the wing. *Courtesy of The Museum of Flight*

Ship Three (PA002, c/n 19014, l/n 3) during assembly at Plant 2. Behind the aircraft's right wing center fuel tank assemblies await installation on subsequent aircraft. This aircraft was delivered to Lufthansa on December 27, 1967. *Courtesy of The Museum of Flight*

Lufthansa flight attendant Heidi Michalski christens Ship One on January 17, 1967. *Courtesy of The Boeing Company*

Flight attendants from the early 737 customers christen the first 737 as Boeing and airline representatives look on. *Courtesy of The Museum of Flight*

The only short-range jet with big-jet comfort.

That's the Boeing 737's big plus for passengers.

The new 737 is the smallest member of the Boeing family of jetliners. Yet it's as wide and roomy as the big 707 Intercontinentals. It's the only airliner that can bring passengers on short-range routes the same wide-cabin comfort travelers enjoy aboard transcontinental and over-ocean flights.

Equally important, the new 737 inherits all the benefits of Boeing's unmatched experience as builder of the world's most successful jetliners.

Newest, most advanced short-haul jet in the world, the 737 is currently undergoing an intensive flight test program. Pilots describe it as a delight to fly. The 737 takes off quickly, quietly. It cruises at 580 miles an hour, and carries up to 113 passengers.

The superb new Boeing 737 goes into service early next year. It has already been ordered by: Avianca, Braathens, Britannia, Canadian Pacific, Irish, Lake Central, Lufthansa, Malaysia-Singapore, Mexicana, NAC-New Zealand, Nordair, Northern Consolidated, PSA, Pacific, Pacific Western, Piedmont, South African, United, Western, Wien Air Alaska.

BOEING 737

Flight Testing

An intensive flight test program commenced with six aircraft: one 737-130 prototype, three production 737-130s, and two production 737-222s. Each aircraft was used to thoroughly and systematically test all flight regimes and aircraft systems. While these parameters were tested two additional items—"cockpit efficiency" and "inlet vortices"—were monitored concurrently "in the background," as these items were a hot topic with the Federal Aviation Administration (FAA). The engineers refined and improved cockpit efficiency by observing the workload and collecting data from pilot questionnaires. The information was then analyzed to assist creating better methods for pilot procedures. Since the aircraft was intended to be certified as a two-pilot aircraft this was of paramount importance. The design goal was to create less individual pilot workload for the 737's two person crew than the 727 with its three person crew. To this end, many systems were designed for simplicity, redundancy, or to be automatic while in flight. The FAA and the airlines were also concerned about the close proximity of the engine inlets to the ground. They noted that under certain taxi speed and wind conditions the

This 1967 advertisement touts the advantages of the 737 design and the wide passenger cabin. *Author's Collection*

running engine occasionally formed a small tornado (or vortice) underneath the inlet that could conceivably suck debris into the engine and possibly damage the engine's compressor blades. This condition was evaluated on an ongoing basis throughout the program to ensure no damage would occur.

The testing workload was split across the six aircraft in the test profile, with each aircraft being assigned a unique number and specific area of operation. Internal to Boeing, all aircraft since the introduction of the 727 carried an "Effectivity Number" used to identify a specific aircraft. These numbers are different from the aircraft serial number and the tail number. The Effectivity Number and serial number for specific aircraft never change, while the tail number may change as the aircraft leaves flight test, or gets sold from airline to airline. Examples of this are Ships 2, 3, and 4, which changed registration when they were delivered to Lufthansa after completing the test program. Each of these six aircraft exhibited various issues during testing that were addressed and corrected prior to FAA certification.

Ship One
First Fight of the Boeing 737

Ship One was the first of her kind, and though built from production drawings, was often referred to as the 737 Proto-type. This aircraft was a 737-130 and carried tail number N73700 (Serial Number 19437), and was issued Effectivity Number PA099 by Boeing. She was involved in the first rollout, was christened by airline representatives, and was present for many other public functions.

On April 9, 1967, the Boeing 737 prototype was tested in flight under the command of Capts. Brien Wygle and Lew Wallick.

The handling of the aircraft was reported as generally good, with two minor issues noted. First was the aircraft's tendency to "Dutch Roll" when the Yaw Damper system was switched off. Dutch Roll is exhibited by most swept wing aircraft and is identified by an alternating yaw and roll motion from side to side. The Yaw Damper

This cover was carried on the first flight of the 737-100 prototype. *Author's Collection*

The first of the breed: Ship One in manufacturer's colors as it appeared during flight testing. *Courtesy of Jennings Heilig*

From left to right: Capts. Brien Wygle and Lew Wallick discuss an early test flight with Flight Test Engineers Fred Pittenger, Scott McMurray, and Ray Utterstrom. *Courtesy of The Boeing Company*

Ship One takes off on an early test flight from Boeing Field. Notice the "bomb" attached to the belly of the aircraft for instrument calibration. Today, a small drogue and tube assembly is attached to the vertical stabilizer and serves the same purpose. *Author's Collection*

Ship One in flight over the Seattle area. *Courtesy of The Museum of Flight*

the proper approach speed. Most aircraft begin to give the pilot tactile warnings of an approaching stall, usually felt as a mild vibration or shaking in the aircraft's pitch (nose up and down) axis. As a rule, this vibration usually begins about ten knots above a stall and will become more pronounced as the aircraft's airspeed decreases. It was noted on the test flight that the onset of the stall buffet occurred much earlier than desired at about twenty knots prior, and when in the stall the aircraft exhibited a fairly sharp roll to the left. Although these issues required some aerodynamics work to rectify, they were not considered serious and the flight was deemed a success.

Behind the scenes, Ardell Anderson (Boeing, retired) was an aerodynamics engineer assigned to record the drag data on the flight. This test was conducted—as most first flights were back in those days—with the landing gear extended for the duration of the flight. Anderson took readings and found that even with the landing gear down the drag numbers were not as expected. The aircraft exhibited between nine and twenty-five percent more drag than anticipated, which was a serious performance problem. Ardell Anderson remembered the time:

system automatically uses the rudder to null this effect. Testing must occur with it off to evaluate the true handling qualities of the aircraft, and to verify that pilots can fly the aircraft after a yaw damper failure, or with the yaw damper inoperative. Second, while validating approach speeds an issue with the aircraft's stall behavior arose. Most aircraft use an approach speed of 1.3 times the lowest speed the aircraft can fly. This lowest speed is called "stall speed" and is referred to as Vs. To determine the exact Vs speed during a test, the aircraft must be stalled and the speed noted. Then the 1.3 margin needs to be factored in to determine

A press conference was held after the first flight of the Boeing 737 prototype. From left to right: Division General Manager Ben Wheat, Capts. Brien Wygle and "Lew" Wallick, and Boeing President Bill Allen. *Courtesy of The Boeing Company*

Capts. Brien Wygle and Lew Wallick with Ship One. *Courtesy of The Boeing Company*

I came back to the supervisor, Bill Huntington, and I showed him a chart which was a percentage deviation of drag predicted versus Mach number. It was like nine or ten percent high at the low Mach numbers, then as you went up in Mach number it went up to fifteen percent, twenty-five percent more than predicted. I remember bringing the data back to Huntington. . . . He began rubbing his head and said, "Andy, Andy, Andy, that's gotta be wrong, that's gotta be wrong. . . . You check your numbers?" That just started all of us on a crusade on the drag.

Throughout the flight test program constant experimentation was being conducted by aerodynamicists to mitigate the 737's high drag numbers. Hours of testing, both with the actual aircraft and in the wind tunnel, were required to improve drag and lift while not adversely affecting aircraft handling.

During and after Ship One's first flight only Boeing personnel were allowed onboard until a Type Inspection Authorization (TIA) was granted by the FAA. Boeing Engineer (retired) Larry Timmons explained the rule:

In the FAA system, a TIA is issued once the manufacturer has completed "all" development and company testing to assure compliance with the regulations and all of the structural testing to support that the airplane's limitations are substantiated. First flight and company development flights are conducted under an "Experimental–Research

and Development" airworthiness certificate per FAR [Federal Aviation Regulation] 21.191. This permission to fly allows the gathering of flight data to support the company's obligation to assure the airplane meets FAR regulations prior to any FAA crew flying. Once documentation of the airworthiness of the airplane (per the regulations) is submitted to the FAA another airworthiness certificate is issued. This is identified as "Experimental - Showing Compliance with the Regulations." This certificate and its specific limitations are coupled with the Type Inspection Authorization (which defines the testing that the FAA requires) and allows the compliance flight test program to proceed with FAA participation.

After the TIA was granted testing for FAA type certification continued for several months; the aircraft logged 274 hours and 9 minutes for this purpose.

Ship One was the primary aircraft used for high speed testing. The maximum design speed was referred to as Maximum Design Mach Number (Md) or Maximum Design Indicated Airspeed (Vd), and was well in excess of the normal operating maximum speeds (Mmo and Vmo). The 737-100 was certified with a Maximum Indicated Airspeed (Vmo) of 350 knots and a Mmo (maximum Mach number) of Mach .84, representing eighty-four percent of the speed of sound. Test Pilot Al Jones commented on the handling of the early test 737s: "It was pretty neutral as I recall…. All of the flying qualities I thought were really good…. It took a bit of a technique to land it properly. A lot of the guys, when we first started, made hard landings until they got used to it."

The High Speed Upset Incident

On May 13, 1967, Brien Wygle and Ralph Cokeley conducted a high speed test that involved airspeeds well above Vmo and approaching Vd. The objective of this task was to test the aircraft's resistance to "flutter." A potentially destructive vibration, flutter has a tendency to manifest itself at very high speeds. Therefore, the aircraft's target speeds were set between Mach .81 and .86,

The 737 cabin configuration as seen during flight testing. The consoles were temporarily installed to allow engineers to monitor aircraft data in real time. *Courtesy of The Boeing Company*

During high-speed flight tests the leading edge slats were pulled out by aerodynamic forces, resulting in significant damage. This incident caused the redesign of the hydraulic slat actuators, incorporating mechanical "up" locks. *Courtesy of the Boeing Company*

Here is another view of the slat damage that caused the loss of the A hydraulic system but resulted in a safe landing by test pilots Brien Wygle and Ralph Cokeley. *Courtesy of The Boeing Company*

with indicated airspeeds of 406–430 knots. The test began at 21,000 feet, with a dive angle of about eight degrees nose down and with all hydraulics to the flight control systems in operation. Control inputs for pitch and roll were initiated at an airspeed of 430 knots at 17,000 feet. Quite unexpectedly, the aircraft departed controlled flight, yawing, rolling, and pitching simultaneously. Due to the aircraft's intense gyrations, the airflow into the engines' intakes was disrupted and the engines began to compressor stall. The test crew heard loud bangs from the engine and immediately brought the throttles back to idle. Despite the harrowing events the aircraft decelerated and the pilots regained control.

Brien Wygle described what transpired during the routine test:

We were doing flutter testing. . . . In flutter testing you do some at a high Mach number and you do some at high indicated airspeeds and low Mach number. In between, usually at about 16,000 feet, there is an area where you get the critical Mach…which becomes the basis for the operating redline. And that is where the max Mach and the max indicated airspeed "Vq," as we call it, meet. It is the most demanding condition…most true airspeed. So I had done a lot of 737 flutter testing and this was near the end. It was under this condition that an incident occurred. It was pretty shocking. Tommy Edmonds was flying the F-86 [chase plane]. It was no help that his radio wasn't working. Anyway, from my point of view, you had to dive the 737 pretty sharply to get up to the higher Mach numbers, and the higher Mach numbers were not very high by that day's (or even today's) standards. The 737 was very draggy in the high Mach region. So I went to pick up this last point [of data] at very high speeds. We would get to the target condition speed and then kick the flight controls in various directions to see if there was any evidence of flutter. Actually, the 737 was very good for flutter and didn't have a flutter problem… . All of a sudden, this most dramatic event occurred, of which I had no idea what was happening. The airplane yawed violently. .

.yawed so violently that both engines, even though we were up at very high speeds, surged. I didn't think that such a thing could happen. A surge was normally a low speed thing. They both surged because the airplane yawed so sharply. . .and all of this at max speed. It pitched up and it pitched down. I seemed to have no control over it! The airplane was simply out of control and rolled sharply, and it didn't do this consistently. I'm sure that the whole thing was over in seconds, but for those seconds my feeling was the only thing that I could think of…that I was familiar with was flutter programs where the tail came off or broke in two. I thought I had lost a big chunk of the tail; otherwise why would it be doing these things? I think that Ralph Cokeley, my co-pilot, was halfway out of his seat…He was going to bail out, but I don't think that would have been successful…we couldn't readily get out of those kinds of airplanes. It was that kind of thing that was so stunning. Of course I throttled back to get the speed down and things at least stabilized. That was because all of the damage was done, with no more to do. I landed without difficulty. We found that the leading edges had come out. The reason that I had so much pitch, roll, and yaw was that they [leading edge slats] each came out asymmetrically and randomly.

Visual inventory was taken of the aircraft and the crew found that the leading edge slats, only used for low speed flight, had somehow deployed. An associated loss of hydraulic fluid in system "A," which powered the slats, was noted and observed venting from the leading edge of the wing. Since this system also powered the normal landing gear extension, prior to landing the crew used the alternate "free fall" system to extend the landing gear. The alternate, electrically actuated system was used to extend the trailing edge flaps and a safe landing was accomplished.

According to post flight reports, the episode was quite violent and deceleration was such that items left unsecured in the rear part of the cockpit were later found forward of the rudder pedals. After analyzing the data, engineers identified a strong low pressure area just forward of and below the leading edge slats when the aircraft was at extremely high airspeeds. The design of the slat actuators relied on captive hydraulic pressure to keep the slats in the up position. The strong low pressure had overpowered the actuators and sucked the slats out into the fully extended position. The excessive air loads on the extended slats caused them to be severely damaged and bent them back under the wing. This destroyed the actuators, causing the subsequent loss of "A" System hydraulic fluid. The issue was later rectified with a revised actuator system that integrated a mechanical lock to secure the slats in the up position. Since the revised actuators were not available until January 1968, all subsequent high speed testing was conducted with the slats secured in the "up" position with steel pins before each test flight.

The venting provisions for the fuel system needed some modifications, as flight at high speeds caused the pressure in the center fuel tank cavity to become excessive, damaging the tank's bladder. Several flight test hours were spent rectifying this issue until a revised venting system remedied the problem.

Low speed performance was another area of concern, as drag and stall speeds were found to be high and needed to be optimized. Most modifications were centered on the leading edge Krueger flaps, with a focus on the shapes of and gaps behind the leading edge slats. These items continued to be modified even into the much later Advanced 737 program.

The primary aircraft for takeoff performance and Vmu testing was PA099. Vmu stands for Velocity, Minimum Unstick, and defines the lowest possible speed at which the aircraft can become airborne on takeoff. A wooden skid was attached to the bottom of the fuselage under the tail to protect the aircraft from damage. During the tests the nose was raised prior to obtaining normal takeoff speed (Vr), causing the tail with its protective skid to drag on the runway. Interestingly, the oak skid cartridge needed to be replaced with a new one every fourth test, as it wore down very quickly. In this condition, the speed at which the aircraft's main landing gears lift off the runway is determined to be Vmu. The aircraft must be able to takeoff, remain readily controllable, and climb to thirty-five feet above the ground at this pitch angle before lowering the nose and accelerating. This aircraft capability became a requirement for all future jet transport certifications after problems with the underpowered de Havilland Comet 1. One example of the Comet 1's ill behavior occurred on March 3, 1953. CF-CUN (c/n 6014) rolled off the end of a runway in Karachi, Pakistan, in a nose high attitude. During its delivery flight to Sydney, Australia, this brand new aircraft failed to become airborne because of the extreme amount of aerodynamic drag caused by this condition.

The de Havilland Comet 1 prototype (G-ALVG) while on an early test flight. The Comet taught airplane designers many difficult lessons, but this pioneering jetliner led the way to much improved future designs. *Courtesy of The Museum of Flight*

Other tests conducted using this aircraft included:

- Landings with a simulated jammed stabilizer trim and a forward center of gravity (nose heavy) condition, with wing flaps set to position 15.
- Simulated runaway stabilizer trim at low and high speed, with wing flaps fully deployed to position 40.
- Manual reversion: In this condition, both hydraulic systems "A" and "B" are depressurized. Ailerons and elevator control

are actuated manually by the pilots using the cable driven, servo tab backup. During this condition the rudder was powered by the emergency "standby" hydraulic system. Wheel brakes are powered by stored accumulator pressure. Stability was found to be good with hydraulics on and off.
- An in-flight simulated "A" system hydraulic failure during slat movement.
- Actual flight with all leading edge slats extended on one wing and all retracted on the other wing.
- A trailing edge flap asymmetry, with flaps on one wing set to position 15 and the other set to position 22, to check controllability (note: The 737 has flap settings of Up, 1, 2, 5, 10, 15, 25, 30, and 40, but intermediate positions were selectable during flight testing).
- Flight with an outboard flight spoiler (#2) locked in full up position while opposite spoilers were in the down position.
- Roll rates measured with and without flight spoiler assistance.
- Testing with simulated ice shapes attached to the wings and stabilizers to check stall characteristics.

Some of the major changes to the aircraft based on these flight tests were:

- Vortex generators were added to the wing to cure pitch issues at high speeds.
- Elevator control forces were reduced to match aileron forces.
- Elevator servo tab rigging was adjusted to lower control forces and make transition from hydraulic power to manual reversion less abrupt.
- A Mach trim system was added to prevent Mach tuck, a tendency for the airplane to lower its nose during acceleration through the higher Mach number speed region.
- The centered position of the elevator was changed to match requirements for the new Mach trim system.
- Spoilers 1 and 8 (outboards) were removed from the roll control, but were still retained for use as ground spoilers to assist in landing and rejected take off (RTO) deceleration.
- Rudder control authority was reduced by adjusting hydraulic control pressure from 3000 psi to 2600 psi. This was to aid in controllability during sideslip (crosswind landing) maneuvers.

After FAA type certification, 314 hours and 56 minutes were logged for added testing and demo flights.

This aircraft was in service with Boeing's Flight Test department until it was acquired by NASA's Langley Research Center in 1974. Here, this historic aircraft made numerous research contributions to aviation technology and safety (see chapter 7). Research on the Microwave Landing System (MLS), Global Positioning System (GPS) navigation, weather radar, wind shear avoidance technology, airborne datalink, and electronic "glass cockpit" instrumentation was pioneered with Ship One. Due to the hard work and persistence of those at Seattle's Museum of Flight, it was placed on loan from NASA in September 1997, and displayed at Boeing Field. The Museum of Flight Pavilion was completed to house this special aircraft, as well as many other historically significant aircraft.

Ship Two

Ship Two was a 737-130, and the first production 737 built. This aircraft was later delivered to Deutsche Lufthansa at the end of the

Test pilots Lew Wallick (left) and H. C. "Kit" Carson prior to the first flight of Ship Two. *Courtesy of The Boeing Company*

certification and testing program. Ship Two carried the temporary registration N2282C (later to become D-ABEA), Serial Number 19013, and Effectivity Number PA001. It logged a total of 304 hours and 48 minutes of flight time during the flight test program.

Ship Two was outfitted with the most test instrumentation of any of the six initial test ships, including:

- Two magnetic tape systems
- Two fifty channel oscillographs
- One direct-write oscillographs
- One nose-mounted APACS camera
- One airborne TOL camera
- Three Millekan cameras
- TV camera with onboard monitor
- Twenty barrel ballast system

This state-of-the-art equipment provided a total of 1,096 data measurement input channels for the test program.

One of the main tasks for this aircraft was to test the 737's performance during a rejected takeoff (RTO). In revenue service, a crew faced with the need to abort or reject a takeoff would use all available tools to stop the aircraft, including brakes, thrust reversers, and speed brakes (spoilers). During testing and certification, the required takeoff distance was determined and allowed a rejected takeoff without credit for the reverse thrust, thereby providing a conservative factor to the performance of the airplane. Even though no credit was given for reverse thrust in calculating the required runway, the flight testing and certification needed to explore the behavior of the airplane while considering all systems (the early 737 exhibited some unusual reverse thrust characteristics). These tests required the aircraft to be heavily loaded to maximum takeoff weight. To accomplish this, the aircraft's cabin was fitted with twenty water barrels that could be filled to meet specific weight requirements. The tests called for the aircraft to be accelerated to takeoff decision speed (V1) and then the thrust levers were retarded to idle. A maximum effort stop was then executed by using maximum wheel braking and different combinations of reverse thrust, along with flight and ground spoilers. Some of these configurations approached the

design limits of the brake assemblies. Brake energy was measured in foot/pounds of braking energy, and on these early aircraft the design limits were set at 31.5 million foot/pounds of brake energy. Naturally, a very rapid stop from high speed at high weights would create an enormous amount of heat via braking friction. If a tire heated to the point of failure, the exploding tire could cause severe damage to the airplane and emergency equipment near the aircraft, so aircraft wheels were designed with a safety feature called a "fuse plug." The fuse plug was designed to melt before this could happen, letting the air out of the tire in a far more controlled manner. Since brake energy above 21 million foot/pounds caused enough heat for this to occur, many sets of brakes and tires were replaced during this phase of the test program. An RTO is one of the most abusive maneuvers an aircraft needs to demonstrate safely and reliably. During these trials the aircraft was pushed all the way to its design limits. Consequently, it was not uncommon for a few flaws to become apparent over the course of these evaluations. Improvements to the thrust reversers, landing gear, and the braking system were found necessary.

As the RTO procedure was accomplished, the aircraft's thrust reverser system was typically used to aid in stopping the aircraft. The thrust reversers on the very early 737s were more or less identical to the system used on the 727, but because of their underwing position they created an adverse effect. As the reverser was activated and engine thrust was increased, an area of relatively high pressure under the wing was created. This high pressure had the tendency to lift the aircraft's weight off its main landing gear wheels, diminishing the braking effectiveness and effectively nullifying the reverser's benefit. Boeing's engineers also found that when the aircraft was rapidly switched from high forward thrust to maximum reverse thrust, high loads were levied on the offset links used to move the thrust reverser blocker doors into position, causing them to fail. These issues were later solved by the retrofit of the completely redesigned Rohr target type reversers. The new system reversed the engine's exhaust flow behind the wing, instead of pressurizing the area underneath.

The aircraft's main landing gears were also found to need modification during tests conducted at Edwards Air Force Base in California. The braking system employed an "anti-skid" system similar to anti-lock braking on a car, which was designed to release braking from a wheel when the start of a skid was sensed. A valve was used to release the pressure and cycled several times a second during heavy braking, especially on wet or slippery surfaces. The aircraft's main landing gear assemblies began to shimmy at high speeds, generated by side to side play and inadequate dampening action. This, combined with the active modes of the anti-skid system, caused the entire landing gear assembly to move rapidly forward and backward in a phenomenon called "walking." This violent action was enough to create "high compression and tension" forces on the landing gear's drag strut, causing the spherical bearing assemblies on the forward trunnion to shatter. Boeing experienced a six-week delay in testing while this problem was worked out by the engineers. Three changes were made to solve this issue:

- The spherical bearing assemblies were made out of a stronger, less brittle material.
- Modifications were made to the landing gear's dampener assembly.

- The anti-skid system was de-tuned to change the frequency of the anti-skid valve cycling to prevent the "walking" tendency. This had the adverse effect of degrading the performance of the braking system to an unacceptable level. The final fix was to simply reduce the orifice size in the anti-skid valve from .07 in. to .05 in.

Meanwhile, another landing gear issue was also discovered. During landing gear extension and retraction hydraulic pressure surges were noted, sometimes in excess of 4,500 PSI. Since the maximum normal pressure was 3,400 PSI, a solution was quickly sought. Engineers solved the problem by adding small restrictions to the hydraulic lines used for landing gear extension and retraction.

Electrical System: Eighteen of the twenty water ballast barrels served a dual purpose, being equipped with high capacity electrical resistors. This allowed the aircraft's generators and their associated cooling systems to be tested under maximum output conditions.

The cabin of Ship Two, showing the test equipment and water barrels used for simulating different center of gravity and weight parameters during flight testing. *Courtesy of The Boeing Company*

Engine Testing: Testing of the Pratt & Whitney JT8D engines on the airframe was required to rule out any problems with the harmony of the engines, their cowlings, intakes, and the airframe systems. In-flight engine shutdowns and restarts with and without the electric fuel pumps operating were required to prove the ability to perform this important function in case of a multiple malfunction emergency.

Jet engine power was typically referred to as "thrust" and usually measured in pounds. Tests to measure the thrust output of an engine on the airframe were required for many of the performance calculations, and were later used to predict the aircraft's performance in a variety of weather and aircraft loading conditions. Many of these tests had already been conducted when a flaw was discovered that invalidated the data. A large turbine compressor was used to pressurize air for combustion inside the jet engine. This compressor had a provision to tap some of this air for use on aircraft pressurization and anti-icing systems, referred to as "bleed air." After the fact, it was discovered that this aircraft had a leak in the bleed air ducting that transported the very hot, pressurized air to the air conditioning and anti-ice systems. This allowed more than a normal amount of bleed air to be extracted from the engines and invalidated the performance data. These tests were carried out again with Ship 3 to gather accurate information.

Additionally, the airflow into the engine itself was also tested. Instrumentation was installed to check for differences in air pressure across the compressor face of the engine. This measurement was critical to ensuring that the engine ran smoothly at all speeds and flight altitudes. This pressure measurement (also known as a DC-60 parameter) was found to be unstable. At first an indication error was suspected, but later it was discovered to be an actual airflow disturbance. Some of the small holes in the inlet's acoustic shrouding were covered up and the problem was cured.

Auto Flight Testing: This aircraft was the primary testbed for the SP-77 autopilot and FAA certification for CAT II (low visibility) landings. These tests went well, but a small modification to the hydraulic actuators for the elevators was necessary to provide adequate control authority in the event of an "A" system hydraulic failure. As part of this testing, the autothrottle system was thoroughly tested with no problems noted.

Ship Two was also used as the backup for low speed testing, but saw very little use in this role.

After leaving Boeing Flight Test, this airplane served with Lufthansa until 1983, when it was operated by Far Eastern Air Transport. From April 1984, America West Airlines operated Ship Two until 1987. Subsequently, it was operated by Ansett Airlines until being broken up for spares in 1995.

Ship Three

Ship Three was the second production 737-130, later seeing service with Deutsche Lufthansa after completion of the certification and testing program. This airplane carried the temporary registration N2286C (later to become D-ABEB), Serial Number 19014, and Effectivity Number PA002. A total of 302 hours and 54 minutes flight time was logged by this machine for flight test.

Ship Three spent the bulk of its flight test hours exploring the low speed end of the 737's flight envelope. One of the major issues the flight test engineers attempted to solve was the higher than expected stall speed while in the landing configuration. This condition led to higher approach speeds and translated into longer landing roll distances. These performance numbers were of utmost importance to Boeing and the airlines, as some of the airlines needed to use the 737 from runways that were short and performance restrictive. Thus, it was imperative these minimum speeds were as low as possible, since every knot counted.

There was another factor that had to be balanced with the desired low stall speed. An aircraft's "stall characteristics" is a term that describes how the aircraft will handle for the pilot during an accidental stall and recovery. Stable handling and the airplane's tendency to recover from a stall easily are an important part of the FAA's certification requirement. In short, good handling characteristics would dictate that the aircraft's nose would tend to pitch down in the stall, facilitating a positive recovery. It was found that the opposite was initially true, and the nose continued to rise during the stall when the aircraft was loaded to an aft (tail heavy) center of gravity. Many different high lift device configurations were tested to make the aircraft's stall more docile and pilot friendly. There was also a marked tendency for the airplane to bank to the left in the stall. Aero Engineer Jay Ferrell recounted the story:

This profile shows Ship Three (c/n 19014, l/n 3) in flight test livery. Upon delivery to Lufthansa the tail logo was modernized with an all blue background. *Courtesy of Jennings Heilig*

> There were three principle problems at low speed. Stall characteristics were not saleable due to losing [lift on] the left wing early, the stall speeds were too high at most flap angles, and in the stall the nose of the airplane continued to briefly rise, rather than fall out as we expected and wanted. Since airflow about an airplane is extremely complex, we tufted the wing so there were visual hints of possible problems. The 737 had powerful leading edge slats which were programmable. All of these problems were successfully solved by reprogramming the two outboard slats, removing the fairing strip between the slat and the front spar, and extending the inboard Krueger flap to the side of the body. (Author's note: The Krueger flap extension was added later in preparation for the Advanced 737 program.)

A significant amount of focus was directed toward the position of the leading edge slats and their effect on the stall. After many hours of testing, the lowest full flaps stall speed was realized with only slats 1 and 6 (outboard panels) in a fully extended position, with a small gap between the back of the slat and the wing. The two inboard slats on each wing (panels 2 through 5) were in a slightly less extended position, with the trailing edge faired with the leading edge of the wing. This made the performance data people happy, but caused an unacceptably pronounced pitch-up at the stall break. Further testing showed that having only the inboard slats (panels 3 and 4) slightly retracted and faired and all of the outboard slats (panels 1, 2, 5, and 6) fully extended and gapped provided the best results. This generated a better stall break, with a stall speed that was only one to two knots higher. It is noteworthy that the slat scheduling was sightly different on the 737-200.

In the early wind tunnel testing it was found that the 737 exhibited a marked nose-up pitching tendency at high Mach numbers. Jay Ferrell recounted the story:

In the wind tunneling of the models we had seen stability problems (stick-lightening-pitch up) during cruise. That tendency was fixed in the model stage by lifting the horizontal tail. That resulted in most of the body closure taken on the underside of the body. We were concerned, but from wind tunnel testing had concluded that the flow was satisfactory.

The airflow over the outboard portions of the swept wings became unstable as Mach number increased, separating from the upper wing surface. As airflow there became more disturbed, it moved the center of lift toward the forward portion of the wing. If you imagine the airplane balancing on the center of lift, one can see that as its location moves toward the front of the wing the balance becomes disturbed, and the nose will tend to rise. In addition to the design of the rear fuselage, Boeing's engineers used devices known as "vortex generators" to dispense with these undesirable handling characteristics. These were small vanes attached at angles to the airflow that created small, high-energy vortices of air behind them. Effective at preventing airflow separation, they were added to the top of the wing to help stabilize the aircraft's handling at high Mach numbers. The vortex generators were used to assist the high speed airflow adhere to the top of the wings, helping to nullify the pitch-up effect. As with all compromises in aviation, this too came with a cost. The vortex generators, protruding into the airflow over the wing, created additional drag which cost fuel efficiency in cruise flight. Jay Ferrell continued:

> During flight test we saw stick lightening at high speed. That was not much of a surprise, as we had seen the same thing on the 727. It was not an aft-body problem, but a complicated flow problem stemming from span-wise flow due to the swept wing and transonic flow on the upper wing surface (under the right conditions the shock waves could be seen from inside the cabin). Using the experience from the 727 we put a lot of vortex generators all over the wing… We covered the wings with pretty big ones, then we would go up and fly it. We had. . .a guy with a steel nose on his shoes go out and kick them off. And so we kept kicking off vortex generators and go fly, kick off some more, and go fly, kick off some more, and go fly. We finally found where we were okay, then we asked ourselves, do they need to be this big, because we were fighting drag. So we started putting smaller [vortex] generators on. Finally, we had the pitch-up problem satisfactory, so we didn't

get any stick [control pressure] lightening as the speed was going up. There was little or no discernible drag penalty. All of our later models have used the same fix.

The aerodynamics engineers were going to extraordinary lengths to reduce drag, so this was a small compromise required to improve the 737's handling. The engineers experimented by moving the vortex generators around the wing in an attempt to get maximum stability and minimum aerodynamic drag. The final solution was to move them rearward on the wing. By moving them a mere eight inches aft drag was reduced markedly. Another compromise had been successfully made.

Another takeoff related parameter measured by this aircraft was Vmcg (Velocity Minimum Control on Ground), the minimum speed the aircraft can remain under positive directional control with one engine not producing thrust (failed) and the other producing rated takeoff thrust. The rudder and nose wheel steering are used together to counteract the imbalance of thrust, causing the aircraft to tend to swerve away from the operating engine. Although an aircraft should never experience this in normal operation, this minimum speed must be determined to derive safety margins for safe engine out speeds for takeoff. Different conditions were simulated, such as wet and icy runways, so that the data could be used in all weather and aircraft weight conditions.

Cruising drag was studied extensively on this aircraft. The aircraft was exhibiting more aerodynamic drag than anticipated by the engineers. Key areas on the aircraft that were believed to be causal were the wing to body fairings, gaps in the Krueger flaps, air conditioning pack door inlet deflection, and the lower inboard surface of the wings. These areas were tufted with short pieces of yarn taped in rows to visually see the direction of the airflow in flight. A chase plane flew in formation with the test aircraft and recorded the airflow patterns. Disruptions to the straight airflow in an area helped engineers see where drag was being generated. These drag (read fuel efficiency) shortfalls were never completely solved in these early flight tests. Many of the changes to the later (1971) -200 Advanced concentrated on continued drag reductions. You will see as we go that drag reductions are still a priority on even the most modern 737 MAX. Less drag means less fuel, plain and simple.

An aircraft's pitot static system uses air pressure to measure altitude, airspeed, and how quickly the aircraft is climbing or descending (vertical speed). Outside air pressure (static pressure) is used to measure the airplane's altitude. The vertical speed is sensed through changes in this pressure over time, determining the rate at which the aircraft is climbing or descending. The airspeed indicator uses static air pressure and compares it to ram air pressure (striking the front of the aircraft) to determine indicated airspeed. Static pressure is sensed by a series of small holes in the lower fuselage, forward of the wings. The ram air pressure is received through "pitot tubes" mounted on each side of the aircraft's nose. Static and ram air pressures are delivered to the aircraft's air data computer (ADC). The ADC sends this information electronically to the pilot's flight instruments and to aircraft systems (i.e., Mach trim). The final production version, the Rosemount pitot static system, was installed and tested extensively on this aircraft.

To correct shimmy problems with the main landing gears during brake application, the revised landing gear/brake combination was installed on this aircraft. No problems were noted with the revised design.

Ship Three spent sixty-three of its testing hours hunting for suitable in-flight icing conditions. This required significant icing to test the aircraft's ability to tolerate extensive buildup of ice on unprotected surfaces. The de-icing system's ability to keep the slats, engine inlets, windshields, and various instrumentation probes free from accumulation was also evaluated. Due to the shape and dynamics of the vertical stabilizers, horizontal stabilizers, and inboard sections of the wings, it was found that thermal deicing systems would not be required on the leading edges of these areas.

Upon completion of rigorous flight testing Ship Three launched into the skies, traveling the world to provide demonstration flights for potential customers, including United Airlines, Eastern Providential Airways, South African Airways, Cyprus Airways, Braathens, and Wien Air Alaska. Additional flights were also conducted for the FAA to validate and certify training procedures.

After finishing Flight Test duty with Boeing, this aircraft was delivered to Lufthansa in December 1967. Ship Three moved on to Far Eastern Air Transport, Magnacharters, and finally flew for Aero Contenente until 2005, being the last operational jet of the -100 series. The aircraft was then sent to storage in Lima, Peru.

Ship Four

Ship Four was a 737-130 built with Serial Number 19015, and was given temporary registration N2289C with the FAA. The Boeing Effectivity Number applied to this machine was PA003, indicating it was the third aircraft built to Lufthansa's specifications. A full interior was installed, and the aircraft conducted its testing in full airline configuration.

The first flight of this aircraft had a few glitches. As the aircraft leveled off at its maximum certified altitude of 35,000 feet, the auxiliary power unit (or APU) was started to check its ability to come on line at high altitudes. As the start cycle progressed an APU fire indication illuminated on the center pedestal, just below the throttles. A fire bell sounded. The start was terminated by the pilots and the fire indication quickly extinguished. There were also some pressurization fluctuations due to a cycling pressurization outflow valve. Thorough refinement and additional testing soon worked these problems out and this aircraft's work continued.

An aircraft behavior known as "vertical bounce" was occasionally noted on early test flights. This was a two cycle per second pitch oscillation/vibration which caused a bouncing sensation to be felt in the cockpit during cruise flight, and was also a characteristic of Ships One and Five. On Ship Four, it was especially pronounced with the speed brakes extended. It is interesting to note that according to flight test records not all 737 aircraft exhibited this tendency, so it was very much an aircraft specific phenomenon. In other words, one aircraft might have a vertical bounce issue, while an otherwise identical aircraft might not. The theory was that it was being caused by airflow separating from the rear fuselage at higher airspeeds. After a thorough investigation and many trial and error flights vortex generators were added on the lower surface of the horizontal stabilizer (one on each side). Additionally, three more were added on each side of the lower fuselage just below the horizontal stabilizers, yielding much improvement. Initially these were only fitted when deemed necessary and were not installed on all early aircraft.

Ship Four (c/n 19015, l/n 4) in flight immediately prior to delivery (note the absence of "Experimental" placards next to the service doors). This aircraft was used for cockpit certification during the "Golden Triangle" trials (see "Richard W. Taylor and Crew Compliment by Peter Morton," page 60). *Courtesy of The Museum of Flight*

Much of the testing of the compatibility of the avionics with the airframe was conducted using Ship Four. Levels of electromagnetic interference were noted and not found to be of any concern. The FAA required demonstrations of a few of the electronic systems, such as the Bendix RDR-1E weather radar and the function of the flight data recorder, for which this aircraft was used. After testing the Sperry SP-77 autopilot, the gain on the roll channel—which controls banking left and right—was reduced to achieve normal maneuvering with the autopilot engaged.

Airliners spend significant amounts of time flying in less than ideal weather. This aircraft logged several hours flying through heavy precipitation to measure the buildup of static electricity, which can cause interference on navigation and communication radios. High speed aircraft use small masts on the wingtips and tail called static wicks to dissipate the buildup of static on the airframe. Most aircraft at the time used a radio navigation instrument called an automatic direction finder (ADF). This instrument operates on and near the AM radio band and is very susceptible to static interference. Using the audio portion of the ADF as a gauge, different locations and configurations of static wicks were tested until the best combination was found. Also tested were the audio system and cockpit voice recorder (CVR) for noise levels and interference.

A bank of tests consisting of several flights was designed to determine how air tight the aircraft's baggage compartments were for FAA certification, because (at that time) they required no active fire extinguishing systems. A small amount of air leakage over time was allowed. To test this, the compartments were filled

with CO_2 and then levels of this gas were recorded by sensors in each compartment so the rate of leakage could be directly ascertained by the engineers. This was done many times with different air conditioning and pressurization configurations so the measurements could be taken over a wide range of operating environments. After numerous adjustments to seals in the compartments the testing was complete and certified.

Additionally, this aircraft was used for function and reliability testing and certification, which involved the testing of flight crew

The Boeing 737 first entered airline service with Lufthansa on February 10, 1968. This first flight cover is dated April 1, 1968, and was flown onboard during the inaugural service between Koln and Paris with the "737 City Jet." Since this time Lufthansa has operated 155 different examples of the 737. *Author's Collection*

workload (described later in this chapter). After leaving Boeing, this aircraft was the first 737 delivered to Lufthansa on December 27, 1967. Surprisingly, Ships Two and Four went from Lufthansa to Far Eastern Transport, and on to Ansett Australia together. After being retired from Ansett in September 1993, Ships Four and Two were scrapped in 1995 in Marana, Arizona.

Ship Five

Ship Five was a 737-222, and was the first of the -200 series built. This aircraft was given Serial Number 19039, Effectivity Number PG001, and was registered as N9001U with the Federal Aviation Administration. This aircraft first took flight on August 8, 1967.

was flooded with one-half to three-quarters of an inch of standing water. The aircraft was then taxied through the flooded pad at varying rates of speed. The results of each run were recorded on film from different angles so the engineers could later analyze the tapes in slow motion. While this parameter was especially critical with the 727 and its tail-mounted engines, the wing-mounted engines of the 737 were well outboard of the spray pattern, making it a non-issue (see photo below left).

During the course of flight test, the stall characteristics of the longer

An artist's rendering of Ship Five (N9001U, c/n 19039, l/n 6) after completing flight testing and certification. This aircraft was the first of the 737-200 series. *Courtesy of Jennings Heilig*

bodied -200 were studied and found to be slightly different from the -100's. An amended slat extension schedule yielded better results for the longer aircraft. The change had the leading edge slats go to the intermediate (EXT) position when the trailing edge flaps began to extend, and then they would sequence to fully extended (FULL EXT) when the trailing edge flaps approached position 25. In the FULL EXT position, the outboard slat on each wing (only panels 1 and 6) would extend farther and become gapped, away from the wing. The 737-200 basic aircraft was certified with this flap/slat configuration, though it should be noted the slat extension schedule would once again change with the later 737-200 Advanced.

The handling characteristics of this aircraft were evaluated with several modifications, the most important being the new Rohr "target type" thrust reverser system. This system proved to be much more effective than the original 727 style reversers and their extended tail pipe reduced drag at the same time.

Ship Five undergoing water spray pattern tests. Cameras are installed on the top of the vertical stabilizer and on each wingtip to document the data. Notice the spray patterns are well inboard of the engine inlets. The "blow-in" doors just behind the inlets were a feature of the early Original series 737s and were deleted early into the Advanced 737 program. *Courtesy of The Boeing Company*

For flight testing it flew 183 flights while logging 149 hours and 13 minutes of flight time. In February 1969, the aircraft was prepared for revenue service before being delivered to United Airlines.

As an aircraft will frequently take off or land at high speeds on wet runways, testing must occur to study the spray patterns of water kicked up by the landing gear, particularly the nose gear. Large amounts of water being ingested by the engines could cause rapid compressor blade wear, or worse, an engine flame-out. To test the aircraft's performance in these poor weather conditions a special run of taxiway was used incorporating a large area that

This photo shows the original 727 style thrust reverser, which directed reverse thrust blast under the wing and thus tended to lift weight off the aircraft's main wheels, limiting wheel braking ability significantly. *Courtesy of The Boeing Company*

The revised Rohr thrust reverser system, which redirected reverse thrust blast over the inboard portion of the wing and outboard behind the wing, was much more effective. All Original series 737s were eventually retrofitted with these improved units. *Courtesy of The Boeing Company*

Boeing was offering unimproved runway capability (gravel kit) on the 737-200, and this aircraft was used to test and certify the associated features, as well as other modifications:

- Flight with the inboard trailing edge flap seal plates removed to check for proper handling.
- Since this aircraft exhibited the vertical bounce characteristic, potential fixes, including the tail cone mounted vortex generators and "test strips," were installed to help stabilize the effect.
- After testing minor enhancements to the braking systems and the autopilot, both were certified on this machine.

Additionally, components of the Unimproved Field Kit (described later in this chapter) were tested and are listed below:

- For gravel runway operations, the nose gear, adorned with a large gravel deflector, was tested for shimmy tendencies and water spray patterns.
- For gravel runway operations, vortex dissipators were tested and needed some adjustment before certification. Follow up testing for the dissipators would occur later on Ship Six.

Boeing also flew this airplane to conduct demonstration flights for General Mills Foods, United Airlines, Transair Canada, American Airlines, the Iranian Air Force, KLM (Royal Dutch Airlines), the United States Air Force, and Senator Barry Goldwater. After Ship Five's tour of duty at Boeing she was prepared for revenue operation with United Airlines, starting on September 9, 1969. Remaining with United until early 1997, Ship Five was operated by Air Philippines as RP-C2021 and has been stored in Manila, Philippines, since 2008.

Ship Six

Ship Six was a 737-222 and the last of the initial Flight Test certification aircraft. Registered with the FAA as N9002U, it carried Serial Number 19040 and was given Effectivity Number PG002. Taking flight for the first time on August 31, 1967, this machine served the Flight Test program until December 2, 1967. A total of sixty-five flights and 109 hours and 49 minutes were logged.

This aircraft was used for additional high speed testing that was required for 737-200 certification. If you recall from the testing of Ship One, the original slat actuator design did not have a mechanical lock to keep the slats retracted in flight. This was the flaw that allowed the high speed slat deployment event to occur. New actuators were being designed that would solve the

Ship Six (N9002U, c/n 19040, l/n 8) seen in flight after completing the flight test program. The early style thrust reversers are evident. *Courtesy of The Museum of Flight*

issue, but they would not be ready until January 1968. To prevent delaying high speed testing further, the slats were locked in the up position prior to takeoff with steel pins. This worked well, but facilitated a non-standard slats up takeoff and landing on each of these flights. With the slats pinned in the up position several high speed dives were conducted with the wing-mounted retractable landing lights extended to check handling and for aerodynamic flutter. Speeds between Mach .84 and .89 were achieved satisfactorily with no major issues noted.

To test the aircraft's response to extreme ice buildup, the engineers installed simulated ice shapes on the leading edges of surfaces that were not going to have thermal anti-icing protection. The aircraft exhibited no unorthodox behavior. Further testing of the aircraft's dutch roll characteristics and autopilot were carried out with no abnormalities. The function of the revised center fuel tank vent system was evaluated once again and found to be within pressure differential limits.

Boeing also used Ship Six to demonstrate the 737's two-pilot cockpit to representatives of the Air Line Pilots Association (ALPA). This was very important, as the ALPA was one of the major opponents of the two-pilot cockpit.

After completing the Flight Test program this airplane served with United Airlines from December 1967–June 1985, when it was flown by America West Airlines for less than four months before being returned to United and subsequently scrapped.

Aerodynamic Drag Reduction Studies

The schedule of tests for Ships One to Six included in-depth cruise speed drag evaluations. Upon completion, the data revealed higher than anticipated drag and attendant fuel burn. The areas of the airframe suspected of contributing drag were the lower inboard portion of the wing and the lower rear fuselage. The leading edge slats and Kruger flaps were key areas, as air leaked around their seals and into the spaces behind them, causing an enormous amount of drag. Aerodynamicist Jay Ferrell participated in an experiment to determine the extent of this drag effect:

The seals between the slat segments were collapsing, so we had the total air pressure all along the front spar and behind the slats. (Author's note: It was this force that overcame the hydraulic actuator retention load in the flight test incident recounted by Capt. Wygle). That led to drag. I am a licensed pilot, and I had a lot of time in older airplanes with fabric-covered wings, so I got thinking about that and I said, "Why don't we fabric up the leading edge to do some test investigations on the source of drag?" Of course we couldn't use the slats on those flights, so we kept the slats in and covered up the whole system with fabric. We rounded up some guys on the other side of Boeing Field who still did that kind of work and had them come over and they absolutely sealed up that leading edge. Just as a side note Copenhaver was the chief engineer.

I finally decided that I should tell him what I was doing. I went over and told him, but I didn't tell him until the airplane was ready to fly. When he said, "Cancel that and tell them to take all of that stuff off," I called up our lead guy, Ted Nixon, at flight test. He said, "Jay, I'm sorry, I just can't hear you…something is the matter with the connection…but we're ready to taxi." And so I sat back down and waited until I was sure they were out on the runway, and I walked into Copenhaver's office, which overlooked the runway at Boeing Field, and told him, "Stand up here with me and look, you can watch this airplane take off." So we stood there and watched the airplane go. The interesting thing is that we recovered more drag from that one test than any other one thing that we tried. Again, we were back to the seals that had given up in the upset maneuver, so we began to see how things tie together. It wasn't just having to keep the slats in, the whole system was leaking aerodynamically, which led to a number of changes.

Aerodynamicist Ardell Anderson remembered:

The idea, like Jay was saying, was to make sure that there wasn't any pumping between the various cavities inside the leading edge, causing drag. I didn't realize until later, Jay told me the story about Copenhaver almost canceling it. But here again, I was taking the drag data on that flight. So we got all of our drag data, and were coming in [to land], and all of a sudden I look out the window and the fabric on the leading edge…is flapping all around…just flapping in the breeze. Lew Wallick [the pilot] says, "Can you give me an approach speed…let's see, for flapping fabric on the leading edge?" Between Ted Nixon and I we gave Lew a speed, and I think he added ten or twenty knots and landed. Jay always talked about that as the fastest landing on a 737.

Engineers accomplished thirteen hours of flight testing with tufts of yarn affixed to key locations on the aircraft to observe airflow and high drag areas. These tests revealed an unforeseen phenomenon caused by the open main landing gear well. Normally the lower fuselage and wing to body fairings between the wings prevented one wing's airflow from interfering with the airflow of the other wing. This situation was markedly different than expected when uneven pressure was detected on the bottoms of the left and right wings during roll and yaw maneuvers. Openings on each side of the landing gear allowed air to "tunnel through" the well and exit the other side, even with the landing gear retracted. Aerodynamicists referred to this as one wing "talking" to the other through the landing gear well. This caused a significant amount of drag. The problem was eliminated by installing modified gear doors and seals. In an attempt to further reduce drag, engineers looked at sealing other areas in the main landing gear well. When fully retracted, the outboard wheels and hubcaps were exposed, but flush with the bottom of the airplane. There was a small gap around the edges of the tires that created drag when air flowed around them. Engineers installed small inflatable devices to reduce drag, but they proved to be troublesome in service. Later in the program a compromise was found that still assisted in drag reduction by using small rubber flaps instead of inflatable seals.

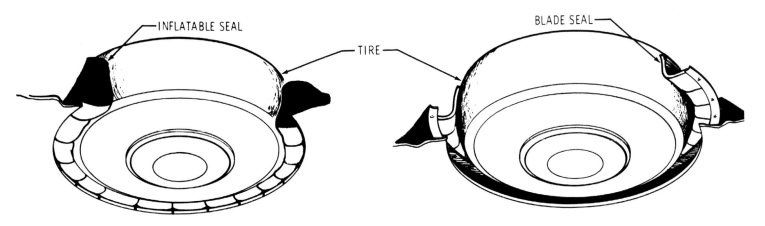

INFLATABLE SEAL

TIRE

BLADE SEAL

EXISTING CONFIGURATION (DETAIL A)

NEW CONFIGURATION (DETAIL B)

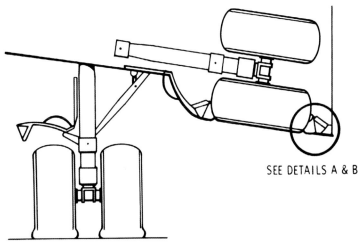

SEE DETAILS A & B

This diagram shows the short-lived inflatable landing gear seals which proved problematic in service. Eventually these were replaced with small rubber flaps that were simpler, yet still effectively reduced drag. *Courtesy of The Boeing Company*

Additional areas were explored to reduce drag. Jay Ferrell reflected on the results of the drag studies:

The [engine] nacelle was a problem, but we really got around most of that… . We had to do a lot of redesigning. You know, so many of the pieces that we are going to talk about all affected each other. The way we changed the thrust reversing [with the later Rohr reverser] actually helped the drag. Lengthening the nacelle, and associated with it, we completely redid the fairing that connected the nacelle to the wing, so there were things that were serendipitous. When we fixed one thing we helped in some other places.

Solving the Vertical Bounce Tendency

The "vertical bounce" characteristic was a low frequency bounce most noticeable in the aft cabin at speeds around Mach .75—toward the high end of the cruise speed range for the early 737 aircraft. Some individual airplanes exhibited it more than others, but it happened most often on the 737-100, because of the shorter coupled nature of the aircraft. It was known to make the aft lavatory seats bounce up and down. Although it was never seen as a safety issue, it would certainly cause issues with passenger comfort.

Boeing Test Pilot Al Jones recalled vertical bounce on the 737:

There was quite a difference between the -100 and -200. The -100 model was kind of a short coupled airplane. It was shorter by six feet. It was a lot more sensitive; in fact, that is where we picked up the vertical bounce on the -100 model…more so than the -200. It was kind of a weird thing, because it was [transitory]. It wouldn't happen all of the time. It would just come in at certain times. That's why we thought it was just turbulence, but it would happen too often.

Boeing used a wind tunnel model equipped with microphones to help solve the vertical bounce issue. *Courtesy of Vic Page/Boeing*

Jay Ferrell added his experience with vertical bounce:

I soon received a video provided by Lufthansa considering something called vertical bounce. They had the -100, which was a little shorter airplane. What they did was film the toilet seat on the aft toilet and it was back there bouncing up and down. Since the airplane pitches sort of around the nose of the airplane the pilots weren't feeling that as much…nothing like the people in the back of the cabin were. Vic Page and Bill Easterbrook had a wind tunnel model built; the most expensive wind tunnel model Boeing had ever built. Instead of using pressure instrumentation they used microphones on the aft body. We had tried pumping dye out of the airplane to see where the dye would spread out on the aft body of the airplane. We also had all sorts of air pressure taps back there. We were picking up nothing, but we did know the back side was different from any other airplane that we had flown. Vic and Bill took this new model to a NASA pressure tunnel at Ames and flew it down there, and we found out what the problem was. We were getting an intermittent and quite high frequency disconnect of the air and the fuselage, but it would close right back up again. It was too quick for pressure instrumentation, but the mics got it. The cause was the separation on the aft body was the same frequency as the natural frequency of the horizontal tail, so when that quick disconnect hit the horizontal tail, the horizontal tail would begin to vibrate, because it was its own natural frequency that was hitting it. That horizontal tail was driving the airplane in this pitching mode. We solved it finally after the seventy-first flight! Everybody was happy, but it took seventy-one flights, plus this expensive wind tunnel model to figure out what in the world was going on back there.

Now 19 other airlines want this airplane.

The plane is the Boeing 737, a new short-range jet. And at this date it might be hard to believe that it almost wasn't built at all.

If it weren't for Lufthansa, it probably wouldn't have been.

We'd asked Boeing to build a short-range jet. (We even suggested some specifications.) Then, when they showed the design to us—and other airlines—we were the first one who agreed to buy. It was only after our 21-plane order that Boeing went ahead with production.

If you ride in one, you'll notice that its passenger cabin is as wide as those on the transcontinental jets, that the cabin stays more level during descents, and that the plane makes smooth, low-speed landings. It'll be nice to ride in one.

And sooner or later you're bound to do it: 189 of them have already been ordered by 20 airlines in 13 countries.

For those who want it sooner: 10 of the first 15 delivered will have the name Lufthansa on the side.

Lufthansa
The German Airline

This Lufthansa ad featured the 737-130 and told of the humble beginnings of this incredibly significant jetliner. *Author's Collection*

The later vortex generator installation that effectively cured the vertical bounce phenomenon. *Author's Collection*

Richard W. Taylor and Crew Complement by Peter Morton

Dick Taylor was a marvelous person: a WWII veteran, design engineer, flight test engineer, refueling boom operator, experimental test pilot, engineering manager, and vice president in a great variety of assignments during a forty-five-year career with Boeing. Among his accomplishments we can use the number "two" to celebrate conspicuous differences he made in the aviation industry, with influence far beyond Boeing. He was the leader of initiatives to establish two-engine aircraft as the preferred configuration for commercial transports that fly over water, and he led the investigations, analysis, design, and demonstrations that established two as the default number of flight crew members in modern jet transport design. Today, all new transport designs are twin-engine, two-person crew configurations, except in the rare case where, for very large aircraft, engines of sufficient thrust are simply not available.

Dick Taylor's career intersected with the 737 a number of times: first in the 1960s as director of engineering for the initial program; later as part of the sales team that sold the 737 to the military as a navigation trainer, and for all practical purposes saved the program from cancellation; and later as the VP general manager of the 707/727/737 Division that manufactured all three models concurrently at the Boeing Renton, Washington, plant. With regard to crew complement, he later led the Boeing response to a presidential task force convened to determine if a crew of two was a satisfactory solution to manage the flight deck of the 757 and 767. Subsequently, all modern transports from all manufacturers were designed for a flight crew of two.

The 737 was originally designed at a time of transformation of certification rules from the original CAR series into Part 25 for transport category aircraft. Previously, a number of excellent two-crew designs went into service, among them the DC-9, BAC-111, Caravelle, and others. The flight decks of these aircraft reflected a qualitative assessment by a small team of manufacturer and regulatory pilots. The new FAR Part 25 rules imposed for the first time a "rational" crew workload requirement involving analysis and demonstration; the 737 would be the first transport to run this gauntlet. The 737 and subsequent designs all benefit from intensive analysis of crew activity, crew member hand and eye activity, and inference of cognitive workload. Additionally, airline labor relations formed a political backdrop, since powerful labor union forces were—in the absence of data and proof to the contrary—strong advocates for a flight deck with stations for three crew members: a pilot, copilot, and flight engineer.

The author had the opportunity to interview Dick Taylor extensively in the writing of this book, and in the narrative that follows, the reader will find a number of his first person observations on the crew complement issue. Unfortunately, Dick Taylor passed away between the time of the interviews and publication; he is sorely missed by an industry to which he contributed great insights and perspective in this and many other areas.

In 1967, the Boeing 737 had been certified by the FAA as a two-pilot aircraft under the quantitative requirements of FAR part 25. Some airlines immediately flew the 737 as it was certified—with a crew of two—straight from the beginning. Others, like United Airlines, had pilot groups that felt the addition of a third crew member in the cockpit would contribute to safety. From 1968–1970, the pilots of United, along with the Air Line Pilot's Association (ALPA), conducted an evaluation on crew complement. Disagreements abounded and the decision went to arbitration,

Richard W. "Dick" Taylor during his tenure as a Boeing test pilot standing with a Boeing B-47 strategic bomber. *Courtesy of The Boeing Company*

which allowed the flight engineer to remain in the cockpits of United 737s, while also conceding that a two-pilot cockpit should be an eventual possibility. This decision was reinforced in 1970, when United pilots once again went to arbitration and saw an extension of the flight engineer position for the 737 through the next contract. It is believed by some that the outcome of the United arbitrations influenced the policies of other airlines like Frontier, Wien Air, and Western Airlines. In 1971, Aloha Airlines began operating their 737s with a two-person cockpit, but the decision was influenced based on the predominantly good weather on their routes. It was not until 1976 that the pilots of Frontier Airlines ratified a contract eliminating the flight engineer from 737 cockpits. The first presidential intervention came in 1979, when President Jimmy Carter enacted a presidential emergency board that settled a strike by the pilots of Wien Air and ultimately required the pilot group to accept the two-person cockpit. It is worth noting that there was no dedicated panel for a flight engineer in the design and the third person sat on the observer seat, facing forward and interacting with the two pilots.

Soon after the DC-9 Super 80 was under development, and would no longer be riding on the qualitative CAB 4b type certification of the earlier DC-9 variants. In this time frame the 757 and 767 were in early development and the former was intended to be a two-pilot jet. The 767 was being designed for three because the launch customers had negotiated an agreement for three with their pilot unions, though Boeing's intentions were to create a two-person version of the aircraft for overseas customers with a design substantially similar to the 757. At this point United 737s were still being flown by a crew of three, and with these new technology aircraft forthcoming the unions advocated with their respective airlines that the flight decks be designed for three crew members, with a dedicated flight engineer's station. ALPA petitioned for a national study to establish standard policies based on the relative safety of two and three crew member flight decks then in service. On March 5, 1981, President Ronald Reagan established the Task Force on Aircraft Crew Complement. This committee, chaired by John McLucas, had 120 days to study the controversy between the aircraft manufacturers and airlines against the concerns of ALPA and the Flight Engineers' International Association (FEIA). The committee adopted a position from the outset that both sides of the argument had a common goal, which was safety, and neither was driven solely by economic factors. Numerous interviews were conducted with airline management, pilots, flight engineers, manufacturers, union leadership, and NASA personnel. The study drew heavily from the NASA Aviation Safety Reporting System (ASRS), a program that allows pilots to report safety issues and errors with anonymity. Specially trained people were allowed to observe operations in two and three pilot aircraft, studying the dynamics of each. Public comments and suggestions were also taken into account during ten days of public hearings. Dick Taylor recalled:

The conflict on crew complement was a true battle. It is just a natural thing. If you have unions it's a natural problem. Not only did we have to design an airplane for better human performance, but we also had to fight the political battle. All of us on both programs [the 737 in 1967 and the 767 in 1978] were engineers. It wasn't in our DNA…to fight politically, we wanted [a solution] on the basis of what was safest and the best product. So that's the way we tackled everything. United Airlines, our first [customer on both the] 737 and 767 [program] had a…union that was the strongest in the nation. The union was very aggressive and skilled, and they had negotiated a contract with United on the 737 to have the third guy [flight engineer] in the cockpit on the basis that the third crew member will … report on what is necessary for safe operations. So that is the way it started; we were always supporting the airline in crew complement negotiations. The UAL 737 negotiation was one in particular that we were able to convince the [external arbitrator] judges that two was safe. (Author's note: the 737 went into service with United using a third crew member, though other US airlines operated with two, as eventually did United.)

Much later, in the eighties, ALPA made their big move. (Author's note: the four launch customers for the 767 had agreed in the late 1970s with their ALPA unions to operate the aircraft with a crew of three, so the basic design of the 767 was for three crew. The 757 was launched only a few months later with a crew of two for Eastern and British Airways.) ALPA went to the president and said they would like for a decision to be made on two versus three and said they would stand by the decision. I thought that we were pretty unlikely to prevail, even though we believed a two-crew cockpit was superior. The president appointed a federal committee to study this and chose John McLucas to head it up. I knew John McLucas very well…McLucas called me up and asked what was going on. I said the union thinks that there should be three crew members in the cockpit. I said come visit Boeing and go visit Douglas and others. Visit the people who build airplanes, and I'm sure you will want to talk to some airline people as well. If you decide to do that, I can get together a cadre of airlines that can brief you on what they are finding. He said, "How long do you think you want for a presentation." I said, "Well, how about two hours." He said "Well, they (the union) want a week." "Say again…the union wants a week to testify?" I said, "I don't think we need that much time. A couple of hours would be enough." When we got in the middle of that they had a series of hearings in Washington, DC. They gave the unions all day. Their story was to recite anecdote and opinion. We tried to go down a completely different basis using design, data, and analysis; and besides the 757 and 767, the certification of the DC-9-80 was yet to come up as one of the chores that the committee was getting to.

Back to the previous history on crew complement for twin jets, I thought all of the Task Force work would hinge around the 737, but that wasn't the way it was reported in the end. ALPA didn't want it to be about just one airplane, they wanted a decision for three forever. We had heard about the [original] DC-9 being certified without much technical analysis. It was a subjective decision on the part of the FAA. The people in the certification process were pilots just like the test pilots of the Douglas Company… . One of the interesting things about the 737 is that we put flight trackers in the jumpseat to see what they [the pilots] were doing in flight. They found that [the pilots] spent one percent of their time managing the systems of the airplane…one percent! It blew everybody's minds to think that it was that low, but it really was, because we worked at designing it that way. It was designed on the basis of a quiet, dark cockpit. It didn't have anything showing that you didn't need. Then the next element was redundancy. Be sure you put in a system that has redundant features, because the reliability of structure, electricity, and mechanics is not perfect. An example of that was the electrical system. We had a generator on both engines and one on the APU in the back. In the third place we had automation. If redundancy is not sufficient we will make it automatic if it does not have to have an action at the failure of a system, because it is going to take care of itself while you take care of the next thing. So you have those three elements in the basic design and it didn't take an extra guy. I think that ALPA thought that all we did was move the [727] controls and indicators from the flight engineer's panel [to the] overhead [panel]. It wasn't designed that way and it was a lot different.

But they really had certified it the correct way… (Author's note: crew members were a mix of Boeing and FAA pilots, the latter recruited at the last minute.) We didn't put in a six month training program for these [FAA] guys, mostly because we didn't have that much time. But to say that you could take an FAA pilot and train him in two weeks to be a captain is pushing the state-of-the-art pretty far. But if you think about it, if that guy can cut the muster after having been trained for two weeks, that will speak well for the [crew workload, and for future pilots from the] airlines. Train them for two weeks and turn them loose. I went on every flight…I was the only one, but I felt like we were being tested. Can you guys do this with minimal help, and I wanted to know the reason why they were not going to approve if they weren't going to. I wanted to have that experience. So it was a morning flight and an afternoon flight. They had a Boeing pilot and an FAA pilot on each flight. This was Newark to Washington, DC, and Boston Logan. (Authors note: The "Golden Triangle"; crew workload tests run during the 1967 Thanksgiving holiday weekend between Newark, Washington National, and Boston was an element in the FAA's plan to be able to point to something when you got the certificate data that verified the certification basis.) Then they would have a new set of pilots: one Boeing and one FAA. (Each flight introduced airplane system or ATC "failures" to add to workload and test the Minimum Equipment List, including an incapacitated crew member event.) They would tap the Boeing guy on the shoulder and [tell him he]…was dead. They were tough tests. [Much later during the 767/757 time period] the McLucas committee that was set up took that all into consideration. The one thing they did say about the airplane was that the FAA had used a stringent set of certifications for the 737 and that same requirement with a couple of tweaks would be adequate for certifying the 757 and 767. So we got that sort of assurance out of the whole thing. It was well done and McLucas had John Lauber, who was the NASA human factors guy. John Lauber is a very good human factors guy.

Test Pilot Brien Wygle had this observation about the FAA and the "Golden Triangle" tests:

The FAA felt that they had to be 100% clean if they approved this. Until they got to that position they were going to keep our feet to the fire. As far as the "Golden Triangles" went, there was the FAA pilot—at the time, on the Flight Operations side, Charlie House…I flew him back to the Golden Triangle. We didn't do any fancy stuff, but I just wanted to say to him: "If we fly this using Newark, Boston, and Washington National…I think that's what we should do. If I demonstrate the workload in North Dakota, you might say: 'Well, that doesn't prove anything.'" So he agreed to that. That was the attitude that we had. We were going to go for broke on this, and we were not going to stop.

Dr. John Lauber, who was in Human Factors Studies at NASA Ames, recalled:

My perspective on the two versus three crew issue basically stems from the work I did with the president's task force. That was a very interesting exercise, because it was less about technology and more about what I sometimes refer to as the "bio-politics of aircraft design and operations." At the heart it was not so much of an engineering or human factors issue as it was a labor and political issue. There was a lot of interesting give and take during the task force's look at the issue. We wanted to hear from everyone who might have a credible view on the matter. We went to Toulouse [Airbus], and we talked to all of the manufacturers down in Long Beach and up in Seattle. Various industry and labor organizations would also visit us at our temporary offices in Washington, DC, at the old DOT [Department of Transportation] building. We had situations where we would have a group of union guys waiting in one room and a couple airline guys in another room, and we had to take steps to make sure they didn't accidentally cross paths. Not that our work was a big secret, but we tried to avoid direct confrontation. It was clear pretty much from the outset that there was not a major safety issue associated with the two-crew complement. The data to support that just wasn't there. You could look at the safety record and there was nothing. There were technical arguments made that an extra set of eyes and ears were better than not having them, but counter to that, we learned that as you increase a team from a size of two to a size of three, you are not just adding one extra link in the network that comprises the team, it's an exponential increase. By increasing crew size you greatly complicate the issues of crew communication and coordination; the kinds of things that lead to accidents far more frequently than technical and engineering issues. We concluded that there might actually be an offsetting increased risk of accidents due to the increased complexity of larger multi-crew operations. Three is much different than two, and not necessarily safer.

In conclusion, the president's task force on crew complement had the following findings and recommendations:

- The DC-9-80 (later known as the MD-80), operated by a two-man crew, was safe, and a third flight crew member was not required for safety.
- The FAA's certification of the DC-9-80 with a two-person crew was "proper and in compliance with the applicable provisions of the Federal Aviation Act of 1958."
- The Boeing 757, 767, and the A310 "potentially could be operated by a crew of two. The addition of a third crew member would not be justified in the interest of safety."
- "The present process, improved and strengthened as recommended, will ensure proper certification of such aircraft as the 757 and 767, and a proper review of the certification of such foreign-made aircraft as the A310 from the standpoint of crew complement."

The task force recommended guidelines for certification of new aircraft with respect to crew complement. Modern technology improved the interface of the pilot with the aircraft and merited new procedures for certifying these systems. The task force also advised the FAA to use the "Task/Timeline" technique to study crew performance for the certification of new aircraft. The use of line pilots in the design and certification process, as well as evaluating factors such as air traffic control and weather, were suggested. The possibility of combined aircraft systems failures and how they effect pilot workload should be accounted for when developing the aircraft's Minimum Equipment List (MEL), a document that allows flight with inoperative equipment under certain circumstances. There were also several recommendations for airport, navigation, and air traffic control in addition to aircraft certification. These findings were a pivotal event for the two-crew cockpit and soon heralded the end of three-crew operation of the 737. Some airlines, such as Air France, were hesitant to order the 737 because of this important economic issue. However, with the two versus three issue drawing to a close Air France submitted their first order for twelve 737-228s in 1981.

Improvements and Optional Equipment for the 737

Two interesting changes made available on early 737s were the redesigned reverse thrust system and an Unimproved Field Kit. These items were highly desirable because of the short fields and remote rugged places that some airlines were needing to take the 737. To truly make the 737 a "next generation DC-3," its performance into and out of short and/or gravel runways needed to be augmented. The 737 was about to become an aerial SUV!

First and foremost, the 737's reverse thrust system needed to be redesigned to achieve good short field landing and takeoff performance. The term "reverse thrust" is a bit misleading, and tends to make people assume the engine itself is reversing its rotation. This is actually not the case, and is in reality much simpler. The engine continues to draw air into its intake in the front and provide jet blast out the tailpipe. The thrust reverser is a device that moves into position to block the jet exhaust exiting the rear of the engine, deflecting it forward at about a forty-five degree angle. The engine is then typically accelerated to about seventy-five percent of maximum thrust. This high velocity jet exhaust that is deflected forward, against the oncoming wind, creates a powerful stopping force for the aircraft. This is usually used in conjunction with the aircraft's wheel brakes to bring the airplane to a stop. On early 737s, a 727-style thrust reverser system was used. This system worked very well on the 727, but did not interface effectively with the 737 airframe. The early reversers were tucked under the wing, just forward of the trailing edge flaps, and when deployed would transmit hot, high pressure exhaust gasses under the wing. This caused a significant air cushion to form under the wings, lifting a fair amount of the aircraft's weight off its wheels. This negatively affected wheel traction and braking, making runway use longer than desired. Test pilot Brien Wygle once said jokingly, "It was the first time I have been able to get constant speed data in reverse thrust." It was true that a fix had to be found and fast!

Boeing teamed up with Rohr Industries, which specialized in providing engine accessories and cowlings for aircraft manufacturers. After assessing the 737's situation, they felt that a "target type" thrust reverser design similar to the one currently in use on the DC-9 would fit the bill. The problem was that it would be expensive for Boeing to design and implement installation of the revised reverser system...to the tune of about 22 million dollars! After much collaboration with test pilots and engineers it was decided that the expenditure was necessary and the go-ahead was given. Marketing Manager Peter Morton talked about changing the reverser design:

The reason we could do that is Douglas had outsourced the reversers to Rohr. Rohr had the ownership and we could buy them from Rohr. Boeing inserted a fixed tailpipe extender between the rear portion of the engine and the trailing edge of the wing and installed the Rohr reverser behind the wing, cocked at an angle. With this arrangement the reverse thrust was blown upward over the inboard wing and downward outboard the wheels, which made it much more effective. Later on, when we were marketing the airplane, we would take it down to Boardman, Oregon's, 4,000 foot runway. We went from having the worst jet transport reverser in the world to having the best. It was almost like a turboprop and deceleration was very pronounced. You could stop the airplane with reversers alone within the FAA runway length. Tommy Edmonds used to take pilots into Boardman and demonstrate it [without using wheel brakes]—reversers only! And it could back up without [the engines] surging. That was the other thing, there was no [exhaust] flow into the inlets because the reverser was so far back. Eventually we got to the point that we could use the reversers on a gravel runway!

Retrofitting the Rohr system on existing aircraft was very involved. The engine itself could remain where it was mounted, but the jet pipe would have to be extended past the trailing edge of the wing to avoid the area under the wing becoming "pressurized" during reverse thrust action. The engines being so close to the ground was another issue. For the reverser clamshells to clear the ground while in use they were mounted at about a thirty-five degree angle from vertical to make space. Even with this, pilots were cautioned that the nose wheels should be on the ground before deploying the reversers. Otherwise, it was possible the reversers could potentially scrape on the runway. The angling of the reversers had a negative and a positive effect. Since some of the reverse thrust was directed toward the rear fuselage it generated more noise in the cabin. Sharp-eyed airplane spotters will remember seeing exhaust stains on this part of the fuselage on the Pratt & Whitney powered 737s using this system. The positive side was the fuselage deflected the thrust again, creating more drag and helping to stop the airplane.

As far as aircraft systems were involved, many changes were required to the pneumatic and hydraulic systems. The new Rohr installations relied on hydraulic pressure to actuate the thrust reversers and the aircraft had to be modified accordingly. Primary

Ship Four (in 1972) taken in Prague, Czech Republic, clearly shows the non-advanced engine pylon. By this time this aircraft had been retrofitted with the updated Rohr "target" type thrust reversers. *Courtesy of P. Popelar*

The optional rear airstair on Ship Four. *Courtesy of P. Popelar*

The rear airstair in the retracted position from inside the cabin. This installation differed from the optional forward airstair, which was stored under the cabin floor when not in use. *Courtesy of The Boeing Company*

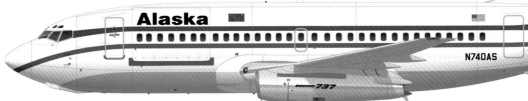

hydraulic pressure was supplied by the "A" hydraulic system, with alternate power being supplied by the standby hydraulic system in case of an "A" system failure. The pneumatics for the old system were consequently removed. In all, the efforts and money spent paid off handsomely. It was found that the new reversers, operating at about half thrust (1.5 EPR), provided twice the stopping power as the older 727-style reversers at full power. The first factory new 737 with the improved Rohr reverser system was delivered to United Airlines on January 3, 1969. This aircraft was a 737-222 given Serial Number 19933 and Line Number 135. All Original series 737s were eventually retrofitted with the new reverser.

The Unimproved Field Kit (often referred to as the "Gravel Kit") received FAA certification in February 1969. This kit was a combination of several items added to the aircraft to allow safe operation from dirt and gravel runways. The most noticeable addition was a large plate mounted to the nose gear low and behind the nose wheels. This shield (sometimes referred to irreverently as the nose "ski") was designed to deflect rocks and debris, preventing them from impacting the airplane's lower surfaces. It was a fairly complex addition and would retract with the landing gear into a fairing around the nose gear well. The shield also acted as the gear door when the landing gears were retracted, facilitating the removal of the two standard nose gear doors.

Gravel Runway Capability

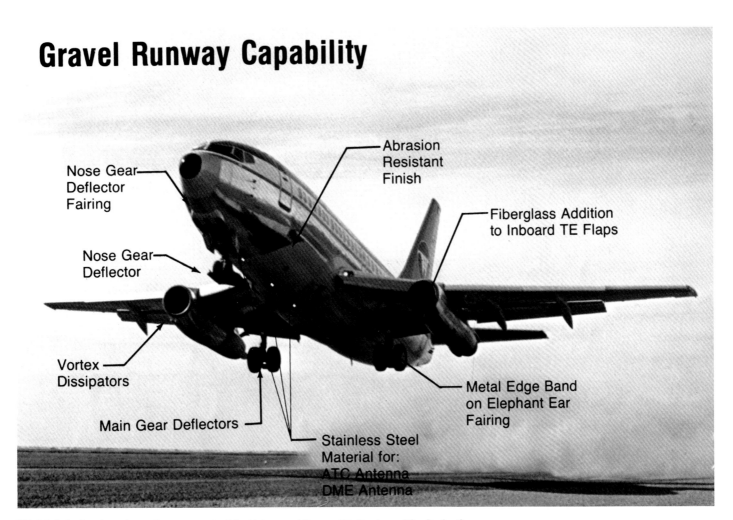

This labeled sales photo shows the components of the Unimproved Runway Kit. *Courtesy of The Boeing Company*

The complex Nose Gear Deflector component of the Unimproved Field Kit. *Courtesy of The Boeing Company*

The possibility of debris ingested by the engines was a concern from the beginning of the program because of the close proximity of the engine inlets to the ground. This concern was heightened when the aircraft was taxied over unprepared surfaces. If you watch a running jet engine taxi over a puddle on the ground, often times you will notice a small vortex or "tornado" form under the inlet. The water in the puddle makes it visible to the eye, but

737 TIRE COMPARISON
(WITH GRAVEL DEFLECTOR)

BASIC TIRE
40 X 14-16

LOW PRESSURE TIRE
C40 X 18-17

737 WHEEL, TIRE, & BRAKES OPTIONS

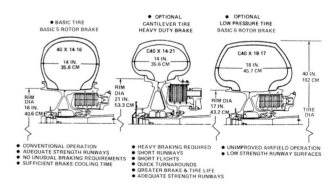

Prominent under the inlet is the vortex dissipator seen on PG199. High pressure engine bleed air is expelled out of the orifice at the forward end of the mast, interrupting the formation of the vortex which could otherwise lift debris and cause foreign object damage to the engine. This solution was quite effective. Note the experimental conical screen inside the inlet for testing purposes. *Courtesy of The Boeing Company*

The tire and brake options available for the Original series 737. The low pressure tire option was used by carriers such as Air Zaire, which operated into unimproved runways with great regularity. Note the gravel deflector installed between the tires. *Courtesy of The Boeing Company*

they are often present even when invisible. It is this phenomenon that introduces foreign objects into the engine's inlet, potentially causing damage. If this vortex can be prevented from forming in the first place then foreign object ingestion becomes a non-issue. Boeing devised a very clever way to facilitate this. A small tube was mounted under each engine's inlet, on the end of which was an orifice for channeling high pressure, thirteenth stage engine bleed air directly under the inlet, where vortices would normally form. After extensive testing the correct combination of position

and air spray was achieved and proved to be quite effective. In fact, this configuration was so successful that aircraft with this modification operating on unpaved surfaces statistically had less foreign object damage than standard 737s operating only on paved surfaces.

No detail was left unaddressed. Boeing installed a retractable rotating beacon on the kitted aircraft, as this was found to be vulnerable to damage during unimproved field operations. The position of the light was controllable from the cockpit. *Courtesy of The Boeing Company*

This view of the main wheel well shows the tire screens designed to protect the hydraulic systems from foreign object damage. Screens were also installed on some Original series 737s without the Unimproved Field Kit. *Courtesy of The Boeing Company*

The Unimproved Field Kit also incorporated other small changes to the airframe, such as protective coatings on the undersides of the trailing edge flaps and special metal shielding on brake lines, hydraulic lines, and control cables. The #2 communication antenna was relocated and a retractable rotating beacon was installed. Slightly oversized main landing gear tires were retrofitted with small gravel deflectors added between them. Boeing also offered a low pressure tire option that allowed operation on runways with low surface bearing capability, which were used extensively by Air Zaire. Additionally, special screens were installed in the main landing gear wheel wells on many Original series aircraft. These were intended to protect the delicate hydraulic reservoirs and associated plumbing from a burst tire or debris kicked up during takeoff or landing. Although they were not specifically part of the Unimproved Field Kit, they helped protect the aircraft when operating on gravel runways.

The left main landing gear shown from the front with the shielded brake lines as part of the Unimproved Field Kit. *Courtesy of The Boeing Company*

Now we look as good as we are.

A new look and a continuing commitment to being the finest airline in the sky.

Nordair advertised its attractive new livery in 1984. Nordair ceased operations in 1987, after being purchased by Pacific Western Airlines. *Author's Collection*

CF-NAB (c/n 19847, l/n 84) in flight, featuring the Unimproved Runway Kit and yet to receive the Rohr thrust reverser retrofit. This example later served with CP Air, Canadian Airlines, TAT, Ardennes Gamma, AirAsia, and Air Mediterranean before being stored in 2005. *Courtesy of The Boeing Company*

Extreme Service with
Boeing Field Service Engineer Bob Bogash

Nordair of Canada was an airline formed in 1947 from the merger of Mont Laurier Aviation and Boreal Airways. Based at Montreal-Dorval Airport in Quebec, Nordair operated international and trans-atlantic services with Lockheed L-1049 Super Constellations. In addition to these operations, Nordair also flew scheduled flights deep into the Arctic Circle with four-engine, piston-powered Lockheed Constellations and Douglas DC-4s. Nordair became the first Canadian airline to purchase gravel-kitted 737s to replace most of their piston engine service.

Flying the 737 into some of these remote Arctic airstrips was significantly different from the type of flying most other jetliners performed. Most major airline airports, even in those days, were equipped with an instrument landing system (ILS), but these remote airports were operating with few navaids or old fashioned non-directional beacon (NDB) approaches. These NDB approaches were challenging and lacked precision, especially when crossing a shoreline, due to interference with the navigation signals. Perpetual snow and ice crystal conditions caused bad P-static problems that made ADF needles swing wildly. Some of the destinations were so close to the Magnetic North Pole that compass systems would become confused and always indicate a northerly heading, causing pilots to use some very interesting navigation procedures.

Bob Bogash tells about operating the 737 in the Arctic Circle:

You were on your own, ATC-wise… . This was the real world. The weather was bad and it was dark half of the year…twenty-four hours dark! There was an ILS at Frobisher Bay and that was it. You were using NDB approaches everywhere else. Most of the runways didn't have electric lights. The airport manager went up and he had flare pots. He would light the flare pots along the sides of the runway. The problem was it was very windy and the flare pots would blow out. He was trying to keep enough of them lit so that we could come in and land. There was no en route communication with Air Traffic Control since there was no VHF radio coverage. You would be cleared north of sixty degrees north latitude and that was it. You would climb and descend all by yourself.

We modified the airplanes with a switch. You would disconnect the compass system, uncoupling the HSI from the fluxgate compass transmitter. At some fields we would fly a "cloud break" procedure using a stopwatch. For example, from Ft. Chimo, you would time an hour and fifteen minutes going into Deception Bay, assuring you were then over the sea. We were depending on the slow precession of the aircraft's directional gyros. At a certain point you would uncouple the gyro from the compass system and your HSI would be getting heading information based on the slow precession of these gyros. You would then descend through the overcast, breaking out of the cloud base over the sea. When you broke out below you would turn south, find the coastline, and fly back along the coast to find the fjord and fly up to the

Nordair Capt. "Red" Martindale monitors aircraft instrumentation during a flight in the Arctic Circle. Attached to the side window is an Astro Compass, used to measure sun angles with reference to an ephemeris to cross check the aircraft's position. *Courtesy of Bob Bogash*

airfield and land. It was a lot of fun creating from-scratch Instrument Approach Plates for remote fields where there were no officially published procedures.

Resolute, the world's most northern airline airport, was only about 111 nautical miles from the Magnetic North Pole. Compass-wise, everything was "South." Therefore, in the North, all of the headings utilized "True" headings. We would also use an Astro Compass… and would shoot sun lines. You would pull out an ephemeris from under your seat and go through the date and time to figure out Sun angles, and that was how you would navigate! There was no VHF communications anywhere, so you depended on HF, which was often a problem. Nordair made up their own approaches and you navigated this way. This was all in the 737.

At the end of these approaches landings were made on icy, gravel runways. Some were quite short (5,000 feet) and NO reverse thrust was allowed on gravel runways for the first few years, even when covered with ice and snow. The 737 proved itself to have capabilities unique and well suited to the airlines operating in the extreme conditions in Arctic regions. Besides "plain old gravel" runways, Nordair also flew their 737s off strips that were essentially just beach (where they sometimes got stuck in the sand!), and also off rivers—frozen during the winter—and sea ice. Some locations had gravel

runways for summer use and in winter, after the sea froze, a road grader was put on the ice and scraped out an ice strip. In all, many of their operations more closely resembled those flown by a Super Cub or a Cessna 180, and not those of a big jetliner!

The importance of the 737 to people in the High Arctic, in their tiny villages and settlements, cannot be overstated. With little communication with the outside world, no phones, and a very long, unpressurized, piston-engine plane ride back to civilization, the inhabitants were always at risk when it came to accidents and health issues. The 737's speed and comfort were a genuine paradigm shift, far more important than a businessman taking a United flight from Newark to Cleveland.

After Nordair acquired the gravel equipped 737s for their revenue operations, several other operators began to see the outstanding benefits of this special aircraft. Eventually, gravel equipped 737 equipment would be operated by Alaska Airlines, Northern Consolidated, Pacific Western Airlines, Transair, and

This is the typical Arctic boarding scene in the late 1960s and early '70s. Note the details of the gravel kit nose gear deflector and the fairing built into the nose of the aircraft to streamline the installation while the landing gear was retracted. *Courtesy of Bob Bogash*

Queen Elizabeth II flew to the Arctic Circle on a Boeing 737, landing on the gravel runway at Resolute Bay, Canada (CYRB), during a tour in 1970. *Courtesy of Bob Bogash*

The baggage claim situation was a bit different in the Arctic, as passengers wait for their luggage plane-side in Great Whale, Canada (CYGW). *Courtesy of Bob Bogash*

This Nordair 737-200 is in its element during operations in the Arctic Circle, Resolute Bay, 1970. *Courtesy of Bob Bogash*

Wien Air Alaska. As of 2017, Air Inuit, Air North, Northern Air Cargo, Nolinor Aviation, and Canadian North Airlines were still providing service with gravel kitted 737-200C aircraft because of this unique and outstanding capability. Combined, these airlines are still operating eighteen gravel equipped aircraft that are regularly flown on revenue passenger or cargo service on to gravel or ice runways. Some other airlines in Africa (such as Cameroon Airlines) also acquired gravel-kit 737s to fly off dirt and gravel runways in bush country. Bob Bogash continues:

> There is a special uniqueness to these operations. Nordair, for one, along with many of the other Arctic 737 operators, had never operated a new aircraft. All of their machines were second-hand or tenth-hand. And they were old. In many ways, flying with Nordair was a throwback in history. Big airlines, like United, had many new airplanes, and their crews were transitioning from much more modern equipment.
>
> I was lucky to be exposed to this era in aviation. More than that, the flight crews were basically a throwback

in history as well. So, in addition to the relatively modern Super Connie, we had a large number of pilots who were moving directly from DC-3, DC-4, and C-46 aircraft into the 737—a large, modern, high-performance jetliner. And they did so with aplomb. In the twenty plus years that Nordair operated the 737 into the Arctic, they experienced no serious accidents—a testament to the pilots, but also to the flying qualities of the airplane.

Between its friendliness toward flight crews [and passengers] and its rugged capabilities and dependability, the 737 proved to be a hard airplane not to fall in love with. In those early days, it was anything but a smashing success; in fact, it was often a rarity when it showed up someplace and people would come to look her over. Boeing even considered ending production after 400 units. Her transition over the subsequent years to become the world's best selling airliner, with two produced every day, is a source of great personal pride to me—a person who knew her greatness would eventually be recognized by all.

737 Production Moves from the Thompson Plant to Renton

Boeing's Renton, Washington, assembly hall was built well before the 737 was even a dream. In 1941, a marshy property on the northeast side of Renton airport was procured by the US government, as American involvement in WWII was becoming inevitable. Upon this property an assembly plant was built to produce an aircraft called the XPB-1 Sea Ranger. The Sea Ranger never saw production, but the Renton plant was soon used to build the famous B-29 bomber en masse. In 1948, the Renton facility was used to produce the B-377 Stratocruiser and its military derivatives, the C-97 and the KC-97 tanker. Six years later, Renton would be used to produce the first Boeing jetliner prototype (Boeing 367-80), which was the basis for the Boeing 707 and KC-135 Stratotanker. The 707, KC-135, and later the 727 were assembled here.

The first eight 737 airframes (prototype, six production aircraft, and the static test airframe) were built at Plant 2 on Boeing Field, near Seattle, Washington. This facility had very low ceilings and required the aircraft to be fully assembled without its vertical stabilizer, which was added later in the parking lot that is now

The 737 assembly line inside the Thompson assembly hall at Boeing Field in late 1967. *Courtesy of The Boeing Company*

The 100th 737 to be built (c/n 19920, l/n 100) was delivered to Pacific Southwest Airlines (PSA) on November 25, 1968, as N380PS. *Courtesy of The Boeing Company*

The 737's new home at the Renton assembly hall in November 1973. The parallel 727 line is visible in the background. *Courtesy of The Boeing Company*

Taxiway B at Boeing Field. Thereafter, the next 264 Boeing 737 airframes were built entirely at the Thompson site. According to Boeing corporate historian Michael Lombardi, in 1970, a severe downturn in aircraft sales occurred and Boeing was still struggling to absorb the enormous development expense of the Boeing 747 jumbo jet. The 707 and 727 were still being produced in the Renton facility and the decision was made to combine 737 production with the 707 and 727 lines. This arrangement was made to increase efficiency and reduce overall costs. After the monumental task of moving the 737's final assembly to Renton, the first 737 built there was a 737-2A8 (VT-EAI, c/n 20482, l/n 272) delivered to Indian Airlines on December 23, 1970. Since that time the Renton factory has seen the 707, 727, and 757 jetliners come and go, but the 737 abides. As of January 31, 2017, a staggering 9,095 Boeing 737 jetliners have been produced in the Renton assembly hall, with many thousands to come.

The Advanced 737 Program

Aerodynamic drag caused shortfalls in climb and cruise performance with the early aircraft. During the 737 Basic test program (with Ships One through Six), enormous amounts of effort were spent reducing drag while balancing aircraft handling. The Basic 737 was greatly improved because of these efforts and was considered by many to be a true "pilot's airplane" due to its maneuverability and excellent flying qualities. Still, the 737 and DC-9's performance capabilities were a close match. After initial certification in 1967, Boeing began modifying PG199 (a 737-222 retained by Boeing) to achieve the lowest drag and highest lift configuration possible. Modifications were made, most notably to the engine-to-wing fairings, leading edge devices, and gap seals. By 1970, the culmination of these modifications and the advent of higher thrust versions of the bulletproof JT8D engine brought about an aircraft that was a real performer and highly competitive against aircraft such as the

All Nippon Airways was the launch customer for the 737 Advanced program. Pictured is a 737-281 (JA8417, c/n 20563, l/n 296) seen on a pre-delivery test flight. *Courtesy of The Boeing Company*

Douglas (later McDonnell-Douglas) DC-9 series. In January 1970, Boeing examined the improvements that were becoming available and launched the Advanced 737-200 program.

Aerodynamicist Vic Page worked on the 737 program and recalled the situation:

Initial 737-100 certification flight testing in April '67 showed the airplane did not achieve estimated performance objectives. Both cruise drag and stall speeds were too high. This negatively impacted the range and field length performance being quoted to customers… . From April 1967–January 1970, when the 737 Advanced program was given the go-ahead, there were many wind tunnel and flight tests that contributed to developing the 737 Advanced configuration. Stall speeds and airplane drag were reduced, and 737 Advanced performance exceeded the original objectives. This development included tailoring the wing leading edge devices and the surface on to which they retracted. We originally designed the wing leading edge to be a totally smooth contour with the slats retracted. This resulted in a slight step in the remaining wing contour when the slat was deployed. This step was removed. The step at the slat trailing edge was accepted in the retracted position to provide a smooth remaining wing contour when the slat was deployed. It also included tailoring the forward portion of the nacelle strut, modified thrust reversers [all Advanced 737s had the later Rohr reversers], and we also developed a Gravel Runway Kit [for the 737-200]. The aerodynamic drag and stability problems were eliminated with sealing and vortex generators positioned on the wing and the aft body, forward of the flow separations. The vortex generators added energy to the flow and eliminated the separations.

Boeing's aero engineers identified the engine mounting as a major target area for drag reduction. Many experiments were done to reduce the aerodynamic drag in this area. Engineers looked for ideas and noticed the marked resemblance between the 737 and the Messerschmitt Me-262. The Me-262 was one of the most advanced fighters of WWII and was the first operational jet fighter in history. It featured twin jet engines closely mounted to the underside of each wing, which was very similar to the 737 configuration. The wing and leading edge slat configuration of the Me-262 also happened to have a strong resemblance to the Boeing jet. The German fighter was studied by engineers and generated some new ideas. To modify the 737, the most successful studies involved a trial and error method. On wind tunnel models the basic wing and engine mounting was modified in front and behind the wing with clay. This process of modification and wind tunnel drag tests was conducted until the best

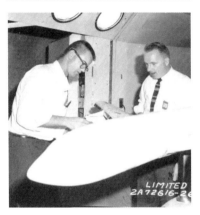

The various efforts to reduce drag and increase performance of the early 737. Tufts of yarn were taped to the wing to allow aerodynamicists to observe airflow while in flight. *Courtesy of Vic Page/Boeing*

The German Messerschmitt Me-262 was the first operational jet fighter and shared a similar engine and wing relationship to the Original series 737. *United States Air Force*

737 High Lift System

ORIGINAL PRODUCTION LANDING CONFIGURATION

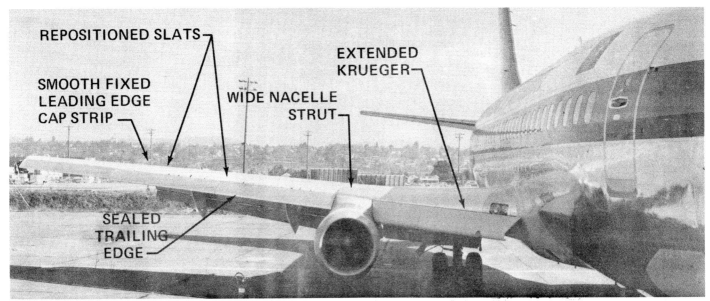

REPOSITIONED SLATS

SMOOTH FIXED
LEADING EDGE
CAP STRIP

EXTENDED
KRUEGER

WIDE NACELLE
STRUT

SEALED
TRAILING
EDGE

ADVANCED LANDING CONFIGURATION

The original configuration and the Advanced 737 wing modifications. Notice the Advanced engine to wing fairing closes the gap between the slat and the pylon, forcing the air over the wing, both increasing lift and reducing drag. *Courtesy of The Boeing Company*

configuration was found, leading to the Advanced engine-to-wing "glove," which was designed to serve two very important functions. The first was to reduce cruise drag. In the basic configuration, a lot of the passing air was forced to go underneath the wing, where it would cause drag along the engine pylons. The new glove forced more of this air over the wing, creating additional lift and reducing aerodynamic drag. Takeoff and landing speed and performance were also very important for the 737's short field takeoff and landing abilities. The wing glove and the leading edge Krueger flaps were designed to have no gapping between them when in the extended position. This was key, as it forced all of this air over the top of the wing, energizing lift and allowing decreased takeoff and landing speeds. The Krueger flaps were also extended farther toward the fuselage under the fixed landing lights to capture extra lift in this area.

Flight Testing for the 737-200 Advanced Program

Flight testing for the 737-200 Advanced program was accomplished by a 737-222 with registration number N1359B and previously registered by Boeing as N737Q. This aircraft was given Serial Number 19758 and Effectivity Number PG199. PG199 was the sixteenth 737 off the assembly line and was retained by Boeing for further testing. From September 1970 to December 1971, this aircraft accumulated 181 hours and 20 minutes of flight time specifically to test the performance enhancements that would truly bring out the best results and make a great airplane even more competitive.

Tests in the low speed regions of the performance envelope were conducted and were of paramount importance, because of the redesigned engine pylon glove and its aerodynamic interaction with the leading edge slats and redesigned Krueger flaps. As a

This shows PG199 (c/n 19758, l/n 16) prior to its tenure as the Advanced 737 testbed and demonstrator. While at Boeing this aircraft wore test registrations N737Q and N1359B, and is often mistaken for the 737 prototype because of its similar paint scheme. PG199 was delivered to National Airways of New Zealand on February 15, 1974. *Courtesy of The Museum of Flight*

Experiments with many configurations were conducted during the flight test program. Here Ship One's Krueger flaps extended under the landing light and wing-to-engine fairings are similar to the final Advanced 737 configuration. The larger experimental trailing edge flaps were tested but never saw production. *Courtesy of The Boeing Company*

The ceremony commemorating the delivery of the first 737-200 Advanced aircraft to All Nippon Airlines (ANA) occurred on May 20, 1971. Jack Steiner shakes hands with executives from the airline as they take possession of the new aircraft. Times were very tough for Boeing, and because of this the ceremony occurred with little fanfare. *Courtesy of The Boeing Company*

result of this testing, the slat extension schedule (with regard to the trailing edge flap position) was changed to achieve ideal stall speeds and handling characteristics. This change had the slats transit to the fully extended position with the trailing edge flaps moving to position 10. Once fully extended, the outboard slat panels (1 and 6) would "gap" away from the wing slightly to provide the best low speed performance for the Advanced configuration. Because of these slat scheduling changes modifications to and testing of the stall warning system were also required.

For every takeoff of a commercial jet, performance data is reviewed to ensure that if the aircraft were to have an engine failure at the worst possible time, not only would it be able to lift off on the remaining runway, but it also must be able to climb well enough to clear all obstacles with ease. Occasionally, there were situations when the runways being used by airlines were plenty long, but because of high altitudes and temperatures the aircraft would struggle to meet the climb requirements. Under these circumstances it was advantageous to accelerate to a higher speed while still on the runway with less trailing edge flap extension (i.e., position 1 versus position 5). This would reduce aerodynamic drag sufficiently to allow for a slightly faster and steeper climb in

the event of an engine failure. This concept was tested on this aircraft to acquire data to improve the 737 Advanced's load carrying capability in adverse airport conditions. Vmu (Velocity, Minimum Unstick) tests were also conducted to prove the ability of the aircraft to become airborne after a tail strike on the runway. The Advanced 737 featured the new Hydro-Aire III Antiskid package, a closed-loop system designed to make braking smoother and more effective. Heavy duty brakes and wheel assemblies were also retrofitted to improve stopping performance. Due to these brake changes RTO (Rejected Takeoff) testing was also conducted to validate performance.

One of the new features on the Advanced 737 was the auto brake system. There were four different settings for the system selectable from the cockpit: OFF, 1 (minimum), 2 (medium), and 3 (maximum). OFF would have the system disarmed, with the only braking provided manually by the pilot. Settings 1, 2, and 3 would automatically apply braking at the moment of touchdown and maintain a scheduled deceleration rate corresponding to the setting selected. On average, auto brakes reduced the aircraft's required landing distance because the brakes were applied immediately upon touchdown, whereas a pilot would typically delay brake application by two seconds. This feature was thoroughly tested throughout the program and has become a standard feature on subsequent aircraft designs.

Since the "vertical bounce" phenomenon was still noticeable additional vortex generator configurations were tested, leading to the new production standard arrangement. The large vortex generators were removed from the lower surfaces of the horizontal stabilizer and a total of eight (four on each side) were installed on the upper fuselage between the horizontal and vertical stabilizers. This configuration was effective, and was standard equipment on all subsequent 737s until the emergence of the 737 MAX in 2016.

In addition to the above tests, studies with simulated ice shapes glued to the aircraft were undertaken to check handling and maneuverability in simulated heavy icing conditions. High speed tests were performed to speeds up to Mach .90 to check the revised vortex generator configurations. Fifteen different tests were conducted on the engines:

- In-flight shutdowns and restarts
- Thrust calibration
- Simulated go-arounds from idle to thrust lever stops to check "slam acceleration" performance
- Vmcg (engine out steering) tests using only aerodynamic controls (no nose wheel steering) to simulate icy runway conditions
- Autopilot and autothrottle performance with the higher thrust JT8D-15 engine

After PG199 had finished its flight test duties and extensive use for sales promotion of the 737-200 Advanced it was placed in airline service. Although built to United Airlines' specifications, the aircraft never saw service with that carrier. On February 15, 1974, the aircraft was delivered to National Airways of New Zealand and later went to Air New Zealand.

Sales Challenges

Selling the 737 initially proved a difficult endeavor. Orders were not coming in fast enough, and the production rate was in the neighborhood of one to one and a half aircraft per month. This was not enough production to sustain the program indefinitely and the 737 was losing a lot of ground to the Douglas DC-9, which had a two-year head start in getting to market. It was around this time the 737 program was once again in serious jeopardy.

Airline mergers during this period did little to help the plight of the 737. Lake Central Airlines had placed an order for 737s to replace their fleet of Convair propliners, but the order was canceled in 1968, when Lake Central was absorbed into Allegheny Airlines, an already established DC-9 customer. A similar disappointment occurred the same year with Pacific Airlines, an established Boeing customer. Their plan to order 737s to supplement their 727 operations was scrubbed when the carrier merged with Bonanza Airlines and West Coast Airlines. Bonanza and West Coast had been early DC-9 operators with a combined fleet of seven Douglas jets. The newly consolidated airline, known as Air West, became well known for its sizable DC-9 operation.

Boeing management was constantly analyzing the situation, and was literally teetering on the fence between continuing the 737 program or canceling it. In addition to this challenge, Boeing's product line had expanded so quickly that internal restructuring in the sales department was required to maintain the company's

This 737-159 (c/n 19680, l/n 94) was one of two examples purchased by Avianca Columbia in 1968. Both aircraft were sold to the West German Air Force in 1971. *Courtesy of The Boeing Company*

robustness. In this situation, Boeing began to look to other businesses that had similar issues with multiple brands under one roof. Frequent meetings were held that would decide the fate of the 737, and eventually had remarkable impacts on the future of airline operations.

Newly appointed 737 Marketing Manager Peter Morton remembered his involvement in a set of meetings to determine the fate of the 737:

The Boeing product line was getting so complicated that the sales department was confused. Boeing concluded if there are several brands in a single company you need a brand manager for each. Senior product development executive Don Hufford was assigned to create a marketing management organization to advocate and support each model airplane inside the sales department. Instead of trying to borrow program engineers to support sales in specialized areas like noise, fuel burn, or cockpit systems, there would be marketing managers who would be expert on technical aspects of the airplane. Don recruited specialists on the 727 (Mark Gregoire), the 707 (John Brown), and the 737 (Tom Lollar). Each had assistants—Tom's included Ray Randall, Borge Boeskov, and myself—each of us with a geographic focus. When I joined the group Mr. Hufford said, "I have a special assignment for you. You are going to serve on a task force that will provide a recommendation to corporate management as to whether the 737 program should continue." I had given up my life and career as a big frog in a small pond in customer service to come over and decide if the 737 was going to continue, not to mention my job! The task force went for three weeks, and we met in secret, because this was volatile information. We met over and over, and ran numbers, and made the recommendation that the 737 should be continued at Boeing. The reasons were: 1. Even though there seemed no way we could get the program sunk costs back (the non-recurring costs), right now, at one and a half airplanes a month, the airplane was kind of paying for its recurring costs; 2. We think that this new, Advanced version of the

Death in the Andes

-- art by Rick Goettling

A true story from the early career of an ops engineer

by Peter Morton

On Page 260 of the recent history of Boeing, *Legend and Legacy,* I described the controversy surrounding the initial campaigns to sell the 737 in South America for operation out of high-altitude airports. We had the monopoly on three-engine jet transports, and the Sales organization really preferred to sell a 727 for these operations. No one wanted to enter into a bidding war of twin jets against the DC9. So our salesman, Jim Robinson, invented the "Death in the Andes" slogan, dramatizing the dangers of twin jet operation out of high/hot airfields.

As we all know, it isn't the number of engines that counts, it's the number of pounds of thrust packed into each engine and the resulting thrust-to-weight ratio that makes or breaks that kind of operation.

But the original marginal operation by a twin jet reached its all-time extreme when Robinson's boss, John Broback, sold a 737 to Avianca for operation out of Bogota, Colombia.

I was the operations engineer for Avianca, and **Gene Bolin** was assigned as the lead training pilot. The 737-200 was too heavy for the operation, and the JT8D-9 engine was not yet available. The 737 advanced wing configuration was still only a gleam in Bob Norton's eye. So an under-powered 737-100 with JT8D-7 engines, was proposed and, unfortunately, bought by the airline. The reputation of that operation still taints the 737 in Colombia.

It fell to Gene and me to prove to the airline and a rebellious pilots' union that the operation was feasible. After flight training was complete, we ferried the airplane to Baranquilla on the Caribbean coast of Colombia for the proving runs. The sea-level operation was just fine, but the big question was: Could the 737 fly from Bogota to Baranquilla with a full passenger payload at the warm day condition of 20 degrees C? I still remember the gross weight requirement: 90,000 pounds exactly.

Gene and I carefully planned the flight with Mr. Perez, the Avianca operations engineer. He trusted us implicitly. We would ballast the airplane with fuel and newspaper bales to the fateful 90,000 pounds. With air conditioning packs off, we would make a V_1 engine cut, the airplane would accelerate to V_R, rotate per the book, and climb in a vast circle around the Bogota valley basin.

Retracting flaps, we would not exceed five minutes of takeoff thrust and would use final segment

climb performance to clear the mountains toward the now-infamous Medellin, our alternate destination. We had 225 mph tires installed, operating near the *coffin corner* of tire speed, brake energy, field length and climb limit at the maximum certified improved climb speed. We were even taking credit for the unusually high barometric pressure which prevails at Bogota: good for an equivalent reduction in airport elevation from 8,300 feet to about 7,900 feet!

This operations engineer was in hog heaven! There couldn't be another place in the world where all these wonderful parameters came together. Gene and I had actually simulated the operation at Moses Lake to see if Mr. Newton's f really equals ma, and he was a willing, if not enthusiastic, participant in this one-act play.

> **All I could see were 40 very large eyes as we executed what must be the lowest ever jet transport tour over downtown Bogota.**

Things don't always go as planned. The number of newspaper bales available fell about 3,000 pounds short of the required ballast. Oh well, that's OK; 3,000 pounds equals 20 150-pound passengers, and we found some campesinos who were cutting airport grass coming off shift. "How'd you like to go for an airplane ride?" (What's that you say about insurance release forms?)

With the 737 fleet chief pilot, Captain De La Cruz, in the left seat, Gene in the right, myself in the observer's seat, and our 20 enthusiastic sightseers, we taxied out for takeoff. The other observer's seat (if such it can be called on a 737) was occupied by the chief of the pilots' union who had, he said, "made his peace with God that very morning."

As I remember, V_1 was 150 knots indicated, V_R was 154, and V_2 was 152. Yes, V_2 was lower than V_R, and it was legal. You see, correcting for static position error due to ground effect V_2 was actually a knot or two higher than V_R in calibrated airspeed. Delightful!

Captain De La Cruz started the takeoff roll, I

started my timer, and we lumbered down the runway. The acceleration was perceptible. The runway was rough, and we seemed to indulge in as much vertical as horizontal motion. Some 55-or-so seconds later, Gene cut the left engine to idle. The lack of acceleration was shocking. In one sense, we seemed to be frozen in space, but the runway was going by at an incredible rate. Sure enough, the airspeed crept on up to 154 knots, De La Cruz rotated, and the airplane lifted off with the requisite runway still apparently in front of us. The indicated airspeed did, in fact, appear to slightly *decrease!* But as soon as the gear retracted, it stabilized and we saw a positive rate of climb -- as I remember, 50 feet per minute more than we needed to make good the 2.4 percent climb gradient.

Well, f was, in fact, still equal to ma. The airplane climbed out to our selected level of height, we retracted the flaps within the five-minute takeoff time limit, and we made the wide turn at 15-degrees bank as we headed over the mountains toward Medellin at *max continuous thrust.* Oh, rapture!

I looked back into the cabin at our happy campesinos, and all I could see were 40 very large eyes as we executed what must be the lowest-ever jet transport tour over downtown Bogota.

The story has a mixed ending. The pilots' union reluctantly accepted the results of the test, the airplane went into service and gained a horrible reputation as a *runway lover.* Avianca sold the airplanes about two years later and used 727s exclusively on all domestic departures from Bogota. For the 737, it took the advanced wing configuration, the -17 engine, and many years to live down a bad reputation and finally bury Jim Robinson's "Death in the Andes."

Today the 737 is an excellent performer in high/hot airports and is the airplane-of-choice for developing route systems in austere surroundings. But this ex-ops engineer will never forget that moment when all the flight manual charts in the sky came together for one magnificent limited takeoff.

Peter Morton

(Peter Morton has been Director of Customer Training for nearly seven years. He's been a board member of the Bellevue Philharmonic.)

Courtesy of Peter Morton/Boeing

aircraft will sell well, and Peter here is going to make sure that happens; 3. If you take all of the spares that will ever be sold to support each airplane and credit it to the airplane financially, it does provide a reasonable return; 4. We don't have anything else to do with the resources that are currently working on the 737, so if we did cancel it there would be a serious layoff. The executives weighed in on the recommendation and the decision came back to continue. In the meantime, Dick Taylor and Bob Norton got a sale of airplanes to the Air Force as a navigation trainer and turned over the new 737-200 Advanced to the sales department. It kept things going.

The early 737-100 and 737-200 were really great airplanes for many operations, but the most promising markets for these aircraft were in more rural and largely undeveloped nations. Many of these places had short runways, some unpaved, and were nestled in mountainous terrain. Often the aircraft would need to take off from very high altitude airports, climbing above higher terrain, and be able to do it all safely in case of an engine failure. One of the early customers for the 737 was Avianca Columbia. The operations desired by this airline with the early Basic 737-100 (with the original JT8D-7 engines) showed the need for improvements in aerodynamic drag reduction, lift, and engine power, as evidenced by Peter Morton's "Death in the Andes" article, which recounted a story when he was a performance engineer, long before the marketing manager job offer.

PG199, the Advanced 737 demonstrator, is seen while on a sales tour. Ballast was routinely loaded onto the aircraft to simulate a fully loaded condition, allowing airline representatives to see the performance of the aircraft firsthand. *Courtesy of Peter Morton/Boeing*

With the introduction of the Advanced model in 1970, the 737's aircraft performance was maturing nicely. While the earlier "Basic" 737-200 was more or less on par with the McDonnell Douglas DC-9-30, it was widely known the Advanced aircraft had a 3,000 pound load carrying advantage over the DC-9 given the same engines being hung on the airframe. This benefit was won by continually improving the aerodynamics and structural

71-1403 (c/n 20685, l/n 317) was the first T-43A built and was delivered to the USAF July 31, 1973. *Courtesy of The Boeing Company*

strength of the 737. Even though it had formidable performance capabilities over the Douglas machine, sales of the 737 remained slow at best. This was due to a large extent because of the previously established DC-9 customer base. The United States Air Force gave Boeing an order for nineteen T-43A Advanced Navigation Trainers. Many believe this order saved the 737 program from closure, or being sold off to other companies. This order brought the production rate up to two aircraft a month in the 1972 time frame. Another "stay of execution" had been won, but the benefits would only last a short while. Additional orders had to be achieved.

Even in early 1973 the 737 program was still in jeopardy. Constant analysis of costs and sales revenues were still being frequently looked at by high management in Boeing. Production of the aircraft was still minimal at two aircraft per month, a rate at which it was extremely difficult to reap a profit. Even with the 737's performance advantages, raising the cost of the aircraft more than the baseline six percent per year (for inflation) would cost Boeing sales. It was predicted that even raising the price of the 737 eight to ten percent would cut already slow sales in half. The only way to extend the program was to aggressively pursue sales abroad. If aircraft production could be increased to five per month enormous cost savings would be realized by Boeing, and the program's non-recurring costs would also be spread over a larger order base. At this point it was believed domestic markets had already been tapped out.

Anglian 737s

Back in Britain, the BAC One-Eleven was proving to be too small for several airlines, such as Aloha Airlines, Britannia Airways, and Aer Lingus. Many had requested a higher capacity version of the One-Eleven. The initial inability to meet this requirement was due to the lack of a more powerful version of the Rolls-Royce Spey engine to which BAC was seemingly committed. This eventually caused these three One-Eleven operators to look seriously at the 737, promptly leading to orders. Britain's own Britannia Airways also shifted in favor of the Boeing jet. After catching wind of this, the British government put significant political pressure on the airline to purchase the One-Eleven. In defiance of the government's demands Britannia Airways ordered three 737-204s, with an option for one additional aircraft. Pursuant to the Duty Act of 1958, the

Labour Government levied a fourteen percent "import tax" on the aircraft to dissuade a further order. Completely ignoring this, nineteen more 737-204s were eventually ordered, with an additional twenty-two aircraft either being leased or bought on the used market. This in itself was evidence of the operational advantages the Boeing 737 had over the BAC One-Eleven.

A British Airways 737-236 Advanced (G-BGDB, c/n 21791, l/n 626) on a pre-delivery test flight in 1980. British Airways became an important customer for the 737 program, eventually operating 144 examples since 1979.

Even British Airways was showing interest in the 727 and 737. Both their Spey-powered Hawker Siddeley Tridents (which were built specifically to British Airways' specifications) and the BAC jets were proving to be too small. More capacity and larger jets were becoming more desirable. This situation sparked a strong push to "stretch" the One-Eleven, and pressure was put on Rolls-Royce to make a more powerful version of the original Spey Mk. 506 that powered the BAC One-Eleven 200. The eventual evolution of this engine would see a thrust increase from 10,410 pounds to 12,550 with the Spey Mk. 512-14DW. This allowed BAC to do what they had been wanting to do for some time: stretch the One-Eleven. The resultant aircraft was the BAC One-Eleven 500 series, featuring a fuselage stretch of 13 ft. 6 in. Lift was also enhanced with a small wingspan increase of five feet. This aircraft was much more competitive than earlier models and won the British Airways order.

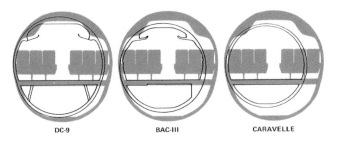

The 737 fuselage size compared to the DC-9, BAC One-Eleven, and Sud Aviation Caravelle. *Courtesy of Peter Morton/Boeing*

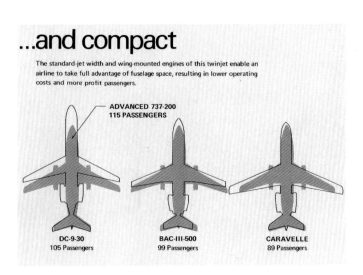

The ramp space required by the 737 when compared to its competitors. *Courtesy of Peter Morton/Boeing*

This 737-248C (EI-ASL, c/n 21011, l/n 411) was delivered to Aer Lingus on May 2, 1975. This example is still in service with Canadian operator First Air and has been fitted with the Unimproved Runway Kit. *Courtesy of The Museum of Flight*

This kept the One-Eleven program alive for several more years, and it even saw limited production in Romania. Unfortunately for BAC, this improved aircraft was still too little too late, as many sales had already been lost to the 737 and DC-9. British Airways later became a large 737 customer for Boeing, operating them alongside their remaining fleet of One-Elevens.

Western Airlines

Western Air Express was founded in July 1925, and commenced operations on April 17, 1926, flying air mail in a Douglas M-2 biplane. A colorful and storied history saw Western Air Express merge with Standard Air Lines and later join Fokker Aircraft and Transcontinental Air Transport to become Transcontinental and Western Airlines (TWA). By 1934, Western Air Express had separated from TWA and was renamed Western Airlines in 1941. The airline grew after WWII and operated Douglas DC-6s, Convair 240s, and Lockheed L-188 Electra turboprops. Western Airlines, provided its first pure jet service with two Boeing 707-139 jetliners leased to Western after orders for these aircraft were canceled by Cubana de Aviacion, subsequent to the airline's takeover by Fidel Castro's new Cuban government. The airline soon expanded its jet operation with the addition of larger Boeing 707-320s, 720s, and Boeing 727-200s. To add to its growing fleet, once Boeing "went firm" on developing the 737 Western's President Terry Drinkwater became interested in the 737. He insisted that the new jetliner be able to lift high gross weights out of the high-altitude airports in Denver, Colorado, and Salt Lake City, Utah. This caused Boeing to revisit the 737's wing—still in the paper design stage—and to add three additional feet to each wing. Although this did come with a small weight increase, the wing was able to provide higher lift with minimal drag. Western also strongly considered the Douglas DC-9, with Dick Ault and others internal to the airline favoring the Douglas jet. Because of Boeing's

Author's Collection

Boeing's Ben Wheat presented Dick Ault of Western Airlines with the carrier's first 737-247 (N4501W, c/n 19598, l/n 33) on June 11, 1968. *Courtesy of The Boeing Company*

willingness to listen to their customers the order for sixteen Boeing 737-200s was won and the airplane became a better performer in the process.

Western's fleet grew to encompass fifty-four examples of the 737-200 series, and they later operated thirteen 737-300s to supplement their McDonnell Douglas DC-10 wide body, trijet service. Western Airlines became caught up in the "merger mania" of the late 1980s post-deregulation environment and was merged into Delta Airlines on April 1, 1987. Delta continued to operate Western's 737 aircraft and is still an important 737 customer today, operating 156 737NGs as of March 2016.

The Californians
Pacific Southwest Airlines

In 1946, a Californian businessman named Kenny Friedkin started a flying service called Friedkin Aeronautics that specialized in flight training. By 1948, the small company evolved into Friedkin Airlines, providing charter service in a war weary Cessna T-50 nicknamed the "Bamboo Bomber" because of its wooden construction. The company's name was changed to Pacific Southwest Airlines in 1949 and

back into aviation. Stewardesses (as they were called at the time) wore miniskirts and hot pants, and told jokes to their passengers. This fun-loving, low fare service became extremely popular and spurred the addition of more jetliners to its fleet. On September 20, 1968, PSA's first Boeing 737-214 N378PS (c/n 19681, l/n 68) was delivered to the airline. This was the first of eleven 737s purchased new from Boeing, while three additional airplanes were leased from Air California and the GATX-Boothe Aircraft Company. It is interesting that the Boeing fleet replaced the airline's two DC-9-30s by 1973, when the airline transitioned to their newer fuchsia, orange, and red paint scheme made famous by the smile painted on the nose of all of its airplanes. By 1976, PSA had replaced their fourteen strong fleet of 737s with additional 727s and the reacquisition of two Lockheed Electras for its services to Lake Tahoe. This was a rare situation, with 737s being replaced by older technology aircraft, but was due somewhat to PSA's highly specialized route structure and the increased capacity of

N379PS (c/n 19682, l/n 78) was delivered new to Pacific Southwest Airlines on October 5, 1968. Here it is shown in the later fuchsia paint scheme. *Courtesy of Jennings Heilig*

PSA's first 737-214 (N378PS, c/n 19681, l/n 78) shown during a pre-delivery test flight. *Courtesy of The Museum of Flight*

The same aircraft shown on the flight line at Boeing Field prior to delivery. *Courtesy of The Museum of Flight*

became widely known as "PSA." Through the years this intrastate carrier grew with the use of Douglas DC-3 and DC-4 propliners that were later replaced by six Lockheed L-188 Electra turbo props. The company moved into the jet age with the introduction of five Boeing 727-100s and the acquisition of two Douglas DC-9-30 series jetliners. PSA soon became famous for bringing fun

the 727-200 Advanced aircraft. PSA eventually replaced its 727-200 aircraft with McDonnell Douglas DC-9 Super 80s and augmented them with smaller BAe-146 four-engined jetliners. PSA was absorbed into USAir on April 8, 1988.

Air California

Air California was another Californian intrastate airline that was formed to provide service from the Los Angeles Basin to the San Francisco Bay area. This was (and still is) a very lucrative and heavily traveled route for airlines. January 16, 1967, the first day of operations at Air California, was not without its challenges. The first service from Orange County to San Francisco was made difficult by both airports being shrouded in low visibility weather. "The show must go on," and this first service was accomplished by bussing passengers to nearby Ontario Airport, where they boarded the company's Lockheed L-188 Electra. Aboard this aircraft the customers were flown to a small airport on the California coast called Half Moon Bay. Another bus ride on a winding road shadowed by redwood trees took the travelers to San Francisco International Airport. This company was determined to be a tough competitor. In March 1968, Air California entered the jet age with two ex-Continental Airlines DC-9-14 jets leased from Douglas. These aircraft were short-lived at Air California, only serving thirteen months before they were replaced by the 737-200.

Air California began 737 service in 1968, when six 737-293s were leased from the GATX-Boothe Aircraft Corporation. The company ultimately operated twenty-nine different examples of the 737-200 series, including two 737-210C aircraft that came

Air California leased N463GB from GATX-Boothe and took delivery of the aircraft on July 10, 1968. This aircraft was originally bought by Pacific Airlines, but was reassigned when that carrier merged with Bonanza Air Lines and West Coast Airlines, established DC-9 operators. *Courtesy of The Boeing Company*

from Wien Air Alaska. This pair of aircraft had a cargo door installed in the forward fuselage and seating for passengers was behind the wing. This aircraft used the optional, yet rarely seen, rear airstair. This feature allowed the aircraft to be self sufficient, since the cargo configuration did not allow passenger access to the forward entry door. Also of interest was Air California's acquisition of the two 737-159 airplanes originally bought by Avianca (see Peter Morton's "Death in the Andes") for use on its Californian route structure in 1977. In 1981, Air California was re-branded into AirCal, with a complete change of the airline's paint scheme.

In later years, AirCal went on to operate the McDonnell Douglas DC-9 Super 80, which was eventually replaced by the 737-300, with its quieter and more fuel efficient turbofan engines. On two different occasions in the history of Air California and AirCal they replaced a DC-9 product with a Boeing 737 version. AirCal was later merged into American Airlines on July 1, 1987.

Two 737-291s shown in close formation. N570GB (c/n 20070, l/n 124) and N571GB (c/n 20071, l/n 131) were leased by the carrier from GATX-Boothe until being operated by Frontier Airlines in January 1970. Through airline acquisitions both aircraft served with Continental Airlines before being retired. *Courtesy of The Museum of Flight*

The Venezuelan VIP aircraft (c/n 21167, l/n 442) purchased for President Carlos Andres Perez in 1975 is still active with the Venezuelan government, registered as 0207. *Courtesy of The Museum of Flight*

Venezuelan Sale

Peter Morton, a Boeing 737 marketing manager in 1971, told of the extraordinary lengths they were going to sell the Advanced 737 to Venezuela:

> Bob Brog was the Boeing salesman for South America and was determined to sell Boeing airplanes to the Venezuelan airlines. Douglas dominated our commercial business with the Venezuelan airline Viasa, who operated DC-9s. The Venezuelan Air Force wanted an airplane with gravel capability to support operations into Canaima. Canaima was the airport by which access to the Venezuelan Tepuys and Angel Falls could be obtained (currently a tourist attraction). Bob thought that if he got a presidential airplane sold that would open the door for commercial sales to the Venezuelan airline. In fact, the Advanced 737 had so many capabilities in short field and high altitude airport performance that it would have made an excellent airplane for them.

We took PG199 (N1359B, c/n 19758) for a demonstration to President Carlos Andres Perez, who in his first term (1974–1979) was called "The Walking President," because legend had it that he walked to every major Venezuelan city, campaigning to get elected, and liked to continue to visit the populace frequently. He flew around in an Avro twin turboprop and was receptive to the idea of a jet. Perez was scheduled to deliver a major speech in Barinas and we timed our visit accordingly.

We had installed some couches and reclining chairs in the front of PG199 and flew to Venezuela. Tom Edmonds was the Boeing pilot, with Tommy Twiggs along as copilot. Because we were going to visit a president the sales department decided we needed to take a Boeing president with us, so Tex Boullion and VP of Sales Clancy Wilde were part of the Boeing delegation. Brog's strategy was to win over the Venezuelan presidential pilot as an advocate, so our plan included having him (Col. Mendoza) in the cockpit when we visited Barinas for Perez's speech. Mendoza was used to flying the Avro, so we allocated sufficient time to familiarize him with the 737. It was quite a challenge, providing transition training to Mendoza in three days or so. Mendoza had the habit of declaring any flight in which he was a crew member as "Air Force One," even when the president was not aboard, so we gave the air traffic control folks a fit because they had to clear the airspace ahead of us. My memory of the activity is that we went to Isla Margarita one day, Merida the next, and Barinas the third to prepare Mendoza to act as "captain" in the left seat when the big day came. This was an amazing expenditure of Boeing resources, both personnel and financial, but Bob Brog was persuasive that the demo would open a new market for us.

I went on all of the flights as a translator in the cockpit and remember several instances in which Tom's diplomatic skills were challenged, trying to keep us safe,

The interior of the Venezuelan VIP aircraft. *Courtesy of The Boeing Company*

and at the same time satisfy Mendoza as he was gaining proficiency flying the 737. These were challenging airports, by the way. The runway slope at Merida was I think four percent (see what sticks in the mind of a performance engineer?), and landing would be uphill and takeoff would be downhill. I remember observing a very high power setting on final approach because we were basically flying level into an uphill runway. We had an APU failure in Merida, so the Boeing mechanics had to do some clever things to get the engines started after our tour of the city.

According to Bob Brog, the evening before the flight for Perez's speech in Barinas there was a meeting at the Casa Rosada (Pink House, which was the equivalent of the White House). Tex told Perez that Col. Mendoza (who was present at the meeting) had acquired all of the skills necessary to fly the 737 and offered, "If you would prefer to make this a private flight with no Boeing people aboard, we would be happy to oblige." Perez replied, "I plan to take my entire cabinet with me on this trip and I would like you to be my guest in the cabin." Mendoza reportedly said, "And I would like Capt. Edmonds to be my guest in the cockpit."

The next day we took off for Barinas with all of those folks aboard. I made a presentation in the cabin to the president and his cabinet members about the 737 and how it would serve Venezuela's needs for international and domestic travel. We also discussed how it could operate into unimproved strips, such as Canaima, and how we proposed to outfit the interior of the airplane appropriate to their needs. This was the first time I had pitched to a head of state. When we reached Barinas, the Venezuelan government officials took off for town in automobiles with a motorcycle escort.

There we were at the airport in Barinas, in our cool, air conditioned airplane. It was hot outside, and we had a very restless Boeing president aboard for several hours. Midway through this time Tex said to me, "Peter, I think we can sweeten this deal a bit: give Bob Brog (he stayed back in Caracas) a call and tell him to add (I don't remember how much) in spares and other concessions, and to meet us when we land in Caracas with a new contract proposal for President Perez to sign." Well, this was all before cellular phones, and in fact landlines in this section of Venezuela. I went hunting for a military officer and told him I needed to call Caracas. He took me into the village of Barinas on his motorcycle. We went to a small office where there was a radio telephone with a line of people waiting to use it. We busted the line and I called Brog. Sure enough, he met us on our return to Caracas with a new contract proposal. PG199 did not have the gravel kit installed at the time, so a week after the demo I got a call from Mendoza, indicating that there was skepticism about the unimproved runway capability. I assured him that it was capable and certified, but to no avail. So I invited him to Seattle and made arrangements with Alaska Air to fly us to Kotzebue, where they had daily service with gravel equipped 737s. Col. Mendoza saw the operation first hand and by golly,

they bought the airplane. Regrettably, the sale did not bring the Venezuelan airline around and they continued to operate DC-9s.

Sales Victories....At Last
Sabena

With the T-43A production run nearing completion more volume was required to keep Boeing's 737 program afloat. Sabena Belgian World Airlines had a fleet of aging Sud Aviation Caravelle VI-Ns coming due for replacement. The DC-9-30 and the emerging Dassault Mercure were counterparts to the 737 Advanced and were providing strong competition for Boeing. Sabena was one of the last major European carriers that had not yet committed to a modern twin-jet. In 1973, Sabena submitted an order for ten 737-229 Advanced aircraft to replace its four remaining Caravelles and five Boeing 727-29s. On the production lines the whistles blew

The Sabena order was an important victory for the 737 program. Pictured is OO-SDA (c/n 20907, l/n 351), the first 737-229 Advanced delivered to the Belgian carrier to replace their aging Sud Aviation Caravelles. *Courtesy of The Boeing Company*

An artist's impression of the proposed Frontier 737. *Courtesy of The Museum of Flight*

Frontier Airlines' first 737 (N7371F, c/n 20074, l/n 170) was leased from GATX-Boothe. *Courtesy of The Museum of Flight*

and the PA system came alive with the news. This triumph signaled the end of slow sales for the 737. The combination of improving market conditions and the 737 Advanced efficiency improvements began to draw in substantial orders. With the 737 finally in its element the program quickly increased in sales volume.

Southwest Airlines and the 737

Southwest Airlines began as a business concept hatched by Rollin King in 1966. With the help of attorney Herb Kelleher extensive research was done, primarily focused on the Pacific Southwest Airlines (PSA) operation in San Diego, California. With the cooperation of PSA's President Kenny Friedkin, Kelleher concluded that King's idea had merit. The decision to move forward was made and Air Southwest (as it was first named) was incorporated on March 15, 1967. Soon after the fledgling carrier was approved by the Texas Aeronautical Commission (TAC) to provide service from Dallas Love Field to Houston Hobby airport and San Antonio, Texas. The celebration did not last long, as resistance from Continental Airlines, Braniff Airways, and Texas International left Air Southwest tied up in court for three years. By the time the long, arduous battle was won by Kelleher and his team, Air Southwest had depleted virtually all of its start up capital. At this point, in January 1971, a long time airline veteran named Lamar Muse came to work for Air Southwest and changed the company's name to Southwest Airlines. He set out to raise money by bringing in investment capital, starting

A Southwest bumper sticker circa 1995. *Author's Collection*

with $50,000 of his own money, followed by another $250,000 from his friends and business acquaintances. Further funding was raised, with a substantial investment made by Mr. Wesley West for $750,000 to help procure new aircraft.

Initially, the aircraft types considered for purchase were the Boeing 737-100 and -200, Douglas DC-9-30, BAC One-Eleven, and the older Lockheed L-188 Electra turbo-prop. Muse immediately ruled out the Electra because airlines that were using jet equipment would be more competitive than those using slower propeller aircraft. Because of the economics of the BAC One-Eleven the race was soon narrowed to the DC-9 or the 737-200. This was an extremely close race and Douglas nearly won. Muse became aware that Boeing had a minor over-production issue and it had three "white tail" 737s sitting in short-term storage on the ramp in Oklahoma City. King and Muse were whisked from Los Angeles International Airport (LAX) to Douglas headquarters in Long Beach by the manufacturer's limousine. During their ride Muse began mentally comparing and contrasting the DC-9 versus the 737. Upon their arrival Muse slipped away

Three 737-2H4 Advanced aircraft for Southwest Airlines being assembled in the Renton assembly hall. *Courtesy of Southwest Airlines*

N20SW (c/n 20369, l/n 267) was Southwest Airlines' first aircraft and was delivered on June 2, 1971. *Courtesy of Southwest Airlines*

N52SW (c/n 21533, l/n 524) was christened *The Herbert D. Kelleher* in honor of the airline's leader. This aircraft left the Southwest fleet in 1999 and flew for Air Philippines and AirPhil Express before being stored in 2011. *Courtesy of Jennings Heilig*

and called Boeing's Director of Domestic Sales Dan Palmer on a pay phone in Douglas' lobby. Muse laid down the deal he wanted with Boeing for the three 737s. Southwest would pay $4 million for each aircraft, with delivery in May 1971. The terms would be that Southwest would pay $50,000 for each aircraft per month for the first sixty months, with no down payment. The balance due was to be paid at the end of the five year period. Muse gave Palmer an hour to make the deal or he was going to buy the DC-9. Thirty minutes later Boeing responded to Muse via telephone while he and King were in a meeting with the Douglas salesmen. Boeing accepted the terms with some provisions for spare parts and history was made. The Douglas salesmen were disappointed, but kind enough to drive Muse and King back to LAX.

Southwest Airlines subsequently exercised the option for the fourth aircraft (N25SW, c/n 20095, l/n 188), which was used to supplement the first three aircraft and to fly interstate charters. Since Southwest was operating exclusively out of Dallas' Love Field, supporters of the new Dallas Fort Worth (DFW) airport set out to block Southwest's interstate plans and its application to the Civil Aeronautics Board for service from Love Field to New Orleans. Jim Wright, who was Fort Worth's representative to the US House of Representatives, set out to block all interstate airline flights out of Love Field. Kelleher and his team were back in the legal fight for the survival of Southwest Airlines and this caused

the need to sell one of the four aircraft. Southwest's first aircraft (N20SW, c/n 20369, l/n 267) was sold to Frontier Airlines with a profit to Southwest of $500,000. The problem for Southwest was that they needed to do the work of four aircraft with only three. Unfortunately, flying time can only be reduced a small amount through piloting techniques and routing. The extra capacity could only be gained by reducing the amount of time the three aircraft would sit at gates between flights. It was determined by Bill Franklin, Southwest's man in charge of ground operations, that the ground time (referred to as "turn time") would have to be reduced to just ten minutes. Many felt it was impossible to deplane and board 122 customers and move the aircraft in that amount of time, but this would be required to keep the schedule intact. They did succeed, due to the remarkable teamwork among ground crews, flight attendants, and pilots.

Through the trials and tribulations over the years Southwest grew into a low fare superpower. The partnership with Boeing continued, leading to Southwest becoming a launch customer for the 737-300 and later the 737-500 and 737-700. On January 17, 2005, Southwest retired N98SW, the company's last 737-2H4 (c/n 23054, l/n 969), and replaced the older aircraft with the next generation 737-700 series jets. As of January 2017, Southwest Airlines' fleet had grown to 724 Boeing 737 aircraft, with additional 737NG orders being delivered. A record order for 200 737 MAX aircraft was received by Boeing on December 13, 2011, assuring Southwest's position as the 737 MAX launch customer.

"Cactus"

The origins of America West Airlines date back to February 1981, when the Arizona airline was first established. After more than two years of preparation, America West began service with three leased Boeing 737s and operated with radio call sign "Cactus." Edward Beauvais, a seasoned airline industry consultant, guided the airline through its first decade. During its formative years many employees were cross-trained for multiple jobs to create additional economic efficiencies.

At the time, America West was considered one of the few post-deregulation success stories when the airline rapidly grew in size by adding additional Boeing 737s, several new destinations, and a second hub in Las Vegas, Nevada. By the mid-1980s, the company also added Boeing 757s acquired from Eastern Airlines and Republic Airlines to supplement its growing fleet of 737-100, -200, and -300 series aircraft. In the wake of deregulation America West added four Boeing 747-206s acquired from KLM (Royal

Dutch Airlines) for its newly established service from Phoenix to Nagoya, Japan, via Honolulu, Hawaii. On a more local level, the airline also procured a fleet of de Havilland DHC-8 turboprops to feed its Phoenix and Las Vegas hub airports.

In 1990, taking advantage of the demise of Pan Am and the third permutation of Braniff, new Airbus A320 jets destined for these airlines were added to the fleet at significantly discounted prices. Even with this advantage finances began to falter due to the carrier's very rapid expansion, the routes to Japan which soon became unprofitable, the Gulf War causing sharp increases in fuel prices, and high overhead costs with its newly constructed Terminal Four at Phoenix Sky Harbor. The carrier continued to lose money and bankruptcy was declared in June 1991. The airline was restructured, Beauvais was replaced by America West veteran Michael Conway, and the 747s and DHC-8s were removed from the fleet.

By 1994, America West had emerged from bankruptcy, and shortly thereafter Conway was replaced by Maurice Myers as the company's CEO. As part of the recovery plan the airline was rebranded, with a new contemporary paint scheme. Slowly, the company's 737s were replaced by a growing number of A320s. During the course of America West's history a significant fleet of 737s was operated, including three of the Original 737 series flight test airplanes: Ship Two, Ship Four, and Ship Six.

In mid-2005, America West Holdings purchased US Airways, which was operating in bankruptcy at the time. Continuing this trend and still under the watch of CEO Doug Parker, the purchase of American Airlines (AMR) by US Airways Group was announced in February 2013. On October 17, 2015, the combined companies became branded as American Airlines.

All told five 737-100s (three originally delivered to Lufthansa and two from Singapore Malaysia Airlines) were used during America West Airlines' history, along with sixty-one 737-200s and sixty-three later model 737-300 series aircraft.

Brazil

In the South American markets, the Advanced 737 had a real advantage over any other jet airliner. Many of these countries did not have the funding or time available to improve their airfields for conventional jet operations. The gravel runway capable 737 did not have to wait for such amenities. The Unimproved Field Kit option for the 737 clenched the deal for many of these carriers. By 1973, fifteen to twenty percent of airlines that ordered the 737 were citing the aircraft's gravel field capability as a major selling point, according to *Aviation Daily*. To engage these markets Boeing provided many demonstrations using PG199, which was the testbed for all of the 737-200 Advanced modifications. Adorned with the Unimproved Field Kit and the new JT8D-15 engines, PG199 was sent all over the world to show the capabilities of this versatile airplane.

The 737 Advanced demonstrator on the gravel runway in Huanuco, Peru. Huanuco's gravel runway was 6,070 feet above sea level. Boeing Marketing Manager Peter Morton is seen climbing the airstairs. The Peruvian demonstration flights were flown by Capts. Brien Wygle and Al Jones. *Courtesy of The Museum of Flight*

Marketing Manager Peter Morton was involved in many of the sales tours to Latin America and reflected on the situation in Brazil:

After we decided to continue the 737 program we had the Advanced airplane. I went to Brazil in 1971. We had one airplane in the Advanced configuration, PG199, that we used to take all over the place to demonstrate. At the time, PG199 had a gravel kit and the Advanced features, so it could go anywhere… . And we took it everywhere! My personal involvement that was most important to the program was Brazil. Brazil has an airport called Santos-Dumont Airport in downtown Rio de Janeiro. They had an "Airbridge" operation using Lockheed Electras to Sao Paulo Airport. Santos-Dumont was 4,200 feet long, and at the end of it was the famous tourist attraction Sugarloaf Mountain, so it was a challenging airport. We demonstrated the 737 there. It was a very successful teaser for us to go in and show analytically that they could satisfy their "Airbridge" market. In Brazil, there were three airlines that were dominant and competing heavily with each other: Varig, Cruziero do Sul, and VASP. VASP was the first to go for the 737 and the others immediately went after it. We must have sold fifty or sixty airplanes to the three airlines. I got a lot of points for doing that…maybe more than I deserved. My biggest personal contribution was when we were in the active negotiations Douglas started to make noise about putting JT8D-17 engines on the DC-9. We were there on the spot and without authorization from Seattle or Renton. Nobody had e-mail. Back in those days we used telexes. Jack Steiner was the head of the 707, 727, and 737 division. Bob Steiner (no relation) was a German and was the salesman in Brazil. Bob just looked at me in front of the customer and said, "We can have the -17 engine too, can't we, Peter?" I said, "Yes!" I was representing the division in sales. Marketing management was not a sales organization, it was an organization that represented the division in sales. I said, "Yes!," and it was one of those things where it was better to apologize afterward than to ask for permission. That cinched the sale. As soon as VASP signed VARIG and Cruzeiro signed, and it was a huge order for the Boeing Company. When I returned to Seattle I did not know if I'd be fired for committing resources without authorization or be treated as a hero. Fortunately, it was the latter, and I think that event greatly helped my career in Boeing.

Peruvian Demonstration Flights

PG199 was also taken to Peru, with Capt. Brien Wygle in the left seat and Al Jones as copilot. Marketing Manager Peter Morton was also on board, and was not only responsible for selling the aircraft to prospective customers, but was also doing the bulk of the performance planning. Because Peter grew up in Costa Rica and was fluent in Spanish he was given the opportunity to serve as interpreter for Capt. Wygle and the Peruvian Air Force officer who flew as copilot on the demonstration flights. The aircraft was taken from airport to airport on a highly choreographed

demonstration schedule to prove to potential customers that it had the short runway and single engine performance Boeing promised. The sequence of airports and fuel usage was planned so the aircraft would arrive at each airport at the requisite high weights to simulate actual revenue operations. The flight went to Lima, Cusco, Andahuaylas, Arequipa, Cajamarca, Iquitos, and Huanuco, among others. At each airport a simulated engine failure at V1 (Takeoff Decision Speed) was executed to show the capability of the airplane to take off and climb out under heavy weight conditions with one engine operating. This was conducted by simply pulling one of the thrust levers back to idle at the appropriate time, just before liftoff. Since the aircraft's fuel load in the left wing and the right wing needed to remain balanced within 1,000 pounds, the engine that was pulled back was alternated each time to maintain this balance. One of these takeoffs at Andahuaylas became very interesting. As the aircraft accelerated past V1 the aircraft sucked a large Andean bird into the left engine—which was supposed to remain at takeoff power—just as Capt. Wygle was about to pull back the thrust lever for the right engine. There was a loud bang and the EPR (a measurement of engine thrust) rolled back toward idle thrust. In a split second the plan was changed and Capt. Wygle pulled back the throttle for the left engine, which had swallowed the bird. The takeoff was continued safely on the remaining engine, although a smell of roasted bird wafted through the cabin for a short time when the air conditioning packs were turned on after takeoff. As a testament to the JT8D engine there was no damage found after landing and the power loss was due to a momentary compressor stall.

An equally challenging situation occurred at one of the last mountain airport demonstrations. Many of these airports were built on the side of the Andean Mountains, at high elevations and usually with considerable runway slope. The procedure was to land uphill and to take off downhill. Capt. Wygle was inclined to watch the radar altimeter carefully on short final, knowing he would shortly be taking off with a simulated engine failure in the other direction. On this occasion he felt the obstacle clearance might not be satisfactory so he called for a conference in the cockpit before turning around and starting the takeoff. Peter

Peter Morton briefs Peruvian government officials during a sales tour of South America. *Courtesy of Peter Morton/Boeing*

Capt. Brien Wygle (left) with an officer from the Peruvian government during a demonstration flight. *Courtesy of Peter Morton/Boeing*

As aircraft sales began to increase the Boeing sales team continued to push forward to gain more customers. The markets in some rural and less developed countries continued to be an area of keen interest for Advanced 737 sales. PG199, the widely used Advanced demonstrator, was taken all over the world to prove its ability to operate in and out of unpaved airports. The Unimproved Field Kit was an attractive feature in these markets, and when installed on the 737, the aircraft was certified for air carrier operations on gravel runways. The Rohr thrust reverser system made this feature more marketable, with its ability to use full reverse thrust down to the allowable sixty knots without risk of ingesting debris into the engine intakes. One operator was even interested in obtaining certification for operations into the grass runway on Norfolk Island, near the mainland of Australia, so a team of Boeing engineers and salesmen decided to test the ability of the 737 to operate in such an environment. The search for a similar airfield for testing ended in Hope, British Columbia. PG199 was taken there by test pilot Lew Wallick and made many takeoff and landing tests. On one of these exercises the nose gear plate, which was installed low on the nose gear, dug into the grass

Morton said the decision was made to wait about fifteen minutes while they burned fuel to reduce gross weight. Additionally, the aircraft was reconfigured to a lower flap setting to reduce drag and improve second segment climb performance after the engine cut. The performance calculations were reviewed and takeoff speeds were adjusted accordingly. The takeoff decision speed (V1) was higher with the lower flap setting, consequently during the takeoff roll the end of the runway seemed quite close when the aircraft lifted off subsequent to the engine cut. The Peruvian Air Force officer in the right seat turned to Morton and said in Spanish, "Mr. Morton, I've come to have great confidence in you and your Boeing people; please do not tell me we could have stopped from V1 on that takeoff."

Peter also recalled the takeoff at Cusco, which was the first of the demonstrations that required no translation in his role as interpreter:

> After the engine cut, and once well away from the airport, the Peruvian Air Force officer leaned across to Capt. Wygle and made the universally understood hand gesture of an aircraft doing a slow roll. Capt. Wygle looked somewhat disappointed and shook his head to the negative, being mindful of Tex Johnston's famous slow roll of the Dash 80 (707 Prototype) over the Seattle Hydroplane Race in 1955 that garnered him lifelong fame. Capt. Wygle was clearly under orders, as were all Boeing pilots, not to repeat that famous maneuver.

Boeing was offering a Business Jet option very early in the 737's career, as evidenced by this pre-1970 ad. *Author's Collection*

PG199, under the command of Capt. Lew Wallick, departs the grass runway at Hope, British Columbia, during testing. The nose gear plate has been removed to prevent it from digging into the soft grass. *Courtesy of The Boeing Company*

operations, the 737 was never certified for grass runways.

Peter Morton, Borge Boeskov, and Ray Randall were the 737 marketing management team assigned to provide technical support for the salesmen and pilots out in the field during sales tours. Test pilots Brien Wygle and Tom Edmonds demonstrated the 737 in Africa, where runway conditions were interesting, to say the least. One day, Peter Morton and the engineering staff received a telex from Borge Boeskov, who was on one of these trips doing sales demonstrations. He was looking for a performance data estimate for the runway they were to use for demonstrations for one of the local airlines when he noticed the runway conditions. He asked, "What is the coefficient of friction of smashed caterpillars?," as this particular runway was just covered with them!

The Chinese airlines also showed interest in the 737 and its special unimproved field capabilities, but at the time a strained relationship between China and the United States made things interesting. Each gravel runway needed to be tested for load bearing ability to determine whether or not it was suitable for 737 operations, and Boeing established a team under the guidance of Eric Lund to perform such surveys in support of

and had to be removed to continue testing. Unlike gravel runways, where load bearing ability could be easily tested, grass was very different. The condition and moistness of the turf made operational predictions difficult, and although it was proven capable of such

sales activities. The Chinese delegation came to Seattle to become acquainted with the aircraft and to observe the building processes and flight capabilities of the 737. To be certain the Boeing jet would fulfill their needs, the delegation asked if their gravel

This 737-2H7C Advanced (TJ-CBB, c/n 20591, l/n 309) is seen on the grass airstrip in Inongo, Republic of Congo, demonstrating the Unimproved Field Kit and low pressure tires. This visit was flown by Boeing test pilot Brien Wygle and photographed on November 24, 1972. *Courtesy of The Boeing Company*

Another view of TJ-CBB in Inongo. Four years later, Boeing test pilot Tom Edmonds demonstrated this aircraft's sister ship (TJ-CBA, c/n 20590, l/n 304) in the same location. *Courtesy of The Boeing Company Archives*

runways would be suitable. Members of Lund's team offered to travel to China and conduct the necessary tests on their runways to determine suitability. Peter Morton recounted the conversation:

> They were pretty paranoid at the time about having Americans go to China other than President Nixon. So when they turned down our offer to come inspect the Chinese gravel runways, I remember their sense of humor, which wasn't much. I said, "Well, OK, just send us a box of rocks from each of your airports and we'll test it here." They didn't laugh; in fact, they didn't even smile.

Boeing left no stone unturned to capitalize on the outstanding characteristics of the 737. This aircraft's high performance wing, high lift devices, and the effective Rohr thrust reverser system made it exceptionally capable in the realm of short runway operations. On short runways, it is imperative that pilots have the ability to land the airplane as close as possible to the approach end of the runway, since the aircraft cannot be effectively decelerated with wheel brakes, wing spoilers, and thrust reversers active until it is on the ground. In Boardman, Oregon, an airport south of Moses Lake, Washington, Boeing employed a unique paint application to the short 4,200 foot runway. The markings on this runway had a 500 foot touchdown window at the approach end of the runway that was visually prominent to the pilots. The rules were simple: if the airplane was going to land past these markings the landing was to be rejected and the aircraft would repeat the approach. These new markings simplified the pilot's decision making process and were later employed at some of the shorter runways used by the 737 during airline operations. Boardman became a favorite stop for Boeing pilots who demonstrated the 737 to potential airline customers because it was only a twenty-five minute flight from Seattle. Perhaps the most spectacular example of this short field operation as a routine airline service

Boeing 737-241 (PP-VME, c/n 21000, l/n 378) is caught on camera departing the short runway in Boardman, Oregon, during demonstrations using the specially developed short runway markings. Interestingly, Varig ordered their aircraft with the vortex dissipators, but without the rest of the Unimproved Field Kit. *Courtesy of The Boeing Company*

The runway in Boardman, Oregon, displaying the special short runway markings developed by Boeing. *Courtesy of Peter Morton/Boeing*

A 737-287 Advanced (c/n 20965, l/n 381) in the striking colors of Aerolineas Argentinas. *Courtesy of The Museum of Flight*

Delta Air Lines was the recipient of the 1,000th 737 to be assembled. N306DL (c/n 23078, l/n 1000) was delivered on December 22, 1983, following the celebration. This aircraft was in production next to the first 737-300 to be built. *Courtesy of The Boeing Company*

was the Maersk Air operation into the extremely short runway at Vagar, in the Faroe Islands. The airport had a 3,700-foot-long runway that accepted daily operations from Denmark with 737s equipped with low pressure tires and heavy duty brakes. Maersk employed the special runway markings developed at Boardman to enhance safety.

As orders for the 737 began to pick up production rates increased to five aircraft per month. During this time the 737 assembly line was moved from the Thompson facility at Boeing Field to the 707/727 assembly hall in Renton, Washington, just

a few miles away. By February 1974, the goal of five aircraft per month was achieved in Renton. Due to the exhaustive efforts of Boeing's sales staff, by 1978, the 737 went from having very low sales numbers to being the best selling jetliner in the world. The accomplishments made by Boeing's people helped the 737 continue on its path to become the best selling jetliner in 1980, 1981, 1983, 1984, and 1985.

The Original Series 737 in Service

737-284 Advanced (c/n 21500, l/n 491, Effectivity PK305), shown in Boeing demonstrator colors, was rolled out on May 4, 1977, and was used by Boeing for a short time for marketing purposes. This aircraft was delivered to Aloha Airlines on September 15, 1977, as N70721 and christened *King Lunaliilo*. *Courtesy of The Museum of Flight*

Piedmont's first 737-201, N734N (c/n 19418, l/n 29), seen with landing gear in transit. Note the "suck-in" doors just behind the intakes on the engines and the short thrust reversers, both features of the very early 737s. From 1965–1970, Piedmont Airlines had nearly tripled its annual passenger miles flown. The 737 was used to augment service provided by the airline's NAMC YS-11As and Fairchild Hiller FH-227 turboprops. *Courtesy of The Museum of Flight*

SAHSA of Honduras operated this 737-2K6 Advanced (c/n 20957, l/n 377) after taking delivery on October 1, 1974. This aircraft was destroyed in a landing accident in San Jose, Costa Rica, on November 17, 1991. All forty-two people onboard survived, but the aircraft was damaged beyond repair. *Courtesy of The Museum of Flight*

A Lufthansa 737-230C (c/n 20254, l/n 230) looking immaculate on a pre-delivery flight. This aircraft was involved in the five-day hijacking of Lufthansa Flight 181 by members of the Popular Front for the Liberation of Palestine on October 13, 1977. This event cost the life of Capt. Jurgen Schumann and three of the four hijackers. The aircraft continued flying until being retired from service with TAF Linhas Aereas in 2008. *Courtesy of The Museum of Flight*

This 737-2H4 (c/n 20336, l/n 239) was originally delivered new to Southwest Airlines on June 15, 1971, as N22SW, twelve days before the carrier began service in Texas. It was acquired by Casino Express, which began service in 1989 and now operates as Xtra Airways, using 737-400 and 737-800 series aircraft. Note the shorter, non-Advanced Krueger flaps inboard of the engine and the early style engine pylon. *Courtesy of P. Popelar*

National Airways of New Zealand operated two different 737-205 Advanced airplanes with this registration. The first (c/n 21131, l/n 428) was delivered in November 1975, leaving the fleet in June 1976. The second example (c/n 22022, l/n 616) was delivered in 1979. Given the updated livery worn by this one the pictured aircraft is likely the latter. *Courtesy of The Boeing Company*

ZK-NAR was a 737-219 Advanced originally ordered by National Airways, but due to a merger was delivered to Air New Zealand on October 12, 1978. This aircraft was stored in Sharjah, United Arab Emirates, in December 2010. *Courtesy of The Boeing Company*

A New Competitor: The Dassault Mercure

Beginning in the mid-1960s, it was determined there was a need for a short range jetliner of larger capacity than the twin-jet aircraft available at the time. Avions Marcel Dassault (later known as Dassault Aviation) took on the challenge of designing and building an aircraft to compete with the Boeing 737. Dassault Aviation officially launched the program in April 1969. Marcel Dassault named the aircraft Mercure, stating, "I wanted to name it for a mythological figure, and I could only think of one who had wings on his helmet and ailerons on his feet—hence the name Mercure." Dassault specialized in building advanced fighter jets, such as the Mystere and the famous Mirage. This vast experience with high speed aerodynamics was put to use on the Mercure design.

The resultant aircraft first flew on May 28, 1971. The Mercure bore a strong resemblance to the 737, with underwing mounted JT8D-15 engines. Sitting much taller on its landing gear, the engines were pod mounted on longer pylons than the 737 configuration. In many ways, the Mercure airframe was ahead of its time. For example, it was one of the first airliners to use a Ram

The Dassault Mercure bears a striking resemblance to the Boeing 737. This aircraft was the second prototype, the last Mercure to join Air Inter in 1983. *Courtesy of The Museum of Flight*

Air Inter's Mercure 100 F-BTTC (c/n 3) is seen on approach into Paris Orly in August 1989. Air Inter was the only carrier to operate the Mercure. *Courtesy of P. Popelar*

Air Turbine (RAT) to provide backup hydraulic and electrical power in case of a serious emergency. If the need arose, a small propeller was automatically deployed from the bottom of the fuselage that used passing air to spin the device, thereby turning an electrical generator and hydraulic pump.

Being forward thinking, Dassault decided to create an aircraft that was slightly larger than the 737, with seating for up to 150 people, whereas the 737-200's typical high density seating accommodated 120 passengers. This was accomplished while using the same JT8D engines employed by the 737 and DC-9. The Mercure used a larger wing that was suited to higher speeds than the 737's wing and similarly featured leading edge slats, but with a slightly simpler trailing edge flap system. Even with a superb wing design, it was necessary for Dassault to make concessions. This compromise was made by sacrificing the ability to carry more fuel, thereby limiting range. The idea that the Mercure's fuel tanks were too small was a common misconception. In reality, it could hold up to 31,300 pounds of fuel, which was just slightly less than a standard Advanced 737-200. Instead, the maximum takeoff weight was the real limiting factor. The airplane was capable of flying a 1,500 nautical mile flight, but only with dozens of seats remaining empty. With a full cabin, the weight limits of the aircraft only allowed a range of roughly 540 nautical miles, hence the Mercure's reputation for having limited range. Dassault did not view this as a major issue, since the typical stage lengths for short range jets were not very long, especially on inter-European routes. Time eventually revealed that the "more passengers and less fuel" compromise was a gamble destined to not pay off. Airlines showed their preference for the flexibility of other designs that were capable of longer range while carrying a full cabin. Had a larger, suitable engine been available at that time the Mercure story may have been quite different.

Another interesting facet of the Mercure story was the international cooperation Dassault fostered while manufacturing the aircraft. For example, CASA of Spain was charged with making the forward fuselage, while FIAT of Italy produced the rear fuselage and vertical stabilizer. Other contributors to the project were Canadair of Canada, Emmen of Switzerland, and SABCA of Belgium.

Similar to the arrangement that SUD had with de Havilland producing the Caravelle, this type of situation set the stage for the formation of the Airbus consortium. Many have made the assessment that the Mercure was a precursor to the later Airbus A320, and even though the two aircraft share similar size and capacity, this was not the case. Dassault and Aerospatiale were typically not in the habit of doing business together and were fierce competitors, so any significant crossover was highly unlikely.

The Mercure was certified as a two-pilot aircraft, although because of union agreements the aircraft was required to be flown with the inclusion of an *Officeur Mecanicien Navigant* (OMN), who fulfilled the role of flight engineer. OMNs were extremely well versed in the mechanics of the aircraft and this led to the easing of some of the Minimum Equipment List requirements. This slightly increased the aircraft's dispatch reliability while operating away from a maintenance base and was very advantageous for on-time performance.

Dassault set up four factories in Martignas, Poitiers, Seclin, and Istres to handle manufacture of the Mercure, but large volumes never came to fruition. Only two prototypes, two structural test airframes, and ten production aircraft were built. All twelve operational Mercures were flown by its sole customer, Air Inter, following conversion of the prototypes into the production configuration. Aside from its limited gross weight there were additional reasons contributing to the commercial failure of this otherwise good airplane. According to Dassault, the devaluation of the United States dollar and the first oil crisis in the early 1970s were major factors. The higher inflation of currency in Europe compared to the United States also gave American aircraft manufacturers an economic advantage.

In the late 1970s, an updated Mercure 200 series was proposed that would use a newly developed engine, the CFM56. This engine, which was a joint venture between General Electric and SNECMA of France, was a new design and had yet to receive a single order. Two variants of the Mercure 200 were envisioned that featured a larger wing design and greater weight carrying capability. The Mercure 200.2 was to have the same cabin size as the Mercure 100, but would use a 22,000 lb. thrust CFM56, with a greatly

The passenger cabin of the Mercure was spacious, with high density seating for up to 150 passengers. *Author's Collection*

The proposed Dassault Mercure 200 is shown in these artists' impressions. This aircraft, if built, could have been a strong competitor to the Boeing 737. The size and specifications for this aircraft showed great resemblance to the later Airbus A320. *Author's Collection*

improved full cabin range. The Mercure 200.1 concept was longer, with a maximum capacity for 184 passengers and uprated 25,000 lb. thrust engines with a slight sacrifice in range performance. In an attempt to get a foothold in the American market and to gain financial support, Dassault approached McDonnell Douglas and Lockheed in 1975. The proposal was to produce the more powerful Mercure 200 under license in the United States. With great similarity to the ill-fated Douglas/SUD partnership in the early 1960s, McDonnell Douglas decided against the formation of a partnership. Instead, McDonnell Douglas chose to move forward with the development and construction of the DC-9 Super 80. Ultimately support for revamping the Mercure and mating it to an engine which might possibly be still-born vaporized without a single example being built. The unfortunate irony for Dassault was that the CFM56 later became one of the most successful aero engines in history. The Mercure airframe, mated to this engine, would have allowed a greatly enhanced weight carrying capability and range. This marriage could have produced an aircraft similar to the specifications of the later Classic 737 series and the Airbus A320, both of which emerged in the 1980s.

During its twenty-two year service with Air Inter, the Mercure gained a reputation for good handling and was referred to by many pilots as the "Air Inter Fighter." This "fighter" reputation may have also been enhanced because this was the first airliner to be equipped with a Head-Up Display (HUD). The Sextant Avionique HUD, adapted from the Mirage fighter, was used to perform takeoffs with visibility as low as 100 meters and landings with 200 meters (CAT III). According to Dassault, by the time the last aircraft was retired in April 1995, the twelve-strong fleet had logged 360,000 accident free flight hours while conducting 440,000 flights. At the time of its debut the Mercure boasted the lowest seat-mile costs of any existing jetliner on short routes of up to 1,000 kilometers, and was profitable with a passenger load of just thirty-two people. In the end, the small Mercure fleet had carried forty-four million passengers with a ninety-eight percent dispatch reliability rate. The Mercure may very well have been the right airframe at the wrong time. Had it been successful, it may have had a marked effect on history, and perhaps even prevented the advent of the later narrow-bodied Airbus series.

Further Refinement

The Advanced 737 was continually improved throughout the course of its long production life. Many aerodynamic benefits were gained when the Advanced configuration was implemented,

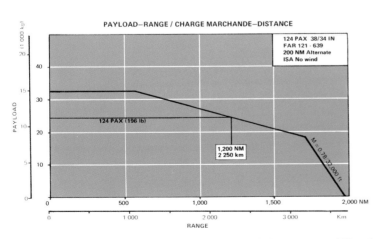
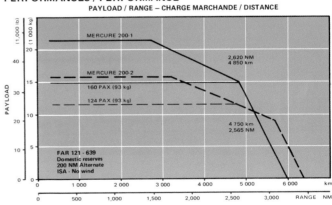

The performance chart on the left details the Mercure 100's short range capability with a full passenger cabin. The chart on the right shows the greatly improved range projections for the proposed CFM56 powered Mercure 200 series. *Author's Collection*

The early 737-200 interior (left) and the newer Advanced Technology Interior (737-300 pictured, right). The newer interior was 940 pounds lighter. *Courtesy of The Boeing Company*

but that was only part of the equation. Many fuel saving and weight reducing changes were made along the way. Some of these items were optional and some became standard.

Weight savings is important on a few different performance fronts. Given identical conditions and engine thrust settings, a heavier aircraft will use more runway for takeoff and landing. This could have an adverse effect, particularly for airlines operating in and out of short and/or high altitude airports. These effects go even deeper, as jets achieve their best fuel efficiency at higher altitudes. A heavier aircraft will take longer to climb and spend more time consuming fuel at a higher rate. This, in turn, requires more fuel to be burned when traveling from point A to point B. All aircraft have maximum structural takeoff and landing weights as well, even when runways are long and temperatures are cool. In all, an aircraft's weight has a direct effect on the ability to achieve maximum revenue with a minimum amount of fuel burn. In extreme cases, sometimes paying passengers need to be "bumped" or removed from a flight so that an aircraft will be within its performance and/or weight limits. This situation costs an airline a great deal of money. The 737 has always been good in this regard, but shedding weight is always advantageous.

In an effort to reduce aircraft weight, composite materials began to see widespread use throughout the aircraft. The Advanced Technology Interior was developed using new composite honeycomb core materials to manufacture fixtures and interior panels in the cabin. In addition, the overhead bins were made larger while giving the 737's cabin a more roomy look. This change alone reduced empty aircraft weight by 940 pounds! Another weight saving measure that reaped great benefits was the use of composite materials to replace metal flight controls, trailing edge surfaces, and landing gear doors on the later

aircraft. Additional changes were made, such as modifications to the rudder system. For proper aerodynamic balancing counterweights were used on the rudder. As time went on it was found that fewer weights were required, especially after carbon fiber surfaces came into production. Removing these counterweights reduced the total weight of the aircraft by a small amount, but every pound mattered. Boeing also developed a composite horizontal stabilizer which saw service on five aircraft (see First in Composite Primary Structures, page 187).

Reducing drag and increasing lift was important, but only comprised part of the performance equation. The Pratt & Whitney JT8D engine used on the "Original" 737s also refined and "grew" with the capabilities of the airplane. The JT8D-15A, introduced in 1982, combined greater thrust capability (15,500 pounds of

JT8D PRINCIPAL CHANGES

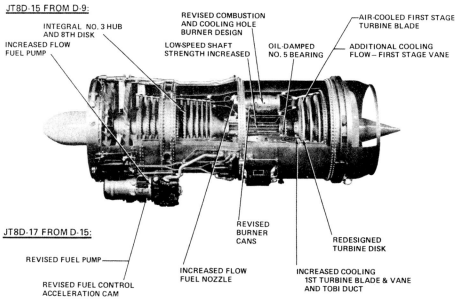

The evolutionary changes made to the JT8D engine. *Courtesy of The Boeing Company*

thrust versus 14,000) than the older engines. Refinements to improve fuel efficiency by 4.2% over a 1,000 mile sector were very significant, resulting in extended range, or a fuel savings of roughly eighty gallons. To achieve these improvements the "A" model engines were modified with the following equipment (also capable of being retrofitted to older engines):

- Re-cambered first stage compressors
- Sermetel coatings on high pressure compressor stator blades
- Improved low and high pressure compressor assemblies
- New carbon seals and inlet case assembly
  Refined first and second stage compressor blades

   In addition to the "A" model improvements, one other variant was developed by 1983. This was the JT8D-17A, with increased maximum rated thrust to 16,000 pounds, and soon became a standard option on the 737. With the advent of the these newer technology JT8D engines higher maximum takeoff weights were allowed. Aircraft equipped with -15A powerplants saw maximum takeoff weights increased to 115,500 pounds, with a maximum landing weight of 103,000 pounds. The maximum weights for -17A powered aircraft were 128,100 and 107,000 pounds, respectively. These weight increases

were significant, because a full cabin could be carried with more fuel, making longer range flights possible.

The Performance Data Computer System (PDCS)

In 1979, Boeing developed the Performance Data Computer System (PDCS). This advanced system incorporated a keypad and computer screen interface for the pilots' use and was designed to help the crew operate the aircraft more efficiently while providing real-time performance data. This easy-to-use system was capable of providing fuel savings of up to 2.3 percent. In some respects, the PDCS was the precursor to the now ubiquitous flight management computer found on virtually all transport and many business jets. Among the features of this system were:

- Automatic speed and thrust limit protection
- Cruise and holding speeds with engine thrust (EPR) information
- Time and fuel remaining computations
- Immediate en route diversion planning in case of adverse conditions at the destination airport
- Best economy speeds and altitudes based on weight and atmospheric conditions

The Performance Data Computer System was an optional enhancement for the Original 737 series. This system was used to save fuel by identifying the ideal engine thrust settings for existing conditions. *Courtesy of Vic Page/Boeing*

Performance Data Computer System (PDCS)

With Automatic Flight Control System (AFCS)

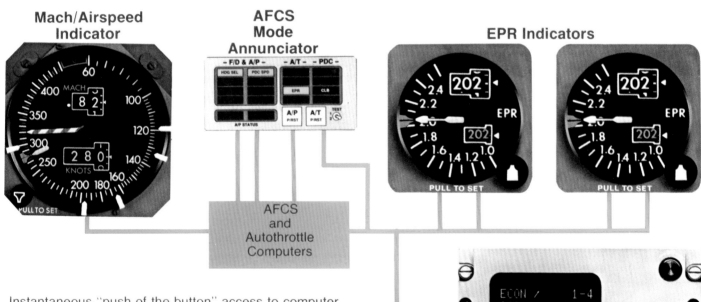

Mach/Airspeed Indicator

AFCS Mode Annunciator

EPR Indicators

AFCS and Autothrottle Computers

Instantaneous "push of the button" access to computer inflight performance data for best economy speeds and altitudes

   Cruise, climb, descent and hold speeds coupled to AFCS

   Thrust ratings for autothrottle

   Demonstrated crew acceptance with 3 – 4% fuel savings

3PD1-8R2

Altitude
Go-Around
Bleed Logic
EPR
Airspeed
Fuel Quantity
TAT

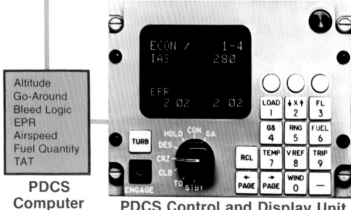

PDCS Computer

PDCS Control and Display Unit

The Advanced 737-200C "Convertible Airplane"

To further the versatility of the 737 airframe Boeing introduced the "Convertible Aircraft." This option allowed operations with an all-cargo configuration, or several different cargo/passenger combinations dependent on the airline's demand on that particular day. The key to this rapid conversion was the use of a large 84.5 in. × 134 in. cargo door installed forward of the wing on the left side of the fuselage. It

Operated by Wien Air Alaska until 1985, this 737-210C (c/n 21067, l/n 414) served with AirCal and American Airlines before migrating north to work with Canadian carriers NWT Air and First Air. This aircraft crashed on August 20, 2011, while on approach into Resolute Bay, Canada, operating as First Air flight 6560. *Courtesy of Jennings Heilig*

Federal Express took delivery of N201FE (c/n 21926, l/n 597) on August 29, 1979. This was the first of four 737-2S2Cs delivered to the carrier that year. This aircraft was sold to Sunland Airlines in 1981, and is currently stored at Ras Al Khaimah Airport, United Arab Emirates. *Courtesy of Jennings Heilig*

was positioned carefully to allow the use of pallet loaders while clearing the inlet of the Number One (left) engine. The main cabin floor featured a built-in roller system and tiedowns to ease the loading of palletized cargo. If a combination cargo/passenger configuration was desired, seat rows attached to pallet-like structures were easily rolled aboard through the cargo door and slid aft on the roller equipped floor, then locked into position. The balance of seats and cargo was adjusted by installing the required number of seat pallets (which were always aft of the cargo), then installing the movable bulkhead or partition. Passenger boarding was accomplished through the left side, rear door, and optional integral air stair. In this cargo/passenger configuration, an aisle way was left free of cargo, allowing crew access from the passenger compartment to the cockpit as needed. In the all-cargo configuration, up to 2,990 cubic feet of cargo space was available for use. Amazingly, Boeing demonstrated that the conversion from all-passenger to all-cargo configuration could be accomplished by a crew of six men in one hour!

Wien Air Alaska was the first airline to operate in the state of Alaska. Wien made excellent use of this gravel runway equipped 737-210C (N4905W, c/n 20917, l/n 344) until 1980. Today, this aircraft is still in service with Bid Air Cargo in South Africa. *Courtesy of The Museum of Flight*

The versatility of the "Convertible" 737 was a major selling point, here showing the rapid metamorphosis from a cargo aircraft into a passenger jet. Note the excellent view of the Unimproved Field Kit nose wheel deflector. *Courtesy of The Boeing Company*

The updated "Optional Flight Deck." Note the PDCS system above and to the right of the thrust levers. *Courtesy of Vic Page/Boeing*

The Optional Flight Deck

Boeing offered an upgraded avionics package known as the Automatic Flight Control System (AFCS), which was certified in 1981. This option included the Performance Data Computer System, but also added several items to improve automation and low visibility approach capability. Sperry's new SP-177 autopilot system, combined with an autothrottle system, were the heart of the package. Two separate autopilots and flight control computers provided the redundancy required to conduct automatic (autopilot flown) landings and permitted the aircraft to land with cloud ceilings of fifty feet and forward visibilities as low as 700 feet. The pilot interfaced with the new system through a revised Mode Control Panel (MCP), through which the various autopilot modes were engaged. Additionally, an improved Mode Annunciator Panel was installed so the pilot could easily verify that the autopilot was correctly engaged in the commanded mode.

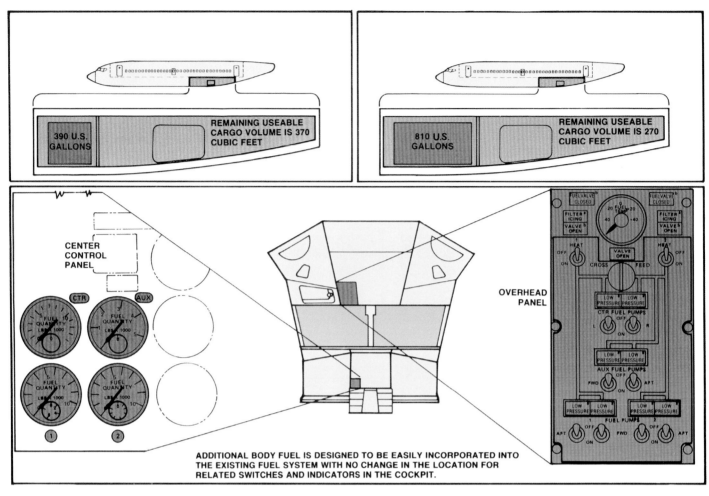

390 U.S. GALLONS	REMAINING USEABLE CARGO VOLUME IS 370 CUBIC FEET
810 U.S. GALLONS	REMAINING USEABLE CARGO VOLUME IS 270 CUBIC FEET

CENTER CONTROL PANEL

OVERHEAD PANEL

ADDITIONAL BODY FUEL IS DESIGNED TO BE EASILY INCORPORATED INTO THE EXISTING FUEL SYSTEM WITH NO CHANGE IN THE LOCATION FOR RELATED SWITCHES AND INDICATORS IN THE COCKPIT.

The optional auxiliary fuel systems for the 737-200 series. Note the additional gauges and "AUX FUEL PUMPS" switches added to the overhead panel in the cockpit. *Courtesy of Vic Page/Boeing*

Auxiliary Fuel Tank Option

As the 737 program evolved, the ability for the aircraft to carry more weight was increased with the advent of the JT8D-15A and -17A engines. Some airlines desired to use this capability to increase the fuel range of the airplane. To allow this, Boeing offered two different auxiliary fuel tank options. The first increased fuel capacity by 390 gallons, while the larger tank option increased capacity by 810 gallons. A modified fuel panel with additional auxiliary fuel pump switches was installed in the cockpit, along with an associated fuel gauge. Although this option was quite useful to some airlines, it came with a price. The rear cargo hold under the cabin floor needed to be reduced in volume from 505 cubic feet to 370 or 270, depending on which size tanks were installed.

Conclusion

In looking at the 737-100, -200, and -200 Advanced programs, it is clear Boeing went the extra mile to create an airplane that was incredibly capable and versatile. From the costly adaptation of the DC-9 style Rohr thrust reverser all the way through the last of the -200 Advanced options, Boeing was committed to making an aircraft for every conceivable type of operation. Along the way constant effort was made to reduce fuel consumption by the use of the later JT8D "A" model engines, the development of the Performance

An artist's impression of an Aloha Airlines 737-297 (c/n 20209, l/n 152) delivered to the airline on March 28, 1969. This aircraft suffered a rapid decompression and subsequent emergency landing in Kahului, Hawaii, on April 28, 1988. The aircraft had 35,496 hours and an unusually high number of cycles (flights) totaling 89,680. *Courtesy of Jennings Heilig*

Data Computer System, and incorporation of numerous aerodynamic improvements to the basic 737 airframe. Takeoff runway and climb performance were steadily improved by aerodynamic changes to the Krueger flaps and slats, reducing the weight of the aircraft through the use of high tech materials, and the certification of the higher power JT8D engines. The "Original" series of the 737 came a long way, and its ability to carry more and go farther even from austere airstrips was nothing short of amazing.

Production of the 737-200 series ended with the delivery of a 737-25C (B-2524, c/n 24236, l/n 1585) on August 10, 1988. The Original series was phased out with a total of 1,144 aircraft, including thirty 737-100s and nineteen T-43A Navigation Trainers. Boeing's 737 experienced enormous success and was utilized around the world. Yet these celebrated accomplishments were not the highest point in the 737's history. They were a solid foundation, but only the tip of the iceberg in Boeing's achievements over the next three decades.

Courtesy of The Boeing Company

The Boeing 737-200 Advanced was a

remarkably competent airplane. Because of constant refinement throughout its production life it was a strong competitor, with many advantages over other jetliners available at the time. Against all odds, this airplane went from low sales numbers and high aerodynamic drag to being a stellar performer on the runway and in the sales books. New engine

Southwest Airlines 737-3H4 (c/n 27929, l/n 2744, Effectivity PS793) was christened *California One* to signify the carrier's large presence in the state. This aircraft was delivered new to the airline on August 4, 1995, and is still in service with this highly recognizable paint scheme.
Courtesy of Jennings Heilig

technology and the growing desire for slightly larger aircraft required manufacturers to adapt their jetliners to remain competitive.

McDonnell Douglas maintained its position as Boeing's primary competitor in the short to medium range markets. The Pratt & Whitney JT8D-17A engine (optional on the 737-200 Advanced and DC-9) had reached the limits of its thrust generating potential at 16,000 pounds and a more powerful alternative was required. Clearly, the airlines desired higher seating capacity and thus required more powerful engines. On the DC-9-50 the limitations of the basic JT8D-17 became apparent. The aircraft required longer runways, and although it safely met FAA single engine climb requirements, it had a shallow climb angle at high takeoff weights. Due to this the aircraft overflew neighborhoods near airports at lower than average altitudes while at very high power settings. The limited engine thrust hampered further capacity growth of this airframe and engine combination, while the noise it generated damaged the public perception of the DC-9. The challenge on the horizon was to develop jetliners with more powerful yet quieter engines that could meet and exceed new noise limits imposed by regulators at various airports around the world.

The continued growth of the DC-9 airframe utilizing the JT8D powerplant had the following progression:

Version	Year	Aircraft Length	Capacity	Max Takeoff Weight
DC-9-10	1965	104.4 feet	79	85,700 pounds
DC-9-15	1966	104.4 feet	109	90,700 pounds
DC-9-32	1967	119.3 feet	127	110,000 pounds
DC-9-40	1968	125.6 feet	128	114,000 pounds
DC-9-50	1975	133.6 feet	139	121,000 pounds

The DC-9 Super 80 and the JT8D-200 Series

By 1971, the JT8D had become the most popular jet engine used for narrow-body airline operations. During this time Boeing conducted studies on the effects of retrofitting a higher bypass fan section to the JT8D. Boeing's objective was to increase power output and simultaneously reduce noise generated by the engine at takeoff power. Boeing hoped to use this higher bypass JT8D for its 727-300 concept. This 727 derivative was to have a stretched fuselage length eighteen feet more than the 727-200. Boeing also considered another new design called the 7N7, which was a twin jet with much larger, high bypass Rolls-Royce RB-211 engines. The 727-300 and 7N7 design studies were compared to determine which would become the next production aircraft. Ultimately, the 7N7 was found to be a better choice and was developed into the Boeing 757. Even though the 727-300 was never built, the higher bypass JT8D idea resurfaced two years later.

An artist's impression of the DC-9 Super 80, which later became known as the MD-80 for marketing reasons. *Courtesy of The Boeing Company*

On July 5, 1973, a collective effort was taken on by Pratt & Whitney, McDonnell Douglas, and NASA to reduce noise emissions and increase the power output of the JT8D engine. The project used the JT8D-9 core as a basis, but the small two stage fan section was replaced with a larger diameter single stage fan unit. Additionally, a new four stage compressor section was integrated into the new engine, nearly doubling the ratio of air that bypassed the engine's hot section from 1.05:1 to 2.03:1. Not only did this create more fuel efficient power, but the increased amount of "fan air" that went around the combustion chambers remixed with the exhaust in the tailpipe to greatly reduce the noise footprint of the engine. The JT8D-9's forty inch diameter fan was replaced with a newly designed forty-nine inch fan section, thus creating the improved JT8D-109. McDonnell Douglas used a DC-9-31 N54638 (c/n 47649, l/n 741) as a testbed for the new engine. This aircraft and engine combination first flew on January 9, 1975. The JT8D-109 was rated to 16,000 pounds of thrust and became the basis for the Pratt & Whitney JT8D-209. This engine possessed an increased thrust rating of 18,500 pounds and a significantly improved noise signature.

McDonnell Douglas recognized that an engineering advantage could be gained over the 737 if the JT8D-209 engine was adapted to the DC-9 airframe. If Boeing were to do likewise and use the JT8D-209, both the 727 and 737 would require a major revision due to its larger fan diameter. Although the 727 had pod-mounted engines like the DC-9, the #2 (center) engine would require a massive redesign to its "S"-shaped intake duct to employ the JT8D-209 engine. Likewise, the 737-200 had minimal ground clearance under its wing-mounted engines. It was almost certain the additional nine-inch diameter would cause numerous technical difficulties for Boeing. The DC-9 could simply be redesigned with the enlarged engine pods mounted to the tail of the aircraft. McDonnell Douglas was keen to wedge itself into the market between the 727 and the 737, and identified this as a great opportunity.

McDonnell Douglas entertained a DC-9 derivative with additional seating capacity using the refined JT8D-209 engine and its attendant thrust increase. Past projects, such as the DC-9-20 through the -50 series, shared a common wing of the same size and shape. The original DC-9 was designed under a similar premise as the 737, with a small, heavily loaded wing that was desirable for its economical, high speed cruising at low to middle altitudes. The same wing reached its limits of efficient operation when it was incorporated into the 121,000 pound DC-9-50. If Douglas was to successfully increase the proposed aircraft's wingspan and weight, the wing would require a significant redesign. Initially, the engineers at McDonnell Douglas wanted to install a high technology, super critical airfoil on the new airplane. Although this plan was marginally more efficient, Douglas could not justify the additional engineering expense, since the aircraft was still intended for short to medium length routes. Instead, McDonnell Douglas decided to use the existing DC-9-50 wing as a basis for a new design. The original wing was extended at the wingtip by two feet and also incorporated a new ten-foot wing root section on each side. These modifications supplied the additional wing area required to support the growing aircraft. Initially, the larger DC-9 concept was designated the DC-9-55. Over time, the marketing decision was made to change the airplane's name to the DC-9 Super 80, because it was to enter service in the early 1980s (later, in 1983, the aircraft's name was changed to MD-80 for marketing reasons).

The DC-9 Super 80 featured the enhanced JT8D-209 engines, a newly optimized wing that spanned 107 ft. 10.2 in., and a fuselage extended to a length of 147 ft. 10 in. Modifications were also required to counterbalance the additional weight attached to the rear part of the aircraft, because the new JT8D-209 was significantly heavier than the older engines. Boeing's Joe Sutter explained the challenges the McDonnell Douglas engineers faced when designing an airplane with heavy engines in the back:

> You have your cockpit and your load carrying passenger seats up front. If you wanted to stretch the airplane, you couldn't do it effectively. The MD-80 was a typical example of this. Even with a modest increase in engine weight, the fuselage was all in front of the wing. It becomes unbalanced very quickly…and you can't grow the airplane very easily. The future is limited.

Conversely, airplanes with wing mounted engines have the concentrated engine weight near the center of gravity of the airframe and have much less restrictive passenger and cargo loading limits. In this situation, an aircraft can be stretched with minimal ill effects to weight and balance. Additionally, in a deep stall situation the larger engines could conceivably cause additional aerodynamic interference with the horizontal stabilizers. McDonnell Douglas mitigated the deep stall risk by installing a hydraulic stick pusher that would force the nose down prior to a full stall.

The first flight of the DC-9 Super 80 occurred on October 18, 1979, with its first delivery to launch customer Swissair on September 13, 1980. This sleek new airplane had a maximum capacity of 172 passengers and was definitely playing in the 727-200's sandbox. Loyal DC-9 operators like Swissair and Austrian Airlines ordered the new aircraft, along with American carriers such as Pacific Southwest Airlines. In comparison to the Advanced 737-200, the new DC-9 Super 80 was quieter and more fuel efficient, increasing its appeal to airlines like AirCal, which had been predominantly 737 operators. As its popularity increased, the Super 80 began to encroach on Boeing's sales in more than just one market.

A New Technology 737

The advancement in engine designs of the mid-1970s and early 1980s opened new possibilities and expectations in the airline industry. Airlines needed improved fuel economy, faster speeds, longer distances, increased passenger capacity, and lower noise levels from designs created by aircraft manufacturers. If Boeing wished to remain competitive, it was imperative to align its 737 design concept with the evolving market, or risk fading into obsolescence. The limits of fuel economy were reached with the 737's utilization of the JT8D-17 engine and new ideas were sought. In Seattle engineering teams worked to meet these challenges. Boeing's John Roundhill recalled the situation:

> The 737-200 and 727 were being developed in the higher thrust and gross weight versions. We ended up with an engine called the JT8D-17R, which was on the 727 … Meanwhile, back at the ranch, Pratt was running these engines and it turned out the pressure ratios were so high at those thrust levels that the -17 in particular and the -15 developed a noise signature with

An early 737-300 concept compared to the 737-200 Advanced. Note that at the time the proposed 737-300 had a different wing planform and exit door configuration. *Courtesy of The Museum of Flight*

something called "shock cell" noise. It was a fairly low frequency noise and it was kind of intermittent. Shock waves [were] creating these little balls of supersonic flow in the exhaust of the engine that were not captured by the EPNDB metric [noise measurement] that the FAA used. When we formed the noise staff in 1974, we went back to Washington, DC. They had a big JT8D-

17 cross section photo on the wall in the FAA office and it said, "Public Enemy Number One." What was happening as we got into the late '70s…the 747… [and later] the 767, and the 757 were committed with high bypass ratio engines, and so somebody finally said one day, "What about the 737?" We've got to get a high bypass engine on the 737 or it's going out of business.

McDonnell Douglas was making great progress with the design and construction of its DC-9 Super 80 paired with the re-fanned JT8D-217. Due to timing, the Super 80 had a significant head start in the short to medium range market and Boeing needed to act quickly in its efforts to regain control. Boeing's team looked into every available option to improve the 737's performance, and ironically found the solution right on McDonnell Douglas' production floor in Long Beach, California. The fleet of classic Douglas DC-8 long-range jetliners had high fuel consumption, were noisy, and required new engines. A consortium called CFMI designed and supplied Douglas with high bypass engines for this purpose. The new CFM56 engine was exactly what Boeing's team needed to pair with the 737 to gain the upper hand over McDonnell Douglas, and they quickly mobilized to procure this high technology engine for the 737.

The CFM56 High Bypass Jet Engine

In the late 1960s, *Societe Nationale d'Etudes et de Construction de Motors d'Aviation* (SNECMA), which specialized in designing and building engines for military applications, researched ideas to create a jet engine for the civilian market. The effort culminated in a design plan for a high bypass jet engine of the ten-ton class, with a target of 20,000 pounds of thrust. Rene Ravaud, a recognized hero of the French Resistance during WWII and head of SNECMA, sought a partner to help create and market the plan. In June 1971, Ravaud met General Electric executive Gerhard Neumann at the Paris Air Show. General Electric had vast experience in the manufacture of jet engines, such as the J79, which powered military jets including the famous McDonnell F-4 Phantom II and the blisteringly fast Convair B-58 Hustler. General Electric's portfolio also included the CF6 series of engines built in the late 1960s and early 1970s for commercial applications on aircraft such as the McDonnell Douglas DC-10 wide-body trijet and the Airbus A300. After discussing a partnership Ravaud and Neumann agreed to form an alliance. Together they created a company named CFMI, where SNECMA and GE held a 50/50 stake. Per their agreement, each company would make contributions to refine the engine plan, build and assemble parts, and market the product.

TAKEOFF NOISE AREA
737-300 / MD-82

- AC91-53 TAKEOFF PROCEDURE
- 500 NMI MISSION
- 95 dB SEL CONTOUR

SIDELINE DISTANCE (1000 FEET)

DISTANCE FROM BRAKE RELEASE (1000 FEET)

| MD-82 AREA = 1.31 MI^2 |
| 737-300 AREA = 0.30 MI^2 |

The difference in the takeoff thrust noise footprint between a CFM56 powered 737 and the MD-82 (DC-9-80) with re-fanned JT8D-200 series engines. The quiet operation of the CFM56 was an enormously important advantage. *Courtesy of The Boeing Company*

PARIS AIR SHOW 1971

SOUVENIR BOARDING PASS

FLIGHT	DATE	SEAT	AIRPORT	SEE US AT	CHALET
747	5/29	9 E	LE BOURGET		9 E

RAYTHEON DATA SYSTEMS, USA

Author's Collection

Their plan was for CFMI to use the core (high pressure compressor and turbine sections) of General Electric's F-101 engine developed for the Rockwell B-1A supersonic bomber as a basis for the new civilian turbofan engine. General Electric would modify and produce this core section and supply SNECMA with a high bypass fan design. The fan, based on the larger CF6-80A engine for the Boeing 767 wide body jetliner, would be scaled down for use on the project. SNECMA would manufacture this fan section, low pressure compressors, and turbines in France. These items would then be mated to the General Electric high pressure compressor and turbine stages. Additionally, the French company would design the gearboxes, engine controls, accessories, and the interface between the aircraft and the engine. Once all of the parts were built they were to be shipped for final assembly to either the GE plant in Evendale, Ohio, or the SNECMA plant in Villaroche, France.

In 1972, General Electric applied for permission from the Nixon administration to export its engine core component. However, this first attempt was rejected by the administration's Security Advisor, Henry Kissinger, on the grounds that the engine core was part of a strategic bomber program and would compromise national security. Additionally, the F-101 project had been funded with US tax dollars and Kissinger feared that job opportunities for American workers would be lost. Senator Barry Goldwater wrote President Nixon a letter. This correspondence, backed by many supporters, expressed the opinion that using the F-101 technology to create a new civilian motor with SNECMA was a solid concept, and they hoped the Nixon administration was not intending to block the project. Goldwater's letter caused the Nixon administration concern. It was possible if approval was not granted then the SNECMA project would continue without American involvement, thereby weakening the United States' strong influence in aero technology. President Nixon realized this project was of paramount importance and decided that the Americans' fifty percent stake in the engine's development was better than none at all. At the summit meeting with French President Georges Pompidou in Reykjavik, Iceland, on May 30, 1973, Nixon offered to approve the engine project, with the stipulation that the French government would not charge tariffs against the import of American jetliners in Europe. Pompidou agreed and CFMI's engine project was approved.

The cooperation and shared resources between SNECMA and General Electric allowed the development of the incredibly efficient CFM56 engine. The CFM56 was so named by combining the traditional GE prefix "CF" (abbreviation for "Commercial Fan") with "M56," which was SNECMA's designation for its commercial engine project. It featured a fourteen stage, dual spool, axial compressor section. Since the CFM56 was a high bypass engine, the vast majority of the air pulled into the engine's inlet flowed around the core and mixed with the exhaust at the aft end of the engine, at a 5:1 ratio. Air that flowed into the engine's core was enriched with fuel and ignited in the annular ring type combustion chamber. This very highly compressed gas was pushed through the turbine section, where it expanded quickly, exacted turning force on the six stage axial flow turbine, and then provided jet thrust behind the engine. By utilizing the high bypass ratio, the early CFM56 models were nearly twenty percent more fuel efficient than the legacy JT8D engine it was designed to replace.

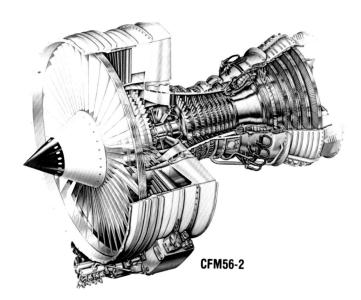

CFM56-2

The 1973 Icelandic Summit Meeting that brought life to the CFM56 program. From left to right: Icelandic President Kristjan Eldjarn, French President Georges Pompidou, and American President Richard M. Nixon. *Courtesy of The Nixon Archives*

This cutaway drawing of the CFM56-2 shows the details of the fan, compressor, and turbine sections. This engine was used to power the re-engined Douglas DC-8-70 series, as well as the KC-135R Air Force tanker. *Courtesy of The Boeing Company*

The CFM56 successfully ran in 1974, and subsequent flight testing began in February 1977, under the wing of a McDonnell Douglas YC-15 experimental cargo aircraft. The first YC-15 aircraft built (c/n 72-1875) was modified to carry the CFM56 under its left wing, slung from the #1 pylon (left, outboard). Interestingly, this same aircraft tested the Pratt & Whitney JT8D-209 engine for the DC-9 Super 80. On March 17, 1977, tests to achieve French certification were conducted in France using a SNECMA-owned Sud Caravelle III (c/n 193). This aircraft was delivered to SAS (Scandinavian) in March 1965, registered as SE-DAH and christened *Torgny Viking*. Later, after SNECMA acquired the airplane, it was re-registered F-ZACF, and was supplied with the standard Rolls-Royce Avon engine on the port pylon and the much larger CFM56 on the starboard side. The aircraft was equipped to monitor 380 different parameters during the extensive test program. SNECMA conducted many hours of flight testing up to 45,000 feet and Mach .82, as these were airframe limitations for the Caravelle III. After successfully passing all of its tests the French authorities officially certified the CFM56 in November 1979. Upon completion of the test program F-ZACF was scrapped in Istres, France, sometime after 1980.

Seen during flight test, this is a United Airlines DC-8-71 with newly installed CFM56-2 engines. Equipped with these high bypass engines, the DC-8-70 series was for some time the quietest four-engine jetliner in the world. *Courtesy of The Boeing Company*

One of the first perceived applications for the high bypass CFM56 engine was to replace the old, noisy, and high fuel consumption JT3D-3B and JT3D-7 engines on the stretched Douglas DC-8 series sixty aircraft. Although this plan would require extensive modifications to the wings and pylons of the airplane, it would make the DC-8 nearly twenty percent more fuel efficient. It wouldn't just make the DC-8 more powerful, it would also make it the quietest four-engine jetliner in the world. Even so, sales interest in the engine was lukewarm at best. The development of plans to join the CFM56 engine to the proposed Dassault Mercure 200 was uncertain, putting the whole CFM56 program in jeopardy. Rene Ravaud was quoted as saying one could "hear the vultures flying around the building." The outlook was bleak, and it appeared the CFM56's failure to attract concrete orders would soon lead to the program's demise.

Fortunately for CFMI, United Airlines saw the value in the DC-8 modernization program and announced an order for the conversion of twenty-nine DC-8-61 jetliners into the re-engined

Although the 707-700 never saw commercial service, it became the basis for the USAF's modernization program for the KC-135 tanker and E-3 AWACS reconnaissance aircraft, which were 707 derivatives. N707QT (c/n 21956, l/n 941) was the last Boeing 707 built. After testing this aircraft was converted to a standard 707-320 and delivered to the Moroccan Air Force. *Courtesy of The Boeing Company*

(and renamed) DC-8-71. Shortly thereafter Delta Airlines and Flying Tigers placed orders for thirteen and eighteen conversions, respectively. Even though this number of engine orders did not push the program past the break-even point, the CFM56 program was pressed forward into production. Soon after Boeing started a program to re-engine the Boeing 707 with the CFM56, touted as the 707-700. One aircraft was eventually modified as a testbed, but no commercial orders ever developed.

The US Air Force saw great benefit in the program. Soon a successful program was launched to re-engine the large fleet of Boeing 707 derivative KC-135 tankers, E-3 AWACS, and E-6 aircraft already in operation. This was a boon for the CFMI consortium and laid the groundwork for the future success of the CFM56. For Boeing this was a good situation, since the engines were soon in service and quickly gained flight hours on four-engine aircraft. The excellent in-service reliability of the new high-tech engine was soon backed by a large number of operational flight hours. This CFM56 rapidly became a known quantity, with many advantages over the older technology JT8D-200 series engines to which the competing DC-9 Super 80 was seemingly married.

While Boeing contemplated a successor to the 737-200, the larger Boeing 757 was also under development. The 757 was an all new design, intended to be a modern replacement for the older 727-200. This narrow bodied twin-jet was capable of carrying 239 passengers in a high density layout. The airplane was already being offered with British Rolls-Royce RB-211-535 and American Pratt & Whitney PW2037 engines. Many times airlines prefer to have a choice of engines for commonality with other aircraft in their fleet, or for political reasons. Boeing wished to offer a third option, in the form of the General Electric CF6-32, but General Electric was hesitant to compete with two other established manufacturers on the 757 and felt it might not be profitable. Boeing pushed hard and made a deal wherein General Electric agreed to provide for the 757 program, under the auspice that it would be the sole engine supplier for the new 737 aircraft under development. Although it was offered, interestingly, no 757s were ever sold with the CF6-32 engine, but General Electric (through CFMI) had made an extremely lucrative deal with Boeing and the 737. Since General Electric owned half of the CFMI company,

737-300

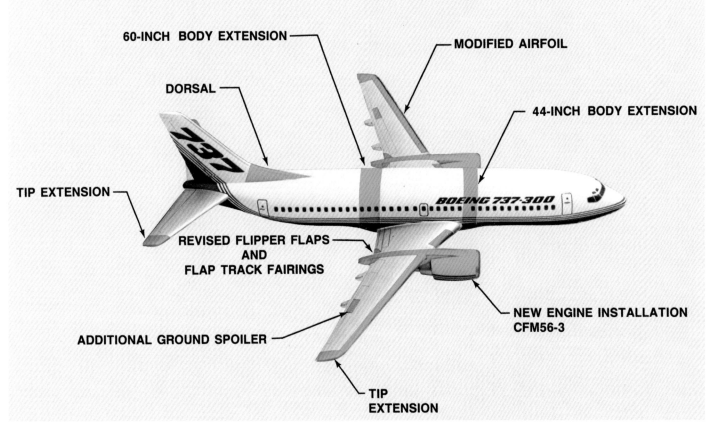

60-INCH BODY EXTENSION

DORSAL

MODIFIED AIRFOIL

44-INCH BODY EXTENSION

TIP EXTENSION

REVISED FLIPPER FLAPS
AND
FLAP TRACK FAIRINGS

ADDITIONAL GROUND SPOILER

NEW ENGINE INSTALLATION
CFM56-3

TIP
EXTENSION

This model shows the significant differences between the 737-200 and the newer 737-300. *Courtesy of The Boeing Company*

which was developing the CFM56 powerplant, the combination of the new 737 with this engine followed a logical progression. Even though this was the ideal new engine for the 737, there were serious challenges in integrating it with the 737 airframe.

The Launch of the "New Generation" 737

The design development of the "New Generation" 737 began in earnest in 1979, as the CFM56 engine had proven itself to be a viable power plant for this high technology 737 variant. Boeing announced its intent to build the new 737 model, later known as the 737-300, at the 1980 Farnborough Airshow in England. In March 1981, as Boeing's engineering department worked on designing the new jet, two airlines showed interest. USAir and Southwest Airlines submitted orders for ten aircraft each, with options for an additional twenty. These orders officially launched the 737-300 program on March 21, 1981.

The new 737 was introduced much later than its main competitor (DC-9 Super 80), and experienced a similar situation to the launch of the Original 737 series. Although marketing challenges were intrinsic to the 737-300's late arrival into the marketplace, there was also a solid advantage. Boeing's John Roundhill explained the benefit of this situation:

When you are not first, you know what the other guys are committed to. This allows you to focus on the customer, the airlines, and what you can use to differentiate your product. The Super 80 had the JT8D-200 series engines (bypass ratio 2-1), so they were committed to that. We had the advantage that if we could come up with a high bypass ratio engine we could leap frog them.

How They Made the CFM56 Fit

Boeing asked its engineers to figure out how to make the CFM56 engine fit, given the small underwing space allowed by the 737 design. This was a daunting challenge, as the diameter of CFMI's replacement powerplant was significantly larger than the JT8D variants, including the re-fanned JT8D-200 series. The underwing mounted Pratt & Whitney engine caused much concern early on due to its relatively small ground clearance. The 737-300 design team's Mark Gregoire was charged with finding a way to extend the life of the 737 design while spending a minimum amount of money. The Boeing Company's resources were once again stretched to their limits, but this time with the development of the 757 and 767 (known as the 7N7 and 7X7 at the time). This mandated that any modifications would have to be kept minimal and made a major redesign out of the question.

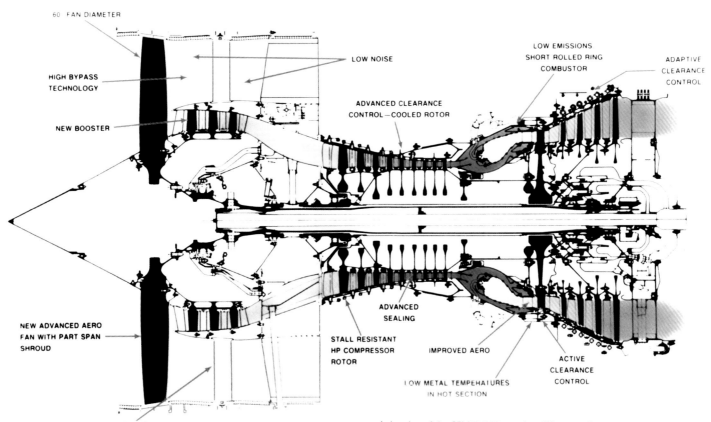

HIGH BYPASS TECHNOLOGY

NEW BOOSTER

LOW NOISE

LOW EMISSIONS SHORT ROLLED RING COMBUSTOR

ADAPTIVE CLEARANCE CONTROL

ADVANCED CLEARANCE CONTROL—COOLED ROTOR

NEW ADVANCED AERO FAN WITH PART SPAN SHROUD

ADVANCED SEALING

STALL RESISTANT HP COMPRESSOR ROTOR

IMPROVED AERO

ACTIVE CLEARANCE CONTROL

LOW METAL TEMPERATURES IN HOT SECTION

NEW OGV

A drawing of the CFM56-3 illustrating differences from the earlier versions of the engine. The fan size was reduced from sixty-eight inches on the CFM56-2 to sixty inches for the CFM56-3. *Courtesy of The Boeing Company*

The Original series 737's landing gear was kept small and simple to limit the weight and complexity of the system as a whole. This seriously constrained the amount of room under the wing, which barely fit the JT8D engine with its forty inch diameter fan section. Since the CFM engine had a fan section sixty inches in diameter, there was physically not enough room under the 737's wing for an engine of this size. It may have seemed that the easiest solution would be to make the landing gears longer. Although this appeared simple enough, the problem became apparent when considering the size of the landing gear wells, particularly where the main wing mounted units were concerned. If the wells were extended outboard, the engines would also have to be moved farther outboard and so on. A complete redesign of the 737's basic wing structure would have been required and was unaffordable for Boeing at the time. Additionally, installing longer landing gears would add increased weight to the aircraft and adversely affect its excellent ground servicing geometry, which made this an undesirable option for the engineers.

John Roundhill described the complexities involving the new CFM56:

It had a single stage turbine which was supersonic…I had never heard of anything like it. It was the right size for engines on 707s, 727s, and 737s. We, at Boeing, considered a number of fan sizes. So then they got together with GE and the CFM56-2. At a sixty-eight inch fan diameter, there was no way that we could see doing that…putting it under the wing… . The breakthrough was to convince CFM that there was a big enough market on the 737 to downsize the fan and make it a diameter that we could handle. The second

Here at ground level the positioning of the engine in front of the wing is obvious. CFMI moved the engine accessory components from the bottom to the sides to allow proper ground clearance. This, combined with the flattened inlet, gave the engine an unusual appearance and made the Classic series 737s easily identifiable. *Author's Collection*

CFM56-3 Engine

- Starter Duct
- Fuel Flowmeter
- Precooler
- Bleed Regulator Valve
- Borescope Ports
- 5th Stage Air Duct
- Starter
- Fuel Line
- Fuel-Lub Oil Cooler
- Generator
- Clearance Cooling Tubes
- Burner Fuel Lines
- Fuel Control
- Constant Speed Drive
- Throttle

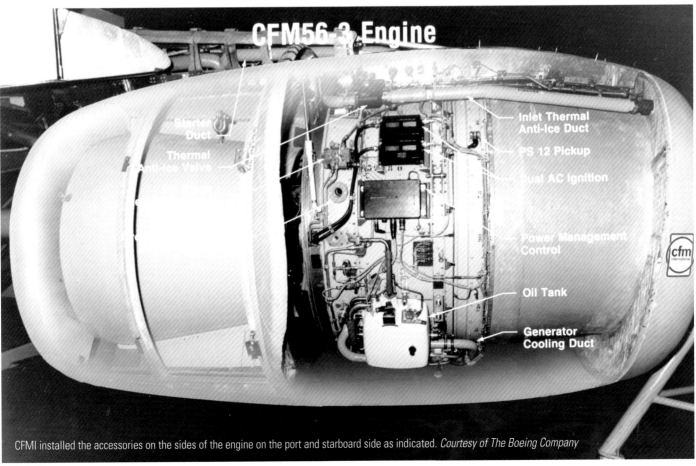

CFM56-3 Engine

- Starter Duct
- Thermal Anti-Ice Valve
- Inlet Thermal Anti-Ice Duct
- PS 12 Pickup
- Dual AC Ignition
- Power Management Control
- Oil Tank
- Generator Cooling Duct

cfm

CFMI installed the accessories on the sides of the engine on the port and starboard side as indicated. *Courtesy of The Boeing Company*

breakthrough was [fitting] the bigger engine under the wing of the 737 without making the landing gear longer. The gear, wing box, [and] fuselage diameter interface are the guts of an airplane. If you take that apart you are starting from scratch. We were able to move the engine forward and up.

The only place that could possibly be considered for mounting the CFM56 engine was entirely out in front of the wing. When viewed from the front, the top of the nacelle for the new motor would be nearly even with the leading edge of the wing. The wing was essentially the same wing as the -200 Advanced (with some small modifications added later) and was a known quantity by this point. The changes made in close proximity to the wing with the placement of the large turbofan unit was the wild card for the aerodynamics engineers, and they worried about the effects this configuration would have on the wings' aerodynamics. How would the new engine nacelle and pylon affect the aerodynamics of the wing throughout the 737's operational speed range? Cutting edge technology in the form of computational fluid dynamics was used to solve the problem.

Computational Fluid Dynamics

Computer technology had come a very long way by the time the 737-300 was being designed. Complex mathematical problems, beyond the capability of the use of slide rules and the like, could be studied and solved rapidly with newly improved supercomputers. Quantum leaps in computing power allowed a concept known as Computational Fluid Dynamics (CFD) to be usable. CFD is the use of numerical simulation to predict the flow of "fluids" (in this case air) around components on an aircraft. Aerodynamicist Jay Ferrell recounts the introduction of CFD technology:

> The idea was: can we compute things without having to wind tunnel them? So what they were doing was writing very complicated programs and comparing them with data that guys like me were getting out of the wind tunnel. By the time I left [CFD] it was still a dream and…it was so complicated. The flow around an airplane is unreal.

Some of the first generation CFD computer codes were developed by Boeing in the 1960s to help design low drag shapes for components of the US Supersonic Transport (SST) program. As early as 1973, Boeing had procured a powerful computer known as CDC6600 for solving more complex CFD simulations. This computer was produced by Control Data Corporation and was widely regarded as the first "supercomputer," costing $7 million a copy. The powerful CDC6600 allowed the use of an improved CFD application known as TA230. This computer program modeled the airflow around a three-dimensional aircraft or object using the so-called "panel method," which approximated the aircraft's actual curved shape via a patchwork of flat panels. Other simplifications were necessary to compute the flow patterns around an entire aircraft. For example, the effects of the increased compressibility of air and the shock waves that appear in the flow when the local airspeed is near the speed of sound were only crudely approximated. The details of complex turbulent flow in the thin layer of air touching the aircraft's skin ("boundary layer")

were ignored. But the engineers developed adjustments for these shortcomings to interpret the kinds of aerodynamic information the simplified numerical model could provide. One of the earliest uses of this program was for the Boeing 747-100 Space Shuttle Carrier Aircraft (SSCA), to explore the aerodynamic effects of the two aircraft while attached to each other. The in-flight separation of the Shuttle and the SSCA was also analyzed using this system. Later versions of CFD became much more capable and caused a shift in the tools used by engineers for aerodynamic designs. Calculations predicted and even replaced wind tunnel testing under certain circumstances. In some cases, it solved airflow problems not even apparent on expensive and sophisticated wind tunnel models. Although CFD was faster and more efficient than dated aerodynamic design methods, it still took experienced designers weeks to devise and run complex test configurations.

CFD technology was also used to analyze the complex workings of turbulent airflows and how they interacted when in close proximity to the surface of the aircraft. A second generation method used in codes called PANAIR and A502 was adopted by Boeing aerodynamicists around the time the 737-300 was on the drawing board. While the airflow simulation model employed in these applications was still classified as a "Panel Method," its more complex theory could accurately represent smoothly curved surfaces when calculating local aerodynamic surface pressures. It proved useful in designing the engine nacelles and pylons for the 737-300. The shapes of these items and the method of attachment to the new jet's wing were of paramount importance where aerodynamic drag was concerned. This interface was critical because of how closely mounted the new engines were to the leading edge of the wing and their aerodynamic interaction with the leading edge flaps and slats.

Sizing Up the Competition

The McDonnell Douglas DC-9 Super 80 (MD-80) had an almost four-year lead in production time over the 737-300 program. Although this was not an ideal situation for Boeing, the company was willing to embark on this venture to gain an advantage over McDonnell Douglas. Boeing intended to build a better aircraft with the incorporation of the newer technology CFM56-3 engine. Despite the challenges of mounting this large diameter turbofan on the existing 737 airframe, its performance advantages over the MD-80's re-fanned JT8D-209 engine were enormous. When airlines considered the purchase of aircraft, specific fuel consumption was a key issue, especially when fuel prices escalated in the 1970s and '80s. The generation of fuel efficient power was where the 737-300 was going to shine, and in many important ways outclass the competing McDonnell Douglas machine. The CFM56-3 relied on a new technology core and was greatly optimized. It possessed a higher bypass ratio than the Pratt & Whitney unit, and also took advantage of small details like variable geometry stator vanes on the first four stages of the engine's compressor. Stator vanes are small blades that are stationary guides in the engine's compressor. Their function is to modify the airflow as it leaves one compressor stage, ensuring it is stabilized before introducing it to the next stage at the optimum angle. Designers were challenged to create an ideal angle of airflow. This angle of airflow varied dependent upon the engine's speed and whether it was accelerating or decelerating. By using fuel as a "hydraulic" control medium, the stator vanes' angle was adjusted slightly to achieve optimum

NOISE REDUCTION FEATURES
CFM56-3

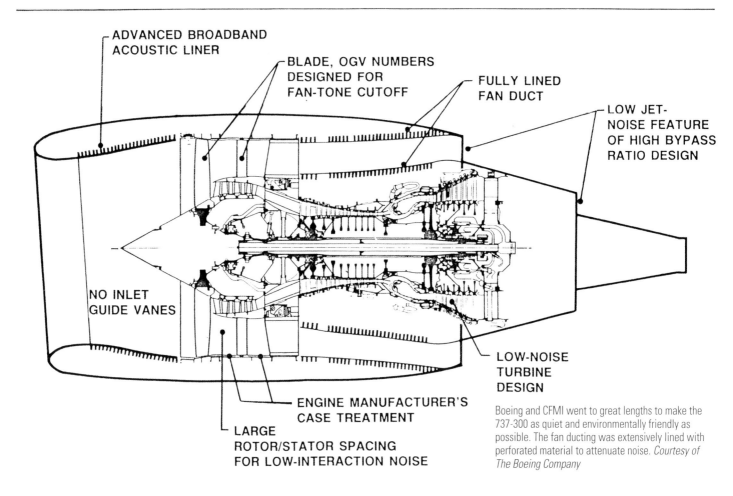

ADVANCED BROADBAND
ACOUSTIC LINER

BLADE, OGV NUMBERS
DESIGNED FOR
FAN-TONE CUTOFF

FULLY LINED
FAN DUCT

LOW JET-
NOISE FEATURE
OF HIGH BYPASS
RATIO DESIGN

NO INLET
GUIDE VANES

LOW-NOISE
TURBINE
DESIGN

ENGINE MANUFACTURER'S
CASE TREATMENT

LARGE
ROTOR/STATOR SPACING
FOR LOW-INTERACTION NOISE

Boeing and CFMI went to great lengths to make the 737-300 as quiet and environmentally friendly as possible. The fan ducting was extensively lined with perforated material to attenuate noise. *Courtesy of The Boeing Company*

engine acceleration and efficiency in all conditions. The CFM56-3 possessed an advanced annular burner design that aided in fuel efficiency and also reduced engine exhaust emissions well below the Environmental Protection Agency's requirements. These features, combined with an advanced Power Management Control (PMC) system, made the CFM56-3 ahead of its time in terms of fuel efficiency, noise footprint, and excellent operating characteristics.

The 737-300's CFM56-3 engine was on average eighteen percent more fuel efficient than the low bypass engines of just a few years back. It also used eleven percent less fuel for a given amount of thrust than the MD-80's re-fanned engines. This was an enormous financial benefit for any airline that would operate the 737-300. Since the advent of the jet airliner, noise was a major concern for public relations at many airports. Noisy jets were a problem for the airlines, since laws requiring lower noise levels were being enacted by legislators. Nowhere was this more apparent than at the Orange County Airport (KSNA) in Southern California. Noise regulations there became so restrictive that most jets had to (and still do) fly a specific profile requiring a maximum thrust takeoff to climb as quickly as possible, then reducing thrust markedly as the aircraft transitioned over the "noise sensitive" neighborhoods in a slow climb. In some cases the engine bleed air was turned off to increase the aircraft's initial climb rate prior to reducing power to decrease engine noise. This procedure required the use of the auxiliary power unit (APU) to supply compressed air to the air conditioning packs. The CFM56 engine

was significantly quieter than even the most recent re-fan engines and gave the new Boeing jet a significant public relations edge over the MD-80. Boeing received the first CFM56-3 engine on September 14, 1983.

More Passenger Capacity

Boeing's replacement of the JT8D with the CFM56-3 improved fuel efficiency, reduced noise, and increased power on its 737-300. The additional thrust enabled the 737-300 to carry more weight while maintaining good takeoff and cruise performance. Boeing utilized the extra weight carrying capability by increasing passenger and cargo capacity. Two fuselage extensions were added to the airframe to accomplish the goal. A forty-four inch plug was added in front of the wing and a sixty inch fuselage section was added behind the wing. The larger extension behind the wing balanced the engines' weight movement from underneath to out in front of the leading edge of the wing. The typical all coach class capacity of the aircraft increased from 122 passengers to 137, all while burning less fuel!

Aerodynamic Improvements

As the size of the 737 increased a few aerodynamic enhancements were required to optimize the efficiency of the aircraft. The most noticeable change was the addition of an extended dorsal fairing near the base of the vertical stabilizer. Less apparent was the slight increase to the height of the vertical stabilizer. These revisions were necessary to provide greater stability to the aircraft's yaw (side to side) axis because of the larger, more powerful CFM56-3 engines. If an engine were to fail at low speed, additional rudder authority and stability would be required to counteract the asymmetric thrust. These additions also helped stabilize the aircraft in case the yaw damper system became inoperative. The horizontal stabilizers were increased in span to allow greater pitch stability due to the larger size of the aircraft.

The new wing on the 737-300 featured several modifications. The wings were extended by eleven inches on each wingtip. This increased lift and the wing's aspect ratio, optimizing the wing's performance. An additional ground spoiler was also added to each wing just inboard of the ailerons, enhancing the aircraft's stopping performance on landing. Less noticeable were the small wing leading edge chord extensions added to boost the wing's performance and weight carrying capability. This 4.4 percent extension improved performance at low speeds, as well as in cruise. Typical cruise speeds were higher due to the increase in the wing's critical Mach number. Turbulence penetration speeds were also increased to Mach .73 from .70 (on the 737-200) because the onset of transonic (nearly supersonic) airflow over the wing was delayed to a higher airspeed. Also, for a given weight, when compared to the 737-200, the cruise altitude was nearly 4,000 feet higher. Since jet engines were more fuel efficient at higher altitudes this was another significant advancement in efficiency. To better optimize the low speed performance of the wing the leading edge slats were re-cambered and the extended positions were refined to reduce typical approach speeds by two to three knots over a 737-200 operating under similar conditions.

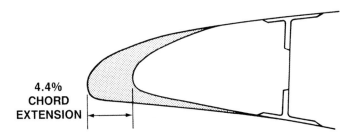

The chord of the wing on the 737-300 was extended slightly compared to the 737-200 to increase economical cruise speed to approximately Mach .745. *Courtesy of The Boeing Company*

The wing of the 737 was originally designed (as with most jet transports) with a forward and rear spar to provide structural strength. The volume between these wing spars constitutes the aircraft's main (wing) fuel tanks. Without intervention this would have placed fuel storage directly above the engine's turbine section. To prevent this a large "dry bay" was isolated on the 737-200 directly above this area to prevent fire hazard in the event of a un-contained engine failure. Because most of the engine is in front of the wings on the 737-300, the previous dry bay is unnecessary and can become part of the wing fuel tank. A smaller volume directly above the CFM56 hot section is isolated as a dry bay. The net effect is to increase the overall fuel capacity of the main tanks from 1,499 to 1,577 gallons in each wing.

Other minor airframe changes were made, such as the addition of a slightly taller nose landing gear, allowing additional engine to ground clearance. The main landing gear wheels were made more

stout, with an option to install forty-two inch wide tires. Significant strength and service life increases due to the use of new aluminum alloys in key areas, such as the wing spars and fuselage keel areas, were incorporated into the new aircraft. Composite flight control surfaces and corrosion prevention improvements similar to those used on the late model 737-200 Advanced were made standard on the 737-300 and subsequent models.

The 737-300 Cockpit

The "New Generation" 737 cockpit was designed to keep commonality with the 737-200. This was done while still taking advantage of newer technology available from other Boeing aircraft, such as the 757 and 767, which were under development at the same time. Aircraft systems possessed enough commonality to allow the overhead panel to be remarkably similar to the 737-200 with a few small differences, primarily on the new aircraft's hydraulic panel. The pilot alerting systems were nearly identical, as was the systems layout on the overhead panel. There were some key differences because of the natural evolution of technology.

The 737 Classic overhead panel retained great similarity with the older 737-200. *Author's Collection*

The overhead panel on the 737-300 was kept as similar as possible to the 737-200. Some changes were necessary, such as the addition of the "SPEED TRIM" and "AUTO SLAT" lights on the flight control panel (top left) and the deletion of the hydraulic "GROUND INTERCONNECT" switch on the hydraulic panel (right of center). Also added were the "VHF NAV," "COMPASS," "ATTITUDE," and "FMC" switches because of the new FMCs and Inertial Reference Systems (middle left). The "STBY RUD

The cockpit of the 737-300 was similar to the 737-200, but one very noticeable difference was the addition of the dual Control Display Units (CDUs), identified by the green screens to the left and right of the thrust levers. These enabled pilots to input information into the Flight Management Computers (FMCs). The electro-mechanical instruments are sometimes referred to as "steam gauges" by pilots. *Courtesy of The Boeing Company*

ON" light (top left) was added as a modification for greater redundancy of the rudder control system.

One of the most obvious differences was the SP-300 Mode Control Panel (MCP), which was on the glareshield above the engine instrumentation. This encompassed one of the major operational changes for the pilots and their interaction with the autopilot. The MCP controlled the flight directors, and in turn the autopilot, when in Command Mode. A heading select knob was installed in the middle of the MCP panel, within easy reach of either pilot. In the older 737-200 aircraft, the captain's heading knob was controlling, and required the captain to set the heading, even when it was the first officer's turn to fly. The autopilot and flight director systems of the 737-300 were more advanced, allowing the autopilot to change altitudes and automatically level off when it arrived at a newly assigned altitude. These details incorporated into the SP-300 autopilot significantly reduced the pilot's workload. Designers retained the Control Wheel Steering system from the older SP-77 and SP-177 autopilots of the 737-100, -200, and -200 ADV as a workload reduction tool.

The engine instruments were naturally different as a result of the new CFM56-3s installed on the 737-300. They were still set up similarly, with the top row showing power output. The main difference was in how the power output was measured. The JT8D powerplant on the older 737s used engine pressure ratio (EPR) to quantify engine thrust. The CFM56 used fan speed to measure power output, which was not as linear with actual thrust output, but was not susceptible to indication errors if a probe were to become blocked by a contaminant or icing. The fan speed was called N1, which was the rotational speed of the low pressure spool and fan of the engine. N1 was measured in percentage of maximum. The next gauges going down the row were exhaust gas temperature (EGT); N2, which was the high pressure spool speed; and fuel flow in thousands of pounds per hour. Arranged from top to bottom just to the right were oil pressure measured in PSI, oil temperature measured in degrees Celsius, oil quantity in gallons, and vibration in meters.

Where some of the Advanced 737-200 aircraft came with the Performance Data Computer System (PDCS), the new 737-

300 featured a Control Display Unit (CDU) which was used to accomplish several tasks (and has continued to gain capabilities throughout the years). It was used to enter the position data required to orient the new Inertial Navigation Systems (INS) and to calculate engine performance parameters. Additionally, the pilot used the CDU to determine the aircraft's optimum and maximum cruising altitudes (based on aircraft weight and temperature) and to enter the aircraft's flight plan route. Since the CDU interfaced directly with the Flight Management Computer (FMC) and the autopilot/autothrottle systems, automatic navigation was enabled. Vertical climb and descent profiles were also calculated, taking into account winds aloft, weight, and temperature. The CDU also incorporated a "bite check" function, which was helpful for maintenance technicians when troubleshooting problems. These functions resulted in easing the workload of pilots and mechanics, as well as providing optimum engine and aircraft performance to enhance fuel efficiency.

The 737 was the first jetliner to be equipped with four dimensional navigation (4D Nav). Also known as time control navigation (T-Nav), this useful function allowed aircraft speed to be precisely calculated and managed so the aircraft would arrive at a specific navigation fix at a precise time. This function could be used to conserve fuel by flying the aircraft at optimum speed when a known delay was ahead. This feature could also advise the crew of the earliest and latest takeoff time to arrive at the destination or a fix at a specific time. A fuel savings of up to .5% could easily be realized with 1985 air traffic control technology, with a possible 1.5–4.5% savings with modernized ATC equipment, allowing advanced arrival metering.

There were other subtle changes made from the earlier 737 designs, such as the pilot's oxygen mask system. The new EROS mask system was stowed in a compartment outboard of the pilot and was easier to don with one hand. When the exposed handles were squeezed pressurized oxygen filled the hollow inflatable head bands, allowing

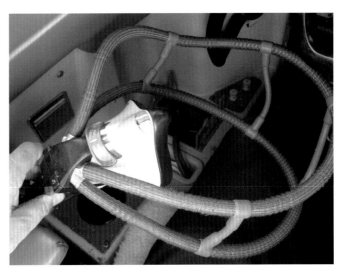

The EROS quick-donning oxygen mask shown with the elastic headbands inflated. *Author's Collection*

the mask to be placed on the pilot's head while retaining the use of the other hand to fly the aircraft. Once the handles on the mask were released the headband would snug down to the back of the head, pressing the mask to the pilot's face and allowing hands-free, automatic operation. It was also equipped with a simplified test function to reduce workload during preflight preparations.

The 737-300 came standard with an advanced wind shear alerting system that was integrated with the flight director system. If the aircraft was equipped with optional Electronic Flight Instrumentation System (EFIS) instrumentation, the wind shear alerting system would provide pitch limit aerodynamic stall indicators. The older vertical speed indicators, which used changes in outside air pressure to derive an indication, were revised and driven by the aircraft's inertial systems. This made their indication

The optional Electronic Flight Instrumentation System (EFIS) cockpit used high technology displays for the attitude indicators, navigation displays, and engine instrument stacks. These displays could also be used to transpose weather radar imagery over the navigation display for increased situational awareness. *Courtesy of The Boeing Company*

instantaneous, with little to none of the lag that was typical of older generation vertical speed indicators. To help the pilot recognize a wind shear condition in a timely manner an audio voice warning, along with red warning lights, were included in the system package.

Many airlines, such as Lufthansa and Ansett, ordered new 737s with the optional Electronic Flight Instrument Systems (EFIS) replacing the traditional electro-mechanical flight instruments. The use of the new technology displays ensured the 737 had more commonality with the newer 747-400, 757, and 767. FAA certification for the EFIS system installation on the "Classic" series was granted on July 24, 1986. The older systems were often referred to as "steam gages" and the aircraft so equipped were sometimes dubbed "hard ball" airplanes by their pilots. The new EFIS instrumentation was less maintenance intensive, since the system was solid-state. Another benefit from a crew workload standpoint was the EFIS system incorporated a map display. This innovation was a huge situational awareness gain for the pilot. Not only could the aircraft's position in relation to surrounding airports be ascertained at a glance, but the routing was presented simultaneously with weather radar. This alone markedly reduced pilot workload.

Aircraft Systems Changes

A substantial amount of commonality existed between the older 737-200 series and the new 737-300. The Classic 737-300 shared sixty-seven percent parts commonality with its older siblings. Some of the improved components of the 737-300 aircraft, such as the main landing gear assemblies, were stronger and more robust. Although these parts were improved, many were engineered to remain compatible as replacement parts for the earlier 737-200 Advanced aircraft. Innovations like these allowed the airlines to stock less parts, further reducing operating expenses. The flight deck design of the 737-300 was kept as similar to the 737-200 as possible, allowing many airlines to use the 737-200 and -300 with a common pilot group, thereby requiring only minimal cross-training. Although there were many efforts to keep the two versions as similar as possible, there were also opportunities for improvement to increase systems redundancy and safety.

The hydraulic system on the New Generation 737-300 was changed to increase redundancy and improve the aircraft's operation with failed systems. On the 737-300, each hydraulic system (A and B) was powered by one engine driven pump (EDP) and one electric motor driven pump (EMDP), allowing hydraulic component loads to be more evenly redistributed. This was a significant change from the 737-200, which had all high-load items on the engine driven (EDP) A system and smaller utilities on the electrically driven (EMDP) B system. In keeping with the entire 737 line, the basic flight controls were still actuated with dual hydraulics, and in the very unlikely event both of these systems (A and B) failed, the ailerons and elevators could be operated manually with a cable-driven backup to execute flight control via servo tabs. The rudder, powered by the A and B systems, could also be actuated by the standby hydraulic system in the event of a dual failure. The wheel brake systems were also changed slightly to allow better braking capability in the event of a single hydraulic system failure.

The 737-300 Is Born

The 737-300 prototype was assembled in the Renton, Washington, assembly hall amongst the 737-200 Advanced airplanes already being built in full force. The construction of the 737-300 prototype went smoothly, and it was completed on time. On January 17, 1984, Boeing's 737-300 was rolled out of the aircraft paint facility and introduced to the world. Resplendent in its bare metal finish with red, white, and blue stripes, the vertical stabilizer was adorned with the now familiar "737" Stratotype logo. This beautiful machine was the 1,001st 737 ever built. The first of its kind, it was more powerful, fuel efficient, and quieter than its predecessors. The 737-300 prototype was flown on February 24, 1984, just five weeks after its official rollout, and marked a new era for Boeing and the 737 program. This aircraft wore the standard test registration N73700 (c/n 22950, l/n 1001 in this case) on its maiden flight under the command of Capts. Tom Edmonds and Jim McRoberts. The second of the 737-300 series was registered as N351AU (c/n 22951, l/n 1007), and became airborne on March 4, 1984, sporting

The first 737-300 (c/n 22950, l/n 1001) being built alongside 737-200 series airframes being assembled in Renton, Washington. *Courtesy of The Boeing Company*

Another view of the 737-300 prototype being assembled next to the 1,000th 737; the latter (c/n 23078, l/n 1000) would be delivered to Delta Air Lines after festivities marking its completion. *Courtesy of The Boeing Company*

Capts. Tom Edmonds (left) and Jim McRoberts photographed with the 737-300 prototype. *Courtesy of The Boeing Company*

Capts. McRoberts and Edmonds emerging from the 737-300 after its maiden flight. *Courtesy of The Boeing Company*

The 737-300 prototype lifting off for the first time from Renton, Washington, on February 24, 1984, under the command of Capts. Edmonds and McRoberts. *Courtesy of The Boeing Company*

A first flight cover flown on the inaugural flight of the 737-300. *Author's Collection*

The 737-300 prototype in flight over the Cascade Mountains. *Courtesy of The Museum of Flight*

This photo shows the third Flight Test 737-3B7 (N352AU, c/n 22952, l/n 1015) lifting off during a test flight. This aircraft was delivered to USAir on April 11, 1985. Note the small drogue chute attached to the tip of the vertical stabilizer for instrumentation calibration. *Courtesy of The Boeing Company*

a modified bare metal USAir paint scheme. During the test program, there was concern that the airframe, with its extended wings, might exhibit flutter, an aerodynamic oscillation which can lead to airframe damage if not properly damped out. As a precaution, 110 pound weights were added to each wingtip in an effort to prevent this phenomenon. During subsequent flight testing it became apparent this addition was unnecessary, as the aircraft exhibited a natural tendency to dampen out flutter throughout its speed range. In total, three aircraft were used in the flight testing of the 737-300 series over a period of nine months, logging 1,294 hours.

Vmu (Velocity, minimum unstick) testing defines the lowest possible airspeed that an aircraft can become airborne with a given weight, center of gravity, and flap setting. The 737-300 prototype demonstrates the aircraft's ability to safely climb after an over-rotation. A wooden skid is used to protect the rear fuselage of the aircraft. *Courtesy of The Boeing Company*

Taken September 18, 1984, are President of Southwest Airlines Herb Kelleher (left) and President and Chairman of USAir Edwin Colodny. Both airlines were launch customers for the 737-300 series. *Courtesy of The Boeing Company*

A JAT Yugoslav Airlines 737-3H9 (c/n 2330, l/n 1136) seen preparing to taxi out in Sarajevo, Bosnia, and Herzegovina in 1986. *Courtesy of P. Popelar*

Piedmont Airlines operated this 737-301 (c/n 23261, l/n 1157) until 1989. This aircraft then saw service with USAir, America West Airlines, and KD Avia of Russia prior to being retired in 2009. *Courtesy of Jennings Heilig*

An artist's impression of Delta's 737-347 N304WA (c/n 23345, l/n 1170), which was delivered to Western Airlines on November 11, 1985, prior to its merger with Delta Air Lines in 1987. *Courtesy of Jennings Heilig*

After 1938 in the United States, and for the ensuing forty years, all interstate airline markets were controlled by the Civil Aeronautics Board (CAB). This government entity determined airfares that could be charged by the airlines, similar to the government regulation of public utilities. CAB was given the authority to approve or deny airlines the right to operate on each route for which they applied. This arrangement created stability in the airline industry, ensuring that each airline had adequate profits. However, airline regulation prevented competition between airlines in a free market and the formation of new interstate airlines was discouraged by CAB, which had complete control over their ability to operate. CAB collected input from airlines that had already established a particular route regarding the entry of another carrier. The established carrier would often resist the new application, citing some deficiency with the newcomer, thus swaying CAB to deny the application. Often times applications for new routes and carriers were denied, or met with very long delays rendering a decision. Although the larger established airlines did well under CAB because profits were virtually guaranteed, new carriers often found it very difficult to gain a foothold.

The governing role of CAB began to be reviewed because of global events changing the landscape of the airline industry. The Oil Crisis of 1973 was a pivotal event, spurring the need for adaptation. The Oil Crisis caused fuel costs for airlines to increase at astronomical rates. To ensure profits, CAB raised airfares to the point where they became unaffordable to a large portion of the population, disenchanting them more with each price increase. In addition, many economists felt government regulation of fares was leading to an airline system with higher operating costs due to the inefficiencies inherent in arrangements designed to guarantee profits. In contrast to the United States' CAB airline regulation, the British carrier Laker Airways began to operate on transatlantic routes with a new venture called Laker Skytrain. This service, the brainchild of Sir Freddie Laker, capitalized on the efficiencies of their McDonnell Douglas DC-10's high density all economy arrangement with ten abreast seating. Laker used these wide body aircraft to provide what is generally regarded as the first ultra low fare service across the Atlantic. Capitalism was being brought to America's doorstep, pushing the need for the US carriers to compete in a free market to survive.

On October 24, 1978, President Jimmy Carter signed the Airline Deregulation Act. This event forever changed the landscape of the American airline industry. While the Federal Aviation Administration (FAA) retained full authority over the safety aspects of airline operations, the authority of CAB over route and fare control was gradually eliminated. During the transition period CAB was commanded to make timely decisions on applications for new routes. Not only were government subsidies for airlines carrying US Mail decreased, but essential air service (EAS) routes were also minimized. The latter had historically been subsidized by the federal government to ensure airline operations were available to smaller communities lacking the passenger volume for air carriers to operate profitably. Although deregulation did not completely eliminate EAS subsidies, the instances where these occurred were greatly reduced. In 1978, 746 communities were involved in the EAS program, but by 2015, only 153 remained subsidized in Alaska and the continental United States.

CAB's governing power was gradually relinquished over the six years following the implementation of the Airline Deregulation Act. By 1981, airlines were given the freedom to choose the routes they would like to serve. In 1982, carriers were given the latitude to set their own fares. These two freedoms caused the major airlines to either adapt and become efficient or to slip into obsolescence. Dozens of new airlines, such as PEOPLExpress, Muse Air, and Sunworld, quickly arrived on the scene, only to be gone less than a decade later. Both fares and airline profits quickly dropped as the major airlines began to restructure. In 1979, the number of passengers flown had increased to 317 million. The boom would be short-lived, as by 1981, passenger numbers fell to 286 million and the airline industry as a whole lost $421 million.

Major airlines tried to survive by attracting customers and reducing costs. Although Texas International was the first airline to offer a frequent flyer program, American Airlines' AAdvantage program, initially offered in 1981, was the first to see widespread success. United Airlines and others soon followed suit. The established airlines struggled to compete against many of the upstart airlines and their lower operating costs. Soon layoffs and pay decreases created internal strife between unions and airline management. Thousands of employees were laid off, while airlines tightened their belts. Iconic airlines like Pan Am, Eastern, Braniff, and later Trans World did not evolve quickly enough, soon fading into the history books.

At Boeing, the effects of deregulation spawned massive changes, as it caused the airlines to change their ideal specifications for new aircraft. Peter Morton spoke of the confusion: "I don't even think our theorists were able to smoke out what it was going to look like at the end of that turbulent time. There are some things that are not simulate-able, you just have to do them. It was a fascinating time." The events which transpired in the decades following deregulation were without precedent and made any kind of future planning extremely challenging. Industry professionals could only guess at what airlines were going to be looking for in future aircraft. Boeing's Vice President of 737 MAX Marketing Joe Ozimek remembered the situation: "Deregulation was a fundamental change, and it caused a lot of airplanes to look differently than they would have under regulation." Based on pre-deregulation metrics, Boeing had estimated the market for the 737-300 to be only 300 aircraft.

The airlines, in their struggle to compete cost effectively, began to use a concept known in the industry as "hub and spoke." Instead of flying direct flights over long range between two cities, the airlines created hub airports at which their market strategy was to become the dominant carrier, providing multiple daily connections to cities within their route structure. Many times, in the post-deregulation environment, the airlines would schedule a stop and plane change in a hub city like Dallas, Denver, Chicago, or Atlanta. This system changed the specifications that airlines had for new aircraft, as slightly smaller aircraft that flew shorter routes became more efficient and desirable. Other airlines, like Southwest, did not use a hub and spoke system at the time, but provided customer service through the use of 737s with increased frequency between cities. Many airlines felt that more flight frequency with smaller aircraft provided the best possible customer service. This also led to larger aircraft, such as the Boeing 757, finding themselves sized out of the market, as their production runs became substantially less than forecast. On the other hand, the 737 gained favor in the post-deregulation environment. Far in excess of original projections, Boeing has built 9,365 Boeing 737 aircraft as of January 2017, and has open orders for 4,430 additional aircraft yet to be delivered. The effects of deregulation drastically changed the airline industry and set the stage for the 737's incredible success story.

A Testament to the Strength and Durability of the 737

On May 24, 1988, TACA Airlines Flight 110 prepared for descent into Moisant Field (KMSY) in New Orleans, Louisiana. The aircraft was a 737-3T0 (N75356, c/n 23838, l/n 1505) and originated in Belize City, Belize. The aircraft's weather radar was used to sense the precipitation inside of clouds and would then graphically show the position of hazardous weather to the crew. The flight's first officer noted there were

TACA Airlines' 737-3T0, N75356 (c/n 23838, l/n 1505) was delivered to the El Salvadorian airline on May 10, 1988. Fourteen days later this aircraft encountered extreme weather and performed a miraculous "dead stick" landing on a levee near New Orleans, Louisiana. *Courtesy of Jennings Heilig*

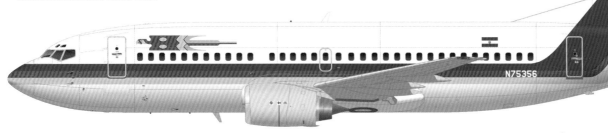

moderate and isolated severe weather cells being depicted so continuous engine ignition was selected "on" as a precaution. Although the flight was maneuvered around the severe weather depicted on their radar screens, an extreme encounter with rain, hail, and turbulence occurred while descending through 16,500 feet. The flight's transgression through extreme weather caused both engines to flame out, forcing the aircraft into a gliding descent. Both engine generators went off-line, leaving the electrical system on battery power alone. The airplane's auxiliary power unit (APU) was started, providing electrical power and pressurized air for attempts at restarting the engines. Subsequently, the turbofan engines were restarted, but would not accelerate up to normal flight idle speed and exceeded exhaust gas temperature (EGT) limits. Since both engines were not providing any thrust and were exceeding temperature limits, the crew elected to shut them down to prevent a more dangerous catastrophic failure. There were no suitable airports within gliding range of the aircraft, so the crew executed a miraculous dead stick landing on a grass levee near NASA's Michoud Assembly Facility. None of the forty-five people onboard were injured in the incident. The aircraft's engines were replaced and Boeing test pilots elected to fly the aircraft out safely using an access road adjacent to the grass. After further maintenance and inspections the aircraft was returned to service. According to the NTSB report, OMB-88-5 and AD 6-14-88 were issued requiring modifications be made to the CFM56-3 engines and procedures to increase the engine's ability to ingest very high amounts of water without ill effects. Subsequently, this aircraft had a long career, seeing service with Aviateca, America West Airlines, Morris Air, and served in the Southwest Airlines fleet until December 2016 as N697SW.

A New and Formidable Competitor

The origins of the Boeing 737's newest and most prolific competitor began long before the first 737 ever took flight. The Sud Aviation Caravelle, which first flew in 1955, was the first successful short range jetliner. This aircraft, built by Sud Aviation in Toulouse, France, was a joint cooperation between the French manufacturer and de Havilland in Hatfield, England. The nose section and some landing gear components from the British Comet program were adapted to the new jetliner. This aircraft proved that a jetliner could be built with an international partnership and was a very important move in the history of commercial aviation.

As time went on, several European aircraft companies were interested in building jetliners, but many had funding problems and found it difficult to engage in these monumental projects on their own with minimal government assistance. In 1964, the British Plowden Commission found that American manufacturers could build aircraft with costs ten to twenty percent lower than British manufacturers. This was mostly attributed to smaller projected production runs, because of the relatively small domestic jetliner market in Britain. Other European countries had similar concerns about the ability to compete with well-established American manufacturers: Boeing, Convair, Douglas, and Lockheed.

At the 1965 Paris Air Show the Studiengruppe Airbus was formed, which was the first use of the name "Airbus" regarding aircraft manufacturing. The group consisted of several historic German aircraft manufacturers, such as Dornier, Messerschmitt, and VFW. They explored the feasibility of producing a large commercial jetliner. In the meantime, the governments of France, Germany, and the United Kingdom had suggested that their top manufacturers study the possibility of joining forces to become competitive in the world's large jetliner market. During this period, British Aerospace had been trying to gain financial support for the BAC Three-Eleven, which would be a much larger follow-on to their already established BAC One-Eleven. Unfortunately, support was never forthcoming, with interests beginning to look toward the viability of a collective European product.

On December 17, 1970, a consortium called Airbus Industrie G.I.E. began operations. The companies involved were Aerospatiale (Sud Aviation merged with SEREB) and Deutsche Airbus (consisting of Messerschmitt, Bolkow, Blohm, and VFW-Fokker). The team

The A300 was the first aircraft produced by the Airbus consortium and was first flown on October 28, 1972. This example (EP-IBC, c/n 632) is a more recent A300-605R model. *Courtesy of P. Popelar*

The A310 was a development of the A300 featuring a new wing and more advanced systems. The aircraft pictured is an A310-304 (OK-WAB, c/n 567) operated by CSA from 1991 until being sold to Mahan Air in 2009. *Courtesy of P. Popelar*

was soon joined by CASA (Construcciones Aeronauticas S.A.) of Spain. Although not an official partner in Airbus, Hawker Siddeley (which had absorbed de Havilland) was employed as a risk sharing subcontractor and was charged with the design and building of wing structures for the proposed aircraft. Intermittently involved from early on, BAC did not officially become a full partner in the Airbus Consortium until 1979. At that point the ownership was split as follows: 37.9 percent Aerospatiale and Deutsche Airbus, 20 percent BAE (BAC merged with Hawker Siddeley), 4.2 percent belonging to CASA of Spain, and the remaining 37.9 percent being owned by other shareholders.

Airbus developed the A300, a twin-engined, widebody jetliner that employed the new General Electric CF6-50 turbofan engine. Launched with an order from Air France for six of the new jets with options to purchase a further ten, it first flew on October

28, 1972. The aircraft was a slow starter in terms of sales, with only fifteen orders at the time of the first A300's rollout ceremony. Many people high up in the industry felt the A300 would not be a successful venture and largely disregarded it. Under the radar things were beginning to gain momentum. A large order from Eastern Airlines in 1977 made industry leaders stand up and take notice. Airbus may have started slowly, but much like an accelerating locomotive, its force has only increased over time. A slightly smaller derivative of the A300 called the A310 was first flown on April 3, 1982. By this point both aircraft were selling reasonably well and left Airbus poised for its next undertaking.

The Airbus A320

As early as 1974, European interest in collectively building a narrow-bodied airliner of the 150 seat class was being seriously

The A320 first flew on February 22, 1987, and featured many advanced systems. Air Inter used this A320-211 (F-GHQP, c/n 337) 1992–April 1, 1997, when the carrier merged with Air France. *Courtesy of P. Popelar*

looked at. The EURAC (Group of Six) was formed, which was a partnership of BAC, Hawker-Siddeley, Aerospatiale, Dornier, MBB, and VFW-Fokker. Although that was not an official Airbus project at the beginning, all involved were heavily vested in the Airbus consortium. Later in 1975, Dassault Aviation joined EURAC. There was a significant move to create a development of the Dassault Mercure slightly stretched, with longer range and employing the CFM56 powerplant under development. This project was known as the ASMR, and was to be a joint venture with McDonnell Douglas, in the United States, shouldering fifteen percent of the costs. Aerospatiale would be responsible for forty percent, Dassault for five percent, and the remaining forty percent to be provided by other partners. The French government was very supportive of a joint venture with an American manufacturer, but by 1977, the ASMR project was terminated. BAC was still trying to develop an aircraft known as "X-11," which was to be a wider, larger outgrowth of the aging BAC One-Eleven, but it did not come to fruition. A deal made between Boeing and Aerospatiale to share in the development of the 7N7 (Boeing 757 concept) and the A300-10 (later known as the A310) also fell through, leaving Aerospatiale to return to their original design concept, the A200.

In 1977, the leaders of Aerospatiale, VFW-Fokker, and MBB began the JET (Joint European Transport) study, commencing development of the A200-like design concept based on a capacity of 130–170 seats. The aircraft specifications featured a single-aisle fuselage which was to be 12 ft. 10 in. in diameter and would be slightly wider than Boeing's 727 and 737. The aircraft was to be offered in three different fuselage lengths to suit the various needs of airline customers. The CFM56 and Pratt & Whitney JT10D turbofan engines were considered as possible options for installation on the new concept. It was clear to the participants that the new jet would have to be built under the control of the Airbus consortium, so leadership of the program was handed over to Airbus in 1980. Notably, the development of the aircraft remained remarkably similar to the Aerospatiale A200 concept. At the Paris Air Show on June 6, 1981, Air France expressed interested in procuring twenty-five of such aircraft, with the possibility of needing another twenty-five airplanes. The long road to the development of the new Airbus was underway, but the launch of the program was not formally announced until March 1984.

The A320 was designed to replace the 727, and was also a direct competitor of the Classic series 737. The size of the aircraft was variable–similar to the JET study aircraft–to efficiently meet the needs of the airlines. The initial version was the A320, with a fuselage length of 123 ft., 3 in. and seating for up to 179 passengers. The CFM56-5A1 was chosen for the design and was capable of producing up to 27,000 pounds of thrust. The wing design of the A320 was, in typical Airbus fashion, provided by BAE systems, and took advantage of the airfoil innovations developed during BAE's canceled BAC Three-Eleven project. There were similarities with Airbus' past aircraft, with each partner responsible for the assembly of assigned components for the airplane. MBB produced the rear fuselage and wing flaps, while Aerospatiale provided the forward fuselage, wing center section, engine pylons, and cabin doors. CASA constructed the horizontal stabilizers and landing gear doors.

To make the aircraft lighter and technologically advanced, the A320 used some technologies typically found on military aircraft. Novel at the time for a jetliner, the flight control system was designed using a philosophy known as "fly-by-wire." Up to

this time conventional airliner designs had employed either cable-driven control systems and/or hydraulically driven flight controls linked mechanically to the pilots' cockpit controls. Fly-by-wire (or Electrical Flight Control System, as Airbus refers to it) was a very different concept using cockpit controls linked electronically to five primary flight control computers. When the pilot applied a control input, a signal was sent to the flight control computers. These computers looked at the flight situation and sent appropriate signals to the hydraulic actuators at the control surfaces. Airbus saw this as advantageous not only for weight savings, but the computers could also protect the aircraft in the rare event that the pilot would mistakenly command a maneuver which would cause the aircraft to exceed pre-established limits. Of course, these protections could be disengaged if aircraft malfunctions caused the need for the flight controls to be commanded directly by the pilot, bypassing the computer protections in a mode called "Direct Law." Because of the lack of mechanical connection to the flight controls, there was no need for leverage to move pulleys and pushrods mechanically. Airbus elected to install a sidestick controller in lieu of the traditional control yoke. The sidesticks sensed pressure and commanded the flight controls through the fly-by-wire system with very little muscle effort on the part of the pilot. This type of control system was also used to augment the aircraft's inherent stability and made the task of flying the aircraft easier for the pilot. The A320 employed an automatic pitch trim function to enhance stability in all flight regimes. An unusual aspect of the A320 control system is that the pilot and copilot sidesticks were not interconnected; one pilot did not experience tactile feedback with regard to control inputs from the other, nor from the autopilot.

The flight instrumentation was the most advanced available at the time. A six-tube EFIS (Electronic Flight Instrumentation System) was employed. One CRT in front of each pilot displayed the aircraft's flight instrumentation in a Primary Flight Display (PFD) format. Just inboard of that was a map display that could be set by the pilot to display the navigation track, terrain, air traffic, and weather radar, among other things. The two center displays were used to present engine instrumentation and aircraft systems status in a schematic format. The overhead panel was a push button interface, with many systems operations automatic. At the time this flight deck was industry leading, and became the basis for cockpit designs of future Airbus models.

After the initial order from Air France many other airlines followed suit, replacing older aircraft with the new, state-of-the art machine. Orders came in from the European carriers at first, but then a big break came. Northwest Airlines was replacing its aging Boeing 727 aircraft, and in 1986, made an enormous order for 100 new Airbus A320s. By the time the A320 prototype had first flown on February 22, 1987, Airbus had won over 400 orders for the new aircraft. This very strong start made it obvious to all involved that the A320 was going to be a significant player in the short to medium range market.

Additional options were offered as time went on. Starting in 1989, the new V2500 engine was provided as an alternative to the CFM56-5, which was, up until that point, standard equipment. The A320 was the baseline aircraft, with different fuselage lengths being introduced later to suit the airlines' capacity needs. The first of these was the A321, which first flew on March 11, 1993. This aircraft featured a significant fuselage stretch of fourteen feet in front of the wing and eight feet, nine inches behind, allowing up to 220 passengers in high density all economy seating. Since the aircraft was much heavier, the development of a new wing design was considered. Fleet commonality was a key factor, and it was found that wing performance could be improved for the A321 by redesigning the trailing edge flaps to a double slotted design and making small changes to the wing area and camber. This allowed use of what was largely the same wing with some modifications, instead of a completely new structure. On August 25, 1995, another new version of that basic design, dubbed the A319, took its first fight. This aircraft was twelve feet, four inches shorter than the standard A320 and shared an identical wing structure with its sibling. More use of advanced composite parts was employed on the A319 for the sake of saving weight. Given the success of the A319, a further "shrink" was employed to produce the smallest Airbus: the A318. The fuselage was seven feet, eleven inches shorter than the A319 and employed a slightly taller vertical stabilizer to offset the aerodynamic effects of the shorter fuselage. After becoming airborne for the first time on January 12, 2002, the A318 entered service with Frontier Airlines in 2003.

An Airbus A319-111 (HB-JZG, c/n 2196) lifting off from Prague, Czech Republic, in 2006. This example has two overwing exits on each side for high density seating egress requirements, where most A319s have only one over each wing. *Courtesy of P. Popelar*

It can be seen that Airbus, in developing the basic A320 design, produced a range of aircraft that directly competed with all of the different variants of the 737, while the A321 attempted to compete with the passenger carrying capability of the Boeing 757, though not with its maximum range. The newer technology of Airbus' aircraft, including high efficiency wing and cockpit instrumentation, gave it a significant advantage over the Classic 737. The Airbus A320 series had positioned itself to be the primary competitor for the 737, forcing Boeing to a decision point on how to address this bold, new competitor.

The 737-400

In a market where short to medium range passenger travel was ever increasing, Boeing recognized the development of the slightly larger Airbus A320 as a serious threat, as Airbus had already

made apparent the development of the eventual A320. In 1984, Boeing salesman Rudy Hillinga had his finger on the pulse of the European market and was working closely with Lufthansa. The German airline saw the need for a 150-seat aircraft for its inter-European route structure, but was unwilling to wait until 1992 to fill this niche with Boeing's planned 7J7. The 7J7 was projected to be a super efficient jetliner in the 150 seat class, with a twin aisle and a 2-2-2 seating configuration. General Electric designed a powerplant called the GE36 Un-Ducted Fan (UDF), slated for use on the 7J7. This revolutionary aero engine used a jet engine core to power two counter rotating rows of un-cowled, large scimitar-shaped blades. Due to concerns of possible blade failure the engines were to be mounted on the tail of the aircraft, well away from the passenger cabin. Doing so required the reemergence of the T-tail design, regardless of its inherent disadvantages. The 7J7 was to employ state-of-the-art technologies, such as an advanced EFIS based cockpit, a fly-by-wire computerized control system, and an advanced wing design. Projections were the 7J7 concept was capable of a sixty percent improvement in fuel mileage over other similar sized jetliners at the time. Hillinga knew that Lufthansa was impatient and feared that Airbus was about to go firm on building the A320. Since the A320 would be in service much sooner than the 1992 projection for the 7J7, Hillinga pushed for the development of a larger 737 derivative which could be delivered much earlier. He hoped to beat Airbus to the market and possibly prevent the launch of the new European jetliner. His insistence played a key role in the launch of the 737-400 in 1985, despite the feelings of many among the ranks at Boeing that the market for a 150 seat 737 would generate few sales.

The desire for a 737 variant of greater capacity was identified and could easily be accomplished by the Classic 737 platform with minimal design changes. The 737-400 was to carry 156–170 passengers, with small penalties in range and performance, when compared to the 737-300 series. To accomplish this, the fuselage length was increased to 119 feet 7 inches. A seventy-two inch fuselage extension was inserted forward of the wing, while an additional forty-eight inch plug was added aft of the wing to balance the aircraft. Due to the increased seating capacity one additional hatch-type overwing exit was installed on each side of the cabin, providing enhanced egress capability. This configuration, along with the optional EFIS cockpit instrumentation package, put the 737-400 in a good position to compete with the new A320.

An artist's impression of G-BSNW (c/n 25169, l/n 2237) with its second operator, British Airways. This aircraft was delivered new to the British airline Dan-Air London on March 12, 1992, just before the merger of the two carriers. *Courtesy of Jennings Heilig*

BRITISH AIRWAYS

G-BSNW

John Roundhill, who at the time was the chief engineer of Pproduct technology for the 737 and 757, recalled the decision to develop the 737-400:

When I came on the scene with the narrow body situation the 737-300 was in service and Boeing had 1,300 people working on a program called the 7J7. That was going to be delivered in 1992. Dick Taylor asked me to come out of propulsion and noise and start working on the 737 and 757 derivative for Jack Wimpress…Piedmont and some other airlines wanted more seats in the 737. So we started working intently on the 737-400… . This was 1985. The 737-400 story was something like this: Boeing had a 150 seat plan. Dick Taylor realized…that you don't have a plan until someone buys it. So what do you do…you study everything. We worked pretty hard on the 737-400… . So anyway, it worked out that we launched the 737-400. Before Piedmont bought it, they said they needed another six inches of length because they could get another row in. So we did that.

The maximum takeoff weight was increased from 124,500 pounds for the basic 737-300 to 138,500 pounds for the 737-400 series. This additional weight caused some structural revisions to be made, since the aircraft was substantially heavier than its predecessor. The wings remained unchanged in shape and size, but were given additional strength by increasing the gauge of the metals and fasteners used in their construction. The center section of the fuselage was also modified by adding structure to fuselage stations 664 and 727, thereby providing greater rigidity to the airframe. The main landing gears were made stronger and more robust than those of the 737-300 series with revised machining, and by extending the stroke of the landing gear strut by one inch. The increased length of the fuselage led to a systems change in the air conditioning system which added a third temperature control zone. This was required because there were times when one part of the cabin would be hotter or colder than another based on where the passengers were sitting and other factors. The third temperature control allowed the pilot to simply choose the portion of the cabin that needed a temperature adjustment, enhancing passenger comfort. Since the longer fuselage increased the possibility of touching the tail on the runway during takeoff or landing, a non-retractable tail skid was added to the bottom of the rear fuselage to protect the aircraft. It also differentiated the 737-400 from the rest of the Classic fleet. The base engine for the 737-400 was the 22,000 pound thrust CFM56-3B2. A higher gross weight option was also soon offered for the 737-400, which increased the maximum takeoff weight to 150,000 pounds with the upgraded CFM56-3C1 engines, which had 23,500 pounds of available thrust each. The resultant changes made the 737-400 a capable competitor to the A320 while retaining ninety-five percent airframe parts commonality with the 737-300 series machines.

Many believed that the development of the 150 seat 737-400 played a significant role in the cancellation of the 7J7 program. However, other issues also contributed to the demise of this otherwise excellent concept. The UDF powerplant was largely unproven for long term use and created concerns about airport noise. The A320 was launched during this same period and was available much sooner than the projected 1992 availability date for the 7J7. This would have given Airbus a large jump on the 150 seat market and a stretched 737 variant could be made available much earlier to compete effectively. Also, some felt that Boeing was more concerned with investing in the larger aircraft market during that period. Boeing's product line had a significant size gap between the Boeing 767-200 (224 seats) and Boeing 747-400 (524 seats), which caused quite a bit of concern for the Seattle airplane maker. McDonnell Douglas was still producing the DC-10 widebody trijet with seating for 285 passengers and was developing the MD-11, which was a larger version with seating for 323. To add to the worries, Airbus was working on their A340, which was also in this size range. Boeing, with limited resources, chose to concentrate on the development of the Boeing 777-200, which went on to compete head to head with these aircraft and eventually dominated this market segment. Because of these issues the 7J7 program was canceled in 1987, but this concept brought about many new technologies which were carried on to later Boeing models. These took the form of improved aircraft technologies like fly-by-wire, a new digital data bus, cutting edge flight deck instrumentations, and composite structures in the vertical and horizontal tail, as well as in other areas of primary structure. New 777 process technologies were also adopted from the work done on the 7J7, with the use of digital product definition and new analytical design tools.

The Birth of the 737-400

The roll-out of the prototype 737-400 transpired on January 26, 1988, in Renton, Washington. Interestingly, this took place the same day as the roll-out ceremony of the 747-400, just a few miles away in Everett. The first flight of the 737-400 series occurred with Capt. Jim McRoberts at the controls on February 19, 1988. The aircraft used was a 737-401 (c/n 23886, l/n 1487) sporting tail number N73700, Boeing's standard 737 test registration. The flight reportedly went well, with no major differences in handling from the 737-300. This momentous event was followed by 400 hours of flight testing for FAA certification.

The 737-400 prototype just prior to the official rollout ceremony. *Courtesy of The Boeing Company*

The 737-400 Prototype lifting off on its inaugural flight. *Courtesy of The Boeing Company*

Piedmont Airlines took delivery of the first 737-400 (N406US) on September 15, 1988. This was soon followed by the first foreign delivery of 737-4Y0 G-UKLA (c/n 23865, l/n 1582) to Air UK Leisure on October 14, 1988. The 737-400 was the most efficient of the "Classic" series based on fuel per seat mile, having twenty-seven percent better efficiency than the 727-200 and seven percent better than the 737-300. Naturally, the tradeoffs were slightly higher takeoff and approach speeds due to its higher weights. To tailor the 737-400 to the individual operations of each airline, the new aircraft was offered with a choice of engine thrust ratings. The available engines were either the CFM56-3B2 (rated to 22,000 lbs.) or the CFM56-3C1 (limited to 22,000 lbs., or the full 23,500 lb. thrust rating). Because of the higher operating weights of the 737-400, the maximum range was slightly less than the others in the Classic series at 2,090 nautical (2,403 statute) miles. 486 737-400s were delivered by the end of the 737's "Classic" production.

The 737-500

Some airlines desired a 737 version with strong hot temperature and high altitude airport performance, while others were looking for a direct seat-for-seat replacement for their aging fleets of 737-200s. Various engine combinations were investigated for the new derivative, including the Pratt & Whitney JT8D-217. Also strongly considered was the Rolls-Royce Tay, with a mixed flow bypass, as an under wing mounted option. John Roundhill, who was involved in the development of the 737-500, recalls Dick Taylor's method: "I will never forget this…. We went to US Air and [Dick Taylor] said: 'OK, we are going to look at every single engine that is available for this class of aircraft and come back and show you what we think.' So we looked at the Rolls-Royce Tay. We looked at the Pratt & Whitney JT8D-200 series, which was about a 2-to-1 bypass ratio. We looked at [noise] suppressing the JT8D because Colodny [USAir's CEO at the time] liked those and the CFM56." Boeing ultimately chose the derated CFM56-3C1 to keep commonality with the other Classic series aircraft. Roundhill concluded, "So now we had a family of [three] 737 models, where we only had two before."

Pursuant to launch orders from Southwest Airlines for twenty, followed by Braathens of Norway for twenty-five aircraft, Boeing officially launched the 737-500. Based on the 737-300 airframe, the 737-500 was noticeably shorter in length with the removal of a fifty-four inch plug in front and a forty inch section deleted behind the wing. The shorter fuselage required the wing-to-body fairings to be slightly revised and a different nose gear tire was chosen for the 737-500. The basic version of the 737-500 had a maximum takeoff weight of 115,500 pounds and used the CFM56-3B1 derated to 18,500 pounds of thrust. A high gross weight option was also offered that increased the maximum takeoff weight to 134,000 pounds with the CFM56-3B1 that produced 20,000 pounds of thrust. The lighter weight of the aircraft offered enhanced takeoff performance and a slightly longer range of 2,420 nautical (2,783 statute) miles.

The first 737-500 is seen lifting off from Renton, Washington, wearing the standard 737 test registration N73700. *Courtesy of The Boeing Company*

The first roll out of the 737-500 occurred with the 737-500 prototype N73700 (c/n 24178, l/n 1718, Effectivity PU001) on June 3, 1989. The 737-500's first flight occurred on June 30, 1989, with Capts. Jim McRoberts and Ken Higgins. On this flight, PU001 was taken to Mach .89—an unusually high Mach number for a first flight—but there was great confidence in the aircraft. This aircraft was the only one used for the 737-500 certification program, and logged 375 hours

Aer Lingus, a long time operator of the 737, took delivery of 737-548 EI-CDF (c/n 25737, l/n 2232) on March 27, 1992. Today this aircraft is serving with Rossiya Russian Airlines under the same Irish registration. *Courtesy of Jennings Heilig*

This aerial photo is of the landing after a successful inaugural flight of the 737-500. This aircraft later became Southwest Airlines' N501SW *Shamu*, painted in the famous killer whale's likeness. *Courtesy of The Boeing Company*

Boeing 737-500 first flight cover. *Author's Collection*

A view of the Renton assembly hall showing the final assembly of 737-300, -400, and -500 series aircraft. Today, after the adoption of "lean" manufacturing, the aircraft move down the line nose to tail. *Courtesy of The Boeing Company*

United Airlines has operated a large fleet of 737s throughout the airplane's history. This 737-322 (N316UA, c/n 23948, l/n 1491) was delivered new to the carrier on December 17, 1987, wearing this striking livery inspired by artist Saul Bass. *Courtesy of The Boeing Company*

Lufthansa, the first 737 operator, had a long history operating the type, including this 737-330 (D-ABXA, c/n 23522, l/n 1246). This aircraft was Lufthansa's first 737-300 series airplane and left its fleet in 2001. Currently operated by Jet2, this aircraft flies for the fourth largest scheduled airline in the United Kingdom. *Courtesy of The Boeing Company*

before being delivered to Southwest Airlines as N501SW. It was also famous as being one of the three aircraft painted as the killer whale "Shamu" during Southwest's partnership with the SeaWorld theme parks. In 2012, it was withdrawn from service and was scrapped a year later in Tucson, Arizona.

The Life and Times of the 737 Classic Series

The 737 Classic series was involved in many advances in jetliner technology, being the first to usher in elements which were (and still are) being incorporated into the Federal Aviation Administration's NextGen airspace system. Among these were the first use of 4-Dimensional Navigation (4D Nav or T-Nav) and the Required Navigational Performance (RNP) operations (see chapter 7). The 737 also became much more advanced with the introduction of the optional EFIS systems. Noise and fuel consumption were both drastically reduced by the use of the high bypass turbofan technology of the cutting edge CFM56-3 engine. New engineering techniques were also put to work on the Classic 737, and it was one of the first uses of Computational Fluid Dynamics (CFD) to optimize the aerodynamic relationship between the CFM56 powerplant and the 737 airframe. The Classic series played a significant role in pioneering all of these technologies which have since become mainstream throughout the years.

The Classic series 737 was extremely successful and enjoyed a long production run. The 737-300 was the best selling of the Classic series by far, with 1,113 built, which was more than the later 737-400 (486 units) and 737-500 (389 units) combined. Production of the 737-300 and the rest of the Classic series ended in 2000, after producing 1,988 aircraft, as the Next Generation 737 series was dovetailed into the Renton production lines.

D-ABXY (c/n 24563, l/n 1801) was delivered new to Lufthansa on December 18, 1989, adorned in the carrier's updated paint scheme. This aircraft, christened *Hof*, served with the carrier until 2014. *Courtesy P. Popelar*

For many years KLM was a devout DC-9 operator before switching to the Boeing 737. The aircraft pictured is a 737-306 (PH-BDA, c/n 23537, l/n 1275) delivered new to KLM on September 30, 1986, being named *Willem Barentsz* in honor of the Dutch explorer. *Courtesy of The Boeing Company*

Hispania Lineas Aereas operated a fleet of eight 737-300s. Interestingly, this pre-delivery photo shows the aircraft sans registration, which was normally painted below the flag. This carrier operated a mixed fleet of Boeing 737s and Sud Caravelle 10s, but ceased operations in 1989. *Courtesy of The Boeing Company*

N3301 (c/n 23181, l/n 1087) was a 737-347, here in the carrier's attractive bare metal paint scheme. After serving Western Airlines for two years this aircraft was taken on by Delta Air Lines after the two carriers merged. *Courtesy of The Boeing Company*

Alaska Airlines has been a prolific operator of the Boeing 737 and now employs an all Boeing fleet, including this 737-490 N794AS (c/n 28889, l/n 3000), which is still active with the carrier. *Courtesy of The Boeing Company*

This 737-4Y0 (G-UKLA, c/n 23865, l/n 1582) has been operated by many carriers, including Air UK, Malaysia Airlines, Modiluft, KLM, and Sky Airlines. Subsequently, this aircraft was converted for cargo and is currently operated by Bluebird Cargo as TF-BBH. *Courtesy of The Boeing Company*

CSA Czech Airlines took delivery of this late model 737-45S from Boeing on January 1, 2000. Since 2010, this aircraft (c/n 28478, l/n 3132) was acquired by UTAir as part of their fleet modernization program, replacing the venerable Tupolev Tu-134. *Courtesy of P. Popelar*

A CSA 737-400 undergoing a heavy maintenance check. The highest level of inspection, called a "D Check," requires the aircraft to be extensively dismantled. Many times these checks involve non-destructive testing for metal fatigue and corrosion using eddy current testing and visual examination. *Courtesy of P. Popelar*

Air Europe operated this 737-4S3 for a short time before being taken on by Dan-Air London and subsequently by British Airways after the merger of the two carriers. Today this airplane is still in service with Comair of South Africa as ZS-OAO. *Courtesy of The Boeing Company*

SmartWings is a low cost carrier based in Prague, Czech Republic. This 737-522 (c/n 26696, l/n 2440) was originally delivered to United Airlines as N951UA in 1993. *Courtesy of P. Popelar*

Looking sharp in a special paint scheme commemorating the Aero A-14 Brandenburg biplane, this 737-55S (OK-DGL, c/n 28472, l/n 3004) was delivered new to CSA on March 18, 1998. *Courtesy of P. Popelar*

A sight that would have seemed very unlikely when the first 737 was built: a 737-59D in Aeroflot Nord colors. This aircraft (c/n 25065, l/n 2028) is currently operated by Kaiser Air, based in Oakland, California. *Courtesy of P. Popelar*

The customary deice procedure being conducted on CSA's OK-CGH (c/n 28469, l/n 2849). *Courtesy of P. Popelar*

In front of The Museum of Flight at Boeing Field, leading the procession is the first 737-500, followed by a 737-300 and a 737-400, showing the size differences between the members of the Classic 737 family. *Courtesy of The Boeing Company*

Courtesy of The Boeing Company

CHAPTER 5

THE "NEXT GENERATION" SERIES: 737-600, -700, -800, -900, AND -900ER

Development of the Next Generation 737

The 737 design had evolved over many years to offer several different passenger capacity options and performance characteristics to meet customer needs. Times were rapidly changing, with the development of superior versions of the CFM56 and improved airfoil designs. Furthermore, a tendency for airlines to use aircraft on longer range flights with necessarily increased time at high altitudes was a growing trend. Airlines sought the latest technology in their aircraft and were generally not brand specific. The Airbus A320, with its CFM56-5 engines, was proving itself to be a formidable competitor. It was selling well, and some airlines were even

An artist's impression of Southwest Airlines' N719SW (c/n 27853, l/n 82, Effectivity YA019), a 737-7H4 which was delivered new to the carrier on August 5, 1998. *Courtesy of Jennings Heilig*

replacing their older 737 models with this distinguished aircraft. To keep sales going strong at Boeing, engineers sought to marry a technologically advanced wing to a first-rate engine and apply them to their time-tested 737 airframe. Boeing set to work on creating an exceptional aircraft that would exceed customers' highest expectations.

The CFM56-7 Engine

As part of CFMI's quest to take advantage of market changes, the company developed a new CFM56 variant with increased fuel efficiency and reduced noise signatures known as the CFM56-7 series. This turbofan engine was similar in basic operation to its predecessor (CFM56-3), but was revised so that it was a more efficient aero engine. The most noticeable change to the CFM56–7 was the fan section. The fan blades were of a wider chord, while the total number of blades was reduced from thirty-eight to twenty-four. These new blades no longer required the mid-span shroud spacer ring evident on the CFM56-3 fan section, and the spinner was a conical shape, in contrast to the dome shape found on earlier engines. The CFM56-7 featured a bypass ratio ranging from 5.5:1 to 5.1:1, depending on the thrust rating, which varied from 19,500 lbs. to 27,300 lbs. Single-crystal blades were used in the high pressure turbine section to improve engine reliability. The earlier CFM56-3 series used a hydro-mechanical unit (HMU), which mechanically scheduled fuel to the engine and was electronically optimized by the power management control (PMC)

computer. The new CFM56-7 series had significant changes made to its control and monitoring systems. Instead of having mechanical linkages between the cockpit and the engine, the CFM56-7 employed a full authority digital engine control (FADEC) adapted from the CFM56-5, as used on the Airbus A320. This was in essence a fly-by-wire control system tied to a digital monitoring system. The FADEC system used many inputs, such as thrust lever position, outside

The heart of the 737NG series was the CFM56-7 turbofan engine, offering higher thrust levels and greater fuel efficiency than the earlier CFM56-3 powering the Classic series 737. *Courtesy of The Boeing Company*

The fan blades of the CFM56-7 engine (left) compared to the CFM56-3 fan blades (right). Notice the CFM56-7 engine has blades with wider chord and the mid-span shroud spacer ring has been deleted. *Author's Collection*

air temperature and pressure, engine rotational speeds, exhaust gas temperature, bleed air extraction, and the use of engine anti-ice, among others. The computer had full authority over the engine's functions, optimizing engine performance based on pilot inputs and current operating conditions.

Captain Ray Craig, a Boeing test pilot, remembered how the CFM56-7 was distinguished from the earlier CFMI engine models:

> Going from the somewhat limited engine control capability on the Classic (CFM56-3) to a FADEC on the -7 makes engine operation carefree. You can just set thrust and the engine will provide. We did have a couple of problems in flight test, and as it turned out that was because one of the vendors had changed a process affecting some of the gears in the hydro-mechanical unit (fuel control), and it was having some failures internally. I guess overall, my experience with the CFM56 has been amazement. It is such a dependable, robust engine. If you don't get 25,000 hours on the wing the airlines are wondering what they did wrong. What they can do with those engines with redesigning and [computer] modeling is tremendous. That's probably the other aspect, besides the wing, that makes the airplane [737] such a great piece of equipment.

The new CFM56-7 series engine offered a nine percent decrease in fuel consumption and fifteen percent lower maintenance costs than the earlier variants. This powerplant also featured easier access for maintenance and longer "on the wing" times, normally in excess of 25,000 hours between overhauls. The CFM56-7 gave the Next Generation 737 significant advantages over the 737 Classic series and was the optimal choice for Boeing's 737NG plan.

The New Wing

The 737NG, a much heavier aircraft than the Classic series, required an entirely new wing and center fuselage section, both in structure and aerodynamics. During the design phase, higher cruise speeds were taken into account by aerodynamicists. Boeing's

Joe Ozimek, vice president of 737 MAX marketing, explained the differences of the wing from earlier designs: "The new wing had more chord and a changed leading edge. The reason for the added chord was to add wing area on the airplane and achieve longer range. Also, the leading edge of the airplane was changed to speed it up. It was a mid-Mach .76–.77 airplane and we wanted it to go .80, so the leading edge was changed, but the wing planform is clearly similar to what we had… ." The size of the wing was increased from 1,135 square feet (on the 737 Classic) to 1,341 square feet, while a minor adjustment was made to the wing sweep from 25 to 25.2 degrees, respectively. Also due to the increased wingspan, two additional flight spoilers and one slat panel were added to each wing.

Boeing Test Pilot Ray Craig worked on the 737NG program and spoke highly of the new wing:

> Another big difference between the Next Generation and the Classic series was the wing. I remember a flight when I was flying one of the first 737NG airplanes (YA231), which was a systems test airplane. It had a full interior, and I was taking it down to the NBAA [National Business Aviation Association] convention. This was 1997, and I was flying it down to Houston or Dallas, Texas. It was the first time a 737NG had been outside of the Northwest. We were at 41,000 feet, doing Mach .80, just cruising along. I remember the controller calls up "Boeing 231, verify type aircraft." [Captain Craig responds] "737." [Controller says] "Is that thing on steroids or something?"

The wing on the 737 Next Generation series was the discriminator from the Classic 737-300, -400, -500 series, and obviously the -100 and -200, with the change in the engine. The testimony is that the MAX wing is not changing. We are adding some split [authors note: "Advanced Technology"] winglets on the tip to make it slightly more efficient, but it is a superb wing. I have had the NG aircraft [during flight test] up to Mach .89 and there was no buffet or issues with the airplane. During the actual test flight program of the NG series I never

New Advanced Technology Wing Improves Performance

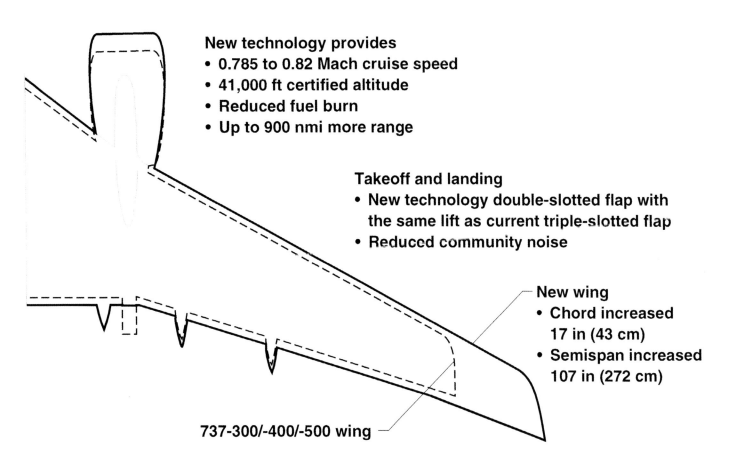

New technology provides
- **0.785 to 0.82 Mach cruise speed**
- **41,000 ft certified altitude**
- **Reduced fuel burn**
- **Up to 900 nmi more range**

Takeoff and landing
- **New technology double-slotted flap with the same lift as current triple-slotted flap**
- **Reduced community noise**

New wing
- **Chord increased 17 in (43 cm)**
- **Semispan increased 107 in (272 cm)**

737-300/-400/-500 wing

The differences between the 737 Classic and 737NG series wings. *Courtesy of The Boeing Company*

737-9AP-410•
5-7-8-DL/LB/LB

had an event that concerned me, or was of issue. We did have some redesigns with the airplane that we found in flight test. We had to go back and do some work on the horizontal tail. They had lightened the structure up too much, based upon the Classic. Because with these new flaps...we had simplified the flap structure, and at flaps 40 we were driving the flaps pretty hard, and had some non-linearity in roll performance. We saw some rapid changes in roll rate [bank] as you got farther out with regard to the aileron and spoiler deflection. It fell back to me with about a month of roll performance on trying to find a nice mix.... There is about a 50 pound assembly in the wheel well called the Spoiler-Mixer. It was a very sophisticated group of cams and was a very reliable system. We spent a good portion of time trying to find the right mix of mechanical cams. We moderated the

non-linearity at flaps 40 and pushed it out farther in the envelope, but we didn't downgrade or degrade roll at other flap settings. Another point: if you extend the flaps, you will see on the flap leading edge what we call "vortilons." Those energized the airflow on the flaps during stalls. I did the actual dispatch deviation guide testing with one wing vortilon missing. You could see the difference in roll performance, because it helps keep the flow attached and eliminates the abruptness [in roll rate] that we had seen.

All Boeing 737s had their main fuel tanks integral to each wing, with a center fuel tank placed between the wing spars in the fuselage center section, just forward of the main landing gear wells. Additional range and fuel capacity was another major factor in the need to redesign the wing for the 737NG. The fuel capacity

Flight Control Changes

On the 737NG, systems were added to the aircraft to enhance controllability in the event of a dual hydraulic failure. The primary flight controls (aileron, elevator, and rudder) were normally driven by both systems (A and B) simultaneously. If the A and B systems failed at the same time, a cable driven backup to the ailerons and elevators was provided for triple redundancy. This situation, called "manual reversion," used pilot muscle power to operate the flight controls through a control surface tab while the standby hydraulic system powered the rudder. Operation in this control regime required substantially more control force by the pilot. Even though this was very manageable, two additional systems were added to assist the pilot. The NG had a second standby yaw damper which could be engaged to stabilize rudder control during manual reversion. Boeing also added the Wheel To Rudder Interconnect System (WTRIS), which used small automatic inputs to the aircraft's rudder system in response to roll control inputs to the ailerons made by the pilot. These operations were invisible to the pilot, but greatly aided in stabilizing the 737NG while in emergency manual reversion flight.

The 737NG Cockpit

Along with new wings and engines, the cockpit of the Next Generation 737 was a major advancement over its predecessors. A full electronic flight instrumentation system (EFIS) was designed by Honeywell (an avionics manufacturer) for installation in the new 737. The liquid crystal displays (LCDs) used light-emitting diodes (LEDs) as backlighting, providing the displays with bright, vivid colors. This technology was a major advancement over traditional cathode-ray tube(CRT) based instrumentation from the 1980s. The full FADEC engine control system (a thrust-by-wire system) was integrated to allow very precise engine management and monitoring. These cockpit upgrades were of paramount importance to the program to keep the 737 competitive for decades to come.

A slight right aileron deflection and the four flight spoilers with automatic cascaded extension on the 737NG. Note the vortex generators on top of the wing. *Author's Collection*

When the speedbrake is deployed by the pilot the flight spoilers deploy on both sides. The black lines on the wing denote the area above the main fuel tank where a small amount of surface frost is permissible due to cold-soaked fuel in the wing tank. *Author's Collection*

volume in the center tank was dramatically increased, allowing a total fuel capacity of 6,875 gallons, compared to the 737 Classic's 5,311 gallon capacity. This increase, combined with the lower fuel burn of the CFM56-7s, created a total range (at maximum payload, not counting reserves) of 3,245 nautical (3,760 statute) miles for the 737-700. This was a substantial increase from 2,270 nautical (2,600 statute) miles for the similarly sized 737-300.

The 737NG cockpit was modern, with a full Electronic Flight Instrumentation System (EFIS), greatly enhancing pilot situational awareness. *Courtesy of The Boeing Company*

A system called Computer Aided Three-Dimensional Interactive Application (CATIA) was developed by Avions Marcel Dassault in 1977 as an in-house tool to digitally design their Mirage fighter jet. After Dassault went public with the software Boeing adopted Version 3 of the software in 1984. This software (Versions 3 and 4) was used extensively in the design of the 777 and was applied to the 737NG to define the aircraft digitally, in three dimensions. This decision facilitated future systems and structural refinements, and helped with the modernization of the cockpit.

The Honeywell EFIS system was selected for the 737NG, but the fleet commonality requirement was still of paramount importance. Boeing had learned lessons on FAA certification and fleet commonality during the Boeing 747-400 program and 757 and 767 programs. Test Pilot Mike Hewett was deeply involved in the project. Capt. Hewett explained:

> I was betting that we could make the same type rating for the Classic and the NG. My job was to take an airplane that had a substantially increased wingspan, more aileron, more thrust—more of everything—and make it feel and fly like the Classic did. The plan was to take the FAA project pilot on the 737NG program and make him part of the team. We brought him in every week to show what we were doing. The agreement that I got with the FAA on same type rating was to bring in thirty experienced line pilots, and with no differences training give them an FAA checkride and measure their performance. The airline pilots came in, walked right through it, and they all loved it.

"Working Together" with the Airlines

Boeing took a proactive stance with the development of the Next Generation 737 and invited airline representatives from around the world to actively participate in the development of this new airplane. Each airline was important, and Boeing listened intently to their needs and desires. Boeing fostered relationships with airlines in Europe, America, and around the world by keeping them informed and seeking input on the planning and development of an exceptional airplane.

In Europe, since many people felt strongly in favor of supporting local jobs, a tremendous amount of political pressure was placed on airlines to buy the Airbus A320. However, Hapag-Lloyd, Germania, and Air Berlin were seeking something else for their fleets. Boeing won them over as customers for the 737NG by displaying a willingness to work with them to create their ideal version of the airplane. Some of the airline representatives who signed contracts with Boeing believed their jobs might be in jeopardy if the aircraft did not develop into an extremely good machine. Boeing's marketing team, recognizing the importance of this trust and the risk these European representatives took, worked alongside them to create a truly competitive airplane. Vice President of Customer Services (at the time) Fred Mitchell remembered: "So we saw a need to bring airline representatives together. Jack Gucker was the Director of Engineering in those days—an old-school kind of guy—and he said, '…So what we are going to do is to bring the customers right along with us.' They were tremendous people who stuck with us through all of the trials and tribulation of inventing an airplane." Boeing's people valued their launch customers' input (including Europeans), and together, they designed the 737NG to the highest standard.

There were several different ideas on how to configure the EFIS instrument presentations in the 737-700 cockpit. Launch customer Southwest Airlines wanted the 737NG cockpit to be similar to its existing fleet of analog 737-200s, 737-300s, and 737-500s. The idea was to have enough similarity to allow a pilot the ability to operate the Originals, Classics, and NGs with ease and be cross-qualified on all of them at once. Any pilot in the airline would then be able to operate any aircraft in the fleet at any time without the need to retrain. Mike Hewett remembered the situation:

> It actually got down to the point where our marketing guy, [our Program Vice President] Gordon Bethune, and the training guys went to Southwest. Not only did they guarantee that it would have a same type rating, but they said in this meeting that the differences training would be less than eight hours...of total training! The whole thing couldn't pull a pilot off duty for more than eight hours.

As one can imagine, it was a monumental task to take what was largely a new aircraft and make it similar enough to meet such strict demands, and have it all approved by the FAA. For Southwest's operation this made good financial sense. For Boeing, it set up a gauntlet of challenges for the designers of the 737NG. The quest for FAA approval of a same type rating for the 737NG went far beyond the design of the aircraft itself. Boeing had to work with the FAA to develop training curriculums and set experience and currency requirements for pilots. Because of the effort put forth by Boeing, the 737NG was deemed similar enough to allow pilots to be cross qualified between the Originals, Classics, and the 737NG with a short differences course.

Air Berlin was one of the earliest customers for the 737-700 and participated actively in the development of the aircraft. D-AHXE (c/n 35135, l/n 2451) was delivered to TUIfly on December 3, 2007, and was being operated for Air Berlin under a partnership agreement between the two carriers. *Courtesy of Jennings Heilig*

Software-Loadable Display Formats Provide Operators Increased Flexibility

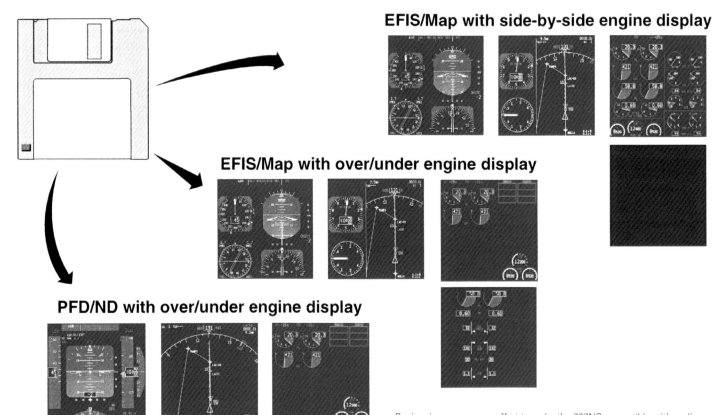

EFIS/Map with side-by-side engine display

EFIS/Map with over/under engine display

PFD/ND with over/under engine display

Boeing, in an enormous effort to make the 737NG compatible with earlier 737 generations, devised a software change that could depict the modern primary flight displays (PFDs) or a traditional "six pack" flight instrument display. Alaska opted for the PFD/ND display option, while Southwest initially used the EFIS/Map with side-by-side engine display. *Courtesy of The Boeing Company*

737-9FD-084•
3-11-6-DH

On the other end of the spectrum, Capt. Steve Fulton of Alaska Airlines had different ideas. Many airports that were served by Alaska had extensive terrain challenges which made traditional ground-based instrument approaches and departures difficult, if not impossible to employ. Alaska Airlines saw the 737NG as their opportunity to pioneer new instrument approaches to satisfy their operational needs. Global Positioning System (GPS) technology was embraced on the 737NG and became the basis for the next generation of instrument approach and departure procedures. The Alaska 737NG required a full electronic flight instrumentation system (EFIS), complete with a moving map and a way for the pilot to monitor the positional accuracy of the aircraft throughout the flight. This could not be done with traditional analog instrumentation effectively, hence the need for a full EFIS system on the 737NG.

The diametrically opposed needs of Southwest Airlines and Alaska Airlines placed Boeing's 737 flight deck design team in a difficult position. Both carriers had good reasons for their cockpit

design preferences and were not able to compromise. This dynamic led Boeing's cockpit designers to make a very interesting decision. They used the new EFIS system, designed with the flexibility to alter the look of the visual displays, to create two distinctly different software packages. One was perfect for Southwest, with a digital representation of the traditional "six pack" instrument setup, designed to mimic the electro-mechanical instrument installation on the 737-200s, 737-300s, and 737-500s serving in their fleet. The inclusion of a moving map with the displays enhanced the pilot's situational awareness and caused only minimal training requirements. For Alaska Airlines, another software package used the innovative Primary Flight Display (PFD) previously introduced on the 777, supplying pilots with more trend information, as well as navigational accuracy scales needed for future GPS-based Required Navigation Performance (RNP) operations. Additionally, an aircraft could be readily switched from one display to another by maintenance technicians. This not only made selling the aircraft from one airline to another simple, it allowed airlines like Southwest to eventually adopt RNP operations and switch to the PFD format after the last of the 737-200 series were retired. At that point, FAA approval to cross-train pilots on the Classics and the PFD equipped 737-700 was obtained. The aircraft required no modifications other than a software change, enabling Southwest to embrace the Next Generation navigation technology eight years later and allowing a pilot to be qualified on all of the aircraft in their fleet. Boeing's Capt. Ray Craig felt the flight instrumentation on the NG "worked right out of the box" with no major issues. Many years of operation proved this system to be reliable, with less maintenance costs than the electro-mechanical instrumentation.

Systems Differences

Boeing sought to keep as much commonality as possible between the Next Generation 737 and the legacy Classic series. Making the airplanes similar from the pilot's perspective allowed them to be cross qualified on both, with minimal differences training. Boeing test pilot Capt. Ray Craig worked on maintaining commonality: "The goal from the Classic to the NG was one day of differences training [for pilots], with no simulator required. So we were striving to keep, as much as we could, similar handling qualities and minimize the training differences for the airlines." Aside from the addition of EFIS flight instrumentation to the flight deck (which could be configured with software to be visually similar to the Classics), most of the other changes made to the 737NG series were not of any major consequence to the flight crew. The aircraft was designed to handle similarly to the earlier models, and Boeing retained a comparable overhead panel for operation of the aircraft systems.

The most significant system changes made were to the electrical system. Higher output integrated drive generators (IDGs) were installed on each engine and in most cases one operative IDG could shoulder most, if not all of the aircraft's electrical loads. This provided greater redundancy compared to the Classic series. The earlier aircraft had generators coupled to the engines by constant speed drive (CSD) units, which fed power to their respective generator busses. If a generator was lost on the Classic, the respective generator bus also lost power. This caused the loss of some interior and exterior aircraft lighting, as well as galley power, depending on electrical demands at the time. On the 737NG, the IDGs fed electrical power directly to their respective transfer bus. In the event of an IDG failure the loads are automatically transferred to the remaining power source, hence the name "transfer bus." Since the NG did not have generator busses like the Classics no systems were typically lost. However, when exceptionally high loads were sensed, power to the aircraft's galleys were shed to protect the system. Because of the higher electrical loads required by the EFIS systems and their associated electronics, higher output transformer rectifier (TR) units were installed. These were used to convert 115 volt AC power into 28 volt DC power for certain electronic systems. There were also some small differences on how the system automatically transferred loads during electrical malfunctions. The Classic and the NG electrical systems were still more similar than different, and for the pilot nearly identical in operation. The fuel system was also slightly different, but like the electrical system, it was operated in the same way by the pilot. The most significant difference between the two aircraft was the larger center fuel tank capacity of the 737NG, which, coupled with more fuel efficient engines, allowed a much longer range.

The 737-700

The first of the 737 Next Generation series introduced into the marketplace (737-700) was ordered by launch customer Southwest Airlines in November 1993. This new aircraft offered seating for a maximum of 149 passengers, but was more commonly equipped for a high density seating of 143. The 737-700 was similar in size to the 737-300, measuring out to 110 ft., 4 in. in total length, just 4 ft. 9 in. longer than its predecessor. Designed with the larger wing, the 737-700 had more lifting capability, available engine power, and volumetric fuel capacity than the 737 Classic fleet. Boeing offered its 737-700 customers three engine options to optimize the aircraft and tailor it to their specifications: the CFM56-7B20 (20,600 lb.), CFM56-7B22 (22,700 lb.), and the CFM56-7B24 (24,200 lb.), with corresponding maximum gross takeoff weight options of up to 155,500 (some later variants up to 171,500) pounds. The 737-700, when equipped with the highest thrust and gross weight options, could carry a full passenger load up to 3,245 nautical (3,760 statute) miles with standard fuel tanks. All versions of the 737-700 had far greater range than the Classic series and could comfortably fly many over water routes new to the 737. This meant that if desired, the 737-700 could travel the 2,226 NM flight from San Diego, California, to Honolulu, Hawaii, with ease.

737-700 Flight Test

During test flights most airplanes have some issues that crop up, and the 737-700 was no exception. Significant alterations were made to the main landing gear so it could support the higher weight limits of the aircraft. Earlier 737 models had a device called a shimmy damper on each main gear leg that prevented the dual wheel assembly from vibrating and cycling back and fourth during landings and heavy braking. Due to the geometry of the newly designed NG gear

The rollout ceremony for the 737-700 Prototype (c/n 27841, l/n 1, Effectivity YA001) occurred on December 8, 1996. Tail logos for each of the airline and leasing company customers were applied to the side of the aircraft, a long-standing Boeing tradition. *Courtesy of The Boeing Company and Jennings Heilig*

YA001, the 737-700 prototype, is seen taxiing out at Renton, Washington. From this perspective it is clear the wings on the 737-700 are much larger than its predecessors. Early 737NGs were delivered without blended winglets and this aircraft is equipped with the original wingtips that are rarely seen today. *Courtesy of The Boeing Company*

off the aircraft. At the postflight meeting I said, 'We've got a shimmy problem and it shook the heck out of the airplane.'" It was extremely fortunate, however, that the cast attachment fittings for the shimmy damper were retained in the design of the new landing gear, because this problem began to crop up again during certification of the Head-Up Guidance System (HGS). Cameras were used to view the touchdown of the main landing gears to certify the accuracy of low visibility landings with the HGS. In the footage, the main wheel trucks were clearly seen vibrating back and forth quite rapidly, along with the intense shimmy that was also felt in the cockpit. Test pilots found it interesting that the smoother the landing, the worse the shimmy became. Eventually, it was deemed necessary to install shimmy dampers to prevent this phenomenon. Production of the damper units began, and in a short period of time they were fitted on to all of the aircraft. At about eighty pounds a piece the damper units added some measure of weight penalty.

High speed testing proceeded without incident until an inexplicable high frequency buzz was felt in the cockpit. It appeared to transmit through the fuselage at airspeeds around 300 knots. Its onset and dissipation was sudden, as the speed of 300 knots was transitioned during acceleration and deceleration. The source of this vibration was not immediately discovered, but the flight test program was allowed to continue as scheduled while engineers researched its cause.

On the other end of the speed spectrum stall testing commenced. Conducting stalls creates a "buffet," or shaking of the airplane when the airspeed is very low. The effect is caused by the turbulent airflow from the wing interfering with the airflow over the tail of the aircraft. As in all new aircraft designs, there was significant

it was believed it would be self-damping, thus the shimmy dampers were removed. Capt. Hewett was there: "I went out on the maiden flight [of the 737-700 prototype]. I had to stay below 250 knots and the airplane flew well. I came in and did the landing and tried to do a smooth landing with people watching me along the runway at Boeing. I managed to actually grease one on the runway and the airplane shook so badly, I thought the panels were going to come

The 737-700 prototype in formation with a Northrop T-38 chase plane. This aircraft first flew on February 9, 1997, under the command of Capts. Mike Hewett and Ken Higgins. *Courtesy of The Museum of Flight*

Capts. Ken Higgins (left) and Mike Hewett (right) seen prior to a test flight of YA001. *Courtesy of The Boeing Company*

flight testing required to develop low stall speeds with acceptable handling qualities. Through the use of aerodynamic devices such as vortex generators and stall strips FAA criteria was met.

Although necessary, stall testing had the adverse effect of creating a lot of stress on the horizontal stabilizers, elevators, and their attached servo tabs. To this end, after the stall program was

This view of the wing of a 737-700 in flight shows the eight small vortex generators installed on top of the wing midspan. *Author's Collection*

Visible just below the inboard leading edge of the wing is the metal stall strip designed to ensure the inboard portions of the wing stall first, effecting a nose-down pitching moment to improve handling. *Author's Collection*

conducted with the aircraft the tail was taken apart and inspected for damage. The inspection revealed cracks in the elevator to servo tab hinges, which turned out to be the cause of the 300 knot buzz. A more robust horizontal stabilizer was created for the production aircraft.

One change that occurred very late in the 737NG program was the redesign of the overwing exit hatches. The older designs required the exit to be lifted, pulled inside the aircraft, and either placed on the adjacent seat row or discarded out on to the aircraft's wing. The new design had the exit open outward, with a lift and hinge mechanism moving the door up and out of the way. The revised exit hatches were a significant safety improvement, allowing faster egress and were extremely easy to open. The 737-700 completed FAA certification on November 7, 1997, and the first aircraft was delivered to Southwest Airlines on December 17, 1997. Type validation was granted by the European Joint Aviation Authorities (JAA) on February 19, 1998.

The 737-800

Boeing created time-tested, exceptional aircraft that gained the innovative company many longstanding customers. Boeing's ability to maintain these relationships was predicated on carefully listening to its customers and striving to meet their needs. Wolfgang Kurth, leader of Hapag-Lloyd, was especially interested in a larger version of the 737 that could be operated in a high-density cabin configuration. He approached Boeing with a request to design a follow-on variant with greater seating capacity than the 143 seats available in the 737-700. To accommodate the German charter's appeal, Boeing revised the 737-700 series airframe with a 19 ft. 2 in. fuselage extension. This modification increased the aircraft's passenger seating by forty-five to a maximum capacity of 189. Similar to the 737-400,

The tail skid assembly as installed on the lower rear fuselage of a 737-8H4. Note the red and green serviceability placard installed. *Author's Collection*

lengthening the fuselage required the installation of a tail skid to protect the rear fuselage against a possible tail strike and subsequent damage during takeoff. A crushable cartridge was attached to the skid with a crush indicator that was visible to pilots and mechanics during a walk-around. The wing on the 737-800 shared the same shape and dimensions as the 737-700, but was enhanced with thicker gauge materials, increasing structur-

al strength for higher operating weights. As with other aircraft in the 737 family, the airlines could choose an engine thrust option to best fit their needs. These available thrust options were: CFM56-7B24 (24,200 lbs.), CFM56-7B26 (26,400 lbs.), and CFM56-7B27 (27,300 lbs.). This robust aircraft, later known as the 737-800, had a maximum range of 2,930 nautical (3,386 statute) miles when equipped with the high thrust CFM56-7B27.

KLM (Royal Dutch Airlines) is one of the oldest airlines, dating to 1919. PH-BXA (c/n 29131, l/n 198) is a 737-806 delivered on February 25, 1999. This aircraft was the first of the series delivered to KLM. *Courtesy of Jennings Heilig*

The 737-800 series was formally launched in November 1994, with an order from Hapag-Lloyd for sixteen aircraft. This was soon followed by an order from Air Berlin for six airplanes in December 1994. The 737-800 prototype (N737BX, c/n 27981, l/n 7) took its inaugural flight on July 31, 1997, under the command of Capts. Mike Hewett and Jim McRoberts. This historic flight departed Renton Municipal Airport at 9:00 a.m. and lasted three hours five minutes. Flight testing was conducted until FAA certification was achieved on March 13, 1998. The first of this series, a 737-8K5 (D-AHFC, c/n 27977, l/n 9), was delivered to launch customer Hapag-Lloyd on April 22, 1998.

The combination of excellent range, economy, and high passenger capacity truly positioned the 737-800 in the "sweet

On June 30, 1997, the 737-800 prototype was rolled out of the Renton assembly hall. This aircraft (c/n 27981, l/n 7) was the 2,906th Boeing 737 built, and after flight testing was delivered to Hapag-Lloyd as D-AHFA on December 29, 1998. *Courtesy of The Boeing Company*

spot" of the market, as passenger numbers have been increasing the last few years. According to *Dallas News*, Southwest Airlines' Chief Executive Officer Gary Kelly spoke of the new aircraft at a company party celebrating the arrival of their first 737-800; "The 800 is a game changer," he said. Southwest's Chief Operations Officer Mike Van de Ven referred to the -800 as a "trifecta win" and continued to say, "It is

A first flight cover flown on the 737-800. *Author's Collection*

good for our customers. It is good for our shareholders. It is good for our employees." According to *PRNewswire*, in 2015, Ryanair's Chief Operations Officer Mick Hickey said: "As Europe's largest airline, the reliability and customer appeal of the Boeing 737-800 aircraft has been the cornerstone of our successful growth over the last sixteen years… . Our current and future Boeing orders will allow us to grow our fleet to over 540 all-Boeing aircraft, which will see our traffic double from 90 million annual customers last year to 180 per annum by 2024."

Boeing's sales numbers for the 737-800 reflect the popularity of this outstanding aircraft. By January 31, 2017, Boeing 737-800 series aircraft sales totaled 5,022 airplanes. Furthermore, it outsold every other single 737 variant by a factor of four and constituted nearly half the total 737 (all series) sales combined! As with the rest of the 737 family, the 737-800 became known for incredible reliability. In fact, in 2012, a CFM56-7B mounted on a 737-800 was the first aero engine in history to remain in service for 50,000 hours without an overhaul visit.

Production Challenges

The incredible growth of 737 sales in the mid-1990s stretched Boeing's production lines to new limits. The facility in Renton, Washington, was working to assemble the 757 and Classic 737 line (-300/-400/-500) on the production floor when the new 737-700 was dovetailed in. Although the Classic 737s were similar to one another, they were not at all identical from a production standpoint. In particular, the 737-400 used thicker fuselage and wing skins, and even had many different landing gear components. Introducing the new 737-700 into the mix dramatically increased these complexities. The 737-700 aircraft had an entirely new wing and many systems components were different. Consequently, there was little parts commonality with other aircraft sharing the production line and crews had to work long overtime shifts to keep deliveries on track. To some extent, it was "the perfect storm" of circumstances when high sales, taxed labor resources, and the introduction of a new model occurred at the same time. The Renton factory used a complex system that required timely parts delivery for successful production. It was called the "Just In Time" parts system, since they did not want extra parts laying around taking up valuable space and cluttering the area. But a worse situation occurred when, even with their combined energies, the crews could not keep up with the frantic pace of the production line.

In late 1997, the production line began to log jam because of a shortage of parts and the situation quickly turned desperate. Peter Morton, who was in charge of leadership training at the time, explained the Boeing mindset, "Delivering airplanes late at Boeing is unbelievably wrong, morally, ethically, religiously…any phrase you want. It never happens." This unprecedented dynamic gained momentum as parts were delivered to the factory out of sequence. The key problem on the production line was that it could not be stopped to wait for a particular component. Consequently, as the first fifteen 737NG aircraft moved through the production line only available parts were installed and the planes exited the line incomplete and only partially assembled. They were then moved to a holding area outside the factory to

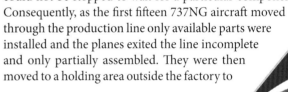

An artist's rendering of Aeroflot's 737-8LJ VP-BRH (c/n 41196, l/n 4665), christened *Kustodiev*, after the famous Russian artist. This aircraft was delivered new to Aeroflot on October 30, 2013. *Courtesy of Jennings Heilig*

wait for the remaining parts. When the requisite components arrived many hours of rework were required, since some of the missing parts had to be installed behind parts already in place. Then, to make matters worse, the European certification agency (CAA) required Boeing install outward-opening overwing emergency exits as opposed to the inward opening hatches standard on the 737 Classic. As Boeing personnel scrambled to create the door they found an already completed design at their facility in Wichita, Kansas, that met these requirements. The door was quickly built to be retrofitted to the existing 737NG aircraft. Ten aircraft that were still in the

Renton factory needed to be modified with the door. Additionally, the fifteen 737NGs that had already left the line to await parts needed to be reworked.

The production issues seemed impossible to fix and turnover was becoming commonplace in management. After Bob Dryden retired Fred Mitchell became Boeing's executive vice president of airplane production, managing the assembly lines in Renton, Everett, and the newly acquired McDonnell Douglas plant in Long Beach. Mitchell devised a plan to recover from the production crisis. A lot of customer contact was required, juggling of delivery schedules, and dealing with ruffled feathers. Fred had previously been VP of customer services, and was well equipped to manage customer contacts. The following year, according to Mitchell: "was a huge recovery program at the Boeing Company. We had to fly about fifteen [737-700] aircraft down to Douglas and we delivered aircraft out of the Long Beach facility. We had to show the customers that we were doing everything within our control to deliver these aircraft." With the incredible effort and perseverance of Fred Mitchell and thousands of others Boeing showed that it was indeed up to the task. Production rates recovered and important lessons were learned.

"Lean Manufacturing" and the 737

Many of the heads and managers in the Boeing Company traveled to Japan in the early 1990s to study the manufacturing practices of companies like Toyota. With the 1997 production struggle behind them, Boeing leaders focused their efforts on finding ways to raise production rates without a repeat of past mistakes. Toyota had incorporated techniques into its assembly line that made it superior to processes practiced in the United States. Bruce Gissing, who escorted Boeing management to Japan, showed them how Japanese companies managed their manufacturing to get more volume with less rework. This concept was coined "lean manufacturing," and could be adapted to a variety of business models and factory types. Touring the Toyota facility was so insightful that after the initial visit all senior management for the 737 production line went to Japan for two weeks to see it for themselves. Managers used ideas generated from Toyota to create their own version of "lean" and identified and corrected weak areas on the production floor.

The lean manufacturing concept originated with the Toyota production system (TPS). It is believed that TPS was developed in 1934, at Sakichi Toyoda's automobile factory, and gained momentum during the 1950s. This philosophy was centered on the elimination of *Muda* (waste) within a manufacturing program. This waste could occur because of *Muri* (overburden), or an unevenness of *Mura* (task loads) along an assembly line. "Load leveling," as it was called, kept each facet of an assembly line working at optimum speed. If a portion of the factory completed its task before the next station was ready to take over then the first station operated under a "push" scenario and a wasteful log jam was created. Boeing's vice president and general manager of the 737 MAX, Keith Leverkuhn, explained how the push scenario affected the production line. "How do I take flow out? I can take flow out here, but up front they are not ready for it because they haven't taken their flow out. That's not so great, because now you have invested something, but you can't take advantage of it." The lean concept encouraged a gain in efficiency by making changes

where the vehicle rolled out the door and then working backward to the beginning to maintain a balance of workload. This was considered a "pull" situation, which was ideal for efficiency when coupled with a just in time (JIT) inventory system. The JIT inventory system saw parts arrive just as they were ready to be installed. The amount of inventory on hand was considered an important metric to gauge the success of a lean program and any extra inventory was considered waste.

Using lean concepts, leadership at Boeing made provisions to effectively recognize and manage flow delays on the production floor. To make the status of a particular station obvious to everyone involved a light system was installed. Green lights meant everything at the station was on schedule and progress was continuous. If amber lights illuminated, this showed a delay of more than a few minutes was being experienced and assistance or additional resources were needed to prevent stopping the line. If a delay became excessive blue lights turned on to indicate that every resource available was required to get that station back on schedule. The Renton factory had three lines, and each aircraft progressed down the line in which it started its assembly. If there was a significant delay on an assembly position it could potentially stop the progression of that entire line, which was highly undesirable. The first priority was to make sure everyone involved was aware of the status and this system did this effectively. Even small details in the layout of the facility had a big impact. For example, the production line managers, because of their job requirements, spent most of their time inside their offices, away from the production line. To stay in tune with the happenings on the production floor the office layout was rearranged. The new layout required managers to walk along the assembly line to arrive at their offices. This small detail had a profound effect on their knowledge and awareness of what was happening on the floor each day.

Boeing's Learning, Education, and Development department encouraged employees to creatively explore lean ways to make manufacturing equipment more compact, easier to operate, and less expensive to manage. Through this venue a program called "The Lean Green Training Machine" was created, consisting of portable learning stations. These mobile classrooms moved around the factory floor, bringing lean educational opportunities right to the employees. Similar to golf carts, these vehicles had fold down tables and were Internet capable for computer-based training. This system saved time which might be wasted for employees to relocate themselves to a classroom. It also reduced costs and provided education on updates while winning the favor of the employee group. Boeing took the opportunity to invest in its people, allowing lean principles and mind-sets to be successfully implemented throughout the company. This philosophy was put into action again at Renton when an employee who was working on the Boeing 757 line came up with an idea. A crew was spending many hours lifting passenger seats up and through the cabin doors prior to installation. He saw this as wasteful and thought an automatic hay bailer might work to deliver the seats to the cabin at a faster rate. Boeing rented one and tried it. It worked beautifully and cut the time spent installing seats at that station by a significant amount.

Factors that made aircraft production different from automotive manufacturing had to be accounted for and caused subtle changes

737 Production Flow

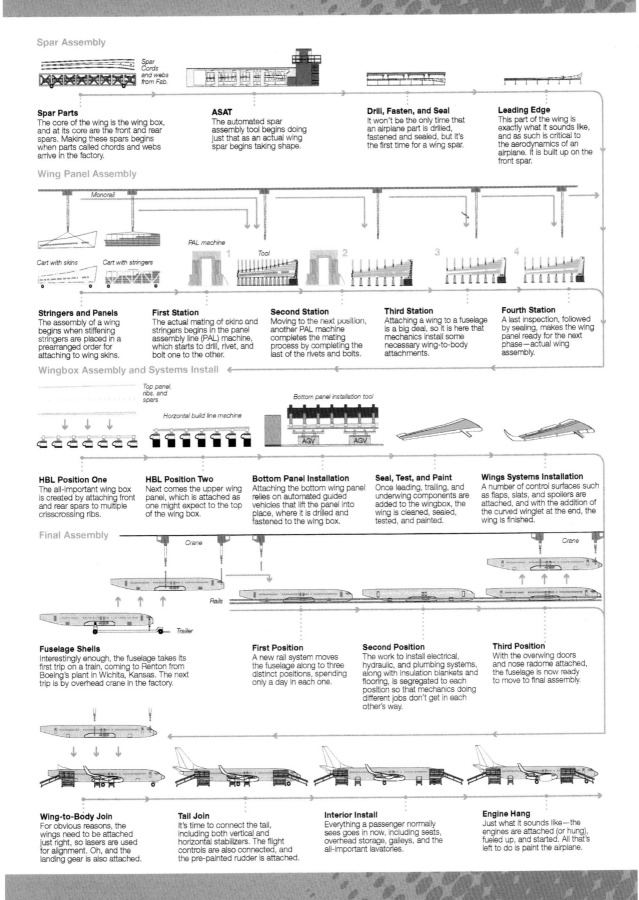

Spar Assembly

Spar Parts
The core of the wing is the wing box, and at its core are the front and rear spars. Making these spars begins when parts called chords and webs arrive in the factory.

ASAT
The automated spar assembly tool begins doing just that as an actual wing spar begins taking shape.

Drill, Fasten, and Seal
It won't be the only time that an airplane part is drilled, fastened and sealed, but it's the first time for a wing spar.

Leading Edge
This part of the wing is exactly what it sounds like, and as such is critical to the aerodynamics of an airplane. It is built up on the front spar.

Wing Panel Assembly

Stringers and Panels
The assembly of a wing begins when stiffening stringers are placed in a prearranged order for attaching to wing skins.

First Station
The actual mating of skins and stringers begins in the panel assembly line (PAL) machine, which starts to drill, rivet, and bolt one to the other.

Second Station
Moving to the next position, another PAL machine completes the mating process by completing the last of the rivets and bolts.

Third Station
Attaching a wing to a fuselage is a big deal, so it is here that mechanics install some necessary wing-to-body attachments.

Fourth Station
A last inspection, followed by sealing, makes the wing panel ready for the next phase—actual wing assembly.

Wingbox Assembly and Systems Install

HBL Position One
The all-important wing box is created by attaching front and rear spars to multiple crisscrossing ribs.

HBL Position Two
Next comes the upper wing panel, which is attached as one might expect to the top of the wing box.

Bottom Panel Installation
Attaching the bottom wing panel relies on automated guided vehicles that lift the panel into place, where it is drilled and fastened to the wing box.

Seal, Test, and Paint
Once leading, trailing, and underwing components are added to the wingbox, the wing is cleaned, sealed, tested, and painted.

Wings Systems Installation
A number of control surfaces such as flaps, slats, and spoilers are attached, and with the addition of the curved winglet at the end, the wing is finished.

Final Assembly

Fuselage Shells
Interestingly enough, the fuselage takes its first trip on a train, coming to Renton from Boeing's plant in Wichita, Kansas. The next trip is by overhead crane in the factory.

First Position
A new rail system moves the fuselage along to three distinct positions, spending only a day in each one.

Second Position
The work to install electrical, hydraulic, and plumbing systems, along with insulation blankets and flooring, is segregated to each position so that mechanics doing different jobs don't get in each other's way.

Third Position
With the overwing doors and nose radome attached, the fuselage is now ready to move to final assembly.

Wing-to-Body Join
For obvious reasons, the wings need to be attached just right, so lasers are used for alignment. Oh, and the landing gear is also attached.

Tail Join
It's time to connect the tail, including both vertical and horizontal stabilizers. The flight controls are also connected, and the pre-painted rudder is attached.

Interior Install
Everything a passenger normally sees goes in now, including seats, overhead storage, galleys, and the all-important lavatories.

Engine Hang
Just what it sounds like—the engines are attached (or hung), fueled up, and started. All that's left to do is paint the airplane.

This diagram shows the production flow of the 737NG and 737 MAX assembly lines in Renton. *Courtesy of The Boeing Company*

One example of Boeing's willingness to apply input from its people resulted in the development of this machine, used to deliver cabin seats to the aircraft cabin at a much higher rate than previously possible. *Courtesy of The Boeing Company*

to the way lean philosophies were implemented. Boeing's vice president and program manager for the 737 MAX Keith Leverkuhn explained:

It really started using the Toyota system. Looking at our current state maps...our future maps with the Kaizens [continuous improvement], it is really a Boeing lean production system. What Toyota does is very valuable and helped us on the journey, but it has really become tailored specifically to what's happening at Boeing now, while its roots were certainly in our understanding of what Toyota was doing, and a lot of the tool sets that they are using have helped us. Transitioning that model to building airplanes is not just a one-for-one graft. So that too has been a journey in figuring out our lean processes. We didn't change the footprint [of the Renton factory], so therefore how did we increase the throughput? It has been an interactive process on the NGs. Listening to the mechanics, working with the industrial engineers, and fully understanding the benefits of taking flow out. You can't put a dollar figure on flow. If we can increase the flow by six hours in this particular job, that might not help me if that job is then bottlenecked at another stage. But then you go through a constant process of trying to figure out how can we take flow out of each step and that iteration allows you

to all of a sudden take advantage. Now we have taken an entire flow day out of the operation. So now I can book that in increasing rates. The zeal about quality, the zeal about flow, and allowing the mechanics and the engineers to work together to figure out how to take the hours out of how we build this thing. It wasn't a big homer on any given day, it has been iterative over the years.

Chihiro Nakao, a leading lean manufacturing consultant, was quoted as saying, "To make planes is to make and develop people." Successes occur when employees are proactive, feel valued, and know they can and do make a difference. Empowering people is an important tenant of the lean system. Today, Boeing's Renton factory practices lean principles on its moving assembly lines to achieve maximum output. At the start of the day crews prepare a 737 airframe for engine installation. Adjacent to and one slot ahead of this point two CFM56 engines are wheeled in on specially designed cradles. During the day the engines are prepared for airframe mounting as accessories and inlet cowls are installed. Overnight, the airframe is moved forward to the next station and the engines are brought out for installation. This process is renewed daily, with two more engines and an airframe being prepared for the next day. Almost always the process clicks along like a sewing machine and works perfectly on time.

Except for the very first airplanes built, the fuselages for the 737 program are built in Wichita, Kansas. This is the early part of the assembly process with a lower forward fuselage section. *Courtesy of The Boeing Company*

The upper forward fuselage section is added to this early 737-700. The later model aircraft (after c/n 32482, l/n 1638, Effectivity YA197) were not produced with the "eyebrow" windows and had vortex generators added to the nose just forward of the windshields to reduce cockpit noise. *Courtesy of The Boeing Company*

This completed 737-700 fuselage is lifted away from the assembly area and prepared for transport to Renton, Washington. *Courtesy of The Boeing Company*

Boeing transports 737 fuselages from Wichita, Kansas, to Renton, Washington, on specially made rail cars. *Courtesy of The Boeing Company*

Boeing's Renton assembly hall as viewed from Rainier Avenue North, across Runway 16/34. *Author's Collection*

The "Wing Join" procedure is being conducted on this 737-800. This procedure has been refined with the use of specialized jacks, allowing accuracy to a fraction of a millimeter. *Author's Collection with permission from Boeing*

The trailing edge flaps and hydraulic systems of this 737-800 are being tested. During the night this aircraft will move to the next station on the assembly line. *Author's Collection with permission from Boeing*

These horizontal stabilizers are prepared for installation on the aircraft. Each one will be wheeled out on the assembly floor, where an overhead crane will lift them off their trolleys and into position on the aircraft. Two of the attach points for the crane can be seen temporarily installed on the upper surface. *Author's Collection with permission from Boeing*

This CFM56-7 turbofan engine has just been installed on a 737-800. Note the temporary scaffolding on top of the wing and fuselage, which moves with the aircraft until assembly is complete. *Author's Collection with permission from Boeing*

737s move through the final assembly areas nose to tail, unlike the forty-five degree parking that was standard during the production of the Original and Classic series. This aircraft is a 737-7H4 for Southwest Airlines. Rudders are painted in advance because they must be carefully balanced prior to installation. Note the early wingtips on this example. *Courtesy of The Boeing Company*

This 737-85C (c/n 40959, l/n 5634) was nearly complete, and would fly for the first time eleven days later on October 17, 2015. This aircraft is now operated by Xiamen Airlines of China. *Author's Collection with permission from Boeing*

These factory fresh 737s are awaiting their first flights. Aircraft are painted in Renton when capacity permits, but the majority have their first flight with only the rudder and winglets painted, never to return to their birthplace. The paint facility at Boeing Field is used to paint most of the 737s produced. *Author's Collection*

This 737-8U3 (c/n 41812, l/n 5613) was beginning to roll on its first takeoff. On October 18, 2015, this aircraft was delivered to Garuda Airlines of Indonesia. *Author's Collection*

BBJ first flight cover. *Author's Collection*

The Boeing Business Jet, Hapag-Lloyd, and Winglets

Boeing Business Jets was in the midst of selling the 737-700 as a factory direct executive jet. In this configuration, the 737 was called the "BBJ," and was modified to allow direct competition with the Gulfstream V corporate jet. The fuel system consisted of nine additional fuel cells in the underfloor baggage compartment areas. These delivered additional fuel to the center fuel tank in flight and nearly doubled the range of the BBJ over a stock 737-700. Still more range was needed to match the 6,200 mile capability of the Gulfstream. Initially, the idea was to add a tenth fuel cell in the aft fuselage, but space in that area of the aircraft was limited because several other fuel tanks had been added in this section. The BBJ had a tendency to be nose heavy because weighty items such as galleys and lavatory options were typically positioned near the front of the aircraft, so adding more fuel space to the aft baggage compartment would help from a balance standpoint, but they were nearly out of space.

Steve Taylor, recently president of Boeing Business Jets, explained how technical problems affected the tenth fuel tank:

> The tenth tank was going to go back where the waste water tank was, [behind] the aft baggage door. The problem with it was...once you put it in, you couldn't get to the waste tank or the potable water tank [for maintenance] without having to take the tenth tank back out. To take the tenth tank out...you had to start by taking the baggage door off, then you had to take the ninth and eighth tank out to get room to slide the [tenth] tank down and get it back out. We were just terrified about what the maintenance implications were going to be with that tank. When Bernie Gratzer [lead engineer with Aviation Partners] came along [with the blended winglet] and said, "We can get you 7%," that completely changed the nature of the airplane.

As Steve Taylor mentioned, this fuel tank and range issue caused one other change to be made to the BBJ airframe: the adoption of the blended winglet. Blended winglets for the BBJ were introduced by a contractor named Aviation Partners, owned and operated by Joe Clark. In the late 1990s, blended winglets

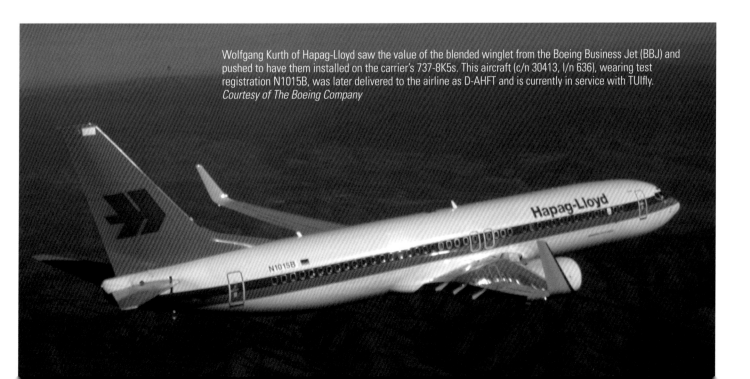

Wolfgang Kurth of Hapag-Lloyd saw the value of the blended winglet from the Boeing Business Jet (BBJ) and pushed to have them installed on the carrier's 737-8K5s. This aircraft (c/n 30413, l/n 636), wearing test registration N1015B, was later delivered to the airline as D-AHFT and is currently in service with TUIfly. *Courtesy of The Boeing Company*

were still quite new and were being retrofitted on several business jets. They were also slated to be installed on all BBJ aircraft. Winglets were an interesting phenomenon that proved some of the limitations of old school wind tunnel aerodynamic development. Since the blended winglets appeared to provide very little aerodynamic drag reduction in the wind tunnel some aerodynamicists were skeptical about the winglets' benefits to the 737 airframe. In addition to wind tunnel testing, Computational Fluid Dynamics (CFD) calculations were fast becoming a mainstream technology with many designs. Where the wind tunnel showed very small improvement (if any), the CFD calculations revealed marked fuel efficiency and aircraft range increases, especially on longer flights. While these calculations were promising, Boeing had yet to test the new blended winglets on the 737NG. President of Boeing Business Jets Borge Boeskov needed some empirical flight test data proving the winglets would increase range. Boeing was trying to effect a recovery from the 1996 production upset and resources were tapped to their limits. Given the challenges that Boeing faced additional research and design capacity was not easily available to accommodate Boeskov's request. Boeskov knew this, but dearly needed hard flight test data so he could advertise solid performance specifications for the BBJ.

Fred Mitchell remembered the day he received a visit from Borge Boeskov:

> Borge was a friend to everybody in the world. He knew Herb [Kelleher of Southwest] personally, he knew Lord King [of British Airways] personally…and he was just this cool guy. So here I am struggling with production issues…Borge had the BBJ [program] and they had been playing around with winglets. Borge had them informally fitted on a BBJ and they seemed to save fuel. He loved them both for fuel savings and because they distinguished the airplane from airline transports. The Boeing Company would not do an official flight test due to resource constraints, so there was not an official fuel saving number. So Borge came to me, because I was the head of production. He said, "Fred, I need to have you take an airplane out of production and put it into flight test to fly the winglets to get a good number that Boeing can stand on. I need to tell my BBJ customers that they will get about a seven percent better [fuel burn]." I said, "You've got to be kidding, Borge! I've got airplanes here, airplanes in LA, trying to get them delivered. I'm behind schedule. There's no way that I can do this." Borge was the coolest, smoothest guy. He says, "Fred, I was over in Europe last week. I had dinner with Wolfgang Kurth." Wolfgang was a real old-fashioned German guy and he was the head of Hapag-Lloyd. Borge said, "Wolfgang likes winglets." I said, "Borge, you wouldn't do that to me!" Borge said, "I don't know, Wolfgang likes winglets, and if I were you, I would think about that." I said, "Goodbye Borge, I've got too much to do," and he walked out of the office. Twenty minutes later my secretary said, "Fred, there's a call coming in from Wolfgang Kurth." Wolfgang said, "I want the winglets! I give you one month! I want the

The 737-800 Prototype (N737BX) was equipped with the blended winglets and test flown to prove that the calculated drag reductions were accurate. The blended winglets have proven to be exceptionally successful in service. Notice the "BBJ" logos on the winglets and yarn tufting applied to the inboard sides of the left winglet. *Courtesy of The Boeing Company*

winglets! Have you got that!" So we, in the middle of all of this chaos, took a Hapag-Lloyd airplane and put some orange wire in the thing (that is the color of flight test wire), bolted on the winglets, and flew it. We were absolutely amazed."

The winglets worked exceptionally well and many people were pleasantly surprised. Peter Morton explained the dynamic:

You have to understand that this is a complicated argument. Winglets don't work well in the wind tunnel due to Reynolds number scaling effects. With Computational Fluid Dynamics you can get a good indication of the improvement in fuel mileage. Our aero guys said, "We didn't get much fuel mileage benefit with simple straight winglets on the 747." However, the blended winglets that Borge wanted on the BBJ and Wolfgang wanted on the 737-800 are different, they are a sculpted shape, carefully tailored to the local airflow; designed by a retired Boeing Aerodynamicist, Bernie Gratzer, who worked for Joe Clark. Wolfgang's mission as an inclusive tour operator really stretched the 737, flying five to six hour flights. If you give him five or seven percent fuel burn that goes right to the bottom line.

According to Test Pilot Mike Hewitt, the blended winglet was the "saving grace" for the BBJ program and made it a truly competitive corporate aircraft. The new data was established on the fuel savings of the blended winglets and Boeskov's jet was able to match the Gulfstream V's range without the necessity of the tenth fuel cell. The winglets were a tremendous success and were later adopted by the airlines. They became a standard factory option on all NG aircraft except the 737-600.

One important difference was to carry all of the required fuel to produce range, the BBJ adopted some of the structure of the 737-800, was heavier, and required more thrust than a stock 737-700. Although both aircraft employed the CFM56-7, the units installed on the standard airliner version were derated to either 22,700 or 24,200 pounds of thrust, depending on airline specifications. The engine was designed to produce a full 27,300 pounds of thrust with only a change to the engine management software. This decreased the maintenance and overhaul intervals on the BBJ engine, but was deemed necessary to make the aircraft competitive. There were some concerns with how the additional thrust would affect the flying qualities of the BBJ. The location of the engines below the aircraft's center of gravity caused a tendency for all 737s to pitch up when power

was applied and naturally pitch down when the engines were retarded to idle. Given this handling characteristic, there was concern that a higher thrust engine would induce excessive pitch changes, particularly when the aircraft was loaded in a tail-heavy (aft center of gravity) condition. Test Pilot Mike Hewett was able to null this potential problem by borrowing an idea from the 777 program. The 777 had a function of the Flight Management Computer (FMC) which proved useful. The FMC could be programmed to calculate the aircraft's loaded center of gravity and was also used to calculate engine thrust based on actual conditions. Additionally, this function could be used to determine thrust limits at times when the aircraft was loaded in an aft center of gravity condition. By using a similar function on the BBJ, the aircraft was certified with the higher thrust engines while compensating for any pitch control issues.

Other important changes were made to the basic 737-700 airframe to support the BBJ program and its specialized mission. The aircraft's requirement to carry more weight was aided by the

Boeing placed this ad in 2013, showing one of the interior options for the Boeing Business Jet (BBJ). *Courtesy of The Boeing Company*

engine's management software, allowing a maximum of 27,300 pounds of thrust. Steve Taylor noted other modifications that were made:

> When we created the original BBJ it was a unique airplane. We had to go into the parts bin and take the landing gear, wing, and center section from a 737-800 and the fuselage from a 737-700 and do quite a bit of structural reinforcement. The reason for that was we needed a really high gross weight to be able to carry all of that fuel. Interestingly, if you put full fuel on a BBJ and an interior you are down to about a three passenger airplane. You are really in a strange part of the envelope. It's a 171,000 pound airplane on a 737-700 sized body. It is really unique. The BBJ also enhanced passenger comfort with a maximum cabin altitude of 6,500 feet compared to the 8,000 feet in the standard airliner.

The 737NG-based Boeing Business Jet first flew on September 4, 1998. As of December 2016, 147 of these aircraft had been delivered to customers all over the world.

Extended-range Twin-engine Operational Performance Standards (ETOPS)

In June 1919, John Alcock and Arthur Brown reached toward new frontiers in aviation by completing the first non-stop transatlantic flight in history. Their twin-engine Vickers Vimy was equipped with Rolls-Royce Eagle engines which were state-of-the-art at the time. The courageous men flew for sixteen hours and traveled 1,777 nautical (2,044 statute) miles from St. John's, Newfoundland, to Clifden, Connemara, County Galway, Ireland. The adventure was fraught with hazards, since the piston engine's reliability was never tested over such great distances. The men successfully traversed the ocean but crash-landed upon arrival. They survived and were presented with an honorary award titled Knight Commander of the Most Excellent Order of the British Empire by King George V. This amazing feat by Alcock and Brown proved that with reliable airplanes people could travel great distances, even spanning entire oceans.

Aircraft and engine technology improved, particularly after WWII, to the point where transatlantic and transpacific passenger service became frequent. Although piston engines experienced significant upgrades after the first transatlantic flight, they were still temperamental. According to 1953 data, the failure rate on piston engines was roughly one every 3,000 hours. To mitigate this risk, airlines used four-engine aircraft, such as the Lockheed Constellation and Douglas DC-6, when traveling long distances over the ocean. This redundancy made it possible for airplanes to provide safe transport on oceanic routes even if an engine failed during flight.

To protect the traveling public, the Civil Aeronautics Authority (CAA) ruled in 1953 that unless authorized by the administrator, twin-engine airliners had to remain within sixty minutes of a suitable alternate airport. This regulation was a safety measure, but it severely limited the usefulness of twin-engined aircraft on routes overwater, or in regions that had great expanses without suitable airports. Out of necessity, some foreign operators like Air Nauru, which did not have to adhere to CAA regulations, flew long overwater flights with twin-engined jetliners. Airlines such as Air Pacific operated twin-engined BAC One-Elevens on routes from Auckland, New Zealand, to Suva, Fiji, with routing that took the aircraft eighty-four minutes from an alternate airport. There were also times when American carriers such as Air Florida were authorized to exceed the sixty minute rule on routing from New York to Santo Domingo, which at its farthest point was sixty-four minutes from a suitable alternate airport. Meanwhile, the United States military was not required to abide by the sixty minute rule. McDonnell Douglas C-9Bs (DC-9-30) and Boeing T-43As (727-200) were used on military flights from San Francisco and San Diego to Honolulu that took them up to 146 minutes from any airport. These flights, which were exceptions to the rule, were monitored, and it became apparent that as engine quality improved so did safety. Two-engine aircraft were more reliable then ever before with the added benefit of better fuel economy than four-engine aircraft.

Boeing's Vice President of Product Development and Marketing Management (1980s) Dick Taylor believed the idea of using twin-engined jetliners for long, overwater routes was safe. Taylor's firsthand knowledge of the proven technology incorporated into Boeing's twin-engined 757 and 767 jetliners supported his belief, and he sought to make oceanic routes with these aircraft possible. After much research Taylor created the framework for what became the Extended-range Twin-engine Operational Performance Standards (ETOPS) program. Dick Taylor recalled the genesis of the program:

> This resulted in a long study, a lot of thought process, and convincing the FAA that the old rule, which said, "Unless approved by the administrator a twin-engined airplane must stay within sixty minutes of a suitable alternate airport on one engine" [was obsolete]. So I worked to figure out what it would take to get this approved by the administrator. I had the best job in the Boeing Company… Bob Bogash and I sat down someplace along in there and said, "We're going to write a document…." The purpose of the document is going to set forth what is necessary for a twin-engined airplane to be superior. So we wrote this document and Bogash's job was to go check it out with each superior person in each subject: the propulsion guy says "well, I'll try"…[So] he's making the chapter. If you want a bulldog to go get something done, Bogash is the one! I could work on the problem with the best there was at Boeing…. It was very, very good.

Boeing's intention was to be able to fly twin-jet aircraft from the West Coast of the United States to Hawaii, the longest continuous overwater route in the world. The Civil Aeronautics Authority (CAA) had transformed into the Federal Aviation Administration (FAA) many years before, but had retained the antiquated sixty minute twin-engine rule. It was a very significant point that the International Civil Aviation Organization (ICAO), which provided rules and standards to most other countries in the United Nations, had been running with a ninety minute twin-engine rule. The ICAO rules also set its ninety minute rule at two engine cruising speed, versus the FAA's rule for sixty minutes at a greatly reduced single engine cruise speed, making it much more restrictive than the international rule. Taylor, along with others at Boeing, set about to prove that the reliability of modern twin-engine jetliners was not only as good, but better than the oceanic airliners of the past. He authored two studies: "Worldwide Operation of Twin-Jet Aircraft (Past, Present, and Future)" in 1983, and "A Progress Report on Extended-Range Twin-Jet Operations" in 1984. These exhaustive documents looked at every conceivable parameter. In-flight engine shutdown statistics for many different jet engines, along with causal factors were charted and explained, and suggestions on how to reduce these very small numbers even further were detailed. Fire warning systems, fuel systems, and other factors which had caused in-flight engine shutdowns in the past were analyzed. Taylor even looked at the robustness of hydraulic, electrical, anti-icing, and navigation, as well as "worst case scenarios." The scope of these reports was thorough, and went well beyond the airplane's performance advancements to include approach procedures into alternate airports. When the sixty minute rule was enacted in 1953, many instrument approaches were much less precise "non-precision" approaches and had significant flight visibility limitations. By the mid-1980s, "precision approaches" were more widespread, with much less probability of not being able to land at an alternate due to inclement weather. All of these improvements in aircraft systems, navigation, and instrument approaches, along with suggestions on how to mitigate the remaining extremely small risks inherent to oceanic flying, led to the adoption of ETOPS rules.

minute ETOPS after one year of reliable service. This extension was necessary to allow twin-jet flights from the West Coast of the United States to the Hawaiian Islands. In 1990, Boeing worked with the FAA on a new concept called "Early ETOPS" for its new Boeing 777 wide body jetliner. Early ETOPS allowed 180 minute ETOPS rules to be used when an aircraft first entered service, bypassing the older rules. The FAA issued Early ETOPS authorization for the 777's first day of service, but the European Joint Aviation Authorities (JAA) disagreed with the FAA's decision. In Europe, the 777 was only granted 120 minute ETOPS authorization until it had been in reliable service for one year. Since then aircraft like the 787 were granted Early ETOPS authorizations by the JAA due to rule changes. The reliability of modern twin-engined jetliners led to aircraft being granted ETOPS ratings up to 330 minutes, allowing direct flights over large expanses of ocean and uninhabited land. ETOPS revolutionized the airline industry and also heavily influenced new aircraft designs like the Boeing 787 and Airbus A350.

ETOPS and the Boeing 737

Aloha Airlines flew an inter-island network in the Hawaiian Islands, as well as longer range 737 flights into Micronesia. For these longer flights, Aloha Airlines was granted 120 minute ETOPS operations with their 737-200 aircraft, beginning weekly service from Honolulu to Kiritimati (Christmas Island) in February 1986. This service heralded the first ETOPS operation for the 737. The Classic 737 fleet followed suit in 1990. The most widely used ETOPS 737 aircraft today are the 737 Next Generation series (-600/-

Aloha Airlines operated N751AL (c/n 30674, l/n 1511) from 2004 until the company ceased operations on March 31, 2008. Aloha was the first airline to operate the 737NG series under 180-minute ETOPS overwater authorization. *Courtesy of Jennings Heilig*

ETOPS in Service

Due to the extensive research efforts put forth by Boeing and the FAA, the first ETOPS authorization was obtained by Trans World Airlines in May 1985. This authorized 120 minute diversion rules for their Boeing 767 flights between St. Louis, Missouri, and Frankfurt, West Germany. The new aircraft was allowed to use a more direct oceanic route, instead of the longer "Blue Spruce Route" over Canada, which was within sixty minutes single-engine divert time of alternates in Greenland, Iceland, and Scotland. This was an enormous triumph for Boeing and the airlines. Initially, this aircraft specific authorization could be extended from 120 to 180

700/-800/-900), which were first granted 120 minute authorization in 1998, beginning service with Air Pacific. 737NG certification of the 180 minute limit was granted on September 1, 1999. The extremely reliable nature of the CFM56, which statistically had an engine shutdown rate of .01 per 1,000 hours, certainly helped achieve approval. This opened up the 737NG to operations between the West Coast and Hawaii, with Aloha Airlines launching this service on February 14, 2000, with 180 minute ETOPS certified 737-700s. Since this time Alaska Airlines, Air Pacific, Qantas, Royal Air Moroc, Sun Country, United Airlines, WestJet, and XL Airways have followed suit, operating 737 jets on daily ETOPS flights.

Portable Maintenance Aid

Boeing put great effort into going digital versus paper for all of its design functions, and made extensive use of Computer-Aided Design (CAD) programs like CATIA. Unfortunately, at the time the rest of the information and maintenance manuals were still produced in very large, heavy paper volumes and on Microfiche for the end users. Small changes were made to the manual as new equipment and techniques became available. This not only caused Boeing to contract massive amounts of printing to distribute to the airlines, but also the personnel at the airline had to spend hours of time replacing pages one by one. The hard copy Maintenance Manual for the 737 Classics consisted of twelve volumes weighing in at a grand total of 104 pounds! On a daily basis mountains of paper were produced for Boeing by subcontracted printing companies.

British Airways led the crusade to turn these cumbersome references into a digital form with easy search functions, all in a compact disc format. United Airlines went a step further and wanted to have the maintenance manuals in a portable computer, so information could be accessed by the mechanics while they were with the aircraft. This saved countless hours during overnight "A" checks. Before a mechanic would have to travel back and forth from the aircraft to the maintenance offices to look at the Microfiche or paper manuals. The troubleshooting and step-by-step instructions had to be researched and then copied to take back to the aircraft. This took valuable man hours before actual maintenance could begin.

The cumbersome "paper" maintenance manual once required. Now this information can be acquired electronically at the aircraft with the PMA. *Author's Collection*

At the time Director of Boeing Technical Publications Fred Mitchell experienced and dealt with these challenges:

A couple airlines were very interested [in the Portable Maintenance Aid], one of which was Lou Mancini of United Airlines. So we sat down and said, "OK, what we want to do is to see if we can become more efficient." One of the things we wanted to do was to have the information digitally available to a mechanic, but we also wanted to have the training aid right there for him. We decided: Let's try some of this, and so the more we examined what a mechanic does at night... . The airplane comes in at 1 o'clock in the morning and he's got until 4 o'clock to dispatch it back to the line. He has three hours. He has a pilot's log and the MEL [inoperative items], so he knows what he's gotta do and central maintenance gets a copy of that. They will say, "OK Joe, you get out there and do this maintenance item." The first thing that he has to do is find all of the information. There's a couple of hours right there. We were taking care of that [with the Portable Maintenance Aid] because you would just press on the ATA chapter and boom, up it would come... . No homework.

The advent of the Portable Maintenance Aid (PMA) was extremely effective at reducing wasted resources. Not only did it do away with bulky paper manuals, it eliminated the workload of maintaining them. Changes to the digital manual on the PMA could be made electronically in minutes. The use of the Portable Maintenance Aid allowed mechanics to have the whole maintenance manual onboard the aircraft, where the maintenance action was being accomplished. Sometimes a mechanic would need to review training information prior to accomplishing some of the more complex tasks, so Boeing elected to include the training materials in the form of Computer Based Training (CBT) repurposed from the maintenance training programs into the Portable Maintenance Aid as well, giving additional support to the mechanics as they accomplished their tasks. Boeing's Lee Hall estimated forty percent of an airline's maintenance costs were attributable to documentation searches before this technology became available.

The 737-600

The most compact member of the 737 Next Generation series was the 737-600. Scandinavian Airlines, a long time DC-9 operator, surprised many analysts when the carrier was named the launch customer for the 737-600. Boeing received the order for thirty-five aircraft in March 1995—later increased to forty-one aircraft—with the first delivery made to the airline on October 10, 1998 (737-683 LN-RPA, c/n 28290, l/n

Air Algerie operates this 737-6D6 (7T-VJS, c/n 30210, l/n 1150), which was delivered from Boeing to the airline on June 12, 2002. Only sixty-nine 737-600s have been delivered to date. *Courtesy of Jennings Heilig*

100). This aircraft was similar in capacity to the Original series 737-200 and the Classic series 737-500, with seating for 100–132 passengers. Based on the 737-700, the length of the fuselage was reduced 8 ft. 2 in., measuring in at 102 ft. 6 in. The wingspan remained the same as the rest of the NG fleet, measuring 112 ft. 7 in. (without winglets). Three different engine options were offered, giving a variety of thrust ratings: the CFM56-7B20 (20,600 lbs.) and the CFM56-7B22 (22,700 lbs.). Boeing also offered a version with CFM56-7B18 engines derated to 18,500 lbs., but this configuration was never certified by the FAA. The 737-600 offered a full passenger payload range of 3,140 nautical (3,611 statute) miles when equipped with the high thrust option. In total, only sixty-nine 737-600 series have been built and delivered to date, the last of which was to Canadian airline Westjet, with 737-6CT (C-GEWJ, c/n 35571, l/n 2045) on September 14, 2006. Aside from the 737-100 series,

Boeing 737-600 first flight cover.
Author's Collection

WestJet Airlines of Canada began service on February 26, 1996. Interestingly, Las Vegas, Nevada, based Allegiant Air was originally to be called WestJet Express, but changed names prior to commencing operations in 1998. C-GXWJ (c/n 35570, l/n 2032) joined its fleet on August 13, 2006, one of sixty-nine examples built to date. *Courtesy of Jennings Heilig*

The first flight of the 737-600 prototype (N7376, c/n 28296, l/n 21) occurred under the command of Capts. Mike Carriker and Ray Craig. This flight, on January 22, 1998, lasted 2 hours and 28 minutes. Note the small drogue trailing from the vertical stabilizer used for instrument calibration purposes. *Courtesy of The Museum of Flight*

Capts. Mike Carrier (left) and Ray Craig (right) prior to a flight in the 737-600. *Courtesy of The Boeing Company*

which sold thirty examples, the 737-600 was the lowest selling of all the 737 series, showing the industry's growing preference for larger, higher capacity versions of the 737.

The 737-900

As time went on, some airline customers were looking for a 737 with greater capacity, even at the expense of some range capability. Thus, the 737-900 was born, the largest and heaviest derivative of the world's most successful jetliner. The new jet was 138 ft. 2 in. long—an 8 ft. 6 in. stretch over the 737-800. A wing of the same size and shape common to the rest of the 737NG fleet was utilized with significant changes to the gauge of materials in the wing structure itself, as well as the fuselage center section. The engines and thrust ratings offered as options on the 737-900 were the CFM56-7B24 (24,200 lbs.), CFM56-7B26 (26,400 lbs.), and CFM56-7B27 (27,300 lbs.). Equipped with the highest thrust option, the standard 737-900 had a maximum range of 2,458 nautical (2,826 statute) miles with a full passenger cabin. The 737-900 features the best fuel efficiency per seat mile of all the 737NG series.

The longer fuselage did cause some concern regarding takeoff and landing, and the possibility of a tail strike (touching the runway with the rear fuselage). To prevent this a higher approach speed was required, which adversely affected takeoff and landing distances. Capt. Ray Craig was responsible for coming up with a solution. He recounted:

> We were geometry limited...we couldn't extend the [main landing] gear any longer. Ed Kane and Bill Williams came up with the concept of a two-position tail skid.

For takeoff, it is retracted up into the airplane...into the normal position that you would see [on a standard 737-800]. When you are coming in to land it would extend six inches. That would give you another two degrees of pitch attitude because the tail skid will hit the runway first, before the body contacted. That knocked off three to four knots on approach speed. Then, for the 737-800 and -900, we went back and looked at the leading edge devices [slats]. On takeoff we were overspeeding the gapped leading edges, so we went to a sealed leading edge for flaps 1 through 25 on takeoff.

This also became an option on the 737-800 for airlines that operate at high weights out of relatively short runways. These two changes improved the performance numbers of the 737-900

significantly and the aircraft began to sell much more rapidly, because maximum performance was being achieved. The first flight of the 737-900 occurred on August 3, 2000, with its higher gross weight sister (737-900ER) taking flight for the first time on September 1, 2006. In total, as of January 31, 2017, Boeing has built 468 examples of the 737-900 and 737-900ER aircraft with seventy-nine open orders.

The 737-900ER can be differentiated from the standard 737-900 with the inclusion of an additional exit door aft of the wing. Notice that this exit does not have the grey outlines normally required because the additional exit is only required when the seating capacity of the aircraft is over 189 passengers. Many airlines with lower density seating have opted to replace the door with a non-operable plug incorporating a normal passenger window. *Courtesy of Jennings Heilig*

Principal Changes of the 737-900
Relative to the 737-800

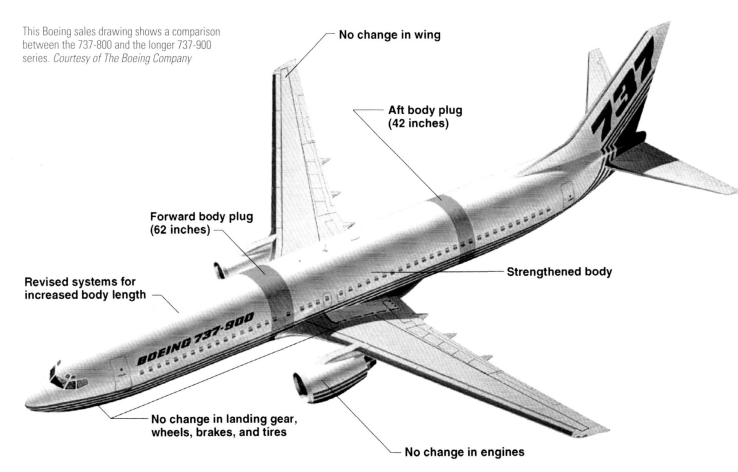

This Boeing sales drawing shows a comparison between the 737-800 and the longer 737-900 series. *Courtesy of The Boeing Company*

No change in wing

Aft body plug
(42 inches)

Forward body plug
(62 inches)

Strengthened body

Revised systems for
increased body length

No change in landing gear,
wheels, brakes, and tires

No change in engines

The rollout ceremony for the 737-900 occurred on July 23, 2000, in Renton, Washington. *Courtesy of The Boeing Company*

Author's Collection

First Flight
737-900

RENTON, WA
AUG
3
2000
98058-9998

33USA

EGG NEBULA

Renton Facility

Building on Success
The Next-Generation 737

Carried on Flight   Takeoff 10:06 am

N495AS (c/n 41728, l/n 5787) was delivered new to Alaska Air on February 24, 2016, resplendent in the new livery of the carrier. In 2001, Alaska was named the launch customer for the 737-900. *Courtesy of Jennings Heilig*

N495AS

The 737-900 prototype first flew on August 3, 2000. This aircraft (c/n 30017, l/n 596) was later delivered to Alaska Airlines on April 29, 2003. *Courtesy of The Boeing Company*

This is a patch commemorating flight testing of the 737-900 series. *Courtesy of The Boeing Company*

Boeing Technology Demonstrator
PROVING THE VALUE OF EMERGING TECHNOLOGIES
BOEING 737-900
Technology Demonstrator
2002
FLIGHT TEST TEAM

BOEING 737-900

Fuel Efficiency Increases and the 737NG Performance Improvement Package (PIP)

In 2011, Boeing continued to look at ways to provide greater fuel efficiency for the 737 Next Generation fleet. A program called the Performance Improvement Package (PIP) evolved to meet these goals. This offering consisted of minor changes to the airframe and engines (internal and external), yielding an additional fuel savings of

Other areas on the plane were scrutinized in search of performance gains. One in particular has been in the crosshairs of aerodynamicists from the very beginning: the main wheel well. On the main landing gears, the outboard tire and its required aerodynamic hubcap were exposed when the wheels were retracted for design simplicity on all 737s. This

around two percent. Many of these changes may seem like small detail changes, but cumulatively make a significant difference to an airline's financial bottom line.

The first of the PIP modifications began to be incorporated in March 2011, with changes intended to reduce aerodynamic drag. Installation of these revisions began with Line Number 3570 (737-8AS, c/n 34986). The wings were looked at with detail for drag reduction. The flight spoilers and slats on the wings were changed structurally to sharpen the trailing edges by replacing the composite honeycomb structure with a thinner aluminum alloy edge. This would cause the airflow to pass more smoothly over the wing in its clean, cruise configuration. The wing modification also called for reductions in the gaps between the retracted spoilers and the upper surface of the trailing edge flaps, optimizing the smoothness of the airflow over these critical areas.

Southwest Airlines operates a growing fleet of 737-8H4 aircraft. N8642E (c/n 42525, l/n 5022, Effectivity YS666), was the first painted in the carrier's new livery and christened *Heart One*. Interestingly, *Heart Two* (N8643A, c/n 42524, l/n 5030, YS667) was the next 737 to leave the Renton factory, but was out of line number sequence. This was due to the July 3, 2014, train derailment which caused the original fuselage for this aircraft (and others) to be damaged and scrapped. N8642A was assembled with a replacement fuselage and a new line number. *Courtesy of Jennings Heilig*

area was targeted once again for a slight revision, smoothing out the small gap between the tire and the wheel well fairings by rounding out the edge slightly. On the NG, the air conditioning system has two large holes incorporated into the area just forward of the wheel wells for the main landing gear. These provide an exit for the exhaust of hot air from the system and were found to produce a small amount of drag. These were revised into a square exhaust with aerodynamic louvers similar to the ones on the Original and Classic series. Installation of these louvered exhausts was implemented on Line Number 4302 (737-924, c/n 36599). The smallest detail was not overlooked by Boeing, as they even changed the shape of the red anti-collision beacons (one on top and one on the bottom of the fuselage) from a cylindrical to a more aerodynamic teardrop shape.

One of the components of the Performance Improvement Package (PIP) was the new, refined exhaust nozzle and cone-shaped plug, here on a 737-8H4. *Author's Collection*

Standard Exhaust Nozzle: the standard nozzle is much longer and shows less of the plug, as seen here on an earlier 737-7H4. *Author's Collection*

Efficiency changes to the CFM56-7s became available on Line Number 3700 (737-81B, c/n 38964) in July 2011. The modified engine was re-designated the CFM56-7BE. The external changes to the exhaust nozzle and conical plug were the most noticeable of the PIP modifications. The new nozzle was eighteen inches shorter than the older design and was combined with a reshaped plug to optimize the flow of exhaust gasses. Included with this redesign was a new oil drain on the bottom of the plug and a redesigned heat shield on the rear portion of the engine strut. This new shield improved heat protection required by the new nozzle design. Internally, changes were made to the shape of the diffuser contours, where the air exits the high-pressure compressor, to optimize fuel combustion and reduce pressure losses. The high-pressure turbine was changed by reducing the number of turbine blades from eighty to seventy-six, with reshaped blades similar to the newer LEAP engine. The low-pressure turbine was made with revisions to the shape of the turbine blades, stator vanes, and rotor. To support the changes made the EEC (Electronic Engine Control) software was changed for optimized performance. These internal changes resulted in a four percent reduction in maintenance costs, with improved fuel combustion and better exhaust gas temperature margins.

The combination of these modifications, combined with the blended winglets, yielded an aircraft that was much more fuel

Another view of the scimitar winglet. Note the re-sculptured winglet tips. *Author's Collection*

efficient than the first Next Generation 737 that rolled off the line. Boeing continued the crusade to reduce drag and increase the fuel efficiency of the 737. This was evidenced by the latest modification: the introduction of the Aviation Partners "Scimitar" Winglet in 2014. This modification is similar to the standard blended winglet, but also incorporates an extension below the wingtip and decreases drag a further two percent. The retrofit 737NG scimitar winglet is similar but not identical to the winglet on the forthcoming 737 MAX. This Scimitar Winglet program was launched by an order from United Airlines.

Every avenue to produce the most fuel efficient aircraft with the 737NG airframe has been explored and many of the modifications were retrofittable to earlier Next Generation aircraft. It was becoming clear that a significant change was on the horizon to make the aircraft more efficient. New engines were being developed which could yield large enough advances to justify a major change to the 737 airframe to allow them to be adapted.

The Next Generation 737 In Service

The late model scimitar winglet. *Author's Collection*

This 737-7BD (c/n 33938, l/n 2863) was painted in AirTran colors, but interestingly was never delivered to the airline. This aircraft was repainted and delivered to Aerolineas Argentinas as LV-BYY on May 15, 2009. *Courtesy of The Boeing Company*

Aloha Airlines was a long time 737 operator and used the 737-700 for overwater ETOPS operations. This 737-76N (N749AL, c/n 32738, l/n 1392) was leased to the carrier by GECAS. Following the shutdown of Aloha this aircraft served with Jet Airways as VT-JGL and is currently operated by SAS (Scandinavian Airlines), registered SE-REZ. *Courtesy of The Boeing Company*

Delta Air Lines currently operates a fleet of 140 Boeing 737NG aircraft, including this 737-732 (N301DQ, c/n 29687, l/n 2667), which was delivered to the carrier on August 1, 2008. *Courtesy of The Boeing Company*

Seen prior to rolling out of the paint facility, this 737-75B was used by Boeing prior to being delivered to Germania in December 1998. This aircraft is owned by leasing agency ILFC and is now operated by Aerolineas Argentinas as LV-CPH. *Courtesy of The Boeing Company*

This formation photo was taken in 1998, with N737BX (737-8K5, c/n 27981, l/n 7), N1791B (737-75B, c/n 28110, l/n 5), and N7376 (c/n 28296, l/n 21) listed in order nearest to farthest. *Courtesy of The Boeing Company*

This 737-8Q8 (c/n 30734, l/n 2477) was the first of two 737-800 aircraft operated by Air Vanuatu. Based in Port Vila, Vanuatu, the carrier operates service to Australia, New Zealand, and the South Pacific. *Courtesy of The Boeing Company*

Ryanair of Ireland is a very successful low cost carrier that currently operates a fleet of 337 Boeing 737-700 and 737-800 aircraft. EI-DHT is a 737-8AS (c/n 33581, l/n 1809) and was first delivered to the airline on October 28, 2005. This photo shows the open thrust reverser detail and the retractable landing lights under the wing to body fairings. *Courtesy of P. Popelar*

Alaska Airlines exclusively operates 737 equipment, including 737-400s, -700s, -800s, and -900s. This 737-890 (N512AS, c/n 39043, l/n 2711), painted in a hybrid "Dreamliner" scheme, is one of 124 737s presently in its fleet. *Courtesy of The Boeing Company*

This 737-924ER (c/n 33531, l/n 2947) is painted in a retro Continental Airlines livery and is seen at liftoff. Post merger, this aircraft is now operated by United Airlines. Notice the view of the open tire-shaped main landing gear wells common to all 737s and the extended 737-900 tail skid. *Courtesy of The Boeing Company*

A unique feature of the 737-900ER is the addition of the exit hatch behind the wing on each side. This hatch has a normal cabin window and no demarkation lines, indicating this exit has been deactivated. This is common practice when low density seating capacity is less than 190 passengers. *Courtesy of The Boeing Company*

CHAPTER 6
THE 737 "MAX" SERIES

Project Yellowstone 1

During 2004, Boeing's research was well under way to replace the 737NG with a more fuel efficient aircraft. This exploratory project, named Yellowstone 1 (also referred to as Y1), was intended to gather technology from the 787 Dreamliner and adapt it to a 737-sized airframe. The Dreamliner featured a nearly all composite airframe made of carbon-fiber reinforced polymer that was lighter and less prone to corrosion. On conventional jetliners, compressed air was tapped from the jet engines to power many systems. The negative aspect of using this high pressure air (called "bleed air") was that it essentially robbed the engine of available power, causing a measurable increase in fuel burn to run the aircraft's air conditioning and pressurization systems. Due to advances made in electrical and battery technology the Dreamliner was equipped with electric air pumps to pressurize the cabin and reaped considerable fuel efficiency benefits. Additionally, other components that were usually powered by hydraulics, such as wheel brakes, were electrically actuated to simplify the system.

Project Yellowstone's design team faced the exceedingly complex challenge of incorporating systems from one type of aircraft into another. While many ideas were considered, few were even possible or cost effective. The systems architecture built for the 787 required a great quantity of volume and would not physically fit into a 737-sized airframe, given the technology at the time. Also the idea of assimilating a carbon-fiber structure into the plan would only yield a maximum efficiency gain of ten percent and required an expensive redesign. Due to the general assumption that a fifteen percent gain in fuel efficiency was needed to spur a new aircraft design Boeing opted to suspend the study in 2008.

Airbus Goes Forth

While Boeing worked on Yellowstone 1, Airbus focused on a project to fully upgrade the A320. In 2006, the research team of project A320E "Enhanced" created a modernized cabin design for the A320, but placed most of their efforts into achieving better weight savings, aerodynamic improvements, and greater fuel efficiency. The project was a success, as Airbus squeezed as much efficiency as economically feasible from the A320 airframe and even applied engine enhancements to reduce fuel burns. In the quest for efficiency Airbus created their own winglet design called "Sharklets" that generated a two percent increase in fuel efficiency over previous designs. Although the limits of what they were capable of were reached with the current configuration, new engine technology was just around the corner.

On December 1, 2010, Airbus announced their intention to launch a highly upgraded version of the A320. The new A320neo ("New Engine Option") was based on two cutting edge engines under development. CFMI was designing a sophisticated engine called the "Leading Edge Aviation Propulsion" (LEAP) turbofan engine, while Pratt & Whitney was developing its own engine called the PW1100G geared turbofan. Airbus studies indicated that by using either of the two new technology engines combined with Sharklets, the company could expect to yield around fifteen percent in fuel savings over previous A320 models. The A320 was the primary competitor to the 737 since the late 1980s. This initiative gave the A320neo a sizable leap into the market ahead of Boeing, who still needed to come up with a complementary aircraft that could compete.

The Birth of the 737 MAX

In response to the Airbus announcement, Boeing personnel assembled to strategically create the A320neo's ultimate competitor. While generating ideas two different schools of thought prevailed. One group believed the best route was to design an entirely new aircraft that used all the latest technology. Others held the strong opinion that a good solid improvement in efficiency could be reaped by modifying the 737NG airframe, while capitalizing on the latest engine, systems, and aerodynamic technologies. As Boeing weighed the merits of each course of action customers' thoughts and ideas were carefully taken into account. 737 MAX Vice President and General Manager Keith Leverkuhn explained:

> This is often the case that there are differing opinions, which is typically a good thing, as long as you can get to a decision quickly…. There was a lot of emphasis on a new airplane and…making sure that we were listening to the customers. The customers wanted the fuel burn economics that the new engine and aerodynamics available to us could provide. They didn't need a different [fuselage] diameter, they needed fuel burn improvement. So those were the conditions under which the MAX was launched.

With the CFMI LEAP engine in development, the technology existed to build a completely new airframe similar to the Yellowstone 1 studies, but when weighing the options time was working against this plan, since the aircraft needed to be built soon to compete against the A320. The second plan called for a new version of the 737 with better fuel economy. This could be achieved while retaining the 737NG airframe modified to accept the new, larger engine. This option would save Boeing time in planning and development while still catering to the customers' need for a superior aircraft. On August 30, 2011 (almost a year after the Airbus A320neo launch), Boeing announced the 737 MAX program, instead of pursuing a completely new airframe design. As work began on the development of the 737 MAX aircraft interest in the new airplane was piqued at Southwest Airlines. On December 13, 2011, Southwest Airlines became the launch customer for the new aircraft with a firm order for 150 aircraft and options to purchase

IF IT DIDN'T OFFER MORE
IT COULDN'T BE MAX.

150 more. Soon other orders were made public from American Airlines, Lion Air, and Aviation Capital Group. Development of the MAX aircraft was not only focused on fuel economy, but as an overall economic package for the airlines. One of the major goals was to retain the excellent 99.7 percent dispatch reliability of the existing 737NG fleet. Since many 737 MAX customers were also 737NG operators, it was imperative this aircraft retain the same FAA Type Rating with the rest of the 737 fleet. This strategic plan to retain commonality would greatly ease training expenses and allow the pilots to transition to the new aircraft with a short "differences" training requirement.

The CFMI LEAP 1B Turbofan Engine

As fuel prices rose to unprecedented levels in the early 2000s, fuel economy emerged as the most critical factor for airlines to consider when purchasing an airplane. On a typical two-hour leg, the Classic 737-300 could burn approximately 849 gallons an hour. Improved wing and engine designs assisted fuel savings on the modernized 737-700 which reduced fuel consumption to approximately 720 gallons an hour, but the airlines needed even greater efficiencies. Engine manufacturers such as CFMI paid close attention to these needs, and while reliability had to be maintained or even increased, they sought to achieve maximum efficiency in their new designs.

In early 2005, CFMI initiated a program called LEAP56 to explore melding the latest engine technology into a replacement for the CFM56-3 and -7. A lengthy development program ensued with a goal to increase the engines' fuel efficiency by sixteen percent using a technologically advanced low pressure compressor and fan section. The end result was the creation of CFMI's LEAP engine on July 13, 2008. This new section was a scaled down version of components from the GEnX jet engine powering the 747-8 and 787 Dreamliner. The fan blades were constructed using the latest "Resin Transfer Molding" technique, which molded the fan blades in a variable shape dependent on the speed at which the engine turned. In previous models rigid fan blades of metal alloys were made with twist angles that, although optimized for some thrust settings, were not ideal across the spectrum. The blades on the LEAP, which were hard mounted to the hub, were designed to untwist as the rotational speed of the fan (N1) increased. This feature allowed the angle of the blades to be closer to ideal over the entire thrust range of the engine. The core of the engine, based on the CFM56, was modified to create optimal fuel economy. Additional components were also modified so the compressors could operate at higher pressures. This high pressure air was fed into the newly forged Twin Annular Pre Swirl (TAPS) combustor section, ensuring nearly complete ignition of the fuel. Not only was fuel consumption reduced markedly, but the engine met stricter NOx emissions criteria set by the FAA. The low pressure turbine section incorporating new Titanium Aluminide blades was designed to be fifty percent lighter than blades used in the CFM56-7. This, along with the composites used in the fan section, yielded a significant weight savings. Although the LEAP 1B engine is heavier than the older CFM56-7, these changes mitigated some of the weight increase by approximately 500 pounds per engine.

After thorough testing, CFMI estimated the LEAP engine could potentially save airlines as much as $1.6 million per year per aircraft. This was a significant data point for the world's airlines

to consider. Another selling feature of the LEAP engine was its increased reliability and longevity. Foreign Object Damage (FOD) was a destroyer of even the greatest engines and CFMI took a proactive stance against it. The company used ejectors adopted from the GE90 engine on the Boeing 777 to protect against FOD. Ejectors deflected material which could get sucked into the engine's core and would prevent costly maintenance while increasing safety. Airlines approved, and variants of the LEAP engine were purchased to power the Airbus A320neo; it is also slated for China's COMAC C919 Jetliner. Capt. Ray Craig explained: "The key driver on [the 737 MAX], as it is with the A320neo, is a more efficient engine. With regard to the CFM56 series -7, they have taken the core about as far as they can take it. So the next step was to increase the fan size... . They have optimized the fan size for the size and weight of the airplane."

When Boeing engineers set out to determine the ideal fan diameter for the new LEAP engine important factors came into play. Regardless of what the fan size was when installed, it required an appropriately sized cowling that would be pulled through the air at high speeds. The aerodynamic drag effects needed to be calculated and factored into an efficiency model. If the fan was made too large, it could potentially increase drag during the aircraft's descent, when the engine produced little thrust. Additional drag could shorten the duration of the aircraft's fuel efficient gliding descent and negatively effect total fuel consumption. Another important factor was engine weight. An engine with a larger fan added significant weight. On the other end of the spectrum, if the fan selected was too small for the airframe fuel efficiency would also suffer, because the engine's bypass ratio would not be optimal. Airbus chose a larger fan diameter for the A320neo, leading to the LEAP 1A engine, with its seventy-eight inch diameter fan. This choice of a larger fan section was driven by the engine thrust requirement of the A321neo, the largest and heaviest of the A320 family. The 737 MAX used the LEAP 1B engine with a 69.4 in. fan diameter, due to its lower thrust requirement. The smaller fan section lightened the aircraft while optimizing efficiency.

Adequate clearance between the engine and the ground was an important feature of the 737 design from the beginning. However, this metric was not the only factor that drove the chosen fan size for the 737 MAX; rather, it was the best size for the airplane's thrust requirement. Joe Ozimek explained the situation:

> Even if we were unconstrained under the wing of this airplane, the fan diameter would be what it is. That is simply because airplanes are three things: wings, body, and engines, and each is dependent on the other. Putting a very large fan on the airplane…(and we have the largest fan in the world by the way: the GE 115B with a fan diameter wider than the body of the entire 737 airplane) may have unwanted weight and drag consequences. We solved for a fan diameter that was optimized for the engine, body, and the wing.

Boeing's engineers had to strike a balance when adjusting landing gear height due to the LEAP 1B's engine size. From the outset, the 737 was designed to sit low on its landing gear and offered operational benefits over competing aircraft. During normal operations, when last minute luggage arrived at the airplane, the ramp crew could load it by hand, rather than wait for a belt loader. Aircraft that sit higher on their landing gear require support equipment to be moved back into position to complete the task. In addition to taking precious minutes away from the airplane's on-time performance when multiplied many times throughout the day, it was also operationally expensive and time consuming. When the wing and landing gear structures were revised on the 737NG, the airplane was raised just enough to give good engine clearance. The same landing gear was also installed on the 737 MAX, but with a much larger engine cowling diameter, the engines were moved eighteen inches farther forward and raised slightly in front of the wing. The nose landing gear was also extended an additional eight inches to augment ground clearance for the new LEAP engines.

Evolution

Many small aerodynamic cleanups had been progressively accomplished during the 737NG production run through elements of the Performance Improvement Package (PIP) program. These enhancements, along with the Aviation Partners' blended winglets, resulted in late model 737NG aircraft being roughly six percent more fuel efficient than the first -700 series entering service in 1997. Gap tolerances between the spoilers and the trailing edge flaps were reduced, and the thickness of the trailing edges of many components on the wings were minimized to mitigate cruising drag. Everything down to reshaping the anti-collision lights was accomplished to achieve these efficiencies. A feature that was an option on the 737NG was the Short Field Package (SFP), incorporating revised leading edge slat scheduling to reduce runway length requirements while optimizing single engine climb capabilities under challenging conditions. The SFP was made standard equipment on the 737 MAX series. Additionally, a two-position tail skid that was optional on the 737-800 series was made standard on the 737-900ER. This will remain unchanged for the MAX -8 and -9, respectively. Many refinements that were developed during the 737NG program were incorporated in the 737 MAX.

Boeing's Michael Teal remembers his first day on the job as 737 MAX vice president and chief project engineer at the August 30, 2011, press conference:

> The presentation shown was describing the changes that we were launching to define the 737 MAX. It showed a new engine, the aft body tail change, and that was pretty much it. We were claiming, at the time, an eleven percent improvement in fuel burn from the best NG airplane. At the press conference Boeing described, "We haven't decided whether we are going to do a sixty-six inch fan or a sixty-eight inch fan." Over 2011–2012, we were doing all of the detailed trade studies to decide on the optimum fan size. We first realized we could do a sixty-eight inch fan by lengthening the nose gear of the airplane and making it eight inches taller. That change gave us two more inches under the engine with a sixty-eight inch fan. That helped: it helped in the optimization of the wing, body, and engine. We also decided that we needed more than eleven percent because the industry was focused on fuel

burn. That's when we decided to change the winglet. The existing NG blended winglet was replaced with a new Advanced Technology Winglet optimized for the MAX. So we went with the Advanced Technology Winglet and optimizing the fan diameter, which is what we have now at 69.4 in. The best fan diameter, plus the winglet, plus the tail change and a few other things for natural laminar flow ended up turning into a fourteen percent improvement. That all took time in the development leading up to firm configuration in summer 2013. From the launch of the program to firm configuration was about two years, during which we also added the fly-by-wire spoilers, a new electronic bleed system, and new flight deck displays.

The Wing

The wing of the 737 MAX series used the same airfoil shape as its predecessor, the 737NG. Boeing Test Pilot Ray Craig said of the NG/MAX wing:

> It is a fantastic wing! Our aerodynamicists did a great job on that wing [and did not need to change it aerodynamically] for…the MAX. To enhance the efficiency we are going from the [current] winglet to a split Advanced Technology Winglet. It's a whole new winglet on which we're maintaining laminar flow.

Laminar flow refers to the air that flows smoothly over an object (in this case, a winglet) and does not separate, creating turbulent airflow and aerodynamic drag. Wind tunnel models did not replicate the function of winglets effectively. This was because of a phenomenon called "boundary layer." Objects, such as airplanes, have a thin boundary layer of air around their surfaces that they pull along with them. Wind tunnel models also have a boundary layer, but it is proportionally thick when compared to the actual aircraft. This difference causes the airflow around a model winglet to give inaccurate results. So instead of relying completely on wind tunnel data, computational fluid dynamics was utilized extensively to create the new winglet. Once the winglet was designed on a computer, a scale model was built and flown in a wind tunnel for validation. A set of equations that model the flow of fluid (air, in this case) called "Navier-Stokes" was then used by the aerodynamicists to convert their wind tunnel model data and correct for boundary layer scaling errors. This technique worked well and created significant fuel savings of 1.8 to 2 percent with the new split winglet.

Outwardly, with the exception of the new winglet, the MAX wing appeared identical to that of the NG. However, there were many internal structural changes made to adapt it to the new aircraft and engine combination. The CFM LEAP 1B engines were larger and heavier than older generation powerplants found on the 737NG series. The fan diameter was increased from 61.8 in. on the CFM56-7 to 69.4 in. on the new LEAP 1B. Because the engines were moved farther forward it caused a requirement for additional internal structure at the engine to wing attach points.

The combination of structural changes to the 737 MAX airframe and the addition of the larger LEAP 1B engine have generated an increase of around 6,000 pounds in operating empty

This photo of the 737 MAX-8 prototype (1A001) shows the new "Advanced Technology Winglet" and the re-contoured tail cone section. After testing this aircraft will be delivered to launch customer Southwest Airlines. *Courtesy of The Boeing Company*

weight over its 737NG counterpart. Although this weight was significant, its addition was a worthy compromise to harvest the efficiency gains the 737 MAX provides. Joe Ozimek explained:

> We want to characterize this properly. You shouldn't describe it as 6,000 pounds heavier. Everyone reads 6,000 pounds heavier and they know that weight on airplanes is death. So they say 6,000 pounds, that is a huge number. The fact is that for that 6,000 pounds, we get fourteen percent more efficient. If we could find another 6,000 pounds to spend on the airplane that got us another fourteen percent, we would spend it too.

The additional structure added to the airframe allowed an increase in maximum takeoff weights, so the 737 MAX is a true transcontinental airplane that is significantly more efficient and capable than its predecessors.

The MAX Cockpit

An important feature airlines looked for in a new aircraft was the ability to retain commonality with an existing fleet. As a cost saving measure and to simplify crew training, airlines wanted their pilots to keep the same pilot certificate (called a Type Rating) when flying the MAX. Boeing has maintained this same strategy throughout each generation of the 737 program. Because of this, the overhead systems panel on the MAX was virtually identical to the legacy 737 fleet. Mechanical switches were utilized for longevity and to

maintain a similar appearance to the legacy. Studies revealed the push buttons in the 757/767/777 needed replacement after an average of 16,000 hours, while the mechanical switches in the 737 tended to last up to 75,000 hours. This feature improved dispatch reliability and required less maintenance action.

When designing the flight instrumentation on the 737 MAX, Boeing engineers looked for common pilot errors during operations with other generation 737s. Ways were explored to mitigate these errors, and much thought was given to keep the MAX and newer NG aircraft operationally compatible with earlier NG and Classic machines. One case in point was illustrated by Boeing Test Pilot Ray Craig regarding the Pitot Heat system, which prevents ice from forming on the airplanes' pitot probes. Ice accumulation on these probes can adversely affect flight instrumentation indications in the cockpit:

> Years ago, we did a study on pitot heat. We had some airplanes take off with the Pitot Heat system off. Our safety folks, practicing due diligence, had gone down their probability analysis. They said that we had to make it automatic like the 757, 767, 777, and so forth. Initially, they came to me and said, "we are going to make it automatic and take the switches off the flight deck." I said, "If you do that, you are going to make your [pilot error] exposure worse." They said, "What do you mean?" [I said] "Because you are going to have a period of time where you are going to have a mixed

fleet situation. You have a pilot who has 15,000 hours in the 737, and he does his flow [cockpit preparation procedures] and turns the switches on. Well, if he were to get in an airplane with no switches, and flew it for a month, and never turns the switches on [it could cause a problem]. Pilots are creatures of muscle memory. So now he gets back on an airplane that does have the switches. You have upped the probability that he will take off [with the switches off]." So they went back and looked at it and said, "You're right."

A very interesting solution to this problem was devised, as Capt. Craig explained:

For the last three or four years all of the aircraft coming off the line have a panel that has two positions on the switch. Before it was "OFF" and "ON." Now it is "AUTO" and "ON." [The "AUTO" position turns on the pitot heat at engine start.] It drives back to the philosophy that the pilots are the primary and the automatics are the backup, so it doesn't matter if you have the new system or the old system, the pilot procedures are the same…. The airplane protects you…. We are enhancing the safety of the airplane. The whole paradigm is to keep the pilot involved with the airplane.

Airframe Changes

When designing the MAX, engineers had the advantage of using Computational Fluid Dynamics to redesign the tail cone (Section 48) into a longer and more streamlined aft fuselage and auxiliary power unit cowling. This new design finally solved the longstanding vertical bounce issue (see Solving The Vertical Bounce Tendency, page 58) and eliminated the need for vortex generators with their attendant aerodynamic drag. To complement this tail cone change, alterations were made to the internal structure of the horizontal stabilizer, and the elevator and tab surfaces were slightly reduced in size.

Systems Changes

Transitioning from the hydro-mechanical flight spoiler system to a computer controlled and hydraulically actuated fly-by-wire system was a significant change to the flight controls on the MAX. This arrangement simplified the complex spoiler mixer system and provided more versatility in spoiler scheduling to improve handling qualities. Weight savings were also realized when the heavy and intricate mechanical spoiler mixer assembly was removed on the MAX. Electronically controlled spoilers were designed to extend or retract to assist with steep approaches or handling in high-speed flight, with the goal of generating a notable improvement in the aircraft's flight characteristics. The spoiler and ground spoiler were also redesigned with multiple electrical redundancies to establish a high level of safety when used to land the aircraft or during a rejected takeoff. If the electrical system of the aircraft became degraded due to a malfunction, it was imperative the new electronically controlled spoiler system remain operative. Thus, revisions to the logic for the MAX's electrical system were made.

To adapt the 737 systems to the new CFM56 LEAP power plant, the mechanical bleed air system on the MAX was replaced with an electronically controlled valve system, optimizing their operation and increasing reliability. Additionally, the 737 MAX was equipped with a new Onboard Networking System (ONS) which Boeing's Jonathan Grant described at the first flight event: "We have added systems to the airplane to really collect a lot of the data to make it useful for mechanics and airline personnel off board. We collect a lot of the data and then we are connecting it to the right people at the right time to keep their airplane reliable and maintainable…." The ONS system was designed to give more real time information to the crew and to airline personnel on the ground. Additionally, the ONS system has the ability to integrate the crew's Electronic Flight Bag, aircraft systems troubleshooting, and data downloading and recording into this single system. ONS will also be installed on late model 737NGs as they come out of the factory.

The Introduction of the Airbus A320neo

On July 1, 2014, Airbus rolled out the first A320neo, the last component of Airbus' A320 modernization program. This aircraft was projected to increase fuel efficiency by ten percent over legacy A320 airplanes while retaining ninety-five percent parts commonality with its predecessors. The A320neo was offered with either the Pratt & Whitney PW1100G-JM Geared Turbofan or the CFM LEAP 1A. In addition to the "Sharklets" affixed to the wings of the A320neo, other aerodynamic improvements were made when Airbus identified the need to enhance takeoff performance. Rio de Janeiro's Santos Dumont airport, with its short 4,265 ft. long runway, combined with obstacles and mountainous terrain, creates a situation that demands exceptional takeoff performance. Boeing met this challenge with the 737-800 by taking advantage of the 737's three position slats. Airbus' Filton, England, facility took a different approach and designed a modification to the wing root fairing on the A320neo to exact additional performance, allowing operations into this significant international destination. This modification was proven to be successful and Airbus has plans to make it retrofittable to other existing A320 aircraft.

The first flight of the Pratt & Whitney powered A320neo occurred on September 25, 2014, using F-WNEO (c/n 6101). This aircraft was soon joined by two other Pratt & Whitney equipped A320neos—D-AVVA (c/n 6286) and F-WWIV (c/n 6720)—for flight testing and certification. Joint FAA and CAA certification was granted for this airframe/engine combination on November 24, 2015, while these three aircraft continued to be tested, simulating actual airline operations. Although the engine was certified and completely safe, some minor issues arose with "uneven cooling" of engine components in the PW1100G-JM powerplant. This situation caused regulators to impose some operational restrictions to the engine until hardware and software changes could be implemented. The result was a delay in the delivery of the aircraft to launch customer Qatar Airways. Qatar Airways was reportedly hesitant to take delivery of the aircraft with operational restrictions, and the company's CEO, Mr. Akbar Al Baker, refused to do so until the restrictions were lifted. As a result, Airbus changed its launch customer to Lufthansa and made Qatar Airways second to begin A320neo operations. Lufthansa promptly launched passenger operations with the aircraft on January 25, 2016, as Flight LH100 on their Frankfurt to Munich route. This occurred just four days before Boeing began flight tests with the 737 MAX prototype (1A001).

On May 19, 2015, the CFM LEAP 1A powered A320neo (F-WNEW, c/n 6419) had its inaugural flight. This marked the first time a LEAP engine was flown on the wing of an aircraft it was specifically designed to power. A second test aircraft (D-AVVB, c/n 6642) joined the test program soon thereafter. On March 31, 2016, the LEAP 1A powered A320neo successfully received Type Certification approval and promptly entered revenue service in August of the same year. This aircraft has proven to be an extremely strong challenger to the Boeing 737 MAX and has captured a sizable portion of the market. A total of 5,069 Airbus A320neo family (A319neo, A320neo, and A321neo) orders have been recorded.

The 737 MAX Flies

On December 8, 2015, the first 737 MAX-8, *The Spirit of Renton*, rolled out with many Boeing employees, photographers, and journalists in attendance. This aircraft was given effectivity number 1A001 (N8701Q, c/n 42554, l/n 5602). Keith Leverkuhn spoke at the rollout:

> Today marks another in a long series of milestones that our team has achieved on time, per our plan, together. With the rollout of the new 737 MAX, the first new airplane of Boeing's second century, our team is upholding an incredible legacy while taking the 737 to the next level of performance.

The prototype (1A001) was joined by three other test airplanes for the year-long test program. After testing and certification, 1A001 is slated to be delivered to Southwest Airlines. Although Southwest Airlines is the 737 MAX launch customer, the first 737 MAX delivery and service is planned for Norwegian Air Shuttle. Southwest Airlines is scheduled to receive its first MAX by July 2017, and begin revenue operations with the new aircraft during October 2017.

Nearly seven weeks later, on January 29, 2016, the 737 MAX prototype departed Renton, Washington, at 9:46 a.m. (PST) and took to the skies amid much fanfare. This historic flight was commanded by 737 Program Chief Pilot Ed Wilson and Boeing Flight Services Chief Pilot Craig Bomben, lasting 2 hours and 46 minutes. An occluded storm front was moving through Washington and created windy, rainy conditions, but the flight departed on time. Accompanied by the Boeing T-33 chase plane, upon landing at Boeing Field the flight was declared a resounding success. At the post-flight press conference Capt. Bomben remarked:

> This is our first airplane of our second century and I just have to say, "Wow"… . The team did an amazing job giving us an unbelievably clean airplane. It flew beautifully. The engines were extremely quiet. We worked our way through the checks very quickly, because honestly we had no issues.

The rollout ceremony for the 737 MAX-8 was held on December 8, 2015, with Boeing employees and members of the press in attendance. *Courtesy of The Boeing Company*

The 737 MAX-8 made its first flight from Renton, Washington, on January 29, 2016, slightly ahead of schedule. *Courtesy of The Boeing Company*

A typical element of caution was exercised on the first flight, with airspeed limited to 250 knots (287 miles per hour) and a maximum altitude of 25,000 ft. This kicked off the test program that was planned to take just under a year for FAA certification. In the following days and weeks the aircraft would be flown faster and higher, expanding the flight test "envelope."

At the first flight event Leverkuhn shared his thoughts on the MAX and the future of the 737 program:

> We think we have a terrific product here, not only in terms of…the fuel savings that we are really confident in achieving, but we think it will be the preferred airplane. We have been at this for a little while now, and the road is going to be long in terms of how we are going to continue to do in the market, and with over sixty customers and over 3,000 airplanes sold already. That is a healthy backlog that we are proud of, a healthy customer base, and we are quite confident that as we step throughout our flight test program we are going to be able to realize and deliver the improvements that we have assured our customers that we are going to be able to provide.

Dovetailing MAX Production with the NG

Lean manufacturing has made the rising production numbers for the 737 possible by increasing efficiency by leaps and bounds.

The "lean" message has also been shared and implemented by many contracted component suppliers, as they are also part of the total system. The factory at Renton exudes a controlled and calm atmosphere. This is impressive when one takes into account the complexity of building a jetliner, each one with 600,000 parts and forty-two miles of wiring being installed, while producing forty-two aircraft a month. The Renton assembly hall has three assembly lanes: two are devoted full time to 737 NG production, while a third lane is dedicated to 737 MAX production. Boeing's goal is to get 737 MAX production up to the same speed as 737NG production before mixing the lines. Soon the 737 MAX will share the same lines as the 737NG, until all NG orders are fulfilled. From then on all production will be MAX airframes at Renton. Production rates at Renton are scheduled to increase to forty-seven per month in 2017, and then on to fifty-two a month, using all three lines during 2018. Vice president of the 737 MAX program Michael Teal explained the challenges:

> Now the question is…back in the supply chain… not everybody has the same ability as we do with the third line. In fact, there's two wing lines that build all of our wings. There are two lines that build the wings, and we are building the MAX wings in sequence with them today. And different suppliers are doing different things. That was one of the biggest challenges of the program, ensuring that the manufacturing system

that you are using today is like a sewing machine. It is clicking away. You have to be able to bring in the changes, which in some cases are large changes—the propulsion system for one—and in some cases are small changes, like in portions of the fuselage where we are adding gauge [increased metal thickness] for the strength requirements for higher takeoff weight. Those are very easy to put into the production system and others create more challenges with the tooling; you have different tools that you have to bring out to do the MAX. Having that whole system orchestrated in such a way that you never stumble on the "sewing machine" that is building the NGs at the same time.

With lessons learned from the past and the implementation of lean principles, Boeing's Renton facility is poised to successfully take on future challenges.

The MAX Boeing Business Jet

Boeing Business Jets (BBJ) plans to continue production with the 737 MAX airframe, with development and sales concentrating on using the MAX-8 and MAX-9 airframes as a basis for the BBJ MAX, as opposed to the shorter MAX-7 airframe. This decision was driven largely by weight and center of gravity (CG) difficulties. The shorter MAX-7 airframe, like any aircraft, is limited on how nose heavy (forward CG limit) or tail heavy (aft CG limit) its loading can be. These forward and aft CG limits are far apart when lightly loaded and allow plenty of loading flexibility at normal airline weights. Notably, as an aircraft gets heavier, these forward and aft limits begin to converge and restrict CG tolerances at very high weights. In fact, a fully loaded 171,000 pound 737-700 BBJ has a seven inch wide balance window. The aircraft must be loaded carefully and precisely to insure it is within its CG range. Because of the larger diameter LEAP engines and the additional structural weight required to accommodate them, a MAX-7 BBJ airframe would have to be roughly 7,000 pounds heavier than the standard 737-700 BBJ. As weight increases, these forward and aft CG limits merge together and make it impossible to load the aircraft to 178,000 pounds legally. Due to these restrictions the MAX-7 airframe would not be an ideal BBJ platform without serious modification. The longer airframes (-800, -900, MAX-8, and MAX-9) have greater tolerances because of their increased fuselage length and thus can easily be loaded to the higher maximum takeoff weights required by their long range missions. Using the longer airframes for the MAX BBJ is not seen as a significant efficiency issue, since the MAX airplane has an eighteen to twenty percent fuel economy advantage over the 737NG-based BBJ aircraft. The MAX-8-based BBJ, because of its greater fuel efficiency, enjoys a range increase to over 6,700 miles, whereas the earlier models were limited to 6,200 miles.

Conclusion

The Boeing 737 is the most successful and longest produced jetliner in aviation history. This special airplane first flew fifty years ago, has sold 14,787 examples, and will soon be produced at a rate of fifty-two aircraft a month. What is it about this airplane that has allowed it to outsell and outlive many newer aircraft designs by decades? The answer to this question lies in the sound fundamental configuration that was conceived in an internal competition between two development teams. These teams, led by Joe Sutter and Jack Steiner, had the same objective: to build the best short to medium range airliner possible. This competition led to the decision to use the wide, six abreast cabin. This not only provided additional passenger comfort, it also brought about great commonality between the 737 and the larger 707 and 727 jets already in airline service. This cabin selection caused the designers to break with convention and adopt the underwing engine configuration, mitigating weight and balance issues. The underwing engine and conventional tail configuration worked well, and created an aircraft that was inherently well balanced and could be "stretched" with relative ease. These are the basic qualities that have allowed the 737 to be improved throughout the years. The aircraft has grown to accommodate twice the number of passengers of the original 737-100 series with a fuel consumption that is less than half the first 737. Range has also increased, allowing true transcontinental and some intermediate overwater operations with the new 737 MAX.

The designers have used the highest level of technology to improve the 737 through four generations, each offering greater reliability and fuel efficiency than its predecessors. This has been accomplished because the product development teams strive to make cost effective aerodynamic and system changes at every opportunity. These goals led to the high lift and super efficient wing on the 737NG and MAX, allowing a fuel efficient cruise speed a full ten percent higher than the earliest 737s. The adoption of high bypass turbofan technology provided by CFMI powerplants has enabled the 737 to become the powerful, efficient jetliner it is today. Boeing designers have made wise decisions, balancing new technology and maintaining similarity to the legacy 737 airplanes. One case in point is the overhead systems panel, which is largely unchanged from the first prototype in 1967. The cockpit design was logical and well thought out from the very beginning, allowing "same type rating" for pilots with very minimal differences training across the generations. The 737 has been adaptable, has pioneered the use of composite primary structures, and has had the flexibility to foster the use of the latest navigation and communication technologies with minimal modifications. Designing and building a remarkable airplane is crucial, but high production rates are also vital to remain competitive. Through the use of "lean" manufacturing principles, Boeing's Renton assembly hall has been able to achieve much higher production rates through proactive elimination of waste and inefficiency.

What has this all meant? The 737s being produced today and tomorrow are faster, have significantly more range, have greater reliability, are more weight efficient, have markedly lower operating costs, are flown by cross-generation qualified 737 pilots, are significantly quieter, have best in class fuel efficiency, and are produced at rates unimaginable in the past. Additionally, newly produced 737s are more than competitive, even with brand new airplane designs in their size category.

The 737 is poised to have a bright future with the introduction of the 737 MAX. The first flight of the MAX coincided with the fiftieth year of 737 production—an amazing milestone by any measure. Due to constant refinement and maturing computational fluid dynamics design techniques, the MAX offers the largest single fuel efficiency improvement between generations in the 737 program. Considering the long production run that is planned for this aircraft and the incredible durability of the 737 design, it

A formation lineup impression of the 737 MAX family, with the MAX-9 (nearest) in company with the MAX-8 and MAX-7. *Courtesy of The Boeing Company*

is entirely conceivable that 737s may still be flying the airways on the type's one-hundredth anniversary too! The success of the 737 is directly attributable to the generations of Boeing people who created an extremely good design as a basis with a constant daily push to improve the aircraft.

Many have asked if there will be a follow-on 737 derivative, and the short answer is that no one knows for sure at this time. Factors likely to determine if the next aircraft to fill the niche will be a 737, or an entirely new design, are many, but are most likely to be technology and airline market driven. Historically, since the beginning of the 737 program, the "sweet spot" for aircraft capacity in this class has increased approximately ten percent per decade. This is made evident by the size progression of the most

popular aircraft of each 737 generation. The 737-300 was the most popular of its generation, with the larger 737-800 being by far the best seller of the Next Generation series. With the recent popularity of the more spacious 737-900 series increasing, it appears this trend will continue. The current 737 design limits further expansion because of landing gear geometry in relation to fuselage length. To make the aircraft significantly longer the landing gear would also have to be revised, which might require a redesign of the landing gear wells and the wings and center section. The desire to expand capacity may lead Boeing to either conduct a major revision to the 737 airframe or possibly design an entirely new aircraft when the time comes. In due time that story will also unfold.

This view of NASA 515's AFD shows the experimental "Brolly Handle" control system and early EFIS displays. *Courtesy of The Boeing Company*

This is a book about the Boeing 737, a remarkably long lived aircraft that has been a transportation system designed by generations of engineers, for generations of passengers, flown by generations of pilots, and maintained by generations of mechanics. We have discussed the airplane from the points of view covering the interests of all these stakeholders, but we have left out much about the evolution of the environment in which the airplane operates. The 737 design has transcended the evolution of air traffic management and the associated avionics development during a period of over sixty years. When the 737 entered service, avionics and ground infrastructure supporting an airplane's need for communications, navigation, and surveillance (often abbreviated "C-N-S") was incredibly primitive relative to the complex system being developed today and the sophisticated environment emerging for the future. While the 737 has by no means been the sole airframe supporting this evolution, its dominance in numbers and operations has often made it the airplane of choice as a development platform for new avionics addressing changes in C-N-S technologies. The NASA 515 Boeing 737 research airplane was dedicated to the exploration of possibilities to enhance operations in the airspace of the present and the future. The 737 was often the first to enter large-scale commercial service bearing new and productive technologies for improving flight safety and efficiency in an airspace that supports burgeoning traffic volume. To understand how airspace infrastructure and C-N-S evolved and applied to the 737 warrants a departure from linear exposition about the airplane and justifies a thorough historical journey from the beginning of "aided" flight that first enabled the routine operation of aircraft at night and in poor visibility.

Although entire books could certainly be written on each of these subjects, my goal here is to give the reader a slightly broader picture of how these developments related historically to aviation's evolution, and how each of these topics pertains to the Boeing 737. It is worth noting that there are many events and key contributors to these advances that will go unmentioned in this chapter due its brief, capsular summary. This qualifying statement is also an apology in advance, most especially to those key individuals and organizations that have inadvertently been omitted. The pioneering advances noted have required many hundreds of pathfinders and dozens of organizations to make the incredibly profound changes that have yielded the safety and efficiency we now take for granted in air transport. The global aviation industry and airline passengers alike owe these pathfinders a tremendous debt. Hence, this disclaimer is offered to note that the omission of any particular event, individual, or organization was a difficult, heart-wrenching decision. It is only possible for a small sample of the many vignettes to be told, acknowledging only a fraction of the key individuals involved in each of those particular events, to better tell the 737's story in context. This chapter reflects the wisdom and memory of individuals who are familiar with this history and the many participating aircraft. In many cases they were and are instrumental in guiding the future. The author is grateful for their insights and assistance.

Ship One: The Later Years

PA099 was the first of her kind. This aircraft (N73700, c/n 19437, l/n 1) underwent the most demanding tasks of the original 737 flight test program and always carried an "Experimental" airworthiness certificate. Although it was built as a 737-100 to Lufthansa specifications, it was never intended to see service as an airliner, and after retirement from testing at Boeing went into storage. It was not until July 26, 1973, that this aircraft was acquired by the National Air and Space Administration (NASA) for airborne research, where it became known as NASA 515 and was re-registered N515NA. The research conducted with this aircraft continues to benefit future airliners, many of which were also 737s, including those still being built decades after this historic aircraft's first flight.

In 1968, long before NASA owned NASA 515, the United States Senate Committee on Aeronautical and Space Sciences issued a report that defined the need for the development of policies regarding aviation research and development. The study recommended that NASA and the Department of Transportation undertake a cooperative study on the problems and possible solutions in the modern air transportation system. Eventually called the Civil Aviation Research and Development (CARD) study, the findings of the group led them to recommend the federal government take a direct role in developing new systems for civil aviation. NASA test pilot John "Jack" Reeder, who was well regarded and an avid supporter of advances in civil aviation, presented his idea for the formation of a research program to

Ship One was repainted in this scheme and became known as NASA 515 after being delivered to the National Air and Space Administration.
Courtesy of Jennings Heilig

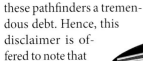

Barry Graves, who was instrumental in the CARD studies. The concepts these two men independently envisioned were merged into a program called the Terminal Configured Vehicle and Avionics program in 1973—later shortened to Terminal Configured Vehicle (TCV). The ultimate goal of the TCV program remained the same: to research and develop advanced technology for aircraft.

When NASA acquired NASA 515 in 1973, the TCV program was started with the goal of creating instrumentation technology for the Space Shuttle and the civil aviation industry. Both of these required predictive instrumentation so pilots would not only have a precise idea of the aircraft's location, but could also see the trends of direction, altitude, and speed. Unfortunately, these projects required displayed information that was difficult to produce with analog, electro-mechanical instrumentation. The origins of the Electronic Flight Instrumentation System (EFIS) began with the research accomplished for the Boeing 2707 SST program, but were developed using NASA 515 to overcome the challenge of testing this new technology in a real aircraft while in flight. To allow this, the aircraft's cockpit was maintained in a fairly conventional configuration, but a second 737-type cockpit shell was installed in the cabin of the aircraft, just forward the wing. This installation was referred to as the Aft Flight Deck (AFD). The modification was completely internal to the aircraft, except for cameras and other required sensors which could, in some situations, give the pilots in the AFD a forward view outside via television screens. It was otherwise a "blind" cockpit, so to speak, because the windshields were blanked out when the television screens were not in use. It allowed various instrumentation combinations to be tried in flight, as the pilots in the AFD could fly the aircraft on the experimental instrumentation while two other pilots in the front cockpit closely monitored the aircraft's progress. Pilot control inputs from the AFD were processed through a mode of the autopilot called Control Wheel Steering (CWS), and in turn the autopilot commanded the aircraft's flight controls accordingly, though the pilots in the front cockpit were able to override the rear cockpit if safety became compromised. Because of some of the special systems being researched NASA 515 had a fourth hydraulic system installed powered by an electrically driven pump for use as needed, depending on the equipment being tested.

Creative efforts were made by designers and engineers to maximize the space available in front of the pilots for navigation displays. It was found that the conventional control yoke in the AFD was positioned in such a way that it blocked the view of the lowest part of the instrument panel, just in front of the pilot. A unique set of control handles were developed which had the left hand and right hand controls for each pilot separately mounted on each side of a central display. They became known as "Brolly Handles," after an English gentleman noted that each one looked like the handle of an umbrella ("brolly" is slang for umbrella in Britain). Although the Brolly Handle concept did not become mainstream in future airliners, a similar approach known as the McFadden Sidestick controller did. The Sidestick controller was tested on 515, and a related design is in widespread use on today's Airbus A320, A330, A340, and A380.

NASA 515 tested various technologies, many of which have become standard equipment on today's jetliners. Not only was the EFIS system developed, but other important systems that greatly enhanced the safety and utility of jetliners were also

NASA 515 approaches a thunderstorm in Colorado in 1992 while conducting wind shear/microburst research as seen from a tail-mounted camera. *Courtesy of NASA*

During tests where the aircraft was being flown from the rear cockpit the pilots in the conventional front cockpit observed. The large console mounted to the center of the glare shield was equipped with a "TAKE OVER" button, allowing the front cockpit to immediately assume control if the need arose. This photo was taken just prior to the aircraft entering a microburst for research in 1992. *Courtesy of NASA*

A NASA Langley crew conducting wind shear and microburst studies from the aft flight deck (AFD) of NASA 515. This cockpit was a representation of a 737 cockpit installed in the cabin of the aircraft to test experimental equipment while in flight. From left to right: Program Manager Rowland Bowes, Research Pilot Lee Person, Deputy Program Manager Michael Lewis, Research Engineer David A Hinton, and Research Engineer Emedio Bracalante. *Courtesy of NASA/Langley Research Center*

conceived. Following the crash of Delta Air Lines Flight 191, the study of the effects of thunderstorms, microbursts, and windshear came to the forefront as a high priority for airline safety. 515 was equipped with advanced systems, such as sensors for Doppler Light Detecting and Ranging (LIDAR), Doppler Radar, and infrared. The goal was to deepen the understanding of thunderstorms and microbursts, and to determine the best methods of mitigating these hazards. Computers were used to record speed and altimeter data during tests while NASA 515 was intentionally flown into and through extreme conditions. Based in part on the technology developed, additional wind shear modes were added to the aircraft's Flight Director, an instrument that gives pilots suggestions on how to maneuver the aircraft depending on the mode selected. Today, the Flight Director is programmed with algorithms that display optimum pitch attitudes based on airspeed and altitude data to the pilot in real time. Based on much research, including NASA 515's flights, wind shear detection and recovery systems were developed that have undoubtedly saved hundreds if not thousands of lives.

Due to increasing airspace congestion causing aircraft delays and lengthy airborne holding times, the TCV program introduced and developed another concept known as "4D Navigation" (also known as Time Navigation, or TNAV). The ability for an airliner to arrive over a starting point on an arrival or approach to a busy

This view of NASA 515's AFD shows the experimental "Brolly Handle" control system and early EFIS displays. *Courtesy of The Boeing Company*

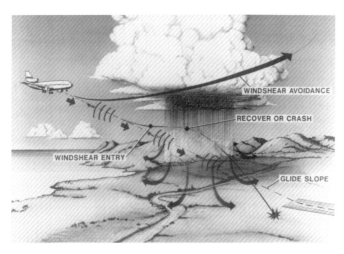

The importance of early wind shear detection. If the aircraft proceeds into the wind shear situation prompt recognition and recovery must occur. Systems developed aboard NASA 515 were the basis of today's Predictive Wind Shear (PWS) systems, which supply early warning and a much safer flight path (thick black arrow). The Enhanced Ground Proximity Warning System (EGPWS) has wind shear recognition functions in case the aircraft fails to avoid the microburst. This system will give the pilots a clear aural and visual "WINDSHEAR" warning, as well as provide optimal pitch guidance to allow the best chance of recovery. *Courtesy of NASA/Langley Research Center*

The infrared sensor was mounted in one of the blanked out passenger windows. *Courtesy of NASA*

The Doppler Light Detecting and Ranging (LIDAR) system as installed on NASA 515. This system was used to detect the rapid wind changes that cause wind shear encounters. *Courtesy of NASA*

way to a newer technology, the Global Positioning System (GPS). These early GPS approaches led to the modern GPS-based Performance Based Navigation (PBN), utilizing Required Navigation Performance (RNP) instrument approaches. These specialized approaches could be designed for curved flight paths with a constant angle descent to terminate at just the right point above the runway. Without the development of the original EFIS systems the precise situational monitoring required for RNP approaches would not be possible.

Preservation of a Legend

After Ship One ended service with NASA, it was placed in storage at Moses Lake, Washington, due to the area's relatively dry climate. Once there, it was kept in operational storage under the loving care of Bob Bogash. Bogash's association with this airplane began long ago, when he worked for Boeing on the 737 program as a liaison engineer at Plant Two, when PA099 was being assembled

Bob Bogash in the captain's seat of NASA 515 (Ship One). *Courtesy of Bob Bogash*

airport at a precise time would improve air traffic control's efficiency, resulting in an increase of aircraft capacity at airports. Additionally, 4D technology could assist pilots by calculating a departure time window with earliest and latest times so they could make travel time constraints without the need for airborne holding. The air traffic controllers at Denver ARTCC partnered with the TCV program to test this technology and its potential benefits, because if the most efficient speeds for time constraints were flown precisely the 4D process would also result in reduced fuel burn.

Many airlines, such as Alaska Airlines, operate into airports where conventional straight-in approaches are not possible because of terrain and other factors. Additionally, some airports have unusually high visibility requirements, making scheduled service difficult, while other airports need curved approach paths to avoid noise sensitive areas or conflicting traffic patterns. The first development of this type of navigation was the microwave approach, which NASA 515 proved was a possible option and saw limited use in specialized operations. The microwave systems soon gave

in 1966. He was there when the aircraft was first set on its landing gears, and he was the first person to close the forward entry door when the aircraft became "shop complete" and was moved to the paint hangar for painting. Over the years, Bogash developed a strong connection to this magnificent aircraft. Since Bogash knew the condition of an aircraft deteriorates quickly with non use, he set up a maintenance schedule that saw him visiting the aircraft over 160 times during a six-year period. All of the aircraft systems were operated, engines ran, and the aircraft taxied around the airport area during each visit. Volunteers from The Museum of Flight in Seattle, Washington and Boeing frequently accompanied Bogash on these missions to keep it running, and after each session Bogash removed its battery and took it home for charging and maintenance. Many parts were upgraded or replaced.

After six years at Moses Lake, agreements were made for NASA 515 to fly to its new home at The Museum of Flight in Seattle. Even though it was still owned by the United States government through NASA, this special aircraft was permanently loaned to the museum. To prepare 515 for flight after six years

NASA 515 at liftoff, showing the blow-in doors behind the inlets indicative of the early Original series. *Courtesy of The Boeing Company*

spare parts were needed, so Japan Air Lines rebuilt the wheels and brakes for the flight. Bogash recalled soliciting help from Alaska Airlines:

> Alaska Airlines was terrific... . Three truckloads of parts were flown in from outstations. They had nine 200s with gravel kits and cargo doors...I wanted to get hold of these guys because I needed parts. I looked in the phone book and tried to get their headquarters or their hangar, so I called reservations. They asked, "Where do you want to fly?" I said, "No, I don't want to fly anywhere. I need parts for my airplane. I need to get through to maintenance." Within twenty minutes I was talking to the right people..."Sure!" they said. I love those guys.

On September 23, 2003, NASA 515 was successfully flown back to its home at Boeing Field and The Museum of Flight. The thirty-three minute flight was commanded by Dale and Mark Ranz, with Bob Bogash as the aircraft's crew chief. Brien Wygle was also on board as the safety observer, more than thirty-six years after the 737's first flight, which he had copiloted with Lew Wallick. The next day, Bob Bogash ran the engines for 2 hours and 43 minutes to burn off the remaining 6,000 pounds of reserve fuel from the flight.

He was onboard for the first engine start and the last engine shutdown of this monumentally significant aircraft. In 2016, a new Aircraft Pavilion was added to The Museum of Flight which houses NASA 515 alongside E1 (Boeing 727 Prototype N7001U), RA001 (747 Prototype N7470), ZA001 (Boeing 787 Dreamliner third Prototype N787BX), and a Boeing VC137B Air Force One (SAM 970), among several others preserved by the museum.

First in Composite Primary Structures

The 737 pioneered many new technologies throughout its long operational life, including the use of a composite primary structure. In July 1977, Boeing took part in a $19 million cost sharing NASA study called the Aircraft Energy Efficiency (ACEE) program. Aircraft manufacturers, including McDonnell Douglas and Lockheed, also took part in different aspects of the program. Boeing was chosen to explore composite technology on the horizontal stabilizers of the 737-200. The criterion for the project was to make this primary structure with excellent strength and durability in all weather conditions, while also having exceptional damage tolerance and repairability.

The new stabilizers for the 737 were produced quite differently from older composites. Many traditional composites were made with aluminum honeycomb, which not only had a tendency to delaminate, but the composite material also had corrosion issues when combined with aluminum. Experiences with these older secondary structures led to some airlines looking at primary composite structures with significant suspicion. Boeing found that when graphite epoxy was used in conjunction with the titanium lug design on the 737, the flexibility of the bonded materials was significantly different and could readily lead to premature structural issues. This problem was specific to the 737 stabilizer design, though, as titanium and graphite epoxy can be used with great success, depending on the design of the interface. The specifics of the 737 design led Boeing to choose a solid piece of graphite fiber with stainless steel lugs and an aluminum leading edge to prevent problems inherent to older processes.

Boeing's John Quinlivan, who was vice president and general manager of the 747, 767, and the composites intensive 777 explained: "There were a lot of people questioning whether we should ever put carbon fiber on a commercial airplane of any type."

Dave Wilson, the senior principal engineer for the 737 Composite Stabilizer Program, remembered the airlines who had mixed experiences with older technology aluminum honeycomb composites: "When you go to the 737 stabilizer structure, instead of having honeycomb, we used a solid laminate. Now you are in a different situation. You don't have this thin face sheet any longer. It is a much more…durable, thick structure, and has a whole new set of properties…."

Boeing engineers had to use some interesting tactics to sell the airlines on the new carbon fiber structures. Quinlivan recalled an event that occurred decades later to prove the viability of composites for the Boeing 787, an airliner made mostly of these materials:

One of the better things that we did: We had a fuselage panel that Gary [Oakes] and others took around the world for the 787 with a half inch peen hammer and gave it to the customer and gave him the hammer and said, "Go ahead and pound on it!"

Gary Oakes, an engineering fellow at Boeing, recalled a memorable event during one such demonstration:

We darn near killed the vice president of engineering at a potential customer airline. He insisted that he wanted to use the sledgehammer, and he wanted to hit it as hard as he could. I knew it would work. We had beaten enough parts over the years. We turned him loose with the panel while I was sitting on one edge of it to keep it from springing back. The hammer sprung back out of his hands, sailed across the shop that we were working in, and went right past his head. That would be great for sales: we just killed an airline vice president! Those hands-on demonstrations were

The composite stabilizers being readied for installation at Boeing's Renton assembly hall. *Courtesy of G. Oakes, D. Wilson, and J. Quinlivan/Boeing*

This MarkAir 737-2X6C Advanced (N670MA, c/n 23121, l/n 1025) was the first of MarkAir's fleet to be equipped with composite stabilizers. This airplane was lost during a training accident on June, 2, 1990, due to pilot error. *Courtesy of G. Oakes, D. Wilson, and J. Quinlivan/Boeing*

without a doubt the most effective way to get past the idea that carbon fiber structures are fragile. The service history of the 737 tails proved it without a shadow of a doubt.

The graphite stabilizers were first flown on N781N (c/n 22275, l/n 687), a factory new 737-201 built for Piedmont Airlines temporarily used for FAA certification. This aircraft flew with the experimental stabilizers on September 26, 1980, and became the first commercial jetliner to fly with a composite primary structure. N781N was returned to a standard aluminum stabilizer configuration prior to delivery to Piedmont on October 27, 1980. Interestingly, this aircraft never entered commercial service with the composite structures that it introduced to the aviation world. Later, after a nearly two-year certification program, the approval to use graphite epoxy horizontal stabilizers was granted in August 1982. Five other 737s were later delivered to their new owners with the approved graphite epoxy stabilizers and entered airline service with them installed beginning in 1984. These aircraft were:

737-232 Advanced	Delta Air Lines	N314DA	c/n 23086 l/n 1012
737-232 Advanced	Delta Air Lines	N307DL	c/n 23079 l/n 1003
737-2X6C Advanced	MarkAir	N670MA	c/n 23121 l/n 1025
	Written Off 6-2-1990 because of a training accident		
737-2X6C Advanced	MarkAir	N671MA	c/n 23122 l/n 1036
	C-GANV with Air North (as of 2015)		
737-2X6C Advanced	MarkAir	N672MA	c/n 23123 l/n 1042

On June 2, 1990, while operating on a training flight, N670MA crashed 7.5 miles northwest of runway 14 at Unalakleet Airport, Alaska. According to NTSB/AAR-91/02: "Deficiencies in flight crew coordination, and their failure to adequately prepare for and properly execute the non-precision approach and their subsequent premature descent" was deemed the cause of the mishap. Fortunately, the four people on board survived, but the aircraft was a total loss, with one engine and the tail section torn from the aircraft. Boeing purchased the graphite epoxy stabilizers from the wreckage to study the effects of a long service life on the composite structures. The outboard portion of the right side stabilizer was damaged from the crash, but its inboard section, along with the left hand unit, were mostly undamaged. Dave Wilson shared the results of the inspection:

> Pulse-echo inspection of the upper and lower skin panels detected no damage. Visual exams of the structure revealed no evidence of surface deterioration… . The teardown focused on each joint to identify structural damage, delamination, wear, fretting, etc., and any corrosion on the Aluminum-Graphite Epoxy surfaces. No damage or delams were found except those resulting from the crash. No corrosion was found on the Aluminum-Graphite Epoxy interfaces; fretting and wear was not apparent. The interior of the box was clean with no moisture. All joints had the original protective system in place with no cracking or degradation. The damage to the right hand structure was limited to the impact area; the remainder did not shatter or exhibit extensive delamination.

Gary Oakes pointed out:

> One of the most important learnings that we got from the 737 stabs, particularly with the first teardown in 1990 to support the 777 design at that time, was that issue of the coefficient of thermal expansion and corrosion protection. For the 737 stabilizers, all of the end ribs are aluminum and the leading edges were aluminum. We had to come up with a galvanic isolation system and how to deal with that local thermal coefficient of expansion difference. They did, but the proof of the pudding was when we brought them back in 1990. They had 19,308 cycles and 17,318 hours and were six years old. One of the first things that we did when we tore it apart was to look at those aluminum interfaces to see what had happened. We looked at the aluminum parts to see if they had fatigued because of the thermal expansion differences. We looked at the corrosion issues. Had we gotten bore corrosion? The system we had put in place was pretty much invented for that stabilizer. We didn't find anything, and that went a long way toward making the case for using aluminum the way we were going to use it on the 777.

The composite studies spearheaded with the 737 never became mainstream on the 737 line, but qualified the extensive use of composite structures in future jetliners, such as the 777-200 and -300, which used far more composite structures than the aircraft Boeing had previously produced. These experiences also greatly influenced the development of the 787 and its primarily composite fuselage, wings, and tail surfaces. The use of composite materials was one of the most important advances in commercial jet design in the twenty-first century, and it all started with the 737.

EFIS Development and History

The electronic flight instrumentation system (EFIS) was comprised of highly refined displays enabling pilots to quickly gather situational and predictive information during flight. Prior to this invention, jetliner cockpits were equipped with electro-mechanical flight instruments which were effective at displaying the aircraft's current state to the pilot, but were limited in providing a clear picture of trends. Additionally, moving maps were not practical on these mechanical displays, requiring the pilot to generate an accurate image of the aircraft's location and where it was headed in his or her mind. This formulated image was then used to decide a course of action. The complexities involved in decision making increased the probability of errors when pilots found themselves in task-saturated environments.

In the late 1960s, Boeing engineers developed flight instrumentation technology using research drawn from the North American XB-70 Valkyrie Supersonic Bomber program. This technology was then further refined while conducting concept studies on the Boeing 2707 Supersonic Transport (SST). During this study, it was agreed that the SST would need to be flown by the pilot with greater precision than subsonic jetliners. The electro-magnetic instrumentation employed for the attitude indicator was comprised of a gyroscopic assembly which utilized a ball marked with pitch and roll angles that was visible to the pilot on the instrument panel. As the aircraft's flight attitude changed, this ball would indicate the current aircraft state to the pilot. The added precision required by the SST would necessitate much wider spaced graduations to be useable for the pilot to achieve the same level of altitude control. It was calculated that the resultant instrument would be far too large to fit behind the instrument panel. This was a challenging situation for the SST engineers and required a "clean sheet of paper" approach to a viable solution. While a resolution was being sought for this problem, engineers elected to use a cathode-ray tube (CRT) as a temporary measure, as other parts of the SST cockpit continued to be developed and simulated.

> Flight Deck Engineer Del Fadden recalled:
>
> A couple of the test pilots that were consulting with Boeing had flown the XB-70. It was a difficult airplane to fly at high altitude. The pitch control was super sensitive. Automatic control was fine, but if you tried to fly it manually it was really, really difficult. Our very first project was to do something to improve the pitch sensitivity on the electro-mechanical [cockpit instruments for the Boeing SST]. There's only so much you can do… . You can't get the mechanical ball to be as big as you need. So as a research task we just did it on a CRT to be able to see what worked and to be able to test various pitch scaling values. We tested scaling that was over twice as sensitive as conventional electromechanical ADIs. That worked so well that we said, "We should just do it that way on the SST displays."

Del Fadden worked alongside engineer John Warner, whose PhD research was primarily on the development of predictive instrumentation. At the time command displays were in widespread use on commercial airliners, where they used an instrument called

The North American XB-70 Valkyrie was a supersonic bomber development capable of speeds over Mach 3. This example (62-0001) completed eighty-three flights before the program was canceled and is now preserved at the United States Air Force Museum in Dayton, Ohio. Its sister ship, 62-0207, was lost in a midair collision in June 1966. *Courtesy of The Boeing Company*

a flight director to give the pilot suggested pitch and roll information based on the task selected by the pilot. This allowed the pilot to simply maneuver the attitude indicator's aircraft symbol on to the translated flight director symbols to maintain and/or resume the correct flight path. The flight director could be programmed to maintain altitude, climb, or descend. It could also be programmed to simultaneously follow a heading or navigational track.

Instrument Landing System (ILS) approaches could also be flown with the flight director, providing pitch and roll commands to bring the aircraft down the approach path with great precision. The command type display (provided that the pilot had programmed it correctly) would furnish good information, describing how to correct the current state of the aircraft. However, this type of display had its limitations, since it gave little information as to where the airplane was actually going and what speed, altitude, and navigational trends existed. Estimations of those trends had to be generated in the pilot's mind if the command display were to be believed, thus raising the cognitive workload for the pilot. This high workload would be especially compounded for the pilot on poor weather approaches.

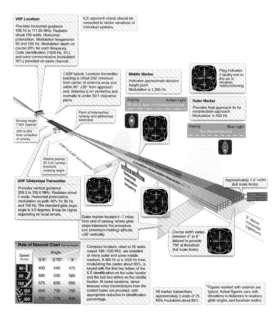

The components of the modern Instrument Landing System (ILS) are shown. *Federal Aviation Administration*

The advent of predictive displays eased the pilot's situational awareness workload substantially by giving them real time predictions on the future state of the aircraft. For example, if the aircraft is descending, the pilot will have set a level off altitude which the computer then uses to present a curved, green line on the moving map display. Since the aircraft's computers know its current rate of descent and groundspeed, it can adjust this line to inform the pilot if it is necessary to increase or decrease the rate of descent to level off at a specific navigational fix. This technology worked effectively with horizontal navigation as well, and the flight path vector was an effective tool used to show the pilot what rate of turn would be required to smoothly intercept a course while hand flying the aircraft. Eventually, this predictive technology was applied to other symbols for showing pilots airspeed and altitude trends.

During these studies, flight deck engineers quickly realized that even small details help the pilot. One common trait of most jet engines at the time was that they were slow in accelerating from idle to a speed producing meaningful thrust. When an experienced pilot advanced the thrust levers, he knew what power setting he wanted to command. On older displays the pilot would move the thrust levers by feel to a position that was "about right," with the engines taking two to four seconds to respond. The pilot would then have to look back at the gauges and make further adjustments to get the final setting. With predictive displays the desired engine thrust could be set, with predictors showing the thrust setting where the engines would stabilize. These small detail enhancements created a cockpit environment that is less task saturated, leaving the pilot with additional mental bandwidth to monitor the flight's progress and make prudent decisions. Del Fadden continued:

At that point, the second and third generation of jets hadn't come out yet and the accident rate was a concern. The NTSB judged most accidents to be caused by some form of pilot error. Basically, we saw our job as: Figure out how to help the pilot do a better job. From the earliest time that we talked about the predictive equipment, I thought that it was absolutely the right answer. Pilots don't make mistakes intentionally. They may make a mistake because they understand the situation incorrectly or incompletely, so our job was to figure out why and find a better way to present information that the pilot could use more effectively… . The trouble with any command display is that there is no sense of what is going on. The display works really well, but it can also work really well for the pilot to do an absolutely splendid job on the wrong task and looking at the command display, he can't tell the difference. My lead engineer John Warner introduced me to the concept of predictive displays and how we could apply them to the SST issues. The neat thing about predictive displays is that the pilot can do almost as good a job as he can with a flight director *and* he sees what the effect on the airplane will be before it occurs. One particular type of failure presented an interesting pilotage task for the SST pilot. If a flight control failure occurred

at supersonic speed, the airplane had to slow down through a very narrow corridor of altitudes and Mach numbers to get back into the subsonic regime, where it could be flown normally. That particular failure left the flight control system in a very basic mode. So John built a CRT-based Mach/Altitude display with a trend predictor. Using that display in the simulator, virtually any of the test pilots, on their first try, could get back through this narrow window. We had great success with it.

In the early 1970s, NASA began a program called the Terminal Controlled Vehicle (TCV) program. Ship One (PA099, the 737 prototype) had long finished its service with Boeing Flight Test and was purchased by NASA to develop new flight instrumentation systems. The SST EFIS displays were developed and improved to benefit commercial aviation and the new Space Shuttle program. Many of the technological goals needed by NASA and Boeing were symbiotic, with advances made for the space effort often benefiting commercial applications and vice versa. Through the cooperation fostered by the TCV program, development of new technologies was exceptionally successful.

The early EFIS systems were based on black and white cathode-ray tube (CRT) displays. As time went on the need to differentiate symbology on the displays led to the introduction of two-color displays featuring red and amber. Two-color systems were a reasonable research tool, but were unsuitable as commercial airplane products. As the evolution of experimental EFIS systems progressed more and more pilots began pushing for a full color display system. At the time, this capability could be achieved only by using a shadow-mask CRT. Initial concerns about vibration of the shadow-mask were quickly resolved, but the problem of brightness remained a significant challenge. Near the equator and at high altitudes the sunlight in a commercial flight deck is incredibly bright, which could easily cause problems for the pilot being able to see the display clearly. Bright sunlight washed out the presentation on the screen, greatly reducing the contrast ratio on the displayed information. Because sunlight is not pure white it has a tendency to shift the color of CRT screen images. Del Fadden continued:

We went on and did a bunch of experiments in high brightness environments with a variety of pilots to figure out what level of brightness they could detect and how much color difference we had to maintain. Unaided, the CRT shadow mask technology at the time was not up to the task, but by adding some exotic filtering on the face of the CRT our equipment supplier, Collins, was able to achieve promising results. To add to the mix, there are big differences between people concerning their individual color sensitivity, even when those people can pass the aviation color blindness tests. While many pilots were reluctant to get involved with color testing, we did get enough volunteers to have reasonable confidence in our test data. We found that we could use only seven different colors and still achieve consistent recognition of the displayed information. We set the test criteria so that the subject had to identify red and amber by themselves with nothing else displayed. For the other five colors the test subjects needed to recognize that a color difference existed. If they could correctly identify the color that was a bonus, but was not required. That test worked, and we got the color space we needed to produce a "full color" display.

An interesting point about the color is that red and blue are at opposite ends of the visible color spectrum. The wavelengths are different. When Collins [Avionics] did the original display, the way they controlled image brightness was to control the amount of time the electron beam illuminated a specific phosphor. Since the blue phosphor was significantly less efficient than the red phosphor, the blue beam had to be turned on for a longer time to achieve a white display image. When our pilots first saw these displays in the simulator and their eyes scanned across the display they would see a color flash associated with what was supposed to be a white display image. We dug into the problem and found that the variable on time was the culprit. The beams had to be on for the same length of time, because if you scanned across it, the color would separate because of the motion of the eye. A subsequent change in the design of the drivers to modulate the beam current instead of the on interval resolved the problem. Today the size of the color envelope is much bigger. The LEDs produce much, much brighter and more pure colors. This opens a huge color space, allowing shading and smoothing of color transitions, and many other visual effects without the need for exotic filters, none of which was possible when we started this.

The EFIS technology, which was developed with the Boeing SST and the NASA TCV programs, has become the industry standard of flight instrumentation in today's jetliners. Through years of research and development engineers were able to correct the problems with the early CRT based systems and went on to pioneer the modern liquid crystal displays (LCD). Using LCD technology, the screens could display many colors with outstanding clarity in all light conditions. Not only were these displays reliable, but they could also display predictive information which would be difficult (and sometimes impossible) to present on the older style electro-mechanical instrumentation. Today the instrumentation technology has enabled pilots to operate the aircraft with a much higher level of situational awareness. The sharp decrease in accidents during the past two decades is evidence of the effectiveness of these high technology systems, as well as more effective pilot training.

Low Visibility Operations History and the 737

The Localizer/Glideslope Approach History

In 1918, commercial aviation began with airmail routes in the United States. During this time period airmail pilots were limited in their ability to make timely mail deliveries due to marginal weather conditions. Because of the lack of electronic navigation equipment these operations were quite dangerous, and pilots risked their lives in poor weather. The first means of long range airway navigation was provided by installing bright lights on the ground which could be seen from the air and followed visually by the pilots. The first lighted airway was installed in 1923 on the New York to San Francisco route, but required clear air and visual acquisition to allow precise navigation. By the time the first transcontinental airmail flight occurred on July 1, 1925, over 300 lighted beacons had already been installed to aid these pioneers on their routes. Although the lighting helped somewhat, the harsh statistics spoke for themselves, as by the end of 1925, thirty-one of the forty pilots hired had been killed in accidents. It quickly became clear that the improvement of navigational equipment was crucial to make this hazardous business safer for pilots. As far back as 1921, the Bureau of Standards experimented with navigational instruments that pilots could utilize for navigation without relying on visual means. By 1926, the airways were equipped with Radio Ranges, enabling pilots to reliably determine their position when flying in the blind. While this was a major accomplishment, pilots still needed visual weather conditions at destination airports to perform safe landings.

Landing aircraft in low visibility conditions, safely and consistently, became a prime focus for early aviation pathfinders. Lt. James "Jimmy" Doolittle conducted the first blind landing on September 24, 1929, in a Consolidated NY2 Husky (NX7918) that was specially equipped with experimental navigation instruments. Among these tools were a Sperry artificial horizon, marker beacon, altimeter (adjustable for changes in barometric pressure), NBS Localizer receiver, and a stop watch. The Husky's airframe was modified with the addition of improved shock absorbers on the landing gears to protect the aircraft during these tests. The first blind landing was successfully accomplished in foggy weather conditions. Later that same day, Doolittle demonstrated another blind landing under simulated conditions by installing a canvas cover over the cockpit during the flight and subsequent landing. This significant event was only possible due to the partnership of several entities working toward this common goal. Those involved in this development were the trustees of the Guggenheim Fund, Sperry Gyroscopes, Kollsman Instruments, the US Army Air Corps, and the US Department of Commerce.

Another critical element in the progression of low visibility navigation was the first "blind landing" employing a Localizer for lateral navigation and a Glideslope for vertical trajectory. This new system was developed by Francis W. Dunmore and G. L. Davies while working for the aeronautics branch of the Bureau of Standards. On September 5, 1931, with an experimental installation in College Park, Maryland, Capt. Marshall S. Boggs executed the first of several instrument landings using a specially equipped Curtiss J-1 Fledgling biplane (registered NS-39). In February 1933, a similar Localizer/Glideslope installation was constructed at the Newark International Airport to continue testing. Two aircraft were outfitted for "hooded" landings with the pilot's view outside blocked, leaving him the instrumentation system as his only reference for landing. These tests were carried out in foggy conditions by Capt. James L. Kinney, while all other aircraft at the field were prevented from operating due to low visibility. The accuracy of the system was proven and required virtually no adjustments to either the ground based transmitters or the airborne receivers during the tests.

It was on this system that Col. Charles A. Lindberg made a blind landing with Capt. Kinney acting as a safety pilot. This technology was even put forth for use on naval aircraft carrier flight operations when on July 30, 1935, Lt. Frank Akers performed the first blind landing with a Berliner-Joyce OJ2 aboard the USS *Langley* off the California coast. Although this technology saw limited use for naval applications at the time, this event certainly proved the accuracy of the new system. During 1934–1936, the Localizer/Glideslope system was put to use in Newark, New Jersey, and Oakland, California. Suitably modified Boeing 247 and Douglas DC-3 airliners were utilized in these operations by United Air Lines and Transcontinental and Western Air (TWA), which executed over three thousand successful approaches on the new system combined.

After successfully demonstrating the viability and safety of the new Localizer/Glideslope system, a similar "Air-Track" system (which later became known as the Instrument Landing System, ILS) was installed in Pittsburgh, Pennsylvania, in 1938. On January 26, a Pennsylvania Central Airlines Boeing 247 made the first commercial passenger approach and landing using the new system under the command of Capt. Cliff Ball and Slim Carmichael. The first operational landings in blind weather conditions began with La Postale de Nuit, a postal carriage division of Air France. Operating DC-3s and DC-4s, they completed over 110,000 flights between 1945 and 1964 without a single cancellation or delay because of low visibility! Landings were accomplished with visibilities as low as eighty meters, roughly equivalent to today's CAT IIIb landing minimums.

The Automatic Landing System

Aviation technology progressed rapidly, with enormous advances in navigation and automation. The use of electronic navigation on lateral and vertical channels presented the possibility of fully automatic landings that could be extremely useful in poor visibility. On August 23, 1937, a Fokker C-14B began an instrument approach into Wright Field, Ohio. Capts. George V. Holloman and Carl J. Crane monitored the approach while their aircraft made the world's first automatic landing using an autopilot system Crane had designed. This was a momentous occasion, and both men were awarded the Mackay Trophy and the Distinguished Flying Cross (DFC). The latter award was presented to Holloman and Crane by none other than Maj. General Hap Arnold. Additionally, in honor of this achievement, Holloman Air Force Base was so named in 1948.

Another monumental accomplishment occurred on September 23, 1947, with a Douglas C-54 of USAAF Air Material Command named *The Robert E. Lee*. Piloted by Capt. Thomas J. Wells, the flight departed Stephenville, Newfoundland, on a transatlantic flight to Brize-Norton, in Oxfordshire, England. The entire ocean crossing, from the commencement of the takeoff roll to the end of the landing rollout, was entirely automatic, with the sole exception of the pilot applying the wheel brakes after touchdown. This aircraft was furnished with state-of-the-art instruments, including a Sperry A-12 autopilot, Bendix autothrottle system, Flux-Valve Compass, radio (radar) altimeter, automatic direction finder (ADF), and a localizer/glideslope receiver.

In the age of early jetliners, Boeing designed an aircraft known as the 367-80, which was the prototype for the Boeing 707 and the KC-135 Air Force tanker. From the outset, this aircraft was intended to be capable of automatic landings. Equipped with the Boeing-Bendix Automatic Landing System, the first automatic landing operation with a jet transport was accomplished in 1959. Meanwhile, in Britain, the Blind Landing Experimental Unit (BLEU), in cooperation with the British Civil Aviation Authority (CAA) and British European Airways (BEA), created a document called BCAR 367, setting parameters and airworthiness requirements for Autoland operations. This document also defined the visibility requirements that became known as CAT I, CAT II, and CAT III (with CAT III being the lowest visibility allowed).

BEA had a large fleet of Hawker Siddeley Trident jetliners which dealt with the ill effects of poor visibility on airline operations on a regular basis. The first approval for CAT II (400 meter visibility) operations in the Trident occurred on February 7, 1968. Sud Aviation was also involved, and gained the first CAT III authorization for the Caravelle on December 28, 1968. The Trident followed suit in May 1972, with CAT IIIa (200 meter visibility) and CAT IIIb (175 meter visibility or less) authorizations in 1975.

CAT III and the 737

Autoland systems are complex and require redundancies for fail-safe operation. Low visibility guidance systems for CAT III operations work differently than autopilots that simply fly an ILS system. With non-autoland systems, the pilot assumes control of the aircraft at the decision point (on a CAT I approach this is typically about 200 feet above the landing surface) and executes the landing with visual references. Conversely, modern autoland systems require additional guidance to properly flare and land an aircraft with precision.

The system on the Boeing 737 works in the following manner: Both Autopilot systems are engaged as the aircraft is maneuvered to intercept the localizer beam. The pilot engages the VOR/LOC mode of the autoflight system, causing the aircraft to turn and follow the localizer signal once it is intercepted. When this occurs, the pilot selects the APP mode on the mode control panel mounted on the glare shield. This commands the aircraft to continue to track the Localizer while locking on to the glideslope and commencing final descent at the appropriate time. At first, the aircraft is flown purely by the signals of the ILS (localizer and glideslope), while the aircraft's autothrottle system maintains airspeed. Initially this works well, but as the aircraft progresses toward the runway the scenario becomes more challenging. Below 100–200 feet above the runway the glideslope signal becomes unreliable, because of the aircraft's close proximity to the runway's glideslope antenna. Momentary interference with the ILS can also cause beam displacement issues at low altitudes. To solve these problems, the Autoland system uses inertial sensors, in conjunction with radar altimeters, to begin augmenting the ILS signals. This begins at about 1,500 feet above runway elevation, after the system completes a self test. Slowly the autoflight computers begin to progressively transfer more authority to the inertial sensors. As the aircraft nears the approach end of the runway the aircraft compensates for variances in the glideslope signal for the landing flare, almost exclusively commanding the autopilots by using inertial information combined with height and descent rate data from the radar altimeters. The flight control computer builds its own path to the runway and issues commands to the autopilot to raise the nose to slow the descent rate just prior to touchdown. At roughly the same time the autothrottle system is commanded to close the throttles to idle. The aircraft then touches down, with its rollout tracking the memorized and smoothed localizer path and signal to maintain the runway centerline.

It is also critical that failures of an autoland system are accounted for, and that the system is tolerant of errors. Safety is built in by using redundant systems and computers that can communicate with each other. Many autoland systems use a triplex arrangement in which three independent flight control computers are fed information from separate sources and work in agreement. If one gives an erroneous solution, the comparison process continues the approach guidance automatically by using the two systems that are still operating in agreement. The third (faulty) system is then ignored and removed from the system, providing the redundancy required for safe Autoland operations. Some aircraft, such as the Boeing 737, provide the same level of redundancy but in a slightly different manner. The 737 possesses dual monitored flight control computers, inertial reference systems, autopilots, and altimetry systems. Each flight control computer provides a monitored independent solution. These multiple outputs are crosschecked and any fault is noticed by the computers. Depending on the fault noted and the type of system installed on the aircraft, the approach is either continued (while safely disregarding the erroneous solution if already below Alert Height), or the system warns the pilot that the autopilot is disconnecting, so as to allow for the pilot to initiate a safe manual go-around and missed approach.

The Head-Up Guidance System (HGS)

In the past, autoland systems on 737s were Fail-Passive designs, with an initial approval down to CAT IIIa weather minima. This allowed a landing in 700 foot horizontal visibility with a decision height of fifty feet above the runway. Later these aircraft were approved for limited CAT IIIb operations that still had a fifty foot Decision Height (DH), but down to RVR 600 feet. (RVR stands for runway visual range and is a measure of horizontal visibility using ground based transmission meters as a measuring device.) While many airlines took this route with their 737 fleets, their aircraft were not approved for automatic takeoffs, so the minimum visibility required for departure was either 600 feet or 1,000 feet at the time, depending on runway lighting or markings. In an effort to reduce takeoff minima, some airlines chose to install the Flight Dynamics Head-Up Guidance System (HGS) to allow lower than standard visibility operations.

One of the first airlines to do so was Alaska Airlines on the Boeing 727-200 trijet. Alaska Airlines Capt. Steve Fulton shared an interesting story from when the HGS was newly certified on the 727 trijet. An elderly Alaska Airlines 727 was holding short with a brand new Boeing 757 on the runway waiting to takeoff in foggy conditions, which were getting worse:

Here is this 727 that is viewed as a "steam jet" in the 1990s. It was a big, noisy beast, huffing and puffing. So here is a brand new 757 that was weeks old that was in front of our airplane. They were cleared on to the runway and the RVR (horizontal visibility) goes below 600. They said that they just wanted to sit there and the controller said, "Negative, we need you to taxi clear of the runway. There is an Alaska 727 behind you that is going to take off." That was a shock wave through the whole industry… . What is going on here? It's not just about low visibility landings, but low visibility takeoffs too.

The Head-Up Guidance System proved itself to be a valuable tool. The Flight Dynamics HGS was already in service on other aircraft types, but needed to be test flown and approved for use on the 737. Alaska Airlines intended to buy the HGS, but in 1993, financial hardships befell the airline. The falling out with their codeshare partner Markair led to the smaller airline directly competing with Alaska Airlines. Two other low fare airlines (Reno Air and Morris Air) also started competing against Alaska Airlines during the same period. Alaska, a higher cost carrier with excellent service, was rapidly losing money, making the airline's management hesitant to spend money on the FAA certification of the HGS. This hesitation on the part of Alaska Airlines gave Morris Air the opportunity to step into the breach. Morris Air saw the HGS as a perfect solution for CAT III operations that were frequently required within their route structure. Morris Air used its fleet of 737-300s, equipped with the HGS system similar to those on the 727, to gain FAA certification on the 737. Southwest Airlines merged with Morris Air in 1994, and soon adopted the HGS system fleet wide. Alaska Airlines emerged from their financial difficulties in 1996, and followed suit by also equipping their 737 fleet with the system. The HGS was a strong choice for many airlines because it not only offered CAT IIIa landing minimums, but also provided runway tracking guidance for low visibility takeoffs. With the use of the HGS, takeoffs with horizontal visibility down to 300 feet RVR were authorized on designated runways. Having lower takeoff minima was also a significant advantage over just having an Autoland system for reduced landing minima.

The HGS system is designed to be intuitive and easy for the pilot to use, even under demanding circumstances. All information available on the pilot's flight instruments is projected on to a glass combiner display between the pilot's head and the windshield. Speed, altitude (barometric and radar), heading, and course guidance are provided while allowing the pilot to simultaneously look through the transparent HGS and the windshield. Inertially compensated flight director guidance is provided with an airplane symbol and a guidance cue. The guidance cue is a small circle that moves in response to the aircraft's displayed flight path. The pilot simply has to maneuver the aircraft to place its symbol on top of the guidance cue. When the HGS is used by itself for low visibility approaches, the entire approach is hand-flown by the pilot, who maneuvers the aircraft to maintain the airplane symbol on top of the guidance cue.

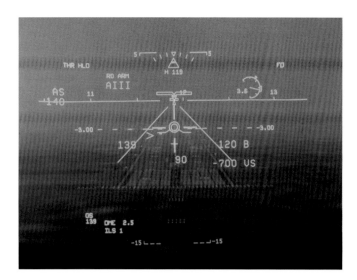

Courtesy of Rockwell Collins

A Category IIIb approach as seen through the Head-Up Guidance HGS-4000 system at 120 feet (above). In the center of the photo the "Flight Path Symbol," resembling an airplane viewed from behind, is observed, showing the present trajectory of the aircraft. Inside the Flight Path Symbol is a small circle, or guidance cue, which is displaying an on course indication. The pilot (or autopilot) simply maneuvers the flight path symbol to overlap the guidance cue, ensuring proper trajectory. On the left "wing" of the flight path symbol is a ">" symbol, which gives airspeed trend information. If it is pointing above the wing the aircraft is accelerating; likewise, if it is below the wing then the airplane is decelerating. Here it is indicating the aircraft's speed is steady.

The altitude above the ground (right) is shown just below the guidance cue and is indicating ninety feet above the surface, based on radio altitude. To the right and slightly below the flight path symbol, "90 B" indicates the aircraft is ninety feet above mean sea level. Since the radio altitude and altitude above sea level are the same, the runway in this example is at sea level. On the top left, "AS 130" is the target approach speed set by the pilot. The "130" just below and to the left of the flight path symbol is showing the actual computed airspeed. On the lower right, the "-650 VS" indicates the aircraft is descending at 650 feet per minute. The projected runway edge lines represent a 200 foot wide runway and appear on the HGS to show the pilot where to look for the runway when the airplane descends through 300 feet and disappears at sixty feet. At about 105 feet a "Flare Cue," which looks like a "+" sign (directly below the flight path symbol), rises from the bottom of the display. When it meets the guidance cue at around forty-five feet, the pilot (or autopilot) follows it by raising the nose of the aircraft to "flare." The word "IDLE" flashes below the flight path symbol, alerting the pilot to retard the thrust levers to idle just prior to touchdown. If the autothrottles are engaged this will happen automatically. On an

approach to Category IIIb minimums, the runway lights may become visible just thirty feet above the runway as the aircraft is being flared out by the autopilot. After touchdown, a runway centerline cue shows the pilot where the actual runway centerline is in case he or she might lose sight of it. Although this system is not approved by administrators for zero visibility operation, it is capable of a blind landing in the event of an emergency.

Hybrid Autoland

CAT III operations with the head-up guidance system and autoland have been used separately in revenue service with excellent safety results. However, Alaska Airlines began to see the potential for reduced landing minimums below CAT III (600 foot RVR visibility) rules by using a "Hybrid HGS/Autoland" equivalent "Fail-Operational" system. Alaska's 737 aircraft were equipped with both systems because the airline was already using the HGS for reduced takeoff weather minimums. The idea was advanced that perhaps the HGS, used in conjunction with the Autoland system (per the FAA's published "Hybrid" criteria), could provide improved landing minimums. Alaska Airlines was the first to apply the method and accomplished the needed "proof of concept" testing, subsequently receiving FAA approval for the use of "Hybrid HGS/Autoland" based on having an "equivalent Fail-Operational" approach capability.

The logic for using a "Hybrid" HGS/Autoland Fail-Operational system was straightforward. Pilots who allowed the aircraft to land using the full autoland system would have the benefit of a fully capable HGS as a backup. The pilot would also have safe rollout guidance using the HGS to track the runway centerline after landing. With the HGS, the pilot had a capable system if the autopilot disconnected for any reason and could have early indications through the HGS that the autoland system was not responding properly. In such an event, the pilot could easily assume control of the aircraft and fly it away under HGS guidance.

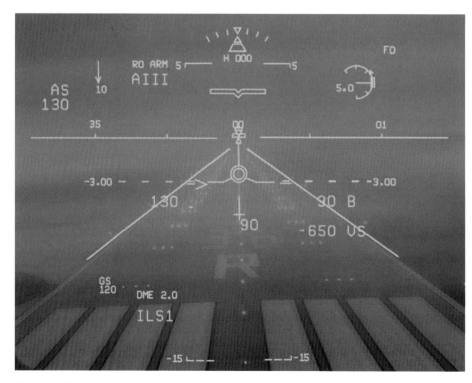

Courtesy of Rockwell Collins

In a dire emergency and following an autopilot failure, the HGS was capable of providing adequate guidance to continue a landing through rollout.

At Alaska Airlines, the additional situational awareness this hybrid system and procedure afforded the pilot was believed to be significant. With the additional OpSpec authorization for CAT III landings using the "Hybrid HGS/Fail-Passive Autoland" system, landings were authorized down to 400 foot RVR visibility with a thirty foot radar altimeter Decision Height. This was close to the lowest CAT IIIb minima available for any air carrier aircraft, including the lowest minima available for the newer 737NGs when utilizing a "Fail-Operational Autoland" with LAND 3 mode (see definition below). It is noteworthy that for any modern Boeing jet using a LAND 3 Fail-Operational Autoland mode, the airline can be eligible for the lowest currently authorized Cat III minima, down to RVR 300 feet. These minima are specified for each of the Touchdown Zone, Mid Point, and Rollout transmissometer (visibility sensor) locations along the runway. Fail-Operational Autoland LAND 3 based operations use an "Alert Height," above which the system assures that full autopilot capability is still available in the late stages of the approach. Fail-Operational Autoland systems that use LAND 3 mode typically do not require a decision height or visual reference. A decision height is only needed for Fail-Passive Autoland or Hybrid HGS/Fail-Passive Autoland systems to assure that adequate visual reference can be established before touchdown.

LAND 3 is an autoland capability possessing the following attributes:

- A Fail-Operational system (only with EDFCS on late model Boeing 737NG and MAX), which means that in the event of a failure the landing will be continued automatically with the remaining operational components of the system.
- Automatic rollout capability
- No Decision Height
- Uses an Alert Height to ensure full operation late into the approach
- Approved down to RVR 300 feet (visibility)

Autoland Using LAND 3 Mode with the Enhanced Digital Flight Control System

The latest 737NG models are equipped with an updated autopilot system known as the Enhanced Digital Flight Control System (EDFCS). This autopilot provided for additional redundancy, engine inoperative autoland capability, more robust crosswind alignment capability, and lateral landing rollout control capability. Collectively, this provided for additional lower visibility landing weather minima authorizations for airlines. The EDFCS autopilot system included customer selectable options at the time of aircraft purchase, depending on the low visibility operations capability needed by the airline. The EDFCS autopilot system could be configured either to allow for full Fail-Operational Autoland with LAND 3 mode, allowing the lowest CAT III minima available, or as with earlier 737s for Fail-Passive Autoland capability without automatic rollout. If the carrier elected to purchase only the Fail-Passive Autoland capability without automatic rollout capability then use of more restrictive CAT III minima applied. The "Fail-Passive only" option was available to allow the operator to use a configuration similar to the 737 aircraft already in the operator's fleet, potentially simplifying the operator's training programs, pilot procedures, fleet deployment, authority authorizations, and manuals. The current EDFCS LAND 2 (see definition below) Fail-Passive Autoland option does not activate the automatic steering for landing rollout capability. LAND 2 is an Autoland capability with the following features:

- A Fail-Passive system (early Boeing 737s and optional on late models equipped with EDFCS), which means that in the event of a hard failure the landing will not be continued automatically.
- No automatic rollout
- Requires a Decision Height and RVR 600 feet (visibility)

If the EDFCS Fail-Passive Autoland option is used in conjunction with an HGS, as with the Alaska Airlines "Hybrid HGS/Fail-Passive Autoland," it could still potentially allow for landings using lower minimums (e.g., RVR 400 feet with a decision height). The EDFCS Fail-Operational Autoland (LAND 3 mode) package has a crosswind align mode, engine inoperative landing capability, and autopilot runway centerline tracking for landing rollout. When using the EDFCS LAND 3 Autoland option all aspects of landing flight control are automatic, even after various failures of autopilot components, sensors, portions of the electrical system, or hydraulic component failures that occur after the aircraft descends below the designated alert height. The pilot needs only to deploy the thrust reversers after touchdown and disconnect the autopilot after the autobrakes have slowed the aircraft to a safe taxi speed. The EDFCS LAND 3 Autoland configuration allows the airline to use the lowest currently approvable Cat III minima down to RVR 300 (e.g., the lowest currently approvable United States FAA Operations-Specifications Cat IIIb minima). These minima are now the lowest available for the 737NG and for other Fail-Operational Autoland capable modern air carrier jet aircraft.

"The Future of Air Navigation: FANS" with Capt. Tom Imrich

With air traffic on the rise, aircraft systems and air traffic services (ATS, also referred to as Air Traffic Control or ATC) need to communicate with each other more efficiently and effectively, providing adequate airspace and airport capacity, safe aircraft separation, and reducing system costs. Improvements are critical for airspace users to assure adequate flexible airspace access while avoiding long ground delays and airborne holding. These inefficiencies and delay issues are even more apparent when the weather at destination airports requires greater aircraft separation due to low visibility, or when the use of alternate arrival routes become necessary, such as during thunderstorms. As ATS evolved, air traffic management attempted to avoid airborne holding by introducing procedures such as Expect Departure Clearance Times (EDCT) during peak arrival periods. ATS applied EDCT to systematically delay aircraft departures at outlying airports and to stagger the arrival traffic flow at busy destination airports. However, this method often left available landing slots unused and wasted airport capacity. Additionally, even with EDCT times many aircraft were still required to enter holding patterns short of the destination while experiencing delays that the system was designed to prevent.

In 1983, while recognizing increasing air traffic congestion and delay occurring globally, the International Civil Aviation Organization (ICAO) formed a committee to study the future of air traffic Communication, Navigation, and Surveillance (C-N-S). ICAO is a subset of the United Nations and is based in Montreal, Canada. This organization sets international standards and recommended practices (SARPS) for use by countries based on a treaty signed in the WWII era by those member nations, as well as being used by the world's airline operators to ensure safe operations internationally. The intent was to address the issues of air traffic congestion and to develop a plan for more efficient flight operations. The study of these elements led to a balanced C-N-S concept called Future Air Navigation System (FANS). The goal was to modernize, optimize, and streamline the air traffic system, and many concepts were explored. Progress toward implementation was extremely slow due to the political nature of this complex international venture. The prospect of a viable outcome looked dim until the early 1990s, when CNS technological advances in aircraft navigation, and communication systems in particular, began to better address some of the implementation challenges with feasible costs.

By the early 1990s, technology had progressed with higher numbers of newer state-of-the-art aircraft in widespread service. Many of these aircraft were equipped with new C-N-S related systems, such as Electronic Flight Instrument Systems (EFIS) based cockpits, inertial systems, flight management s3ystems (FMS), data link (Aircraft Communications Addressing and Reporting System, or ACARS), and interactive collision avoidance systems (TCAS). In particular, the new flight management system capabilities could be used to finally implement some of the recommendations of ICAO FANS studies.

A concept sometimes referred to as "Free Flight" was an additional factor in setting the C-N-S basis for FANS. The three elements of C-N-S needed to be implemented in the correct ratio and proportion with the right capabilities for suitable use by ATS so traffic separation could allow the FANS concept and program to be a success.

In this difficult environment, an informal ad-hoc group of "like minded" airline technical pilots, manufacturer engineers, and ATS and airspace reform advocates sensed what was needed to move ATS forward. They conceived FANS to address the immediate needs of ATS and aircraft separation, and to set a long term foundation for the evolution of ATS and aircraft C-N-S systems. This "ad-hoc" group was formed out of necessity, since there was no formal "state based" panel or organization that had any practical hope of addressing these issues in any reasonable time frame.

Further, there was no practical mechanism through ICAO processes to get the needed simultaneous financial commitment for implementation. Therefore, the group conceived a process and plan to mutually help move FANS forward to implementation on a practically realizable time schedule and limited scale. It was hoped by all parties involved that this limited plan would have a reasonable chance of success. The "ad hoc" FANS development and implementation group consisted of the following primary contributors:

- Dave Allen, the FANS engineering lead from Boeing
- Wayne Aleshire of United Airlines
- David Massey-Greene of Qantas

- Ian Varcoe of Air New Zealand
- Tony Laven of the International Air Transport Association (IATA)
- Tony Maddern of Cathay Pacific Airlines
- Tony Martin, Tom Twiggs, Peter Lemme, and several others from Boeing
- Serge Bagieu of Airbus
- Representatives from the governing authorities of New Zealand and Australia
- Authority Representatives Capt. Tom Imrich, Peter Skaves, George Myers, Roy Grimes, Dave Behrends, and Steve Creamer of the Federal Aviation Administration (FAA)
- Several representatives from FMS and Data Link COM avionics companies working to the specifications or criteria largely defined or set by Boeing engineers
- Paul Fennelly and Vaughan Maiolla from ARINC and SITA, specializing in aviation communication technologies

The ad-hoc group had the backing of some key executives at Boeing, including Dick Peale, who took a leading role in persuading leaders of avionics companies, other OEMs, authorities, and air navigation service providers alike that the FANS program could actually work, and that their best hope of moving forward was committing to FANS. This group had to accomplish an enormous task, with opinions differing widely and globally on how to implement this evolving program. Steering clear of political conflict was especially important for a successful outcome. Ultimately, for navigation Required Navigation Performance (RNP) was key, while for communication, the "datalink" related to the existing Aircraft Communications Addressing and Reporting System (ACARS) was set as the basis. For surveillance, Automatic Dependent Surveillance via "Contract" (ADS-C) was chosen as the primary means. The corresponding needed interfaces with ATS facilities were identified and commitments received allowed the program to be launched. The result was a C-N-S mix called FANS 1 "Package B," which was initially used for the Boeing 747-400. Similarly, a package called "FANS package A" was identified for Airbus aircraft.

Communication

The standard method of communication had long been via duplex party line voice (two-way radio), normally on very high frequency (VHF), as well as on high frequency (HF) for oceanic and long range communication. As air traffic congestion increased steadily throughout the decades busy airspace, combined with numerous aircraft communicating on each frequency, caused an increase in communication delay and errors. Sometimes immediate communication with ATC was not even possible because only one person could transmit at a time on the party line. In oceanic airspace HF communications were often garbled, confusing, delayed, or entirely unintelligible due to range, communication characteristics, or adverse ionospheric radio propagation effects. This caused confusion, delay, and even the increased likelihood of an aircraft taking a clearance intended for another airplane. With data link and satellite technology using Inmarsat, the new FMS systems utilized a textual data link communication system related to the Aircraft Communications Addressing and Reporting System (ACARS). This arrangement allowed pre-defined or text type messaging (rather than voice) introduced through the Flight

Management System (FMS) Control Display Unit (CDU) during long oceanic flights. It could be used nearly anywhere on the globe where suitable communication services were available (e.g., ARINC or SITA). This improvement became the basis for the data link communication element of FANS.

For communication and ADS, FANS "Package B" Boeing 747-400 related tests were well in progress by 1992 at United Airlines, led by Capt. Wayne Aleshire. These tests addressed various "Package B" FANS components, including ADS functions and dynamic re-route flight plan capability (DARPS). These early FANS test flights were typically able to be conducted during normal passenger operations, since the aircraft was also able to routinely navigate and communicate using normal means while still assessing new FANS capabilities.

Navigation

Navigation capabilities have been completely revolutionized by the use of ground-based radio navigation aids first, then by inertial navigation, and finally by GPS based sensors combined in various ways using flight management systems (FMS). Navigation dramatically improved in the 1990s, in terms of navigation trajectory definition, as well as for accuracy, integrity, and availability. The latest stages of navigation capability evolution were in the form of specifying and achieving Required Navigation Performance (RNP) operations, which for the first time since the advent of flight in the early last century could be defined in sensor independent ways. In RNP operations, navigation accuracy, integrity, and availability is assured by the assessments and actions of multiple independent systems that can satisfy the needed navigation capability while alerting the pilot if the system cannot meet these requirements. The detailed development of RNP capability was spearheaded by people like Capts. Tom Twiggs (Boeing) and Tom Imrich (Federal Aviation Administration), dating to the early 1970s. Later development that explicitly displayed and used RNP in FMSs, and depicted RNP and ANP on related flight deck displays, was pioneered by Boeing engineers including Tom Tarleton and Rolan Shomber.

The first practical application of the basic implicit RNP concepts "in service" was with American Airlines operations in Eagle, Colorado (KEGE). American Airlines helped pioneer key preliminary aspects of RNP use with their Boeing 757 operations, flying into and departing back out of Eagle, Colorado. Eagle (KEGE) was a high elevation mountainous region airport constrained in all quadrants around the runway by high, steep terrain. The first "proof-of-concept" tests set the foundation for RNP at Eagle using an American Airlines Boeing 757-223 (N621AN). The tests were piloted by Capts. Bill Syblon and Tom McBroom (American Airlines) on September 6, 1990, and were operationally assessed for approval by FAA operations representatives Capts. Tom Imrich and Jim Enias. With this Boeing 757 aircraft, FMS capability, and a mountain airport location, many of the key aspects of RNP operations were first developed and operationally applied. This allowed American's 757s to be able to routinely, safely, and accurately navigate into landing at that very difficult mountain canyon runway, as well as to be able to later safely depart from that runway on takeoff and accurately navigate through "Cottonwood Pass" while climbing out to a safe cruise altitude. The RNP conceptual design also provided for a safe engine-out missed approach, even if started from as low as the

runway touchdown zone. For takeoff, it maximized the payload by flying an implicit RNP-based safe path even in the event of an engine failure at V1. The RNP path could allow this while providing assured obstacle clearance up to an en route altitude. This initial effort at Eagle, Colorado, then served as the foundation for Alaska Airlines' major pioneering efforts for RNP-based approaches and departures starting in Juneau, Alaska, in 1995.

In broader related industry activities, Capt. Bill Syblon also served in an RNP advocacy leadership role on the ATA/FAA FMS Task Force. That effort supported these kinds of FMS and RNP related developments, along with encouragement and the endorsement of the FAA's Flight Standards Inspector and ATA/FAA FMS Task Force Co-Chair Jim Enias.

Explicit RNP was eventually incorporated into all Boeing flight management systems (FMSs) due to airline requests from Alaska Airlines and others, and as a by-product of the American Airlines 757 Eagle, Colorado, effort. This RNP evolution was also spurred by FANS related developments for oceanic route applications. RNP and its companion assessment Actual Navigation Performance (ANP) were first applied nearly simultaneously on the Boeing

American Airlines Capt. Bill Syblon (right) and Capt. Tom McBroom (left) in Eagle, CO (KEGE), flying the initial "Ad-Hoc" RNP instrument approach and departure procedures for "Proof of Concept" tests with the FAA using an American Airlines B757-223 N621AM, September 6, 1990. *Courtesy of Capt. Thomas Imrich*

N621AM is seen prior to departure from Eagle, Colorado. *Courtesy of Capt. Thomas Imrich*

747-400 and Boeing 737-500. Soon thereafter, the concepts were extended to the 757, 767, and 777 fleets, with major advances in the definitive use of RNP in FMS starting in earnest in 1994.

On August 3, 1994, Continental Airlines 737-524 (N3814, later registered N17614, c/n 27327, l/n 2634) was used by Boeing to first implement, explicitly demonstrate, and ultimately certify RNP and ANP capability using a dual FMS- and EFIS-based system. These tests were flown by Boeing test pilot Capt. Tom Twiggs, with Capt. Tom Imrich serving as the representative from the Operations Authority (FAA). A host of Boeing engineers were onboard to assess the system's performance and record data. The tests used the upgraded RNP/ANP capable FMS with multiple inertial sensors and dual Litton GPS receivers. These were the first significant navigation tests for what later became the certificated FANS-based RNP system used on the Boeing 747-400 and on Alaska's 737-400. The tests served to set the foundation for RNP capable FMS employed on the remainder of the Boeing 737 series and defined the process used for other Boeing models.

This particular RNP test flight was to confirm a variety of RNP related performance aspects, including defining flight technical error limits. The flight was conducted from Boeing Field (KBFI) to the test facility in Glasgow, Montana, and back, with multiple approaches and departures on a four-hour flight. The testing confirmed RNP "normal performance," as well as RNP "non-normal" performance with many kinds of Nav failures, systems related failures, and even engine inoperative failures. Overall, the tests primarily showed consistency with earlier identified results from extensive simulation evaluation. The simulation testing had also included "rare-normal" performance, such as significant winds, turbulence, and wind gradients.

This specific Boeing 737-524 was selected because it was one of the very first aircraft equipped with the optional EFIS flight instrumentation, dual flight management systems, and could serve as the basis for certifying subsequent similarly equipped Boeing 737s. The actual type design change demonstrating RNP capability for the 737-500 was signed off in a test using final production FMS hardware in December 1994. These Boeing 737-500 tests were successful as intended for airworthiness certification and installation of FMS with RNP capability. Furthermore, they set the technical foundation for a much broader installation and operational use of RNP on the 737 and other Boeing types. While the certification of RNP capability on the 737-500 was completed in December 1994, actual operational RNP navigation applications for departures and approaches largely remained on the back burner until Alaska Airlines entered the picture with their 737-400s. Meanwhile, RNP oceanic applications for the Boeing 747-400 had to wait for final FANS certification in June 1995.

At that point in late 1994, with the 737 now having demonstrated airworthiness of RNP capability, the Alaska Airlines effort with RNP and ANP quickly progressed for approach and departure operations. Similarly, since the 747-400's FMS and displays had RNP capability, oceanic navigation applications could start to be implemented with air navigation service providers in the Pacific Flight Information Regions (FIRs) pending certification.

The RNP situation for approach and departure capability evolved dramatically starting in mid-1995, when RNP capability was certified and extended to the Alaska Airlines 737-400 fleet. It was at that point Capt. Steve Fulton led the major advance to operationally implement RNP-based procedures in a major system wide way for departure and approach procedures at Alaska Airlines, whose first RNP operational application for instrument approaches and departures started in Juneau, Alaska (PAJN).

Surveillance

Surveillance (also known as monitoring) is the third component of the critical and pioneering FANS capability triad. Surveillance has gone through a steady and complex evolution, with numerous iterations since the first navigation position reports in the 1930s. Surveillance evolved over time through the era of early primary radars of WWII, beacon transponder mode A radars, and I.F.F. Mode 4 (Identification Friend or Foe) in the 1950s and 1960s. More recent evolutions include the use of secondary radar Mode C, Mode S, the addition of airborne Traffic Collision Avoidance Systems (TCAS) in the 1980s, and currently Automatic Dependent Surveillance (ADS).

The role of surveillance itself in the C-N-S triad is in fact steadily evolving, changing character, and can take on many forms depending on circumstances. In the 1930s, the focus was on periodic and infrequent position reports by air traffic entities to confirm separate trajectories using procedural separation for oceanic and domestic airspace. In the modern era surveillance is vastly different, with ATS actually using a secondary radar to provide a near real time displayed aircraft position as a basis for tactical vectoring of airborne aircraft. Air traffic separation specialists are responsible for metering, sequencing, and maintaining separation in busy terminal areas. In this workload intensive environment, ATS largely substitutes for the role of the aircraft's own navigation capability, with voice communications through a communication-surveillance combination to provide for ATS based "radar vectoring." In the terminal area, this "vector" form of navigation has aircraft essentially led by air traffic service direction, which often lasts until the aircraft is either on a visual approach, or is established on the final segment of an instrument approach. Hence, the role, basis, and requirements for surveillance can vary considerably across airspace domains, from the terminal area, to en route domestic airspace, to the markedly different requirements demanded for oceanic or remote area routes.

The key to successful surveillance is the appropriate balancing of roles for pilots, aircraft, and ATS in maintaining the primary agreed clearance and defined trajectory separation between other aircraft (via navigation) considering terrain, obstacles, and severe weather. If an external agent (ATS) has this responsibility, it has to be via some form of monitoring and display of aircraft positions, and then an air traffic separation specialist must follow rules of separation between airplanes and potential hazards. Unlike where trajectory separation is prime, this latter radar vector method requires expensive and high data rate "surveillance." Furthermore, in a modern "radar vector" era, this concept for the use of surveillance has led ATS to often operate inefficiently in navigating aircraft laterally or vertically within the terminal area. This is done to accomplish their separation goals until the aircraft is sequenced, spaced, and established on final approach.

The FANS effort first recognized and acknowledged the critical set of potentially variable roles for navigation, communication, and surveillance. This allowed for various blends of C-N-S to be used globally in solving airspace and air traffic separation objectives. Whether operating in oceanic and remote airspace, en route in domestic airspace, or even in a busy terminal area, the FANS foundational concepts and components offered a practical and efficient way to help assure aircraft and terrain separation while including numerous benefits for aircraft operators. From the start, FANS conceptually provided for using all three kinds of Automatic Dependent Surveillance (ADS) capabilities: ADS-A, ADS-B, and ADS-C (see following explanation). However, ADS-C was the first element of the evolved ADS surveillance capability to be operationally applied as part of the FANS C-N-S triad, becoming operationally available in oceanic airspace in 1995. Since ADS-C was basic to FANS it was available with most early FANS operations.

- **ADS-A (ADS-Addressable):** Provides that any ATS facility can query an aircraft to essentially trigger a "position report," confirming position or potentially other elements of the aircraft's "state vector," such as altitude, speed, or ETA.
- **ADS-B (ADS-Broadcast):** Provides that an aircraft periodically broadcasts and other nearby aircraft can hear the "state vector" data, such as position, velocity, ID, and altitude. ATS facilities could also listen for that broadcast "state sector" data just as if the ADS-B message was the link of a "pseudo radar" transponder.
- **ADS-C (ADS-Contract):** Provides for an "aircraft to ATS reporting contract" with a specific ATS facility. This allows an aircraft and a particular ATS facility to set up a periodic data link communication data exchange within the ATS facility's area of separation service. This link allows an aircraft to periodically report or ATS to periodically query a specific aircraft for a pre-established series of specified successive "position reports" to confirm position, or other elements of the aircraft's "state sector" as needed. Typical parameter exchanges include the identification of the past Waypoint (WP), next WP, following WP, and altitude and airspeed/Mach existing at the most recently past WP, along with subsequent ETAs. Establishing the contract between aircraft and ATS also allows for establishing a related Controller-Pilot Data Link Communication (CPDLC) link to support exchanging clearance messages or aircraft based flight plan requests in addition to ADS-C reporting.

A major, more recent evolution of ADS emphasizes using Automatic Dependent Surveillance-Broadcast (ADS-B) to allow aircraft to "see" all nearby surrounding aircraft. ADS-B also allows for ATS to electronically view aircraft and in turn provide "pseudo radar like" position and path assurance. Some air navigation service providers (ANSPs) also propose using ADS-B for "radar vector like" services in additional airspace. An example of this might be where radar does not presently exist (e.g., northern Canada), or where ANSPs would like to replace some secondary radars due to their high cost (parts of domestic US airspace). The ADS-B system implemented to date heavily depends on global positioning system (GPS) data and a Mode S transponder data link to determine and exchange position, speed, and identification data for each aircraft. Aircraft that are equipped with appropriate "ADS-B in" reception capability can also receive certain weather data and traffic information from the FAA's ADS-B ground elements. The FAA has currently specified that by 2020, most, if not all, aircraft flying in certain parts of US airspace will need to be equipped with "ADS-B out" capability.

The Utility and Key Concepts of FANS1/A

The first practical applications of combined FANS based communications, navigation, and surveillance capabilities in a complete system were demonstrated for initial certification credit on November 24, 1994. For that initial FANS certification test (identified as Red Label 3) a Qantas Boeing 747438 (VH-OJQ, c/n 25546, l/n 924) was flown under the command of Capt. David Massey-Greene (Qantas) with Capt. Tom Twiggs (Boeing) serving as Flight Test DER (FAA Designated Engineering Representative). This was a historic event, leading to the refining of the C-N-S concepts that FANS pioneered over the next two decades. On board for the dedicated, non-revenue test flight were an array of Boeing engineers and Qantas representatives, as well as authority representatives for data collection and for assessing and verifying system performance. After decades of disjointed C or N or S efforts, this aircraft had finally been configured with a completed array of related and balanced navigation, communication, and surveillance elements the FANS "Package B" offered.

Since the Boeing 747-400 used for this first complete FANS airworthiness installation certification flight test was configured with Rolls-Royce engines, several more subsequent flight tests were eventually needed to address some remedial issues from this test, and for the different engine offerings on other 747-400s. While this round trip flight test between Sydney, Australia, and Avalon, Australia—where the RNP-based approach capability was evaluated—only lasted 7 hours and 16 minutes, it set the foundation for future decades of C-N-S advances. The final 747-400 FANS "Package B" installation certification to address remaining open issues was completed by late spring 1995. That event in turn was immediately followed by authority approval and the first operational FANS flight. Capt. David Massey-Greene was once again in command of the first FANS operational flight from Sydney, Australia (SYD), to Los Angeles (LAX) on June 22, 1995. Capt. Massey-Greene noted it all worked as intended, and that "it was flown on the very next day after the B747 final FANS airworthiness certification. We had HF backup on that flight, but all the primary communications were using CPDLC!"

The 1990 RNP efforts of American at Eagle, the FANS 1/A effort from the early 1990s through the first FANS 1 operational flight in 1995, and the Alaska Airlines early RNP applications to approach and departure were pivotal in evolving airline and ATS capability. They defined the fundamental ability to successfully define and accurately and dynamically fly routes and procedures by RNP. They also demonstrated the reliable exchange of route information, with cleared or requested routes automatically data linked and loaded into the aircraft's navigation system. This conclusively demonstrated the ability for aircraft to reliably and rapidly communicate large volumes of data with ATS ANSPs via a reliable data link.

The ability to have reliable automatic ADS position and aircraft "trajectory state" data reported by "contract" with ATS, without routine pilot intervention, was not just established as fundamental, it also had great potential for reducing errors on the part of pilots and ATS. Secondary forms of ADS for ADS-A and ADS-B evolved from this initial acceptance of the ADS concept.

Only recently is RNP coming into widespread global use for aircraft operations. In some parts of the world Controller Pilot Data Link Communications (CPDLC) and ADS are also becoming mainstream. Since these C-N-S concepts were first pioneered by

FANS 1/A, with each step's success needed for the successful and economic future of ATS evolution, it has taken well over two decades for these key foundational ideas to come to fruition. The ability to receive or request an air traffic clearance via data link, and to have the routing automatically exchanged with an aircraft's flight management system, is now becoming widespread. This has the benefit of avoiding potential human factors in communication errors.

A FANS 1/A Historic Perspective and Postscript

The FANS related CPDLC aspects and ADS are now seeing widespread use, and after two decades of implementation they are being extended to regions like the North Atlantic (NAT). FANS has been safely and efficiently demonstrating the ability to navigate, receive, and request air traffic clearances, address automatic reliable position reporting, and to utilize ADS. Data link based routing or re-routing can be reliably exchanged with an aircraft's flight management computer systems subject to flight crew acceptance. Currently, data link is even used for non-normal communications. FANS related technology has substantially increased the reliability of communications and eased workload for pilots and air traffic specialists while continuing to avoid entire classes of potential communication errors.

The introduction of RNP capability, led by airlines like Alaska (and later Qantas and Westjet), has allowed remarkable progress that improved safe airport access in mountainous regions, schedule reliability, and operating weather minima. In addition, it has simplified pilot procedures while reducing workload. In Oceanic airspace, RNP has allowed for improved separation minimums between adjacent routes for more direct and efficient use of airspace. Within ICAO, the vital central importance of RNP has been recognized as the new global standard for navigation, using the ICAO terminology "Performance Based Navigation." RNP capability likely holds the key to future dynamic flexible trajectory based separation of aircraft from takeoff to landing and for the use of new capabilities like GLS (GPS-based Landing System).

This leads to a historic FANS perspective and commentary on the future of ATS, and how aircraft and ATS need to relate. Capt. Tom Imrich, a recently retired Boeing engineering test pilot and former FAA air carrier ops inspector and manager, was directly involved with FANS and RNP development, implementation, and certification over the decades. He provides some perspective on the role, significance, and future of FANS, RNP, Data Link, and ADS:

> The continued progress toward NextGen and Single European Sky Air Traffic Management Research (SESAR) via implementing the key elements of FANS C-N-S based capability is essential for the future of ATS evolution.
>
> The key FANS related ideas of RNP, data link, and ADS now provide the only practical safe and economic aircraft and air traffic services evolution formula for a feasible modernization path. Using these elements in the right blends is the only effective way to achieve safe, efficient, and economic aircraft and air-vehicle operations. This holds for air vehicles ranging from jet transports, to military aircraft, to general aviation, to gliders, helicopters, and even the tiniest of drones. Any vehicle that intends to operate in mixed use airspace globally

will eventually need to use these fundamental FANS originated C-N-S elements in some form or blend.

FANS is much more than a particular avionics system and is not just a data link. While FANS has been increasingly used in oceanic and remote airspace for the past two decades and is now being applied to more widespread global use, its precepts and various balances of C-N-S elements are fundamental. FANS was and is key as a foundation to be able to use various C-N-S blends to facilitate practical, economic, and safe automated dynamic RNP trajectory based separation. The opportunity for variable C-N-S blends allows for ATS and air vehicles to practically and efficiently relate to each other in different contexts to assure safe separation. This is key to economically providing needed capability and capacity while safely satisfying all the demands being placed on mixed use access to our global airspace. Factors such as limited space for new runways on airports and limited runway availability, combined with complicating variables like convective weather or slippery runways making runway exit times variable, and changing wind directions causing runway changes, each make FANS based C-N-S capabilities fundamental to solving flexible dynamic trajectory based separation. It is becoming increasingly clear that using advantageous combinations of these FANS initiated C-N-S elements is likely the only economically practical alternative.

In fact, for a whole range of various missions of air vehicles and increasing airspace demands, having ATS still continuing to use their present obsolete concept for separation is increasingly problematic. For example, for ATS to try to "hand carry aircraft 1 to 1" using radar vector strategies, now with millions of prospective drones added, is virtually unthinkable. This "radar vector" based ATS paradigm can't possibly work in the future, considering the hundreds of thousands or even more air vehicles that may simultaneously be operating in global airspace. Similarly, duplex party line VHF voice links (as ATS now uses) will simply have exceedingly limited effectiveness in the future. The practical and economic long term solution to our NextGen airspace dilemma now is to use blended C-N-S systems related to fundamental FANS dynamic RNP trajectory based separation concepts. Future ATS needs to instead manage air-vehicle separation using automated dynamic separation of 2-D, 3-D, and 4-D RNP-based trajectories within clearly defined RNP path based limits. In some instances, RNP-based volumes of airspace may even be used, such as for gliders, drone operations, military or security uses, or special purpose operations like search and rescue and medevac.

So from a historic perspective, FANS was the very first successful attempt to establish the fundamental C-N-S principles with the ability to adjust the blends and ratios of C-N-S as needed for various ATS applications. More importantly, FANS set the foundation for RNP-based trajectory definition and operations with "extent," recognizing the role of normal operations, rare normal operations, and certain defined non-normal operations. FANS also first set many of the fundamental RNP-based trajectory definitions and safety analysis assessment methods that will now be used for ATS evolution well into the future.

The key C-N-S ideas of FANS are historically significant. The use of sensor independent RNP with continuously assessed Actual Navigation Performance (ANP, or RNP and EPE at Airbus) to define a 3-D or 4-D path with extent and containment, and for definition of flexible navigation trajectories, is profound and fundamental. Similarly, using closed loop management of ETAs and required times of arrival for waypoints along that RNP trajectory, along with the ability to use planned trajectory speed/Mach and forecast wind accommodation, is crucial.

Using data link for automated clearances and trajectory data exchanges to be backed up for rare-normal and non-normal events by exchange of aircraft "state vector" trajectory data via ADS-A, ADS-B, or ADS-C data set exchanges (and TCAS or equivalent) is central to implementing an effective affordable C-N-S/ATM system. That is also why ADS-B is important now, to serve as a broadcast means to nearby aircraft for trajectory separation assurance (e.g., building on the concepts of TCAS) as separation distances inevitably evolve to closer proximity. ADS-B will increasingly be important to share separation information among the air vehicles in close proximity themselves, and will only be of secondary importance to share ADS-B "state vector" data with ATS ANSPs when, or if, or as needed.

All these considerations need to be explicitly incorporated in setting the foundation for future aircraft avionics design, as well as C-N-S ATS systems definition, for the next century or longer. That is the real legacy of what FANS has contributed. It changed the way we view ATS and how aircraft relate to ATS, and how aircraft need to operate to be safely separated while accomplishing their mission, avoiding adverse weather, or getting to their destination.

The FANS pioneers who faced those overwhelming odds back in the early '90s to set this foundation for C-N-S and to give birth to FANS 1/A should now be recognized as the true pioneers they were, and for the lasting fundamental achievement that FANS and RNP truly represented.

T-43A 71-1403 (c/n 20685, l/n 317) was the first "Gator" delivered to the USAF on July 31, 1973. This aircraft is currently stored at Davis-Monthan Air Force Base (KDMA), Tucson, Arizona. *Courtesy of The Boeing Company*

CHAPTER 8

THE 737 IN GOVERNMENT SERVICE

T-43A Navigation Trainer

The US Air Force (USAF), identifying a need for a new technology navigation trainer, placed a $82.4 million order for nineteen T-43As to replace its aging piston-engined Convair T-29s. This order came at a time when 737 sales were extremely slow and the whole program was in serious jeopardy. Many at Boeing felt

An artist's rendering of 71-1403 (c/n 20685, l/n 317), which was the first T-43A delivered to the USAF on July 31, 1973. *Courtesy of Jennings Heilig*

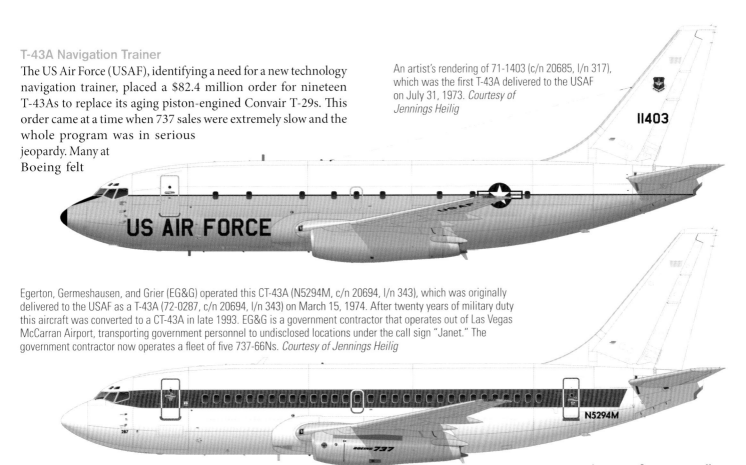

Egerton, Germeshausen, and Grier (EG&G) operated this CT-43A (N5294M, c/n 20694, l/n 343), which was originally delivered to the USAF as a T-43A (72-0287, c/n 20694, l/n 343) on March 15, 1974. After twenty years of military duty this aircraft was converted to a CT-43A in late 1993. EG&G is a government contractor that operates out of Las Vegas McCarran Airport, transporting government personnel to undisclosed locations under the call sign "Janet." The government contractor now operates a fleet of five 737-66Ns. *Courtesy of Jennings Heilig*

this USAF order actually saved the program. The T-43A Navigation Trainer (sometimes referred to as "Gator" by its crews) was based on the 737-253 Advanced airframe, but was highly modified to adapt to its military role.

The most noticeable changes were the deletion of the forward galley door (R1), the aft entry door (L2), and all but nine cabin windows on each side of the aircraft. Internally, there were many more revisions made to the 737 airframe. To allow the extended range required by the mission the optional 800 gallon auxiliary fuel tank was installed in the rear baggage compartment. The cabin floors were substantially reinforced to allow the installation of extremely heavy navigation consoles. Stations for twelve student navigators and accommodations for the two pilots and six navigation instructors were provided. The T-43A was equipped with five celestial navigation sextant stations, as well as the required VHF, HF, and UHF communications equipment for training missions. Electronics were installed to teach navigation using Long Range Navigation (LORAN-C), VHF omnidirectional range (VOR), Tactical air navigation (TACAN), and inertial navigation systems.

The T-43A fleet was initially stationed at Mather AFB, near Sacramento, California, but soon saw duty from Peterson AFB, Colorado, Randolph AFB, Texas, and even on a cooperative effort with the US Navy in Pensacola, Florida. The last T-43A training flight was conducted from Randolph AFB on September 17, 2010, after being in service for nearly four decades. After navigation trainer service with the USAF, many T-43As were converted to transport aircraft. In 1988, 72-0283 (c/n 20690, l/n 336) was reconfigured as a VIP transport. Several were converted to CT-43A standard and used as military transport aircraft. Five of these aircraft—72-0282 (c/n 20689, l/n 334), 72-0284 (c/n 20691, l/n 337), 72-0285 (c/n 20692, l/n 339), 72-0286 (c/n 20693, l/n 340) and 72-0287 (c/n 20694, l/n 343)—found their way to Las Vegas, flying with EG&G (Janet Airlines). One other CT-43A was 73-1149 (c/n 20696, l/n 347), which crashed in Dubrovnik, Croatia, on April 6, 1996, claiming the lives of thirty-five people, including United States Secretary of Commerce Ron Brown. An instrument approach was being attempted when the aircraft deviated from procedure and impacted a nearby hillside. USAF aircraft do not carry CVRs and FDRs, which added challenges to the accident investigation. With the exception of this aircraft the entire T-43A/CT-43A fleet is in permanent storage.

BOEING'S VERSATILE JET FOR MANY MISSIONS.

The military 737 is a multi-mission military derivative of the popular 737 airliner.

HIGH-SPEED TROOP/CARGO AIRLIFT. The 737 can deploy 115 troops and their equipment 2,300 nautical miles, or carry 18 tons of cargo 1,600 nautical miles. Daily operations from short, high-altitude airfields and from gravel or grass surfaces are routine.

AIRBORNE EXECUTIVE SUITE. In its VIP role, the 737 carries key government leaders and their staffs between national capitals up to 3,700 nautical miles at modern jet speeds. Special convertibility features provide for quick installation of the executive furnishings kit.

REFUELING IN THE FIGHTER'S ENVIRONMENT. The 737 tanker refuels fighters in their own environment — high and fast. With refueling stores installed, the 737 can dramatically extend fighter strike range, yet retain full convertibility for other missions.

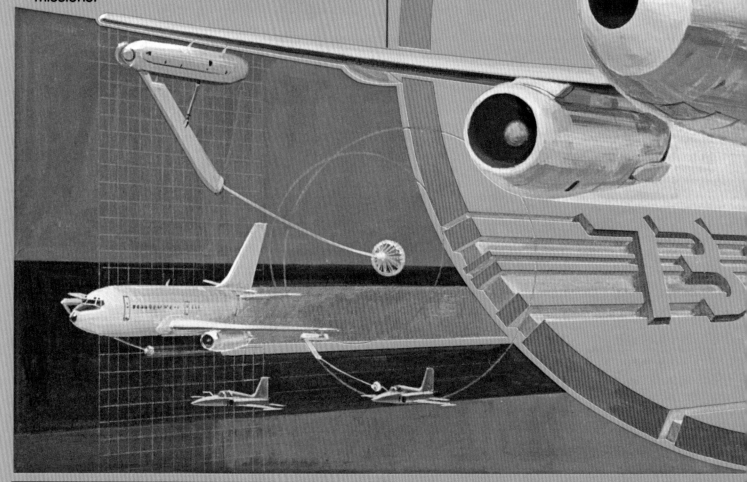

SEA AND LAND SURVEILLANCE. Large enough to carry a high resolution side-looking radar, the 737 can provide high-altitude surveillance of 200-mile-wide coastal waters in a single high-speed pass — and change to low and slow for dropping rescue gear. The 737 side-looking radar can also provide land surveillance for moving targets covering as much as 80 miles to either side of the aircraft.

AT HOME EVERYWHERE IN THE WORLD.
932 Boeing 737 aircraft flown worldwide by
124 operators have logged 15 million hours
in multi-stop short-haul service.

BOEING

Shown with test registration N8288V, AI-7302 was delivered to the Indonesian Air Force on June 30, 1983. Note the flaps appear to be set at position 25 and the landing gear are retracted for low speed surveillance. This is a nonstandard configuration in normal 737 operations, as typically the landing gear must be down with flaps greater than position 10, except during a missed approach (balked landing). *Courtesy of The Boeing Company*

737-2X9 Maritime Reconnaissance Aircraft

In 1982, Boeing delivered three 737-2X9 "Surveiller" aircraft to the Indonesian Air Force (TNI-AU). These maritime reconnaissance platforms were based on the 737-200 Advanced airframe. Surveillers were equipped with the Motorola AN/APS-135 Side-Looking Airborne Modular Multi-Role Radar (SLAMMR), which are covered by long fairings on either side of the rear fuselage. Aircraft AI-7301 (c/n 22777, l/n 868), AI-7302 (c/n 22778, l/n 947), and AI-7303 (c/n 22779, l/n 985) are operated by the Udara 5 Squadron in Hasanuddin, Makassar, Indonesia.

Joint Strike Fighter Testbeds

In preparation for the F-35 Joint Strike Fighter, a 737-247 (N737BG, c/n 19612, l/n 93) was highly modified for service as a flying laboratory after being acquired by Boeing in April 1999. The mission of this aircraft was to test the avionics systems for the

developmental fighter jet. In Wichita, Kansas, Boeing retrofitted the aircraft with a forty-eight inch radar dish secured to the forward pressure bulkhead and an aerodynamic shell was fitted. After over four years of service in this role Boeing sold the aircraft to Jet Midwest, Inc., and it was subsequently scrapped in Walnut Ridge, Arkansas, in 2004.

In 2003, development of the F-35 fighter once again required testing using a flying testbed. An ex-Lufthansa 737-330 (D-ABXH, c/n 23528, l/n 1290) was delivered to Lockheed Martin on October 22, 2003, at the Mojave Spaceport,

The first Joint Strike Fighter avionics testbed aircraft was delivered to Western Airlines as N4515W on November 16, 1968. This airplane was later operated by EG&G, Air South, and Vanguard Airlines before becoming the testbed aircraft. *Courtesy of Jennings Heilig*

and the aircraft was modified by BAE Systems, Inc., beginning in December 2003. This specialized aircraft, called the Cooperative Avionics Test Bed (CATB), was retrofitted with two twelve foot airfoil sections mounted on each side of the fuselage to house the F-35's wing mounted sensors. A long forty-two foot fairing on top of the fuselage and a shorter ten foot housing on the belly of the airplane were also added for testing. Similar to the first JSF Testbed aircraft, a larger nose extension was added to house the experimental radar systems. In 2014, this aircraft was once again modified with new avionics by Northrop Grumman to test the upgraded F-35 Block 3 hardware and software. This aircraft continues to be active in this important testing program today.

C-40 Clipper

Boeing produced a military version of the 737-700C equipped with the reinforced wing of the 737-800 series to fulfill the personnel and cargo transport needs of the United States Navy, Air Force, and Air National Guard. The first was the C-40A for the US Navy, which were purchased to replace the fleet of aging McDonnell Douglas C-9A Nightingales. The C-40A was capable of performing an all passenger role (capacity of 121 people) or a "Combi" configuration with seventy passengers and three standard cargo pallets. The C-40A was essentially a high gross weight version of the 737-700, featuring structural improvements to the landing gear, wing, and center section from the 737-800. A large forward cargo door was installed with a movable barrier between the forward main deck cargo compartment and the passenger compartment behind the wing. Both a forward and rear airstair system were installed on the left side of the aircraft, along with an additional external handle that allowed the captain's side window to be opened in an emergency because of the cargo configuration. The passenger oxygen system consisted of two 1,850 psi bottles and a valved plumbing system to the overhead oxygen system. Electrically operated valves shut off oxygen to the parts of the cabin being used for cargo. A main deck cargo fire suppression system was also added, in addition to the standard lower deck cargo fire suppression systems found on all 737s. To allow for the UHF radio equipment and the additional cargo fire suppression system panels in the cockpit, the pilot's audio panels were relocated from the center console aft of the thrust levers to the outboard side panels near the pilots' oxygen masks.

The first two aircraft were delivered to the Navy on April 21, 2001, and by 2015, all fifteen C-40As ordered had been delivered and were used by squadrons in San Diego, Whidbey Island, Fort Worth, Norfolk, and Jacksonville. Another variant was the C-40C, which is similar to the C-40A, but has the ability to change its interior configuration to seat 42–111 passengers. In October 2002, the 201st Airlift Squadron of the Washington DC Air National Guard received the first aircraft. To fulfill the needs of the USAF for a VIP transport platform an additional model (C-40B) was equipped with sleeping quarters, office space, two galleys, and coach seating. The first C-40B was delivered from Boeing in December 2002. As of 2017, orders for a total of twenty-eight C-40s have been placed with Boeing by the United States military.

This C-40A (c/n 30200, l/n 651) is registered 5831 with the United States Navy. This aircraft was the second C-40A delivered, with the US Navy taking possession of the aircraft on November 2, 2000. *Courtesy of The Boeing Company*

E-7A Wedgetail

The Royal Australian Air Force (RAAF) identified a need for a new Airborne Early Warning and Control (AEW&C) aircraft in a study called "Project Wedgetail" in 1996. The RAAF desired a new technology aircraft similar in function to the classic Boeing 707-320 based E-3 Sentry (AWACS). Boeing made a proposal using the Boeing Business Jet 1 high gross weight 737-700 airframe as a

Wearing test registration N1003M, this C-40A (c/n 29980, l/n 568) was the first of the breed delivered to the US Navy on September 29, 2000. This aircraft served VR-59 "The Lone Star Express" of Fort Worth, Texas. *Courtesy of The Boeing Company*

This "Peace Eagle" (c/n 33962, l/n 1614) was the first of the type delivered to the Turkish Air Force in 2014, and wore temporary American registration N356BJ during flight test. *Courtesy of Boeing*

basis for the new program. BAE Systems of North America provided much of the avionics and mission consoles for the airplane, integrated with the Northrop Grumman MESA radar system. In 2000, Australia submitted an order for four E-7A Wedgetail aircraft with options for three more for delivery in 2006.

Development of the Wedgetail was not without its share of difficulties, including challenges integrating the new technology radar and onboard computer systems. This delayed Wedgetail deliveries until November 26, 2009, when the first two aircraft— A30-001 (c/n 33474, l/n 1245) and A30-002 (c/n 33542, l/n 1232)—were produced. These delays resulted in Boeing paying $770 million in penalties to the Australian government, though by June 5, 2012, the sixth and final aircraft had been delivered to the Australian military. The first operational mission of the Wedgetail occurred on April 3, 2014, when an example from RAAF Squadron No. 2 (A30-001), operating under call sign "Mitchell 11," was used in the search for vanished Malaysian Airlines flight 370. Subsequently, the Australian Wedgetails have seen service over Iraq, in air strikes against the Islamic State of Iraq and the Levant (ISIL), providing 360 degree radar coverage out to a range of over 200 miles through the use of their powerful MESA radar systems.

Australia has not been the only customer for the Wedgetail. The Turkish Air Force (*Turk Hava Kuvvetleri*) ordered four "Peace Eagle" AEW&C aircraft with options on two additional machines for a total of $1.6 billion. The first Peace Eagle (13-001, c/n 33962, l/n 1614) was delivered to the Turkish Air Force on February 21, 2014. South Korea has also shown interest and ordered four 737 AEW&C aircraft, which it calls "Peace Eye." These Korean aircraft are being operated out of Gimhae Air Base, near Busan, South Korea.

P-8A Poseidon

The US Navy had depended on the aging turboprop powered Lockheed P-3C Orion for maritime reconnaissance since it was first introduced in 1962, replacing the Lockheed P-2V Neptune. A large fleet of Orions kept day and night patrol of the waters surrounding the United States for four decades. These sturdy and powerful aircraft were becoming aged and were approaching their airframe life limits. In response, the Navy released a specification for a replacement aircraft. Lockheed-Martin, the heir apparent, submitted a proposal to create the Orion 21, which would be a newly built and updated version of the forty-year-old P-3C airframe. BAE of Britain offered to begin production of the Nimrod MR4A again, but this too was a very old design based on the de

167951 (c/n 34394, l/n 2599, Effectivity YP001) was the first Boeing P-8A delivered to the US Navy, which took ownership on August 12, 2008. During flight test this aircraft wore temporary registration N541BA. Note the extended wingtips standard on the P-8A. *Courtesy of Boeing*

Havilland Comet 4 jetliner. Since the new Nimrod would be an entirely British aircraft a sale was unlikely to the American military, and BAE soon withdrew their entry. Boeing saw the 737-800 airframe as the perfect candidate and proposed a navalized version called the P-8 Poseidon, which ultimately won the US Navy contract. The P-8A is the planned production version and has a bay in the lower aft fuselage to dispense sonobuoys, as well having the ability to carry the AGM-84D Harpoon anti-ship missile, torpedoes, SLAM-ER missiles, and depth charges.

The P-8A is completed in a facility separate from the normal Renton assembly line due to the classified nature of the aircraft. Boeing used a modified 737-800 fuselage, but with the reinforced 737-900 wing assembly for higher weight missions. The P-8A is devoid of normal cabin windows, except for the transparencies on the single overwing exit on each side, and the rear galley door (R2) is deleted. The extended wingtips are a feature specific to the P-8, which are used instead of the blended winglets. According to senior Boeing management, the current plan is to continue to produce the Poseidon with the 737NG airframe for the foreseeable future.

The Poseidon is slated to replace the American P-3C fleet by 2021, as production of the aircraft continues. The Indian Navy has ordered a special version of the aircraft called the P-8I Neptune, and Boeing has also received orders from the Royal Australian Air Force for the aircraft. A possible order from the Royal Air Force is also pending.

The Royal Thai Air Force

The Royal Thai Air Force (Kong Thap Akat Thai) was one of the earliest military aviation establishments in Asia, tracing its roots back to the Siamese Flying Corps in 1911. Today, the RTAF operates an assortment of combat, reconnaissance, transport, training, and rescue aircraft.

The Royal Thai Air Force operated this late model 737-2Z6 Advanced (c/n 23059, l/n 980) delivered new from Boeing on July 21, 1983, as a VIP transport. *Courtesy of The Boeing Company*

This 737-8Z6-BBJ2 (c/n 35478, l/n 1955) replaced earlier examples of the 737 as a VIP transport for the Royal Thai Air Force. Delivered in 2006, this aircraft has been re-registered HS-TYS. *Courtesy of The Boeing Company*

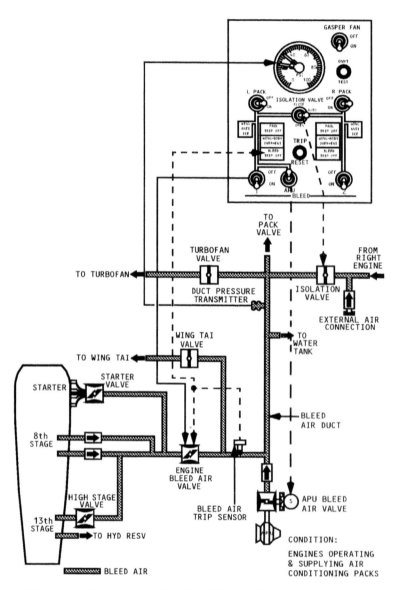

Original series bleed air system (Classic and NG are similar, with minor differences).
Courtesy of The Boeing Company

Aircraft Systems

All airliners need reliable systems to operate flight controls and provide engine control, pressurization, and electrical power. The 737 was designed with the use of leading edge technology, but with a specific eye toward keeping the aircraft simple to build, maintain, and operate. In this chapter we will discuss the various systems of the Original 737 series and give a general overview of how these systems operate. There are some significant changes between the Original and the Classic, Next Generation (NG), and MAX series that will be presented. The 737 MAX systems are being described through research and interviews, since access to official systems manuals has not yet been made available. For more detailed information, *The Boeing 737 Technical Guide* by Capt. Chris Brady is an excellent resource (available at www.b737.org.uk).

Air Systems and Pressurization

The Original 737 series operates at altitudes of up to 35,000 feet and, like all jetliners, requires an effective air conditioning and pressurization system. In operation the system is simple, with the engines' eighth and thirteenth stage compressor sections alternating (based on engine thrust settings) to provide pressurized air for air conditioning, cabin pressurization, and other aircraft systems. The volume of air that travels through the air conditioning system is variable dependent on engine operations. To keep cabin pressurization controlled and constant a large outflow valve is provided. This valve simply controls the amount of air leakage from the cabin to automatically regulate the differential pressure (difference in air pressure between the atmosphere and the inside of the cabin) for climb, cruise, and descent. The main outflow valve is augmented by a much smaller forward outflow valve to maintain trouble-free pressurization.

Bleed Air System

The heart of the 737's pressurization system is the bleed air system. The JT8D engines have two bleed air ports controlled by valves to provide the volume of pressurized air required to run dependent aircraft systems. The engines' compressors squeeze air at a ratio of 14.6:1. This hot, high pressure air is sent to the combustion chambers, where it is ignited and used to turn the turbine section and is eventually expelled and utilized for the generation of engine thrust. Prior to being sent to the combustion chambers a small amount of "bleed air" is extracted from the engine's compressor. The two points where this can occur are the eighth and thirteenth stage compressor wheels. The thirteenth stage compressor generates a much higher pressure than the eighth stage, as it is farther down the flow line through the engine. At low power settings, the eighth stage compressor does not always create enough pressure to operate all of the airplane's systems; in these situations, the thirteenth stage provides the pressure and volume required. At higher power settings, the thirteenth stage bleed valve automatically closes, favoring the eighth stage. If a problem arises and the bleed air temperature becomes excessive the pilot is warned with a "BLEED TRIP OFF" light, and the respective bleed air control valve automatically closes to protect the system from damage.

The bleed air extracted from the engines is highly pressurized and because of this is quite hot. Hot bleed air is used for engine anti-ice to heat the engine's inlet lip and bullet dome, to provide engine fuel heat, and head pressure for the hydraulic reservoirs. The remainder of the bleed air is routed through a heat exchanger called a "pre-cooler." The pre-cooler employs passing air from the engine fan to cool the hot bleed air before sending it into the bleed air manifold. The air conditioning packs, wing anti-ice, and water tank pressurization use this pre-cooled bleed air.

Even though the bleed air is "pre-cooled," it is still very warm. If a leak in the bleed air manifold ducting occurs it is still hot enough to damage nearby structures and components. Pilots are alerted to this condition by the illumination of a left or right "WING BODY OVERHEAT" light. This system is separated into a left and right side for the very purpose of allowing the pilot to isolate a leak on one side by using the provided isolation valve. Each engine (left or right) furnishes bleed air to its respective side of the system and air conditioning pack. The 737's pressurization is easily maintained with one side of the system in operation.

Classic, NG, and MAX differences: The system setup is very similar, but due to the replacement of the JT8D with the CFM56 series the bleed extraction from the engines is from the fifth and ninth stage compressors, but operates similarly.

MAX: The bleed valves on the MAX series are electronically controlled for greater efficiency.

Air Conditioning Packs

The air conditioning pack allows high pressure, high temperature bleed air to be used for cabin air conditioning and pressurization. This apparatus integrates a small compressor assembly to further pressurize the air introduced from the bleed air system. In doing so the air is made much hotter in the process. If this temperature becomes excessive a "PACK FAIL" light illuminates and a control valve will automatically shut off bleed air to the air conditioning pack. When the pack is operating this extremely high pressure and high temperature air then passes through a ram air heat exchanger. In flight this is cooled by outside air passing the aircraft, but while on the ground, or in flight at low speeds, large fans are used to pull air through the heat exchangers. Once the highly pressurized air is cooled by the ram air heat exchangers it is fed into a centrifugal turbine which, via a shaft, turns the compressor at the beginning of the cycle chain. The air exiting the turbine is at a much lower pressure and is very cold. This cold air often contains condensed water, which is removed by the water separator assembly.

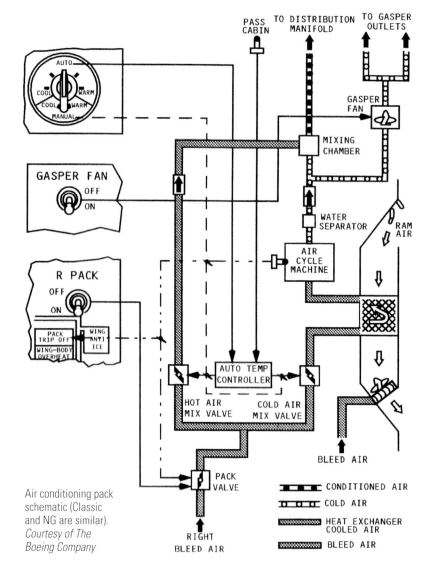

PASS CABIN — TO DISTRIBUTION MANIFOLD — TO GASPER OUTLETS

AUTO
COOL — WARM
COOL — WARM
MANUAL

GASPER FAN
OFF
ON

GASPER FAN

MIXING CHAMBER

R PACK
OFF
ON

PACK TRIP OFF
WING ANTI ICE
WING-BODY OVERHEAT

WATER SEPARATOR

RAM AIR

AIR CYCLE MACHINE

AUTO TEMP CONTROLLER

HOT AIR MIX VALVE   COLD AIR MIX VALVE

BLEED AIR

Air conditioning pack schematic (Classic and NG are similar).
Courtesy of The Boeing Company

PACK VALVE

RIGHT BLEED AIR

CONDITIONED AIR
COLD AIR
HEAT EXCHANGER COOLED AIR
BLEED AIR

passenger cabin. Although these aircraft are only equipped with two air conditioning packs, three different adjustment controls are provided in the air distribution system and are pilot adjustable.

Other Bleed Air Uses

Bleed air extracted from the engines has other important functions. Airframe icing can occur when flying in sub-freezing temperatures while in clouds or precipitation. The accumulation of ice on the leading edges of the wings or engine intakes can cause degraded aircraft performance and an associated reduction in safety. Bleed air is tapped directly from the uncooled eighth stage bleed air manifold to heat the engine's nose dome, stator vanes, and sensors, while hotter thirteenth stage bleed air is selectable to heat the leading edge of the engine inlet. Hot bleed air from the left and right pneumatic manifolds is used to deice the wing's leading edge slats (outboard of the engines) and is selectable by the pilot. The 737 is not susceptible to the ill effects of ice accumulation on the tail and the inboard wing leading edge, thus these surfaces are unheated.

The hydraulic fluid reservoirs are pressurized using bleed air tapped directly from the engines. Pressurization of the reservoirs is necessary to ensure adequate fluid feed to the system and to prevent the fluid from bubbling or frothing. The potable water tank is also pressurized by the pneumatic manifold to produce water pressure for the on board lavatory sinks and coffee pots.

The 737 uses compressed air from its pneumatic system to start the engines. Each engine has a starter featuring a start valve and an impeller that turns the high-pressure spool of the engine up to thirty-five percent of maximum speed. During this process fuel and ignition are introduced, and by the time the starter valve automatically closes, the engine is accelerating to idle under its own power. In the event of an inoperative APU, the required starting pressure can be applied by a pressurized air cart or bottle through a small receptacle in the belly of the aircraft.

Classic, NG, and MAX differences: On these aircraft hydraulic reservoir pressurization is supplied from the pneumatic manifold, instead of directly from the engines. The pneumatic engine starters on these aircraft have slightly higher starter cutout speeds.

Pressurization Control

The pressurization system for the 737 is simple in principle, yet very effective. The engines provide more air volume than required to maintain cabin pressurization under normal circumstances. This valve can be actuated fully open, fully closed, or any position in between to allow a metered "leak" to maintain cabin pressure at the desired setting. The forward outflow valve is provided to augment the main outflow valve and is fully open unless the main outflow valve is nearly closed. At cruise altitude, the 737's pressurization system maintains a cabin altitude of 8,000 feet, although the aircraft can cruise at altitudes as high as 35,000 feet. This equates to a pressure differential (between the atmosphere and the inside of the cabin) of around 7.5 PSI. Both mechanical

Hot bleed air can bypass the compressor and turbine and is used to control cabin temperature. Two valves, one on the cold air side and another on the hot bypass air side, work in opposition to one another under the control of an automatic temperature controller. Once the correct temperature is established the conditioned air is sent into a supply duct and out into the cabin. If the automatic temperature controller fails a "DUCT OVERHEAT" light illuminates and the respective air conditioning pack automatically drives the temperature control valves to a full cold setting. A manual control mode is also installed to allow the pilot to take direct control of the temperature control valves if necessary. A gasper fan system provides additional air volume to the adjustable vents above the passengers' heads. This system receives air volume from the cold air side of the right air conditioning pack. All 737s have a provision for receiving ground conditioned air from external air conditioning units at the gate in the event the aircraft's onboard air conditioning packs are not in use due to a lack of bleed air availability. This situation occurs when the aircraft's engines and auxiliary power unit (APU) are not operating.

400/-800/-900/MAX-8/MAX-9 differences: Due to the longer cabin in these aircraft, a "trim air" system is installed to allow more precise temperature control in different sections of the

over pressure and negative pressure relief valves are installed to protect the pressure cabin from exceeding absolute limits.

Redundancy is set up in the system by providing an alternate automatic controller and a manual mode that allows direct control of the outflow valve by the pilot. The main outflow valve can also be controlled through redundant AC and DC electrical power to insure pressurization control with a wide variety of failures. In the event of cabin depressurization oxygen masks are provided for the flight crew and the passengers via two pressurized oxygen bottles. The pilots are alerted with an alarm if the cabin altitude exceeds 10,000 feet, and the passenger oxygen masks will automatically drop from overhead when the cabin altitude exceeds 14,000 feet. This system supplies oxygen long enough for the pilots to descend to breathable altitudes.

Classic, NG, and MAX differences: The Classic series is allowed a slightly higher cruise altitude of 37,000 feet, while the NG and MAX are authorized up to 41,000 feet. This requires slightly higher cabin differential pressures of 7.8 and 8.35 PSI, respectively. These aircraft are equipped with chemical oxygen generators for each overhead passenger service unit in place of the passenger oxygen bottle and its associated plumbing. The pilot oxygen system is still supplied with a compressed oxygen bottle through improved EROS quick donning masks.

NG and MAX differences: On these aircraft a forward outflow valve is not installed.

Electrics

The 737 electrical system is designed to be redundant and failure tolerant, while providing many automatic functions to ease the workload of the pilot. In general, the electrical system is split into a left and right side to allow system redundancy. Some automatic crossover is available in case of a power failure, but provisions are available to allow the pilot to override the automatics and isolate portions of the system in an emergency. Every electrical user in the aircraft is equipped with a circuit breaker for safety reasons. The system can receive 115 volt alternating current (AC) power from both engines, the APU, or from an external ground power connection. Each engine has a generator driven by the high pressure (N2) spool through a constant speed drive (CSD). The CSD keeps the generators turning at a constant speed (6,000 RPM) regardless of engine speed to keep the AC frequency at 400 cycles. The engine generators can only be connected to their respective generator busses. The APU generator is driven directly by the APU, which operates at a constant speed, thus controlling the cycles without the use of a CSD. The APU generator or ground power may supply both generator busses while on the ground. The APU generator can only supply one generator bus at a time while in flight because of high electrical loads.

NG and MAX differences: Both engine generators are revised and combined with their constant speed drive system, referred to as "integrated drive generators" (IDGs). The APU generator has the added ability to power both transfer busses while in flight. In the cockpit operational differences are minimal, but one obvious difference is the replacement of the analog

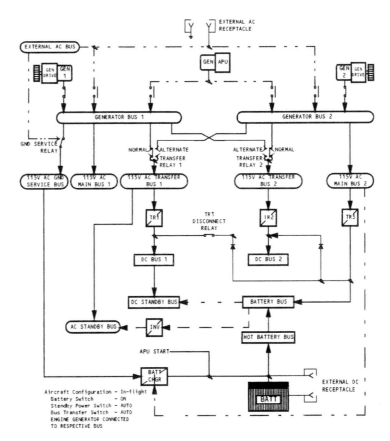

Original series electrical system (Classic series is similar). *Courtesy of The Boeing Company*

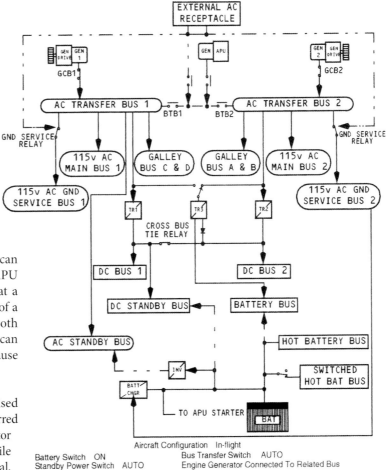

NG series electrical system. *Courtesy of The Boeing Company*

amperage and volt meters with a digital installation. These aircraft also monitor the IDG operation automatically, allowing the removal of the analog generator drive temperature monitors present in the Original and Classic series.

The 115 Volt Alternating Current (AC) System

The two generator busses (1 and 2—left and right—respectively) are used to collect power from the selected generator (or ground power) and distribute it to the respective AC transfer bus and AC main bus. These, along with the AC ground service bus, supply the bulk of the aircraft's AC power needs. Systems considered moderate priority are powered by the AC transfer busses. These are so named because in the case of a loss of supplied power to a generator bus, the respective transfer bus will automatically transfer and use the opposite side generator bus as a power source. This provides redundancy for important electrical items without the need for immediate pilot intervention. Transfer bus 1 supplies power to the AC standby bus, which powers basic items considered essential for safe flight. In the event of the loss of all electrical generators, alternate power to the AC standby bus is furnished by the aircraft's 28 volt battery through a static inverter. The static inverter converts the direct current (DC) power from the battery into 115 volt AC current for this purpose. For aircraft servicing one ground service bus is provided, supplying power to items that might be required while the aircraft's primary electrical system is not powered. This bus allows the battery charger, minimal lighting, and service outlets to operate if AC ground power is plugged into the aircraft.

NG and MAX differences: The NG and MAX series have several revisions to their electrical systems compared to Original and Classic 737s. One of the most notable differences is the absence of the generator busses. Engine generator, APU generator, and ground power are connected directly to the transfer busses through switches, with the role of the generator busses being assumed by the transfer busses. Due to the greater capacity of the aircraft generators fewer items are lost in the event of a failure that leaves one generator powering the entire system. The aircraft is equipped with a second ground service bus on the right side of the system. Each ground service bus is powered by its respective AC transfer bus or by AC ground power.

The 28 Volt Direct Current (DC) System

There are some electronic components which require 28 volt DC power instead of the 115 volt AC power produced by the generators. For the purpose of creating DC power three transformer rectifiers (T/Rs) are installed. Transfer bus 1 feeds T/R 1, which powers DC bus 1. Likewise, transfer bus 2 feeds T/R 2, which powers DC bus 2. The third T/R (T/R 3) is powered from AC main bus 2 and provides power to the battery bus, as

well as backup power to DC buses 1 and 2 if their respective T/Rs fail. The aircraft's battery provides DC power to the hot battery bus, which feeds items that need to be live even with aircraft power off (the engine and APU fire extinguishers, for example). The battery bus and the DC standby bus shoulder the electrical loads for high priority items required either on the ground, in the absence of other power, or items essential for safe flight. These are normally powered by T/R 3, but can be supplied automatically by the aircraft's battery while in flight should a failure occur.

In the event of a complete loss of generating power in flight, the battery can supply the hot battery bus, battery bus, AC standby bus, and DC standby bus with emergency power for a minimum of thirty minutes. This provides emergency instrumentation for the pilots to land but leaves many non-essential aircraft systems inoperative.

NG and MAX differences: These aircraft are equipped with an additional switched hot battery bus and some minor revisions to power sources are built into the system. Some aircraft have an optional second battery which allows for one hour's operation of emergency power with a failure of all generators.

Hydraulics

The 737 uses hydraulic power for many flight control and systems functions throughout the aircraft. Three hydraulic systems (A, B, and standby) are provided to create redundancy where necessary. Each has separate fluid reservoirs, but are interconnected through balance lines on the Original series. Each system operates at a normal pressure of 3,000 PSI, provides the pilot analog indications of pressure, and annunciates warnings if pressure becomes low.

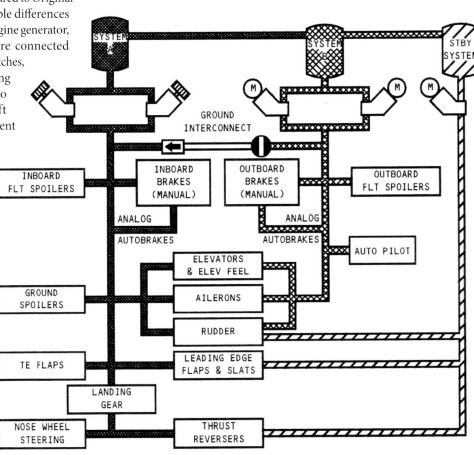

Original series A and B hydraulic systems. *Courtesy of The Boeing Company*

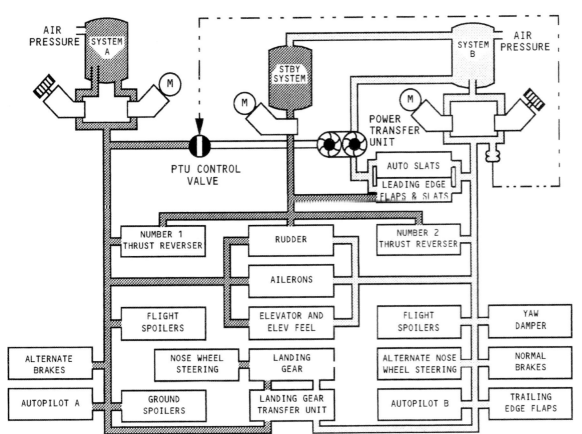

Classic series A and B hydraulic systems (NG is similar). *Courtesy of The Boeing Company*

Please note that later CFM powered aircraft have significant hydraulic differences from the Original series (these major differences will be explained).

The A and B Hydraulic Systems

The A hydraulic system has the highest fluid capacity and is designed to operate utilities that require more volume. This system is driven by two high flow engine motor driven pumps (EMDPs), one on each engine. This system has a heat exchanger in the Number 1 (left) wing fuel tank that uses the fuel in the tank to cool the hydraulic fluid. The B system has a slightly smaller capacity and utilizes two electric driven pumps (EDPs) to pressurize the system. The B system has a heat exchanger in the Number 2 (right) wing tank for fluid cooling. The components powered by the A and B systems on the Original 737 series are as follows:

System A	System B
Ailerons	Ailerons
Elevators and Elevator Feel	Elevators and Elevator Feel
Rudder	Rudder
Ground Spoilers	Outboard Flight Spoilers
Inboard Flight Spoilers	Outboard Wheel Brakes
Inboard Wheel Brakes	Yaw Damper
Thrust Reversers	Autopilot
Landing Gear	Outboard Autobrakes (analog)
Inboard Autobrakes (analog)	Autobrakes (digital)
	Nosewheel Steering
	Leading Edge Slats and Flaps
	Trailing Edge Flaps

Classic, NG, and MAX differences: These later aircraft are hydraulically different from the Original series described above. On these aircraft the A and B systems are more balanced, sharing hydraulic loads more evenly. The reservoirs for the A and B systems are not interconnected like on the Originals and are of a higher fluid capacity. Each system is powered redundantly by one EMDP and one EDP. The A system employs the EDP on the left engine, while the B system uses the EDP mounted on the right engine. Like earlier aircraft, each has a heat exchanger in their respective wing fuel tank for fluid cooling. The components powered by the A and B systems are shown below:

System A	System B
Ailerons	Ailerons
Elevators and Elevator Feel	Elevators and Elevator Feel
Rudder	Rudder
Ground Spoilers	Flight Spoilers (alternating)
Flight Spoilers (alternating)	Right Thrust Reverser
Left Thrust Reverser	Leading Edge Flaps and Slats
Landing Gear	Trailing edge Flaps
Nose Wheel Steering	Alternate Nose Wheel Steering
Autopilot A	Autopilot B
Power Transfer Unit (PTU)	Landing Gear Transfer Valve
Alternate Wheel Brakes	Wheel Brakes
	Yaw Damper
	Autobrakes
	Autoslats

The Standby Hydraulic System

All 737s are equipped with a standby hydraulic system that is used to backup selected items in case of a failure of either or both of the primary hydraulic systems. The standby hydraulic system has a reservoir interconnected with the B system reservoir. This interconnection ensures that the standby system reservoir is always full. If a leak were to occur in the B system, provisions have been made to ensure standby system fluid will not be lost, achieving redundancy. The standby system uses a small electric pump to pressurize the system when the need arises and provides backup power to the following items:

- Rudder
- Thrust Reversers
- Leading Edge Krueger Flaps and Slats
- Standby Yaw Damper (NG and MAX only)

During normal operations the standby system is unpressurized, but will pressurize in the following situations to provide backup hydraulic power:

- Enables alternate leading edge slat and Krueger flap extension when the alternate flaps system is armed and activated by the pilot (manual)
- Enables alternate thrust reverser deployment provided the standby system has been activated
- Enables alternate power to the rudder system under the following circumstances:

  1. When one or both flight control switches is placed in the "STBY RUD" position (manual)
  2. When the rudder force fight monitor detects a disagreement between the A and B rudder actuators on modified aircraft (automatic)

Classic, NG, and MAX differences:
When a loss of pressure is sensed in either the A or B system during takeoff or landing (automatic) the standby system provides power to the rudder.

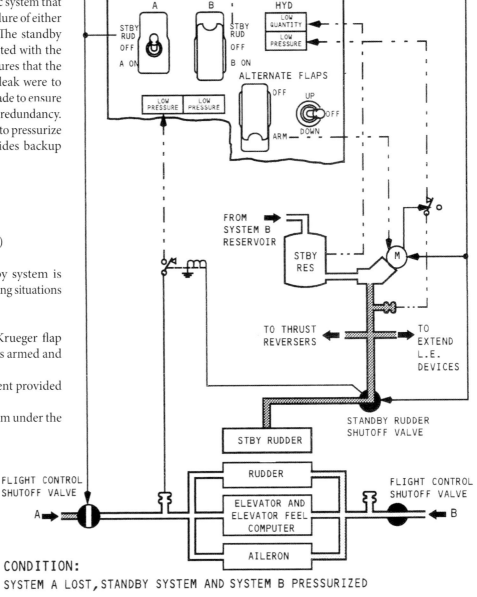

CONDITION:
SYSTEM A LOST, STANDBY SYSTEM AND SYSTEM B PRESSURIZED

Original series standby hydraulic system (Classic and NG are similar, with minor differences). *Courtesy of The Boeing Company*

Flight Controls

The flight control system on the 737 is very effective and provides crisp and sporty handling for the pilots. The primary flight controls (aileron, elevator, and rudder) are all triple redundant, with secondary controls (trailing edge flaps, leading edge Krueger flaps, and slats) having dual redundancy.

Ailerons and Elevators

The aircraft's elevators allow pitch control (nose up and down) for the pilots. Normally, these are powered by the A and B hydraulic systems in concert with one another. Because of this hydraulic power the elevator is equipped with a feel computer and centering unit. This device adjusts the amount of pressure required to deflect the elevators dependent on the airspeed of the aircraft. Similar to the power steering in an automobile, the feel gets heavier as the aircraft accelerates. The feel computer provides an artificial "feel" to the controls and an important tactile indication to the pilots. Elevator trimming is required to allow stable flight at different airspeeds. To enable this, the angle of incidence of the entire horizontal stabilizer assembly (with respect to the fuselage) can be changed by the pilot (or the autopilot) via electric motors and a jackscrew assembly. A provision for manual control from the cockpit is also built into the system.

Ailerons provide roll control left and right, and are powered by the A and B hydraulic systems simultaneously. The ailerons are supplemented with movement of the flight spoilers. For example, when executing a left turn the left aileron is deflected up while the right aileron is deflected down. If the pilot's yoke is moved to the left more than eight degrees two flight spoilers on the left wing will begin to deploy to augment roll control. A right turn works the same way, in the opposite direction.

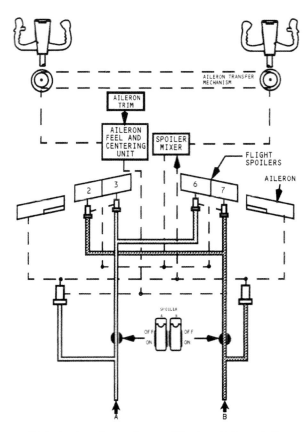

Original series roll control system (Classic and NG are similar, with minor differences). *Courtesy of The Boeing Company*

In the case of failure of either system, the pilot will be alerted by cautions from the hydraulic panel, as well as an A or B system "LOW PRESSURE" and "FEEL DIFF PRESS" lights, dependent on which hydraulic system is failing. The remaining system is capable of providing normal flight control response, however roll might be slightly slower because only one flight spoiler will actuate. If the A and B hydraulic systems were to fail, the ailerons and elevators can be commanded by the pilot directly through a cable backup system using servo tabs to move the flight controls. This makes control inputs much heavier for the pilot, but the aircraft remains very controllable in the absence of all hydraulic pressure. Since the flight spoilers are driven by the hydraulic systems their roll augmentation is unavailable in this condition.

Rudder

The aircraft's rudder is used to control yaw (nose side to side) and is applied by the use of the large, one-piece rudder on the vertical stabilizer. The rudder is controlled with the use of pedals in front of each pilot, and like the ailerons and elevators, primarily uses A and B hydraulic pressure together to actuate. An automatic yaw damper system is used to stabilize the aircraft and to prevent fishtailing. Like the elevators and ailerons, the rudder can operate normally with just one hydraulic system, but in the instance of a complete failure of A and B hydraulics, the third redundancy is executed differently. The rudder uses the standby hydraulic system for power and can be operated normally, although the yaw damper will be inoperative.

Original series pitch control system (Classic and NG are similar, with minor differences). *Courtesy of The Boeing Company*

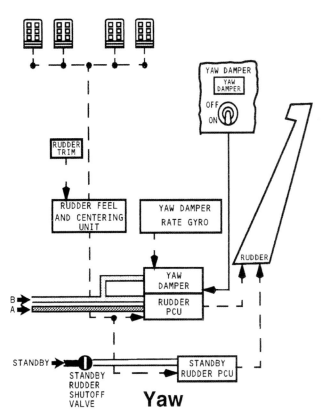

Unmodified Original series rudder control system (Classic and NG are similar, with minor differences). *Courtesy of The Boeing Company*

NG and MAX differences: A standby yaw damper is installed which uses pressure from the standby hydraulic system in the event of a dual failure of systems A and B.

In the wake of two crashes (USAir 427 and United 585) and one other incident involving a Westwind Airlines 737-200, the question of whether the 737 rudder system could "hardover" and cause an uncommanded full deflection was investigated. Theoretically, this situation could cause the aircraft to yaw (and roll) rapidly in the direction of the deflection. The debated question that was argued between Boeing, the Air Line Pilot Association (ALPA), and the FAA was whether these instances were caused by pilot error or an aircraft malfunction. To err on the side of caution, on September 13, 2000, Boeing and the FAA came to an agreement. The decision was made to redesign the rudder system to make a hardover absolutely impossible. The replacement of the original rudder actuator was legislated via Airworthiness Directive 2002-20-07 R1. A new rudder actuator system was installed which had separate A and B system inputs, separate servo valves, and an input to the standby rudder system. With this system the standby rudder actuator automatically acts as an override if a disagreement between the A and B system actuators is sensed. Pilots are alerted with a "STANDBY RUD ON" light if this "force fight monitor" has been triggered.

Ground and Flight Spoilers

Four spoilers are installed on each wing of the Original 737 series. The two middle spoiler panels on each wing (Figure 1: Panels 2, 3, 6, and 7) are called the flight spoilers, while the farthest inboard and the farthest outboard (Figure 1: Panels 1, 4, 5, and 8) are the ground spoilers. During landing, or an aborted takeoff, all of the spoilers extend fully to destroy lift and transfer as much weight as possible to the aircraft's wheels, enabling maximum braking

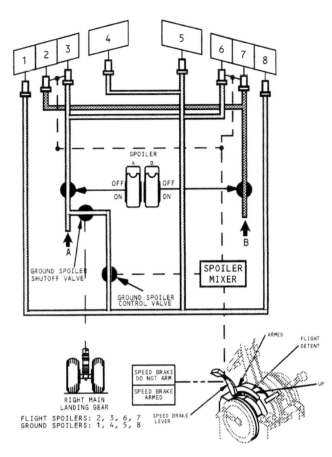

Original series spoiler system (Classic and NG differ in number of spoiler panels). *Courtesy of the Boeing Company*

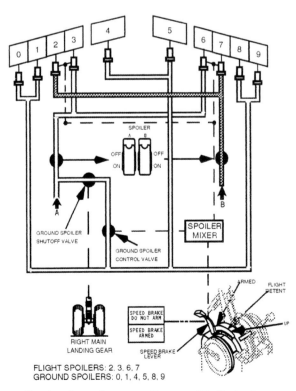

Classic series spoiler system. *Courtesy of The Boeing Company*

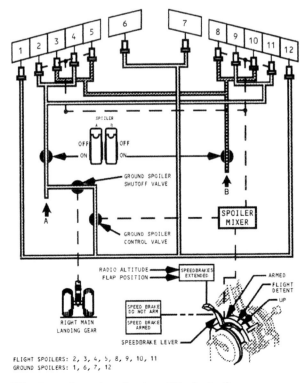

NG series spoiler system. *Courtesy of The Boeing Company*

effect. This is an automatic feature upon landing, provided the speed brake handle is placed in the "ARMED" position. During a rejected takeoff the spoilers can be manually deployed by the pilot, or will automatically deploy if reverse thrust is selected. During flight operations the ground spoilers remain stowed and the flight spoilers are used as speed brakes manually selectable by the pilot. These can be used to slow the aircraft expeditiously, or to descend more rapidly. As previously discussed, the flight spoilers also augment aileron control through the spoiler mixer assembly. On all 737s the ground spoilers use pressure from the A hydraulic system to actuate. To provide redundancy one flight spoiler on each side is driven by the A hydraulic system and the other is actuated through the B system.

Classic differences: One additional ground spoiler was added to each wing (Figure 2: Panels 0 and 9) to enhance stopping ability during landing or a rejected takeoff.

NG and MAX differences: The ground spoiler configuration returned to two panels on each wing, similar to the Original 737 series (Figure 3: Panels 1, 6, 7, and 12). Two additional flight spoilers were also added on each wing and were renumbered. Two flight spoilers on each wing are powered by the A hydraulic system and two by the B system for redundancy. The flight spoilers are Panels 2, 3, 4, 5, 8, 9, 10, and 11.

MAX differences: The 737 MAX is equipped with a fly-by-wire spoiler control system, eliminating the spoiler mixer assembly in the main landing gear wheel well.

Classic and NG aircraft retrofitted with blended winglets: A load alleviation system is installed which limits flight spoiler extension to fifty percent at high aircraft weights to prevent excessive stress to the wing structure.

High Lift Devices

One of the many strong points of the 737 is its takeoff and landing performance. To achieve the goal for minimum runway length requirements an advanced trailing edge flap design, combined with leading edge Krueger flaps and slats, is installed.

The trailing edge flaps are extendable to eight different settings. Up and Positions 1, 2, 5, 10, 15, 25, 30, and 40 are available. Typically the less deployed positions (1, 5, and 15, dependent on conditions and aircraft series) are used for takeoff, while positions 30 and 40 (fully extended) are used for normal landings. The trailing edge flap system is of a triple slotted fowler design, with separate sections inboard and outboard of the engine on each wing. The trailing edge flaps on the Original 737 series are normally operated by the A hydraulic system and are pilot controlled using the flap handle on the center pedestal. In the event of a hydraulic failure all 737s have a provision to lower the trailing edge flaps with an electrically driven motor controllable with the alternate flaps switch on the overhead panel.

NG and MAX differences: The trailing edge flaps on these aircraft are of a slightly simplified, double slotted Fowler design.

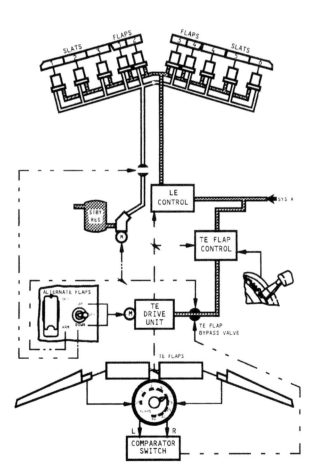

Original series wing flap system. *Courtesy of The Boeing Company*

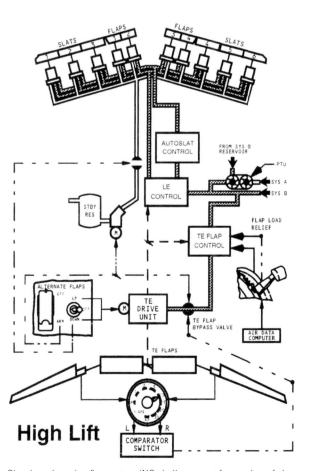

Classic series wing flap system (NG similar except for number of slat panels). *Courtesy of The Boeing Company*

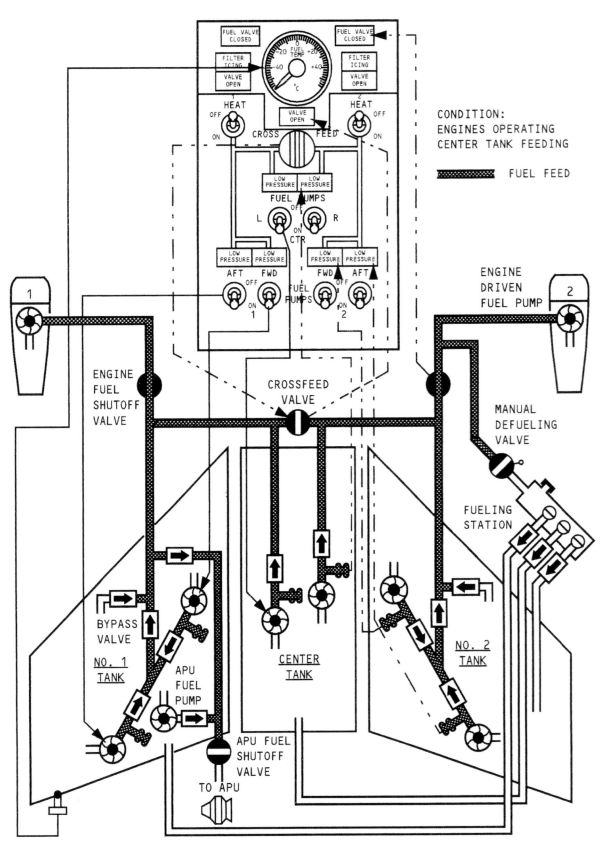

Original series fuel system. *Courtesy of The Boeing Company*

Each wing is equipped with leading edge Krueger flaps installed under the leading edge of the wing, between the engine and the fuselage. When the trailing edge flaps are fully retracted, the Krueger flaps are recessed in a small compartment under the leading edge of the wing. When the flaps are deployed from the up position, these panels deploy from under the wing and extend out from the leading edge of the wing. In doing so they create more curvature (camber) on the inboard portions of the wing.

In addition to the Krueger flaps, each wing is equipped with three leading edge slat panels outboard of the engine. These slide down from the top of the leading edge but create a similar effect to the Krueger flaps, increasing wing camber. The slats deploy automatically to an intermediate "EXT" position when the trailing edge flaps begin to deploy to position 1. This position provides good lift with minimum drag, typically advantageous for takeoff. As the trailing edge flaps are extended to position 10 and beyond, the leading edge slats continue to move to the "FULL EXT" position. This position deploys them farther out and down in front of the wing's leading edge and exposes a small gap between the rear portion of the slat and the wing. The "FULL EXT" position produces more aerodynamic drag, but allows high pressure air under the wing to escape through the gap, energizing the airflow over the wing. This setting is ideal for landing, allowing minimum approach speeds.

On the Original 737 series, both the Krueger flaps and the slats are normally powered by the A hydraulic system. On all 737s the standby hydraulic system can be used for emergency extension by momentarily activating the alternate flaps switch. To improve the 737's handling during aerodynamic stalls an autoslat system is installed. If the trailing edge flaps are in a position which commands the leading edge slats to the intermediate "EXT" position the autoslat system will automatically schedule the slat panels to the "FULL EXT" position if the aircraft approaches stall speed.

Classic, NG, and MAX differences: The leading edge Krueger flaps and slats are powered by the B hydraulic system.
NG and MAX differences: These later series have four slat panels on each wing. Some NG and all MAX aircraft are equipped with the Short Field Takeoff Kit, changing the slat scheduling slightly. The slats remain in the intermediate (ungapped) "EXT" position for flap positions 1–25. This allows takeoffs with more trailing edge flap extension without the added drag of the fully extended slats, enhancing single engine climb capability. For flaps 30 and 40 landings the slats move to the "FULL EXT" position.

Fuel System

The fuel system on the 737 is designed to be redundant and user friendly for the pilot. All 737s have fuel tanks in the wings and also in the center section between the wings, under the cabin floor. These tanks are: main tank 1 (left wing), main tank 2 (right wing), and the center tank. Each of these tanks have two electrically driven fuel pumps. The pumps in each tank have different power sources, allowing fuel to be accessible even after an electrical malfunction. Each of the wing tanks has the ability to suction feed fuel to their respective engine in the absence of all electrical power or a failure of both pumps. The use of center tank fuel requires the use of at least one of the tank's pumps and cannot be suction fed. If there is fuel in all three tanks center tank fuel must be used first, followed by fuel from the main wing tanks. All of the electric fuel pumps maintain the same pressure and pump fuel into the fuel manifold. Because of this, each pump has a spring-loaded flapper valve and check valve. The valves on the center tank pumps have a much lower cracking pressure than the valves on the main tank pumps, ensuring that center tank fuel is used first to exhaustion, followed by main tank fuel. When the center fuel tank is empty the center tank "LOW PRESSURE" lights illuminate and the pilot simply turns off the center tank pumps. A motive flow (suction) pump automatically scavenges any remaining fuel in the center tank and delivers it to the number 1 tank. Once the center tank is empty each engine is normally fed from its respective wing tank. If required, a crossfeed valve is installed to allow both engines to be fed from one tank, or to keep fuel quantities in the wings balanced during single engine flight. The 737 requires no provisions to jettison fuel. The APU has the ability to suction feed fuel from the number 1 (left wing) tank or can receive fuel from the right side of the fuel manifold when fuel pump pressure is available.

Classic, NG, and MAX differences: The center tank fuel pumps operate at a higher pressure, ensuring the use of center tank fuel prior to the consumption of wing tank fuel in lieu of pressure sensitive valves.

Fuel is warmed through the hydraulic system heat exchangers in each wing tank. If the pilot is alerted by a "FILTER ICING" light the respective "heat" switch on the overhead fuel panel can be activated. This switch allows hot thirteenth stage engine bleed air to heat the fuel through an air/fuel heat exchanger.

Classic, NG, and MAX differences: To prevent ice contamination in the fuel (and to cool the engine oil), fuel traveling to each engine passes through an oil/fuel heat exchanger. This action is automatic. The "FILTER ICING" light has been replaced with a "FILTER BYPASS" light in case ice or contamination is sensed in the respective engine's fuel filter.

Fueling is normally provided through the fueling station under the right wing, outboard of the engine. This provision allows a single hose to fuel all of the aircraft's fuel tanks simultaneously. The system features automatic shutoffs to prevent overfilling and aircraft damage. Fuel gauges are installed in this compartment to allow the fueler to load exactly the correct amount of fuel. These gauges are repeaters of the quantity gauges installed in the cockpit and show total fuel in pounds. The de-fueling valve is between the fueling panel and the engine pylon. This valve can be used to pump fuel from the aircraft, or to transfer fuel from one tank to another using the aircraft's fuel pumps.

Auxiliary Fuel Tanks

The 737-200 Advanced can be equipped with an auxiliary fuel tank (either 390 or 810 gallons, depending on the installation) in the aft baggage compartment. When selected, cabin differential pressure, and alternately bleed air, is used to pump the fuel from

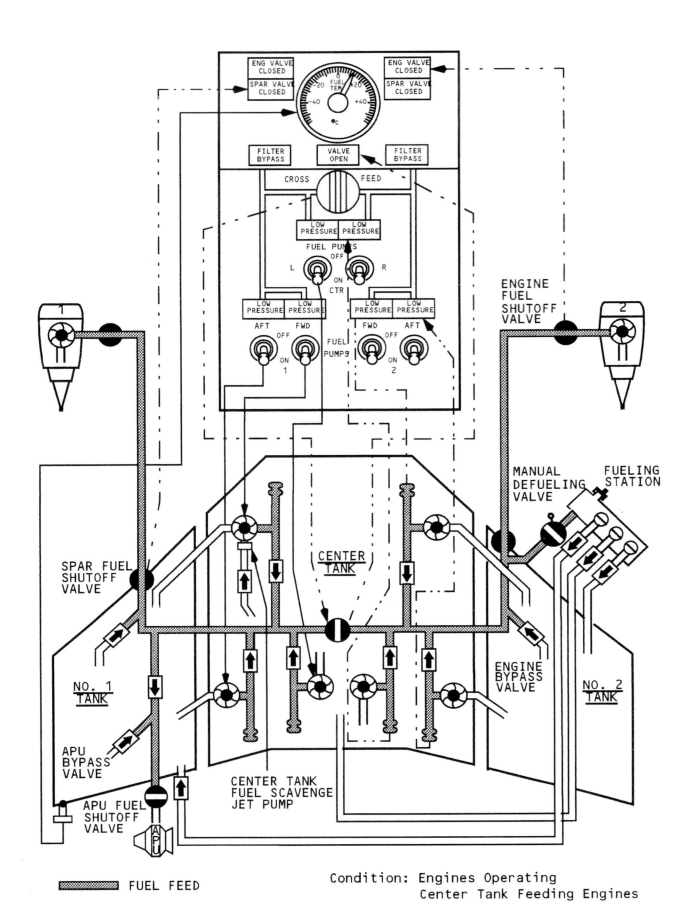

FUEL FEED

Condition: Engines Operating
Center Tank Feeding Engines

NG series fuel system (Classic is similar). *Courtesy of The Boeing Company*

the auxiliary tank into the center tank, where it is picked up by the aircraft's primary fuel system. Fueling of the auxiliary system is provided with a guarded switch on the aircraft's single point refueling panel.

737-200 VIP differences: Optionally additional fuel tanks can be installed. Three cells in the forward baggage compartment and four in the aft compartment can be installed, providing a total fuel capacity of 8,050 gallons and an operational range of 3,500 nautical (4,025 statute) miles. Fuel transfer to the center tank is accomplished using bleed air pressure exclusively.

Classic differences: The auxiliary fuel tank sizes available (in gallons) are 389, 500, 809, and 1,000.

Extended range NG and BBJ differences: Up to nine auxiliary tanks may be installed in the forward and aft cargo compartments, increasing fuel capacity by 3,925 gallons.

Boeing 737 Walk Around

Author's Collection

This is the starting point for a pilot's walk around inspection on the 737-800. The aircraft is always chocked while at the gate so the parking brake may be released. The taxi light between the nose wheels has been deleted on later aircraft and moved into the wing root using an LED lighting system. The drag strut for the nose gear, as well as the mechanical nose gear door linkages, are visible.

Author's Collection

Two pitot tubes are mounted on the right side of the nose. These are used to provide airspeed indication by sampling the ram air pressure through a hole in the front. The top pitot provides information for the first officer's instrumentation, while the lower gives airspeed data to the standby instruments. Below these we find the angle of attack (AOA) vane, which gives information to the stall warning system. These devices are heated electrically to prevent ice accumulation. Under the first officer's side window is the emergency exit handle. This allows the side window to be opened from the outside should the need arise. On cargo 737s there is a handle on the left side as well.

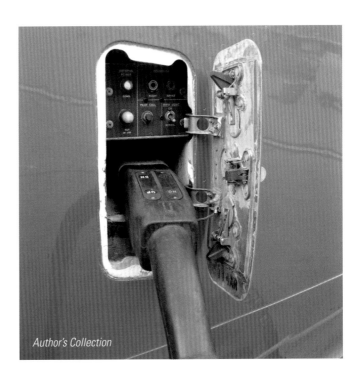

Author's Collection

The ground power plug is found below the cockpit on the right side of the aircraft. This panel is used to apply 115 volt, 400 cycle AC power to the aircraft while at the gate. Located above the plug are provisions for calling the cockpit and audio jacks for direct communication between the pilots and the ground crew. The nose wheel well light(s) can be turned on either with the switch here or from the cockpit.

The access doors to the Electronic and Equipment (called "E & E") compartments are directly forward and aft of the nose landing gear well. Although not part of a normal preflight, this is the view into the aft compartment, which houses many of the electronic modules for instrumentation and aircraft systems.

This is an extended Krueger flap photographed from behind (on a 737-3H4). Note how it seals to the inboard side of the engine nacelle. The small silver circle with red alignment marks on the lower surface of the wing is one of the fuel tank "drip sticks" for manual fuel quantity measurement.

Moving back along the right side of the aircraft is the right wing leading edge. On NG aircraft a long stall strip is installed to enhance the aircraft's behavior during slow flight and stalls. The window for the fixed landing light and runway turnoff lights can be seen in the upper right hand corner. Here the aircraft's Krueger flaps are stowed completely flush with the wing.

This is a view of the right main landing gear through the opening in the wheel well. The chromate colored B hydraulic reservoir is visible in the upper left corner. The orange cord hanging from the well is a grounding cable. During fueling this grounds the aircraft to the truck, preventing issues with static electricity.

A similar view of the left main landing gear of a 737-3H4 shows one of the differences between the Original/Classic fleet and the NG series. The red alignment stripe can be used to verify the landing gear is "down and locked" through a viewer under the carpet on the cabin floor. This is unnecessary on the NG and MAX series because these have two independent electric landing gear indication systems.

The triangular upper torsion link is shown clearly. Slightly left of center, on the end of the torsion link, is the shimmy damper, which was added after early NG aircraft had problems with main landing gear vibration. These are also standard on the Original and Classic series.

The main landing gear as viewed from the front. Between the tires the brake assemblies are visible, as are the separate brake and anti-skid lines. The maximum tire speed on the 737 is 195 knots (224 miles per hour).

The door system as installed on the left main landing gear. On all 737s these doors are mechanically moved into position as the landing gear is retracted using only the visible linkage. These require no special hydraulics, unlike many other aircraft types.

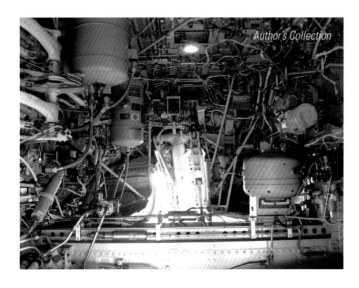

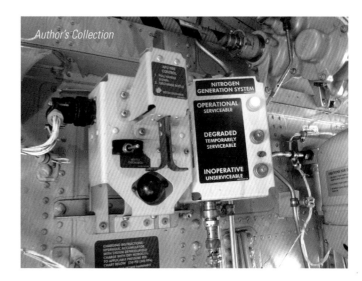

A busy place! This is the main landing gear well, with aircraft forward to the left. The A and B hydraulic reservoirs are seen mounted on the ceiling, with the A reservoir nearest the camera. The structural member that spans across the bottom of the photo is the keel beam. Mounted to this is the standby hydraulic system reservoir. Mounted to the aft wall, above the standby reservoir, is the trailing edge flap motor. The orange and black torque tubes that drive the flaps can be seen extending from both sides of the flap motor. The main landing gear mounting and side strut are clearly seen in the middle.

On the aft wall of the main landing gear well all 737s have an APU fire control. If an APU fire were to occur while the pilot was outside the aircraft during a preflight inspection, the installed red light would illuminate and a siren would be heard. The situation can be handled directly from this station by pulling down the red "T" handle, which cuts off fuel and shuts down the APU. Moving the fire bottle discharge switch to the left causes the APU fire extinguisher to discharge. The APU fire handle in the cockpit performs the same functions. The Nitrogen Generation System (NGS) is equipped on newer NG and MAX aircraft. This system fills the air space in the center fuel tank with inert nitrogen gas to enhance safety.

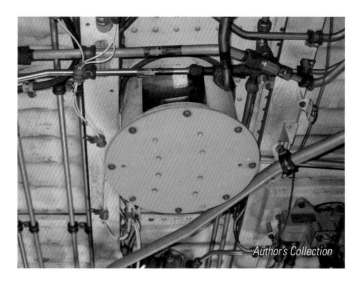

In the main landing gear well, looking at the forward wall. On the left is the hydraulic A system reservoir and its mechanical quantity gauge (silver). Immediately to the right of the A reservoir is the spoiler mixer assembly, which is not required on the 737 MAX because its spoiler system is fly-by-wire and not mechanical. Below the spoiler mixer, recessed into the forward bulkhead is the right center tank fuel pump. The center fuel tank is on the other side of this bulkhead.

On the Original and Classic 737s, on the ceiling of the main landing gear well is a viewer mounted under a small window under the carpet in the cabin above. Looking through this port, a crew member can verify that the main landing gears are locked in the down position by observing the alignment of the red lines on the landing gear side struts. A similar system is installed in the cockpit for the nose gear.

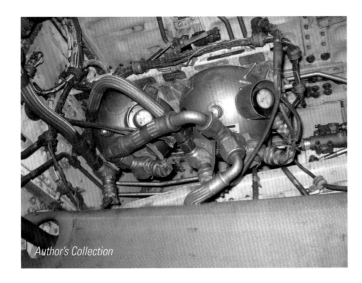

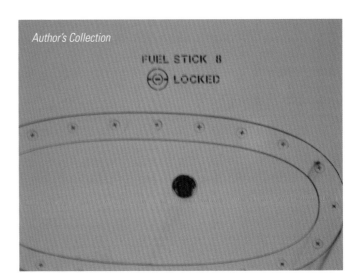

FUEL STICK 8

LOCKED

Two fire bottles are mounted on the port side aft corner of the main landing gear well. These are the extinguisher bottles for the engines. One or both bottles can be discharged to either engine by pulling and turning the appropriate engine fire handle in the cockpit.

This is a closer look at a fuel dipstick installed in the lower surfaces of each wing. These are used for mechanical measurement of fuel quantity in the wing and are normally only used during maintenance issues. The Original and Classic aircraft have this provision for only the main (wing) tanks. The NG and MAX aircraft also have measuring sticks for the center tank. The fuel level can be determined by unlocking the stick and pulling it from the bottom of the wing until the fuel level is determined. The Original and Classic series dipsticks are a hollow tube. When slowly extracted from the wing the top of the tube lowers to the surface of the fuel contained in the tank. Fuel then drips (or sprays) out of the bottom of the tube and the index number is noted. The NG and MAX have a cleaner measuring stick that uses a float and a magnet, and stops the stick at the proper index number. The index number on the stick is compared to a chart and the fuel quantity is determined.

The refueling panel is under the leading edge of the right wing, just outboard of the engine pylon. This panel allows all three fuel tanks to be filled at once with a single pressurized fuel hose. Note the three quantity gauges (2, C, and 1) for the fuel tanks, quantified in pounds. The fueler is facing aft during the fueling operation, hence the reversal of the gauges for tank 1 (left wing) and 2 (right wing). The 737 typically uses Jet A, which is a wide cut fuel similar to kerosene. Jet A1 and military JP5 and JP8 fuels can also be used with no limitations.

The three small vortilons are visible, mounted under the leading edge of the wing to improve aircraft handling. These are not installed on the Original and Classic aircraft because they use a different wing design.

This is the early blended winglet installed on an NG series aircraft. The dual green navigation lights are illuminated. Similar red lights are installed on the left wingtip. Just outboard of the navigation lights is the small window for the strobe light. White tail lights are mounted in the small fairing under the winglet. The two static wicks are provided to dissipate static electricity from the aircraft while in flight. These differ in number depending on the version of the aircraft.

The winglets retrofitted to the Classic series 737s are similar in design and concept to those on the NG. Note the single red navigation light on this aircraft. Most Classics have one on each wing, but later models sometimes have two for redundancy. The Classic winglet is slightly different, with the strobe light mounted to the outboard tip of the winglet.

The later "scimitar" winglet is an option on the NG series aircraft. Winglets are used to reduce aerodynamic drag during flight. The MAX has a bifurcated laminar flow winglet that is similar in appearance to the scimitar design.

The early Classic wingtip. The square strobe assembly is installed behind the clear Plexiglass, just forward of the navigation light (not illuminated). The fairing on the trailing edge contains an optional tail logo light (not visible from this side) and the white tail light.

Author's Collection

Author's Collection

The APU air inlet is on the right side of the rear fuselage, just forward of and below the horizontal stabilizer. This inlet articulates open (shown) to allow air into the APU inlet while in use. When the APU is not in operation the ramp closes to reduce drag. The triangular wedge helps direct air into the inlet while in flight and was not installed on early 737s.

The 737-400 and -800 (shown) are equipped with a non-retractable tail skid designed to protect the tail from a light touch on the runway during takeoff. An excessively hard contact would push the skid up, crushing the shock cartridge, and would be identifiable during a walk around by the absence of the green band shown. A slightly different retractable tail skid is standard equipment on the 737-900 and optional on the 737-800.

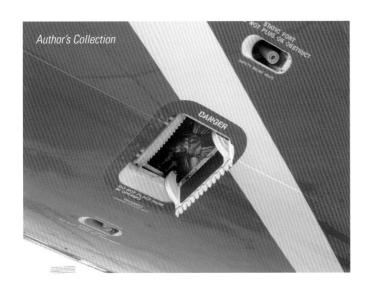

Author's Collection

Author's Collection

The main outflow valve for pressurization control is on the right side, aft fuselage. The valve is in the fully open position and articulates aft to control pressurization during flight. Above and below this are the cabin overpressure relief valves, which protect the pressure vessel in case of a malfunction.

This 737-3H4 shows two notable differences on Original and Classic 737s. The "canoe" fairings housing the flap tracks and actuators are pointed on the trailing edge, while NG and MAX airplanes are slightly more blunt. The fairing behind the engine pylon shows the Classic's heritage with the Original series. The Original 737's engine pylons contained some of the flap drive mechanisms for the inboard trailing edge flap panels. This portion of the pylon is present because the Original series wing and flap system was retained (with slight modifications) for the Classic series. This fairing was deleted from the wing on the NG and MAX but a third canoe fairing was added, slightly inboard of the engine pylon.

Author's Collection

This is the inlet of the CFM56-7 engine on 737NG. Note the strake on the inboard side of the engine nacelle.

Author's Collection

This is a view forward through the engine's fan shroud. The blades and stators are visible in the forward portion of the duct. Immediately behind the fan, the retracted thrust reverser blocker doors and actuator links can be seen in the duct. All of the fan air can be used for reverse thrust when these blocker doors move into position. Near the bottom right, the perforated surfaces inside the duct are to reduce noise emissions.

Author's Collection

In contrast with the NG installation, the inlet on the Classic series CFM56-3C-1 has a more pronounced flattening of the lower engine inlet to give it proper ground clearance. The white markings on the spinner dome serve a dual purpose: they make it obvious to ground personnel the engine is running and also deter birds from flying into the intake.

Author's Collection

Author's Collection

This is a view of the engine core section exhaust. The core exhaust has no provision for thrust reversing on the CFM56 series.

On the lower fuselage, slightly forward of the wing on each side, is the NACA type intake to supply cooling air to the air conditioning pack heat exchangers. These are variable geometry inlets that control the volume of cooling air. Normally they are fully open on the ground and in flight with the wing flaps extended. On Original through NG aircraft, a blue "RAM DOOR FULL OPEN" light illuminates when this occurs. This light has been deleted from the MAX, but the intake operation is unchanged. The small blocker door is in the extended position. When the aircraft senses that its wheels are on the ground this device moves into position to prevent debris being kicked up by the nose wheels and damaging the heat exchangers inside.

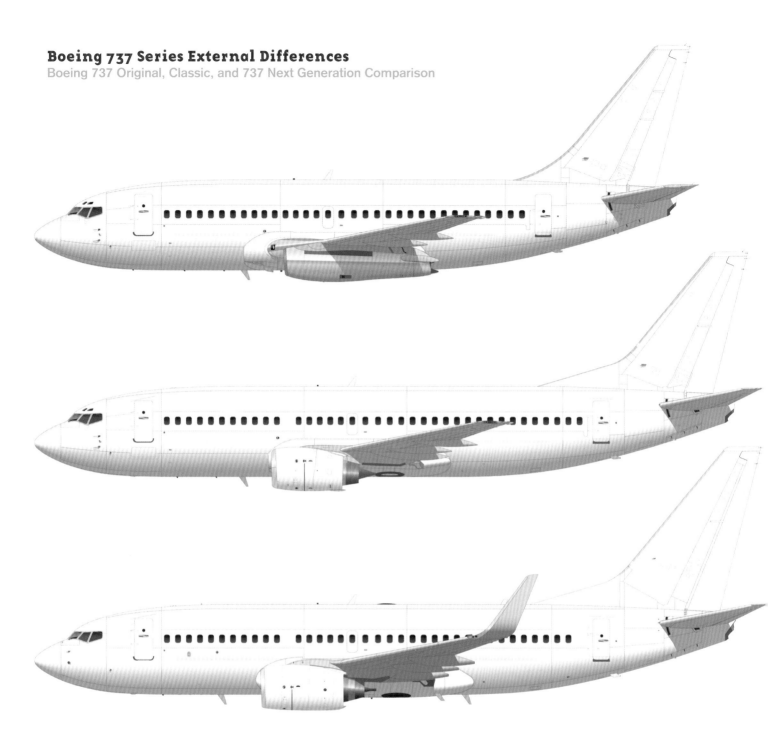

Author's Collection

This comparison shows the evolution of the 737 airframe. Top is the Original series 737-200 (Advanced), which is easily discernible from later versions by the Pratt & Whitney JT8D engines tucked under the wings and the lack of the dorsal extension on the vertical stabilizer. The Classic Series 737-300 (middle) is similar in length to the Next Generation (NG) 737-700 (bottom), but the key visual differences between the 737 Classic and the 737NG are the shape of the trailing edge flap canoe fairings, along with the much larger wingspan of the 737NG. Additionally, the position of the pitot tubes (below the cockpit windows) is farther forward on all 737NGs. As viewed from the front, the Classic series has inlets that are more "flattened" in appearance when compared to the 737NG. The 737 MAX (not shown) has larger engines with inlets that are nearly round, bifurcated "Advanced Technology Winglets," and a more pointed tail cone.

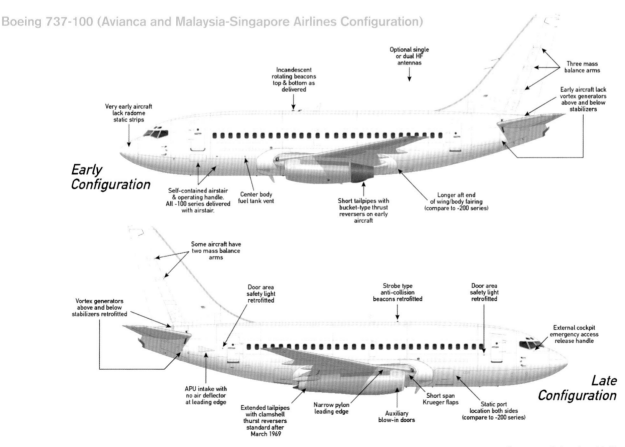

Early Configuration

Very early aircraft lack radome static strips

Incandescent rotating beacons top & bottom as delivered

Three mass balance arms

Early aircraft lack vortex generators above and below stabilizers

Self-contained airstair & operating handle

Center body fuel tank vent

Short tailpipes with bucket-type thrust reversers on early aircraft

Self-contained airstair door on all Lufthansa aircraft & Boeing prototype

Later aircraft have two mass balance arms

Door area safety light retrofitted

Strobe type anti-collision beacons retrofitted

Door area safety light retrofitted

Vortex generators above and below stabilizers retrofitted

APU intake with no air deflector at leading edge

Extended tailpipes with clamshell thurst reversers standard after March 1969

Narrow pylon leading edge

Auxiliary blow-in doors

Short span Krueger flaps

Static port location both sides (compare to -200 series)

Late Configuration

Courtesy of Jennings Heilig

Very early aircraft lack radome static strips

Incandescent rotating beacons top & bottom as delivered

Optional single or dual HF antennas

Three mass balance arms

Early aircraft lack vortex generators above and below stabilizers

Early Configuration

Self-contained airstair & operating handle. All -100 series delivered with airstair.

Center body fuel tank vent

Short tailpipes with bucket-type thrust reversers on early aircraft

Longer aft end of wing/body fairing (compare to -200 series)

Some aircraft have two mass balance arms

Door area safety light retrofitted

Strobe type anti-collision beacons retrofitted

Door area safety light retrofitted

Vortex generators above and below stabilizers retrofitted

External cockpit emergency access release handle

APU intake with no air deflector at leading edge

Extended tailpipes with clamshell thurst reversers standard after March 1969

Narrow pylon leading edge

Auxiliary blow-in doors

Short span Krueger flaps

Static port location both sides (compare to -200 series)

Late Configuration

Courtesy of Jennings Heilig

Boeing 737-200 (Early Basic Configuration)

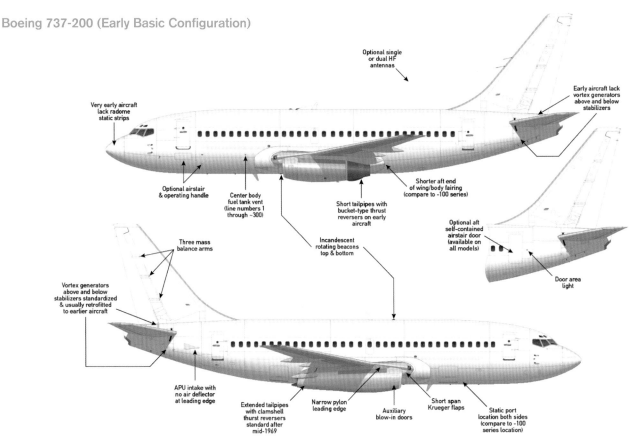

Optional single or dual HF antennas

Early aircraft lack vortex generators above and below stabilizers

Very early aircraft lack radome static strips

Optional airstair & operating handle

Center body fuel tank vent (line numbers 1 through ~300)

Shorter aft end of wing/body fairing (compare to -100 series)

Short tailpipes with bucket-type thrust reversers on early aircraft

Optional aft self-contained airstair door (available on all models)

Door area light

Three mass balance arms

Incandescent rotating beacons top & bottom

Vortex generators above and below stabilizers standardized & usually retrofitted to earlier aircraft

APU intake with no air deflector at leading edge

Extended tailpipes with clamshell thrust reversers standard after mid-1969

Narrow pylon leading edge

Auxiliary blow-in doors

Short span Krueger flaps

Static port location both sides (compare to -100 series location)

Courtesy of Jennings Heilig

Boeing 737-200 (Later Advanced Configuration)

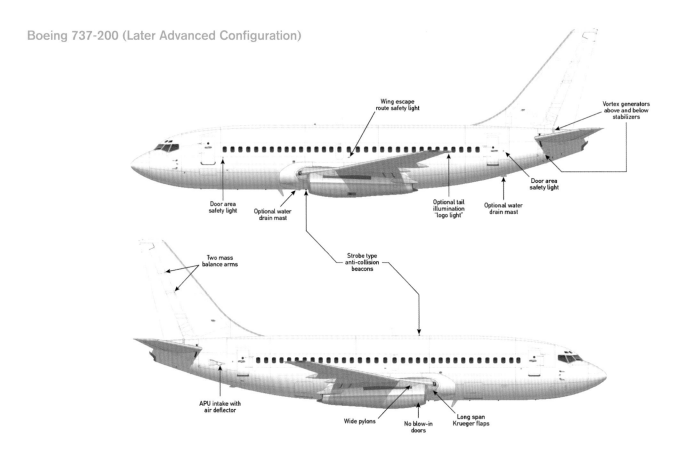

Wing escape route safety light

Vortex generators above and below stabilizers

Door area safety light

Optional water drain mast

Optional tail illumination "logo light"

Optional water drain mast

Door area safety light

Two mass balance arms

Strobe type anti-collision beacons

APU intake with air deflector

Wide pylons

No blow-in doors

Long span Krueger flaps

Courtesy of Jennings Heilig

Boeing 737 ("Combi" Configuration)

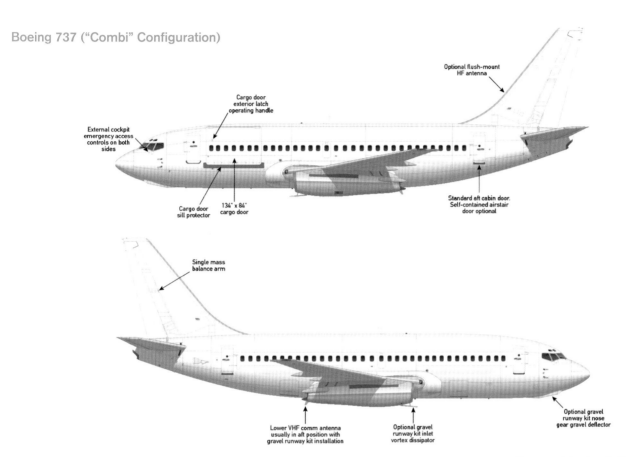

Optional flush-mount HF antenna

Cargo door exterior latch operating handle

External cockpit emergency access controls on both sides

Cargo door sill protector

134" x 84" cargo door

Standard aft cabin door. Self-contained airstair door optional

Single mass balance arm

Lower VHF comm antenna usually in aft position with gravel runway kit installation

Optional gravel runway kit inlet vortex dissipator

Optional gravel runway kit nose gear gravel deflector

Courtesy of Jennings Heilig

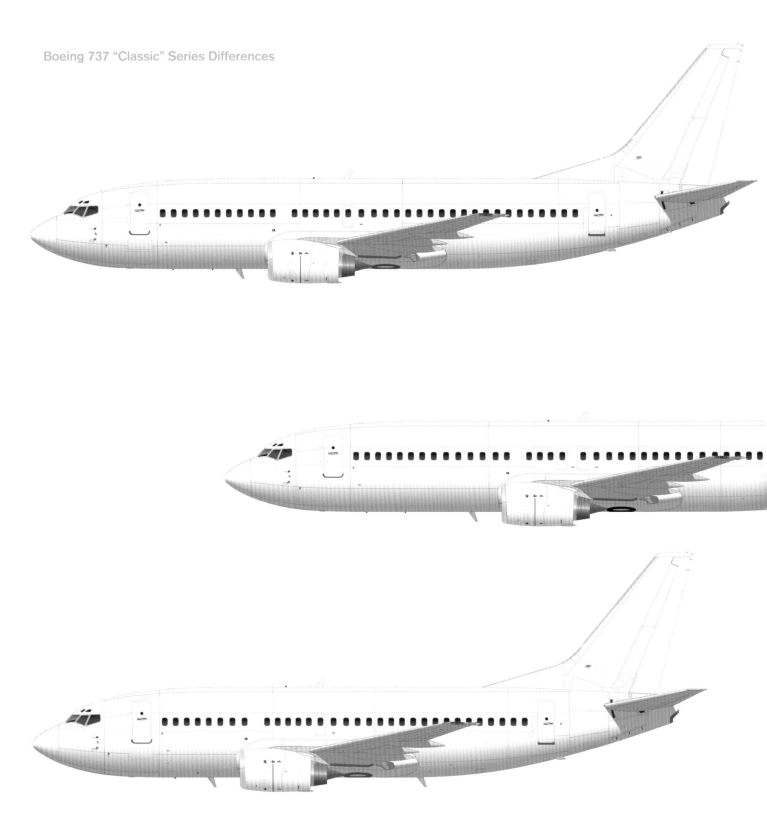

Courtesy of Jennings Heilig

The three members of the 737 Classic series are the 737-300 (top), 737-400 (middle), and 737-500 (bottom), and differ most obviously in fuselage length. The wings of all three versions are dimensionally the same, and can be fitted with optional blended winglets to increase fuel efficiency. The 737-400 can be easily differentiated from the other Classics by noting the tail skid and the installation of two overwing hatches on each side.

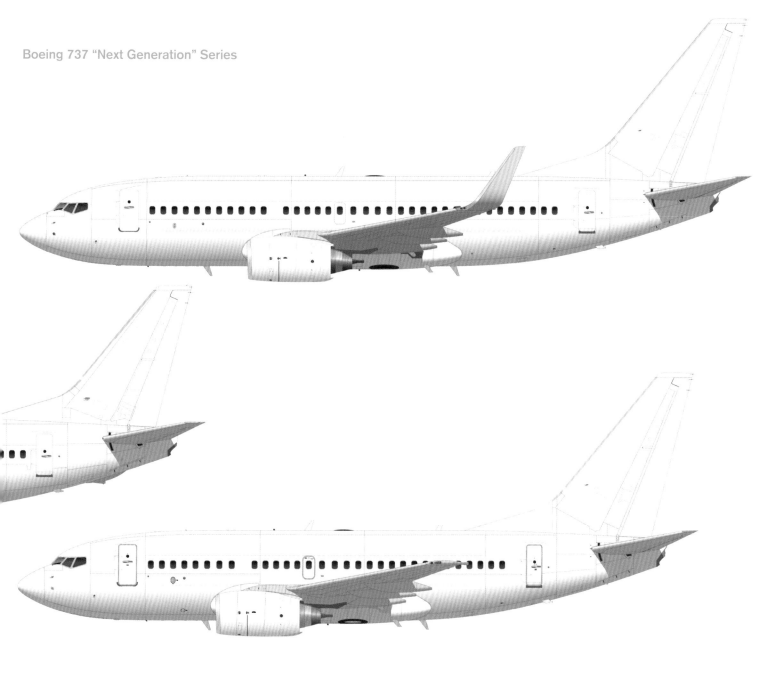

The 737 Next Generation Series began with the introduction of the 737-700 (top), and was later joined by a slightly shorter sibling, the 737-600 (bottom). These aircraft look very similar, but can be told apart by the number of passenger windows forward of the air conditioning duct risers, causing the deletion of one window above the leading edge of the wing; a typical 737-700 will have eleven windows, where a 737-600 will only have eight.

Courtesy of Jennings Heilig

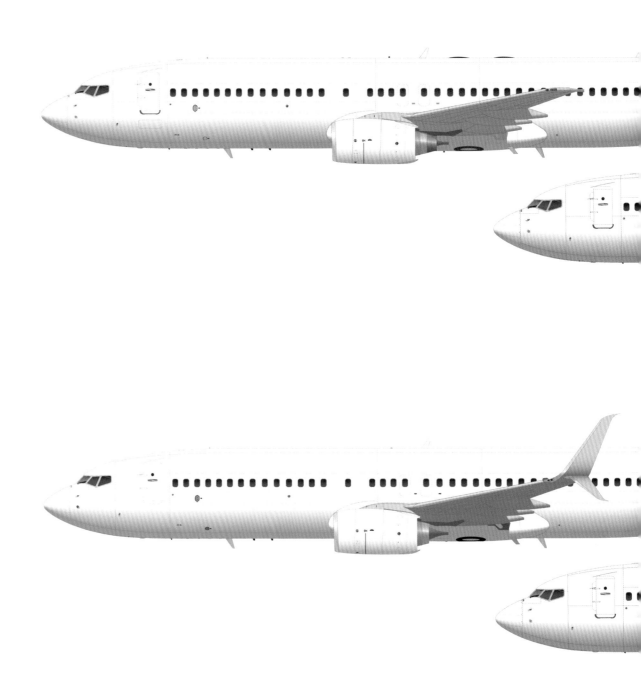

Courtesy of Jennings Heilig

The 737-800 series was introduced very soon after the 737-700 and is substantially longer. The 737-800 differs on the port side, having two blank window spaces instead of one just forward of the wing and the addition of two overwing exits on each side. Also, unlike the 737-600 and -700, the 737-800 has a tail skid because of the extended fuselage length. The top profile shows the early 737-800 configuration without blended winglets and the early style exhaust nozzles. The lower profile shows a late model 737-800 with the "scimitar" winglets and the newer style Performance Improvement Package (PIP) exhausts.

Courtesy of Jennings Heilig

The latest members of the 737NG family are the 737-900 and 737-900ER (Extended Range), which are gaining popularity. The 737-900 is the longest of all the 737s. The -900ER can be identified by the additional emergency exit on the aft fuselage, behind the wing. Depending on the seating capacity chosen by the specific airline operator this exit may have a full size cabin window installed, indicating the exit has been decommissioned and is not visible in the cabin. 737-900ERs with higher density seating require additional doors to be activated. In this case, the door outline will be painted on the exterior and a smaller porthole window is installed on the exit, along with appropriate interior markings.

At the time of writing technical drawings of the 737 MAX were not available to the author, but this series can be easily identified. The 737 MAX has distinguishing features, such as the one-piece bifurcated "Advanced Technology Winglets," noticeably larger engines mounted roughly eighteen inches farther forward on the wing, and an extended nose landing gear which makes a subtle change to the aircraft's stance on the ground. Also very noticeable is the longer tapered rear fuselage. The 737 MAX is currently being offered in three different sizes, with the MAX-7 similar to the 737-700, the MAX-8 roughly size equivalent to the 737-800, and a MAX-9, which is the counterpart to the 737-900.

Boeing 737 Family Comparison

	737-100	737-200	737-200ADV	737-300	737-400	737-500	737-600
Length	94' 0"	100' 2"	100' 2"	105' 7"		97' 9"	102' 6"
Wingspan	93' 0"	93' 0"	93' 0"	94' 8"	94' 8"	94' 8"	112' 7"
Wingspan With Winglets	N/A	N/A	N/A	102' 1"	102' 1"	102' 1"	117' 5"
Height	36' 10"	36' 10"	36' 10"	36' 6"	36' 6"	36' 6"	41' 2"
Max Takeoff Weight - Pounds	110,000 (Optionally 97,000)	115,500 (Optionally 109,000)	128,100 (Optionally 115,500)	138,500 (Optionally 124,500)	150,000 (Optionally 138,500)	136,000 (Optionally 115,500)	145,500 (Optionally 124,000)
Max Landing Weight - Pounds	99,000 (Optionally 89,700)	103,000 (Optionally 95,000)	107,000 (Optionally 103,000)	116,600 (Optionally 114,000)	124,000 (Optionally 121,000)	110,000	120,500 (Optionally 120,500)
Max Standard Fuel Capacity (US Gallons)	4,720	4,780	5,160	5,311	5,311	5,311	6,875
Max Fuel Capacity with Optional Aux Tanks - US Gallons	N/A	N/A	5,970	6,295	6,295	6,295	N/A
Powerplant (Takeoff Thrust in Pounds)	JT8D-7, -7A, -7B (14,000) JT8D-9, -9A (14,500) JT8D-15 (15,500)	JT8D-7, -7A, -7B (14,000) JT8D-9, -9A (14,500) JT8D-15, -15A (15,500) JT8D-17, -17A (16,000)	JT8D-9, -9A (14,500) JT8D-15, -15A (15,500) JT8D-17, -17A (16,000)	CFM56-3B-1 (20,100) CFM56-3C-1 (22,100) CFM56-3B-2 (22,100)	CFM56-3B-2 (22,100) CFM56-3C-1 (23,500)	CFM56-3B-1 (20,100) CFM56-3C-1 [D] (20,100)	CFM56-7B [V] (20,600-22,700)
Vmo - Knots/Mmo	350/Mach .840	350/Mach .840	350/Mach .840	340/Mach .820	340/Mach .820	340/Mach .820	340/Mach .820
Econ Cruise Speed, Approximate	Mach .730	Mach .730	Mach .730	Mach .745	Mach .745	Mach .745	Mach .785
Range, Full Load, Approximate - Nautical Miles	1720	1900	2645	1,635-2,270	1,907-2,090	2,420	3,717
Max Certificated Altitude - Feet	35,000	35,000	35,000	37,000	37,000	37,000	41,000
Seating Capacity (FAA limit)	85-96 (124)	97-124 (136)	102-130 (136)	128-134 (149)	146-159 (188)	108-122 (140)	108-130 (149)
Standard Baggage Compartment Capacity - Cubic Feet	650	875	875	1,068	1,373	822	720

* [1] Projected.
* [D] Thrust derated.
* [V] Various Engine Options

* Sources: FAA TCDS A16WE, Boeing, Wikipedia, Airport Data D6-58326-6, and www.b737.org.uk

737-700	737-800	737-900	737-900ER	737 BBJ	737 MAX-7	737 MAX-8	737 MAX 200	737 MAX-9
110' 4"	129' 6"	138' 2"	138' 2"	110'4" (BBJ-2: 129' 6") (BBJ-3: 138' 2")	116' 8"	129' 8"	129' 8"	138' 4"
112' 7"	112' 7"	112' 7"	N/A	N/A	N/A	N/A	N/A	N/A
117' 5"	117' 5"	117' 5"	117' 5"	117' 5"	117' 10"	117' 10"	117' 10"	117' 10"
41' 2"	41' 2"	41' 2"	41' 2"	41' 2"	40' 4"	40' 4"	40' 4"	40' 4"
155,500 (Optionally 133,000)	174,200 (Optionally 155,500)	174,200 (Optionally 164,000)	187,700 (Optionally 164,000)	171,000 (BBJ-2: 174,200) (BBJ-3: 187,700)	177,000	181,200	181,200	194,700
129,200 (Optionally 128,000)	146,300 (Optionally 144,000)	147,300 (Optionally 146,300)	157,300 (Optionally 146,300)	134,000 (BBJ-2: 146,300) (BBJ-3: 157,300)	145,600	152,800	152,800	163,900
6,875	6,875	6,875	6,875	6,875	6,853	6,853	6,853	6,853
N/A	N/A	N/A	7,837	10,707 (BBJ-2: 10,442) (BBJ-3: 10,966)	N/A	N/A	N/A	N/A
CFM56-7B [V] (20,600-26,300)	CFM56-7B [V] (24,200-27,300)	CFM56-7B [V] (24,200-27,300)	CFM56-7B [V] (24,200-27,300)	CFM56-7B26E (27,300)	CFM LEAP 1B (23,000-28,000)	CFM LEAP 1B (23,000-28,000)	CFM LEAP 1B (23,000-28,000)	CFM LEAP 1B (23,000-28,000)
340/Mach .820	340/Mach .820	340/Mach .820	340/Mach .820	340/Mach .820	340/Mach .820 [1]	340/Mach .820 [1]	340/Mach .820 [1]	340/Mach .820 [1]
Mach .785	Mach .785	Mach .780	Mach .780	Mach .780	Mach .785 [1]	Mach .785 [1]	Mach .785 [1]	Mach .785 [1]
3,245	2,930	2,060-2,458	3,265	6,270 (BBJ-2: 5,630) (BBJ-3: 5,545)	3,825 [1]	3,515 [1]	2,700 [1]	3,515 [1] (With Optional Aux Tank)
41,000	41,000	41,000	41,000	41,000	41,000	41,000	41,000	41,000
128-148 (149)	160-184 (189)	177-189 (189)	174-220 (220)	Variable	138-172	162-189	200	178-220
966	1,555	1,835	1,826	159 (BBJ-2: 711) (BBJ-3: 872)	954	1,543	1,543	1,814

Model building is a rewarding and relaxing hobby millions of people enjoy. For those with interest in this hobby and the Boeing 737, it is good to know there are many kit and livery decal options for the different generations of the aircraft. My goal is to give helpful information to modelers of all skill levels by providing a pictorial step-by-step construction of three different models at different skill levels. Most beginning modelers do not have equipment, such as an airbrush or spray booth, and will most likely desire to use a spray can to create the final finish. Folks with more experience likely have been working with military subjects and camouflage paints. Building airliners with typically glossy finishes and metallic surfaces can strike fear into the heart of even experienced modelers. Techniques will be discussed to aid in the transition to the wonderful world of airliner modeling. When possible, the order prescribed by the kit directions will be followed unless a reason for deviation is presented.

Aftermarket decals and detail sets will also be discussed and employed, allowing customization of the kits. Decades ago, airliner models needed to be built as seen on the box top because few if any aftermarket products were available. In the 1970s, visionaries like Clint Groves, who started a company called Airliners America-ATP, began to transform the hobby, opening doors to many great kit and decal possibilities. Today, many high quality suppliers exist that provide a variety of kits, aftermarket accessories, and outstanding decal sheets.

Modeling is a very safe hobby, but as with any activity, certain precautions must be exercised for maximum safety. First, ensure adequate ventilation while painting; the use of a filtered mask is advisable. Working with gloves while using paints and filler compounds will prevent toluene and other chemicals from being absorbed through the skin. Always read and follow the directions on each product to prevent problems from cropping up. A good hobby knife is essential, but be sure to never cut toward any part of your body in case the knife slips. Lastly, when working with resin model parts use a mask while sawing or sanding to ensure that dust is not inhaled. Be safe and have fun!

The Basic Build: Minicraft's 1/144 Scale 737-300

Minicraft's 737-300 kit offering is perfect for a first model because they are relatively inexpensive, readily obtainable, build fairly easily, and finish into a nice representation of the real aircraft. As a premise, this model will be built using only basic equipment commensurate with the first-time modeler. The use of high quality spray paint and plastic cements will be used widely, while occasional brush painting and sparing use of cyanoacrylate (CA) glues will also be utilized.

The following supplies are required to build this model as shown:

- Minicraft 1/144 Scale 737-300 kit number 14446
- F-DCAL Air France Boeing 737-300 Decal Set FD-144-319 (available from www.f-dcal.fr)
- Authentic Airliners Boeing Cockpit and Cabin Windows 737-700 Decal (available from www.authentic-airliner-decals.de)
- Model Master Spray Paints: Gloss Gull Grey FS16440, Gunship Grey FS36118, German Silver Metallic 291402, and Classic White 2920
- Testors Spray Primer and CreateFX Acrylic Wash
- Tamiya NATO Black XF-69 Spray Paint and NATO Black XF-69 Bottle Paint
- Plastruct Bondene Styrene Cement
- Insta-Cure+ Gap Filling Medium CA Glue (cyanoacrylate)
- Hobby knife
- Assorted sand paper and sanding sticks
- Pledge Floor Care (Future)

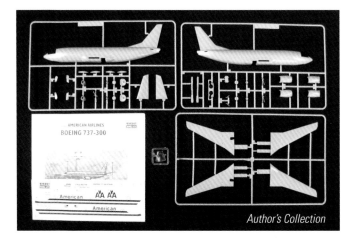

Author's Collection

Any model building project should begin with a few acts of preparation. A thorough review of the instructions is very helpful to allow the modeler to get a "big picture" view of the build. In particular, it is important to note the order of operations and think about the painting requirements. It may be advantageous to paint components such as engines and landing gears prior to final assembly. This strategy may cause the modeler to deviate from the directions a bit on certain kits. Selection of an airline livery may also affect the decision making process and the painting supplies required.

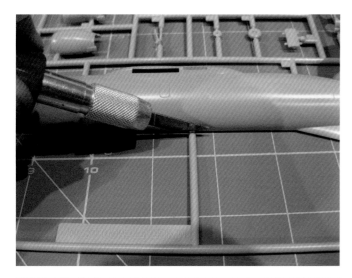

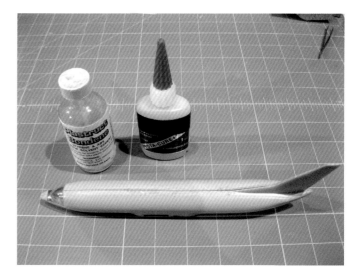

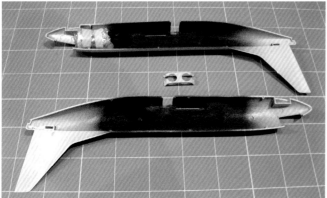

The first construction step led me to glue the two fuselage halves together. Either plastic cement or CA glue can be used to accomplish this, however, a word of caution is warranted for the new modeler. CA glue will set rapidly and may not give the beginner enough time to align the parts perfectly. Styrene cement will allow more time to get things right. CA glue can then be used to fill any gaps present after assembly.

The first step is to remove the fuselage halves from the sprue. The use of a good hobby knife is essential so as not to damage the parts while removing them. Once removed, the inside of the fuselage halves were painted black to create the illusion of depth on the finished model, since the main landing gear wheel wells are open. I will be using cockpit window decals so I did not need to give the cockpit area the same treatment. A small plastic bag filled with BBs was used to supply nose weight. Most model airliners are tail heavy and will be tail sitters unless weight is added. I used CA glue to secure the weight to the inside of the model.

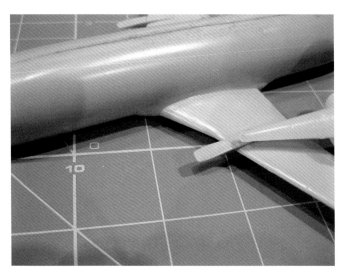

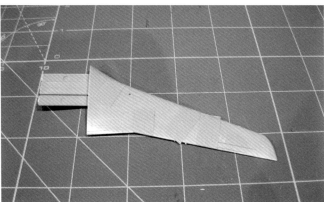

The next step is to assemble the engines. Close attention is required here, as the left and right engines are not interchangeable. Use a piece of tape to mark right and left. I recommend not using a permanent marker, as this can sometimes bleed through the paint and ruin the finish later. Small parts like engines are best cemented together with styrene cement. Here, I chose to deviate from the kit instructions a bit, keeping the engine nacelles separate from the pylons. This eased the painting experience, since the rear portion of each nacelle is tucked under the wing a bit and will be painted a different color.

Like the fuselage, using styrene cement to glue the wings together is advisable so the modeler has time to insure proper alignment. Caution should be exercised because styrene cement works by "melting" the plastic together chemically. Although this causes a very strong bond, excessive application can damage the surrounding plastic. Tape the two halves together and allow the assembly to dry. Since the engine pylons were the same grey color as the lower surface of the wing and I wished to eliminate the seams where the pylons mate to the wings, I elected to attach these first and fill in the gaps with CA glue. Sanding sticks were used to remove excess CA and create a smooth transition.

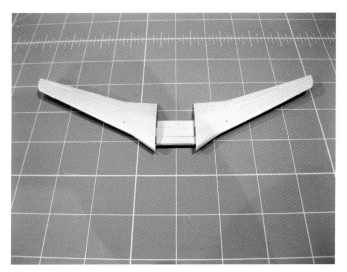

One of the truly nice features of the Minicraft kit is the interlocking system used to ensure proper wing dihedral during assembly (shown prior to attaching to the fuselage). Due to the interlocking nature of these assemblies, when sliding the left and right wing tabs into the fuselage I recommend using styrene cement for the initial bond, since fast-curing CA glue might bond before the wings are in their final position. After assembly conservative use of CA glue was used to fill any remaining gaps.

Although not mandatory, the best finishes can be achieved by filling seams and sanding the model to a smooth surface using sanding sticks and sandpaper. I recommend starting with wet or dry 220 grit and progressing to 320 and 400 so that sanding marks will not be visible once paint is applied. Using damp sandpaper dipped frequently in water will help keep dust to a minimum and irrigate the sandpaper. A technique I like to use involves filling and sanding followed by a very light coat of primer, as the primer coat will make imperfections and unfilled gaps very obvious.

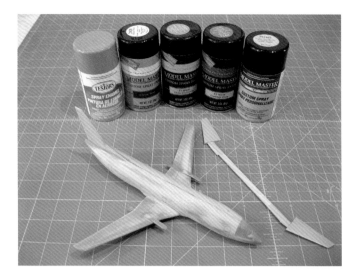

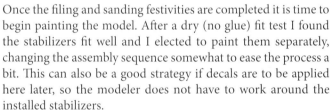

Once the filing and sanding festivities are completed it is time to begin painting the model. After a dry (no glue) fit test I found the stabilizers fit well and I elected to paint them separately, changing the assembly sequence somewhat to ease the process a bit. This can also be a good strategy if decals are to be applied here later, so the modeler does not have to work around the installed stabilizers.

Typically, when using spray paint on airliners I like to start with the wings and paint the fuselage last. The wings have extensive flight control detail, and the paint used on the fuselage is usually a thick glossy paint which can cover up these surface details. One disadvantage of using spray cans is that it is more difficult to control the quantity of paint being applied, but this can be mitigated if some care is taken. Shake the can vigorously for at least one minute to ensure proper mixing of the contents. The spray can should be held twelve to fifteen inches from the model with quick sweeping coats being applied. Keep the can moving at all times while spraying and stop painting frequently to inspect. If not enough paint has been applied the surface will look rough or have poor coverage. Too much paint is indicated by the paint appearing to pool around surface detail. If this is seen discontinue spraying immediately and allow the paint to dry for an hour prior to applying additional coats to avoid dreaded paint run. Best results tend to be achieved by using three coats with some curing time in between. The first coat should be light, will still be slightly transparent, and even a bit rough. This first coat gives subsequent heavier coats a surface with which to bond, helping to prevent runs. The last coat should be the heaviest, but just enough for it to give a shiny surface.

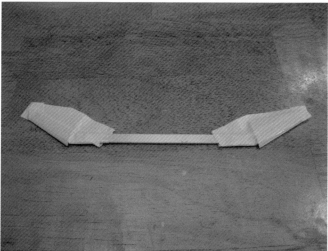

Masking between color applications is best accomplished with high quality modeler's masking tapes such as Tamiya Tape and Pactra Tape. Here, the airplane's grey inspar panels were painted Gunship Grey to simulate the Coroguard coatings typical on the 737 Original and Classic series. After allowing forty-eight hours drying time Tamiya Tape was carefully applied in preparation for the next wing color Gloss Gull Gray, which is close to the standard Boeing Grey color painted on the trailing edges and undersides of the wings. Take your time here, as a missed area can cause grief later. I used a balsa stick to burnish the tape down in the corners, which was helpful in preventing overspray from getting under the tape.

The painting of metallic colors requires a few considerations for good results. First, these paints tend to be sensitive to masking tape, which can mar or pull metallic colors away from the model when removed. Also, certain enamel-based metallics can take a very long time to cure and are also sensitive to fingerprints. Because of this, I always attempt to apply these paints last, even if remasking the whole model is required. The inlets of the engines were difficult because of the compound curves involved. I used Pactra Tape, which is a bit rubbery and worked well here, with Tamiya Tape used to secure it and mask the rear sections of the engines. Several light coats are the best course of action, as the paints tend to be very thin in viscosity and like to sneak under the masking tape if applied too heavily. The horizontal stabilizers were masked and secured to a piece of balsa wood for easy handling. After painting, these items were attached to the model using a sparing amount of CA glue.

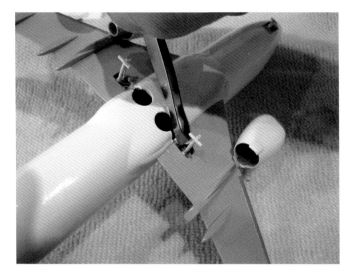

I noticed that there was still some "orange peel" effect on the white paint due to the use of spray paints. This can be solved easily (and inexpensively) with the use of Pledge Floor Care, which also used to be marketed as Future Floor Wax. With a clean, high quality brush this can be applied directly to the desired areas of the model. The finish levels nicely and dries as a very shiny, durable finish that will accept decals well. When finished clean the brush with window cleaner. Pledge Floor Care can also be airbrushed nicely without thinning if you are so equipped.

Small bits like the landing gears and gear doors are best spray painted while taped to a piece of cardboard to insure they are not lost or blown off by the spray. Once dry these need to be carefully installed on the model using tweezers to move them into position. Be sure to check the fit prior to adding glue. Either CA glue or styrene cement will be effective here. Painting tires, especially for people like me who have shaky hands, are best tackled by mounting the wheels on toothpicks and turning them while holding the brush still. Bracing your hands on your table can also be helpful.

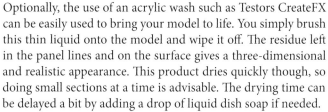

Optionally, the use of an acrylic wash such as Testors CreateFX can be easily used to bring your model to life. You simply brush this thin liquid onto the model and wipe it off. The residue left in the panel lines and on the surface gives a three-dimensional and realistic appearance. This product dries quickly though, so doing small sections at a time is advisable. The drying time can be delayed a bit by adding a drop of liquid dish soap if needed.

In the first image, the wash has been applied to the "flipper flaps," which tend to get very sooty and dirty on 737 Classics. With a paper towel the wash is wiped off, leaving a nice weathered effect. Using a paint brush to apply the wash and cotton swabs for removal is a very effective technique for landing gears and wheel wells.

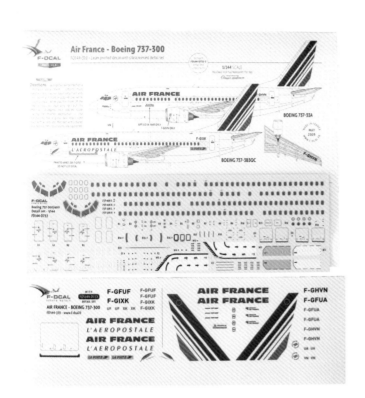

Modern plastic model kits generally come with high quality decals, but many modelers like to have a variety of airline livery decals to choose from to customize their kit. Aftermarket decal manufacturers such as F-DCAL and Draw Decal offer a wide variety of options. Some are screen printed while others are ink jet printed. Screen printed decals use an opaque media, allowing them to be applied over colors other than a white surface while retaining their original color shades. Ink jet based decals must be applied over white surfaces or color distortion will occur because they are somewhat transparent. In certain situations this can be an important factor and is good to know when the modeler devises a painting strategy. In this case the all white fuselage will allow easy use of this ink jet printed Air France sheet. The included detail sheet is cleverly screen printed, as many of these details are on portions of the aircraft which are not typically white.

The Authentic Airliner Decals "3-D" window decals have already been added to the model and are being used in conjunction with the F-DCAL livery sheet. Many aftermarket decals are printed on a continuous carrier film, requiring the decal images to be cut very precisely so as not to allow too much clear film to border the marking. It is best to remove the piece from the sheet first, then do a fine trimming prior to beginning the application process as shown. It is always advisable to read the directions for the decal sheet you are using, but most work best with a soak in warm water. Depending on the decal material used the soak time can be somewhere between ten seconds and one minute. Continue soaking until the decal moves freely on the sheet, but be careful not to allow it to fold on top of itself.

Once the decal has released from the paper transport it to the model and place the decal over the intended position. Carefully slide the backing paper away, leaving the decal on the model. Carefully fine tune the position of the decal on the model. If the decal begins to adhere prior to being in the proper spot add a small amount of water with a clean paintbrush or finger and continue the process. Carefully blot away the water and ensure there are no wrinkles on the decal.

Quality decals such as these are pliable and easy to apply, but any decal can become a bit difficult when going around sharp edges (in this case the vertical stabilizer) and areas with compound curves, such as nose and tail sections. This can be alleviated somewhat with the use of a decal solvent such as Micro Sol. A solvent will soften the decal and allow it to conform to such surfaces. It is always a good idea to test the solvent on a part of the decal that will be unused, as some sheets do not take well to solvents, but most do. Here, solvent is being applied to the decal to help it conform to the stabilizer tip. Many times solvents will make a decal wrinkle, but resist the urge to "fix it." The decal material will be extremely soft and will most likely be damaged if it is touched. Let it dry for at least two hours and you will likely find that the wrinkles are gone and it is adhering nicely.

Small decals can be challenging and a bit tedious, but are well worth the effort on the finished model. My favorite method is to slide them off of the paper and manipulate them into position with a clean, damp paintbrush. Attempt to wick away any excess water without touching the decal and let it dry.

Nice airliner models can be built even with basic supplies by a new modeler. For a person's first airliner models, particularly if one has limited experience applying decals, basic paint schemes like this Air France livery are a good choice. Once the modeler becomes comfortable with the techniques involved more advanced schemes can be used. The best results are achieved by taking your time and most importantly, having fun!

Author's Collection

Intermediate Build: Authentic Airliners 1/144 737-900

The Authentic-Airliners 737-900 kit is a truly professional grade kit that builds well with absolute accuracy and detail. The parts fit is very good and assembly is smooth and drama free. I have declared this an intermediate build because the medium for this kit is resin, as opposed to the styrene plastic that is common and familiar. Authentic Airliners' expanding range of kits are a bit more expensive, but in my opinion they have the shape absolutely right and the parts quality is second to none. Some resin kits have problems with pin holes and warping, but I have never experienced this with any kits from this company. During the course of this build we will look at some more advanced techniques, including airbrush use, as well as the differences inherent to building a resin kit.

The following supplies are required to build this model as shown:

- Authentic Airliners 1/144 Boeing 737-900 kit
  (available at www.authentic-airliners.de)

- Draw Decals KLM 737-900 Decal Set 44s-737-109
  (available at www.drawdecal.com)

- Authentic Airliners Decals 1/144 Cockpit
  and Cabin Windows B737-900
  (available at www.authentic-airliner-decals.de)

- Model Master Classic White 2720, Aircraft Grey 1731, and
  Bright Blue 2766

- Testors Gloss Red 1103 and CreateFX Acrylic Wash

- Alclad II Polished Aluminum

- Tamiya Titanium Silver X-32 and NATO Black XF-69

- Insta-Cure+ Gap Filling Medium CA Glue (cyanoacrylate)

- Insta-Cure+ CA Accelerator

- X-acto type hobby knife

- Small Modeler's Saw

- Assorted Sanding Sticks and Wet or Dry Sandpaper

- Airbrush and Pressure Source

- Small Paint Booth

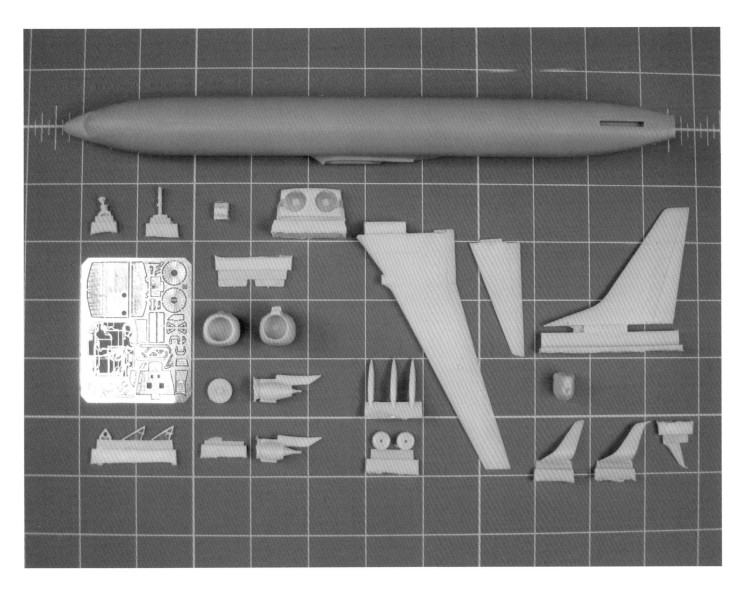

The kit consists of high quality resin and photo-etched detail parts. Optional parts in the kit include resin or photo-etched landing gear doors, standard or PIP exhaust nozzles, and a choice of early wingtips, blended winglets, or scimitar winglets. The kit features resin landing gear parts which bear the weight of the model well.

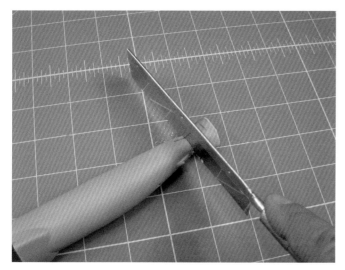

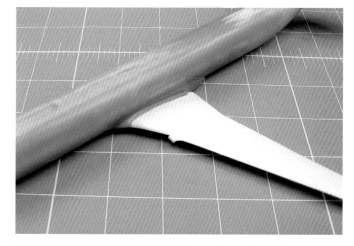

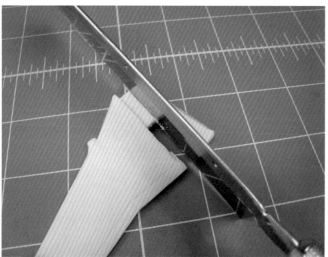

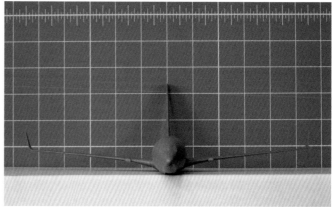

The fit of the parts is excellent, but additional preparation is required to remove the resin parts from the excess casting material. A razor saw is required to prepare the parts for assembly. Light sanding with a medium grit sanding stick may be necessary to smooth out any rough edges.

Test fitting parts prior to committing with glue is a necessity with any model. Since this is a resin kit styrene cement will not be effective. CA glues are my primary means of gluing and filling gaps on resin kits. An accelerator such as Insta-Cure+ is handy, and when sprayed on to CA glues, through a chemical reaction, will harden the glue almost immediately. Be aware though that accelerators can damage painted surfaces, so their use is relegated to primary assembly unless great care is taken to protect paint. A grid pattern in the background is a very effective way to ensure the dihedral of the wings, stabilizers, and winglets are symmetrical and correct prior to the glue curing. Once you have verified that everything is correct, accelerator can be applied and work continued immediately.

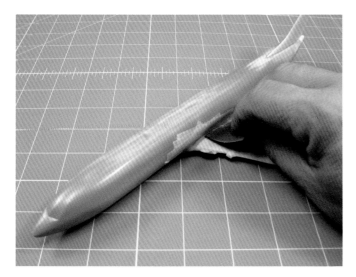

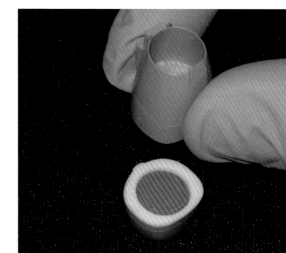

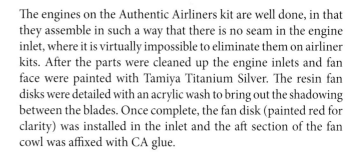

The wing to body fit on this model would allow the wings to be added after painting at the discretion of the modeler. My personal convention is to always paint the model with the wings attached so gaps (if any) can be completely eliminated. Here the right wing was glued, the joint filled with CA glue, and then sanded smooth. Masking tape was employed to protect nearby surface detail from being eroded. Like the Minicraft kit, the fit of the horizontal stabilizers was good and I chose to install them after painting. I did decide to add the vertical stabilizer to allow the very minor gap to be filled completely prior to painting.

The engines on the Authentic Airliners kit are well done, in that they assemble in such a way that there is no seam in the engine inlet, where it is virtually impossible to eliminate them on airliner kits. After the parts were cleaned up the engine inlets and fan face were painted with Tamiya Titanium Silver. The resin fan disks were detailed with an acrylic wash to bring out the shadowing between the blades. Once complete, the fan disk (painted red for clarity) was installed in the inlet and the aft section of the fan cowl was affixed with CA glue.

After assembling the engines a small seam was left, requiring some careful CA filling and sanding. Since the inlets were painted prior to assembly tape was applied to protect the finish during the sanding process. Due to the good fit of the engines to the wings on this model I have elected to paint the engines separately and install them at a tactically chosen time during airframe painting (detailed below).

Although the kit has good detailing in the main landing gear well (molded into the resin), a photo-etch assembly is also included with installation instructions. They must be cut from the carrier sheet with a sharp knife and care must be taken while bending them into shape. Seen here, the photo-etched parts really brought the wheel well to life. Here it has been painted with a mixture of twenty parts Classic White and one part Gloss Red. Boeing wheel wells are nearly white, but a transparent pink anti-corrosive coating is applied, causing the slightly pinkish coloring. The landing gear well fairing was then installed, filled, and sanded smooth. The model was lightly coated with primer to make any flaws obvious. The photo-etched nose gear well parts fit nicely into the solid resin casting.

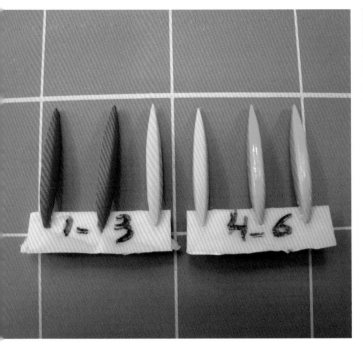

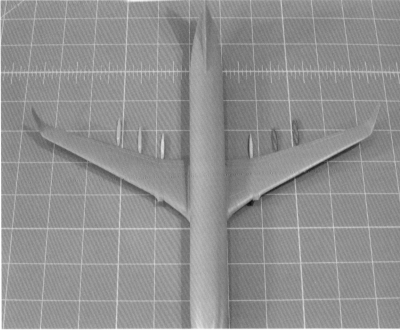

The model is nearly ready to paint, but the canoe fairings for the flaps should be added first and any gaps filled. I have color coded them to show their intended positions to help avoid confusion. These will have to be carefully removed from their carriers with a razor saw.

It is now time for painting and perhaps a first experience with an airbrush. The airbrush is probably the most useful tool that a modeler can possess because it allows for exceptionally nice finishes while being able to meter air pressure and paint flow. Although a complete guide to airbrushing is beyond the scope of this book, I will cover the basics briefly and give suggestions based on my experiences. Other modelers will likely use techniques differing from mine with excellent results. Books, magazines, and online forums are great sources of information on techniques. Try out different ideas and push forward with the ones that work best for you.

My personal preference is to use a single action airbrush, because you are able to manipulate one variable at a time. The Paasche Single Action product is ideal, and it is also easy to clean. This feature is important because it must be cleaned after each use and during color changes. There are three basic ways to supply air pressure to the airbrush: aerosol can, compressor, or a CO_2 cylinder. Having used all three, I give a strong recommendation for the CO_2 cylinder. Aerosol cans are expensive and last for a very limited time. Compressors can squeeze water vapor out of the air which can eventually make its way to the airbrush. Water splattering on enamel paint does not make for a good paint job. If you do choose this route, it is worth investing in a good in-line water separator. A CO_2 cylinder will need a pressure regulator to allow the output pressure to be adjustable between 15–40 psi. They are cheap to refill and one fill up will last through several models with ease.

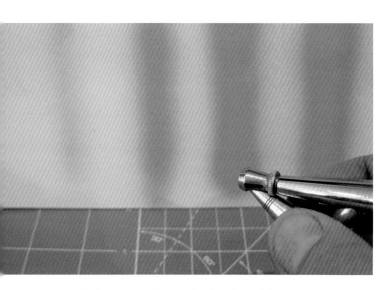

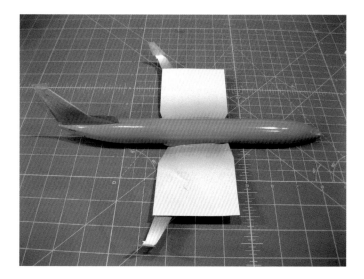

Paint thickness may also need to be adjusted for use in an airbrush, while others are premixed (Alclad II, for example) and are intended for airbrushing. Typically, paints need to be thinned to a consistency slightly thicker than milk for the first coats. Always use the thinners recommended on the bottle to create the correct mixture and beware, using the wrong thinner can invite disaster for your model. Practice with your airbrush on an old model or even a laminated piece of cardboard to determine the right air pressure, paint flow rate, thickness of paint media, and distance from the surface. The key, just like spray painting, is to keep the airbrush moving while paint is flowing to avoid runs. It will take a bit of practice to get the hang of it, but this effort will make an enormous difference in the models you will soon be producing. Airbrushes are also extremely helpful in painting metallics and camouflage schemes.

Airbrushing glossy paint jobs can be daunting, but here are a few techniques which may help. Using enamels such as Model Master Bright Blue (shown), start with a 70% paint, 30% thinner mixture. Set your airbrush using a disposable surface to get the paint flow correct with a full 30 psi airflow. Put down a light coat and do not be concerned about color coverage at this point. This will give the next, slightly heavier coat something to cling to, as well as sealing the edges of the masking tape without the hazard of paint submarining under it. Let the model sit for about half an hour and with the same mixture apply a slightly heavier coat. The finish may have a slight orange peel texture and that is all right. If the color density is still not quite to your liking repeat once more after a short drying period. Once satisfied with the color density you can use a technique that will bring on the high-gloss surface. Drain most of the paint out of the airbrush and use a 20% paint, 80% thinner mixture. Be sure to adjust the paint flow on the airbrush, because this solution will be very thin and fast flowing. Once a workable flow rate has been achieved spray the model until it looks wet, but use caution not to overdo this last coat because runs are still possible. The wet thinner will level the underlying paint, making it smooth and shiny. Another benefit is that this will accelerate the drying process slightly. Still, give 24–48 hours drying time before masking over for the next color. Even though paint control is definitely improved with the airbrush, I still attempt to mask the wings to avoid too much overspray from affecting surface details. Even sticky notes are effective masks (above).

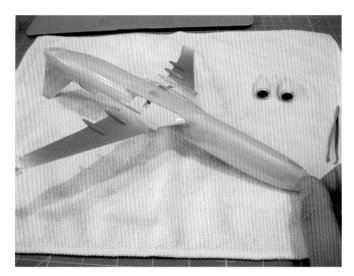

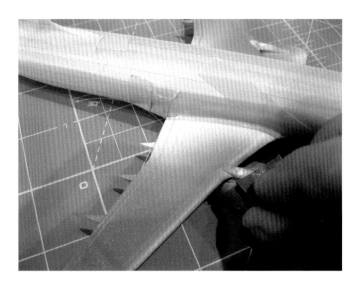

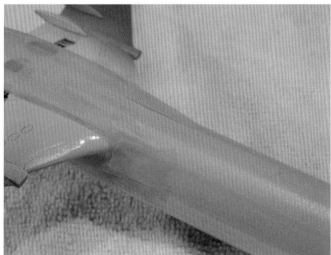

Between colors masking is required. Using a high quality masking tape especially for models is advisable, as some commercially available masking tapes are high tack and can pull your beautiful paint job right off the model. Here Tamiya Tape was applied to the model. An ounce of preparation is worth a pound of cure they say, and it certainly applies here. Note the photo (above) where the tape has not been adequately pushed down to the surface. This could easily be missed and ruin your day. If a piece of tape wants to lift use another piece of tape to seal it down, preventing a possible gap. Burnish down all of the tape edges to insure a good seal.

At this point I have painted the Classic White tail and winglets, the Bright Blue fuselage, and the very light grey (90% Classic White and 10% Aircraft Grey mixture) for the lower fuselage and engine nacelles. The horizontal stabilizers, wings, and engine pylons were aircraft grey, which was the next color to be added. As mentioned earlier, I chose this time, prior to the application of Aircraft Grey, to mount the engines to the pylons. CA glue was used to carefully affix the nacelles and fill the small gaps. This strategy allowed the engines to be completely painted with the very light grey mixture without interference from the wings. Masking tape was being used to protect the paint finish on the engines while I gently sanded the pylons to get a smooth, continuous surface. Once this was done the painting continued with the Aircraft Grey wings and engine pylons. After drying additional masking was required prior to painting the leading edges of the wings and stabilizers.

I am using a product called Alclad II to give the bare metal finish effect on these components. Alclad II, recently marketed by Ammo of Mig (which specializes in weathering products for models), is my favorite bare metal finish because it is realistic looking and once finished is fairly resistant to damage. There is a procedure for successful execution of the finish, though. First, the surface must be smooth and free from imperfections for best results, because metallics show everything! After assuring surface quality and proper masking I started by applying the Alclad II Black Base Coat in three or four thin coats, the first of which was barely more than a dusting. By the third or fourth coat it should look shiny. Allow this to dry overnight. It is imperative that the Black Base Coat not be touched by fingers, as fingerprints will show on the final finish. Try not to touch it at all, but if you must use a cloth or dust-free gloves. Next, the Alclad II Polished Aluminum is applied in *very* thin coats. In my experience heavy coats here can cause surface crazing and a cloudy appearance. Take your time and resist the urge to hurry. (We will cover the use of Alclad products more extensively during the BPK 737-200 build.)

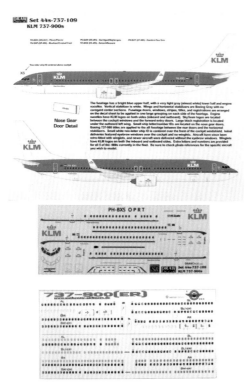

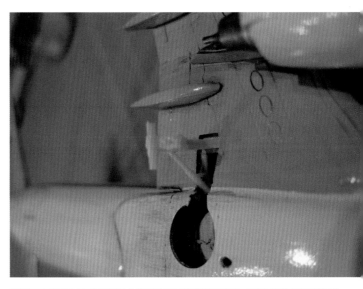

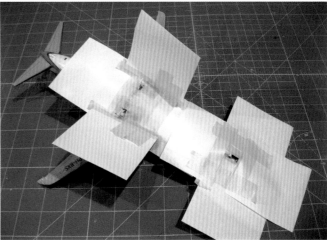

Since many modelers like to choose the airline livery for their models as opposed to just using kit decals Authentic Airliners does not supply decals with its kits, but they do offer excellent window decals that can be purchased separately. I chose to use these because they make a very real representation of cockpit and passenger windows. I have always liked the blue KLM (Royal Dutch Airlines) paint schemes and I sourced the livery decals from Draw Decals. All decals were applied in the same manner as the Minicraft kit, using lukewarm water. Both of these decal sets are printed on a continuous film, requiring the modeler to cut the decals out as close as possible to the boundaries of the decal image so that excess carrier film is not transferred to the model. These decals are high quality and easy to apply.

I opted to use the resin landing gears supplied with the kit, which show great detail for the scale and were easily assembled and installed with CA glue, though I recommend using tweezers because of the small size of the parts. One of the benefits of using an airbrush is having the ability to mix paints prior to spraying and the much more refined control over the spray pattern. I applied the reddish white mixture used to detail the wheel wells for the landing gears as well. With the airbrush I was comfortable using sticky notes and Tamiya Tape to mask the wells off, then painting the landing gears in-situ. After allowing time for the paint to dry the landing gears were treated with a thin wash of CreateFX to simulate shadows and light weathering. Even the most well maintained jetliners tend to have some grime here from tire smoke, brake dust, and grease. The resin wheels supplied with the kit were painted NATO Black. All 737s have smooth "hub caps" on the outboard tires of the main landing gears and standard rims on the inboard, so use caution when installing the wheels. A light wash was applied to the wings, engines, and horizontal stabilizers to bring out the recessed detail provided with this very detailed kit.

Author's Collection

Advanced Build: 1/72 BPK 737-200

Big Planes Kits (BPK) of the Ukraine has produced a beautiful 1/72 model kit of the 737-200 with accurate shape and details. This kit includes window paint masks and a very nice decal sheet. Incidentally, BPK also produces versions of this kit with decals for Pan Am, Piedmont, British Airways, and a T-43A variant. The kit includes a photo-etched detail fret, clear cabin and cockpit windows, rubber tires, and a highly detailed main wheel well. Best of all, the kit includes the Unimproved Field Kit components, which I will be incorporating into my build. For an airliner kit the cockpit is well detailed, and is quite visible through the windows. I consider this kit an advanced build mostly because of the "limited run" nature of the kit and the methods BPK used to integrate the clear window parts with the model. The modeler must make sure that everything is lined up prior to applying glue due to the lack of positive locating tabs. These are not major issues but require a bit of extra care, as we will see.

The following supplies are required to build this model as shown:

- BPK 1/72 Canadian North 737-200 kit #7202

- Authentic Airliners Decals 1/72 707-767 Cabin Windows (available at www.authentic-airliner-decals.de)

- BPK 737-200 Landing Gear Set (inquire at gfactormodels@aol.com)

- Draw Decals Pacific Western 737-200 Set # 72s-737-147 (available at www.drawdecal.com)

- Nazca Decals 1/72 737-200 Detail Set (available at www.nazca-decals.com)

- 72Airliners 737-200 Improvement Set, 1/72 Scale (available at www.72airliners.de)

- Model Master Classic White 2720, Aircraft Grey 1731, and Blue Angel Blue 16473

- Testors Gloss Red 1103, Gloss Green 1124, and CreateFX Acrylic Wash

- Alclad II Gloss Black Base ALC-304, Polished Aluminum ALC-105, Duraluminum ALC-102, and Exhaust Manifold ALC-123

- Tamiya Titanium Silver X-32, NATO Black XF-69, Deck Tan XF-55, and Flat Aluminum XF-16

- Insta-Cure+ Gap Filling Medium CA Glue (cyanoacrylate)

- Super-Cure+ Odorless CA Glue

- Insta-Cure+ CA Accelerator

- Plastruct Bondene Styrene Cement

- X-acto type hobby knife

- Razor saw and jig

- Assorted sanding sticks and wet or dry sandpaper

- Dremel tool with cutting wheel

- Airbrush and pressure source

- Small paint booth

- Pledge Floor Care (Future)

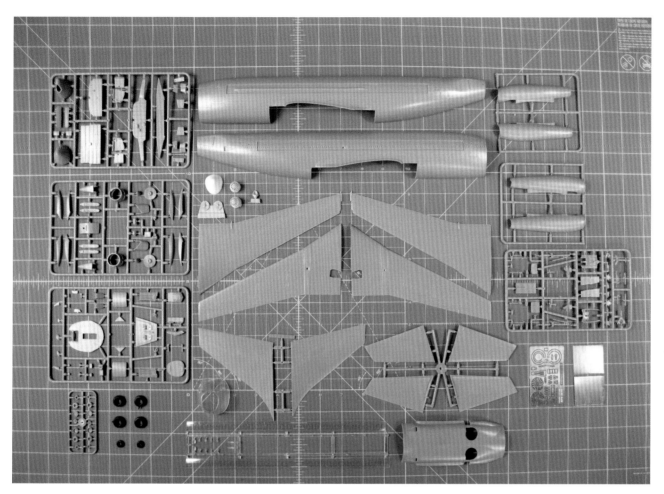

The German company 72Airliners (a subsidiary of Authentic Airliners) produces a very nice detail and correction set for the BPK 737-200 that I chose to use with this build. The all-resin correction kit provides a replacement vertical stabilizer, horizontal stabilizers, engine inlets, engine exhausts with turbine disks, and a re-contoured nose cone. In typical Authentic Airliners style, the parts are of the highest quality and the shape and details are spot-on.

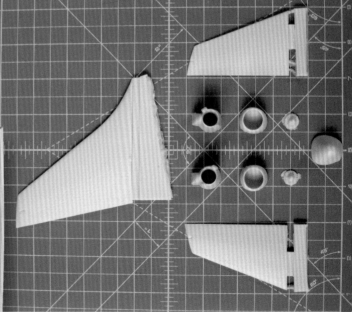

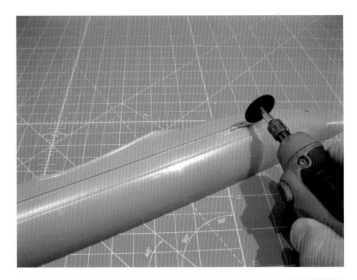

The first step in the building process—familiar to military aircraft modelers—is to assemble the cockpit. This is fairly well detailed straight out of the box and uses decals for the instrument panel details. One accuracy issue is the omission of the jump seat behind the captain's seat in the cockpit, but this is not major due to the limited view through the cockpit windows after assembly. I chose to scratch build the seat using scrap styrene. The cockpit and panels should be a flat dark grey; the seats are typically a lighter grey color. After painting I added approach charts to the yokes and a checklist to the glare shield. These were made by reducing real charts and a checklist with the reduction feature of a scanner. Using thin strips of tape seat belts were added. The pilots' seats have retractable shoulder harnesses so they are not displayed, however, the jump seat uses manually adjusted units, so they are always visible.

One of the more difficult aspects of this kit is dealing with the installation of the passenger windows. To install them the recessed areas needed to be removed, leaving a lip for the clear window piece to be adhered to with CA glue. I was not planning to leave these clear, as cabin window decals were to be used, so the fogging effect of CA glue was not an issue. If I were to use the clear window feature, I might consider using a clear epoxy resin to affix the window panels from the inside to make the assembly strong while allowing the transparent appearance.

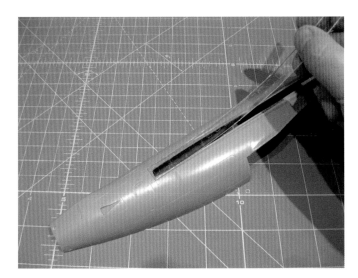

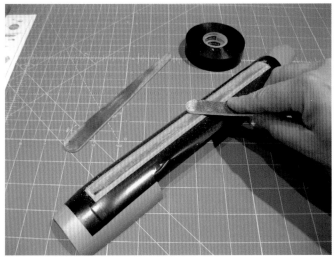

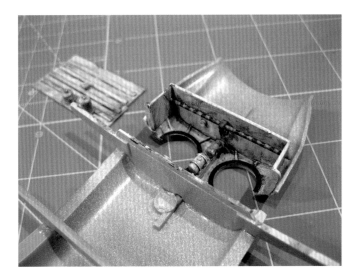

The window panels were glued with caution to maintain proper alignment, using tape to hold them in position while the glue cured. Careful attention at this step will make the sanding and blending process minimal. CA glue was used to fill around the edges and electrical tape was used to protect the surrounding detail during sanding.

The next step in the directions called for the construction of the center section and main landing gear well. Be cautious to align the spars correctly, as these will set the dihedral of the wings during final assembly. This is one of the highlights of this model, with details such as hydraulic reservoirs, the flap drive shafts (orange and black), and surface details. I painted this with a mixture of twenty parts Classic White to one part Gloss Red and added an acrylic wash to bring out the detail and create the typical soiled look of the gear wells.

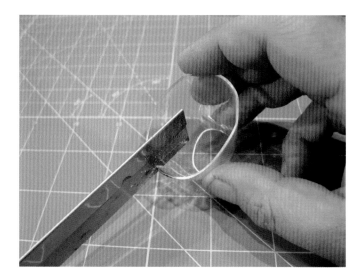

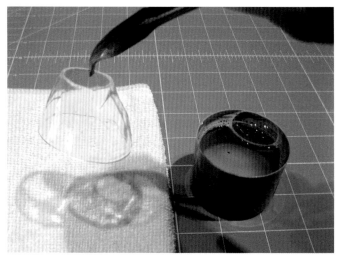

Another typical challenge with short run kits is the lack of locating tabs, which are common on many model kits to ensure proper alignment of wing and fuselage halves. I used tape to ensure proper alignment while using CA glue along one section at a time and CA accelerator to expedite the process. A toothpick was used to separate the parts until the glue could be applied, allowing for a very positive bond. The kit directions indicate weight is needed in the forward section of the fuselage for the finished model to sit properly on its wheels. This is even more critical because of my use of resin stabilizers, which are heavier than the stock kit parts. I used a small container of BBs CA glued to the inside of the forward fuselage to counterweight the model.

The nose wheel well must be cut out to allow a "gear down" configuration. The nose section was modified with a modeler's saw and cut slightly smaller than required, allowing the fit of the nose gear well to be fine-tuned later. The clear nose section was dipped in Pledge Floor Care, set on a towel, and allowed to dry. This technique will bring out the maximum clarity of the windows while preventing the frosting effect CA glue vapors can have on clear parts. The cockpit was then inserted into the clear nose piece and installed on the model using Super-Cure+ Odorless CA glue. With the combination of Pledge Floor Care and the odorless CA I experienced no clear part fogging and was left with perfectly clear cockpit windows. The gaps between the main fuselage and the clear cockpit piece were filled with odorless CA glue and sanded to a continuous finish. The windows were protected with tape to avoid damage to the transparencies.

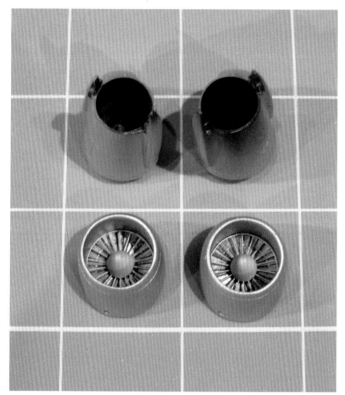

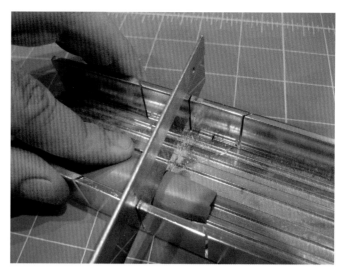

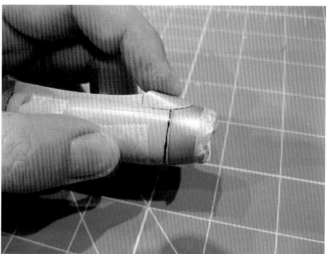

After setting aside the fuselage assembly I moved on to the engines. One of my favorite aspects of the BPK kit is the jet intakes with photo-etched stator vanes. The Authentic Airliners correction set includes seamless inlets and exhaust sections, which I believe are a significant improvement. The photo-etched stator vanes were carefully bent using tweezers and then painted Flat Aluminum while still on the fret to prevent damage. To achieve a dissimilar metal effect, the kit fan disks were painted Duraluminum and the one piece inlet was airbrushed Titanium Silver. After drying, the inlets were assembled with the stators, fan disk, and the bullet fairing, which was painted Deck Tan. Alclad II Exhaust Manifold was airbrushed on the inside of the exhaust and turbine disk.

Mark the insides of the engine halves with their part numbers prior to removing them from the sprue to prevent confusion later. To execute the resin inlet and exhaust conversion the kit engine halves must be marked and cut with a razor saw. The use of a jig made this process much easier and more precise. Note that the resin inlets are marked left and right, so caution should be exercised to ensure proper assembly. I used CA glue as a filler and sanded the nacelles smooth while using masking tape to protect the inlet areas from damage. The nacelles were test fitted to the wings and through the use of strategic sanding I was able to achieve a good fit.

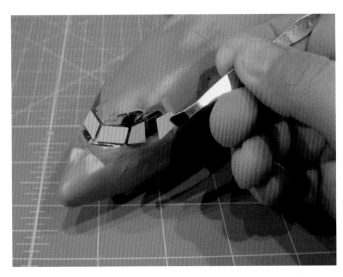

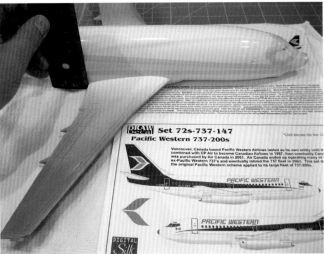

During final assembly I chose to change the order of operation slightly. For ease of painting the horizontal stabilizers and engine nacelles were left off the model until this was complete. Because I found the gap between the fuselage and wings to be a bit too visible for my taste I chose to install the wings prior to painting, so the gaps could be properly filled and sanded. After filling and sanding the airframe the Vintage Flyers cockpit window masks were put to use. I found these were a bit easier to use than the kit masks and were quite effective. The fuselage was painted Classic White using the same techniques as on the KLM kit earlier, progressively thinning the paint to gain a glossy finish. After forty-eight hours drying time it was time to paint the blue stripe. This may seem difficult, but it is fairly easy with proper preparation and patience while masking. Tamiya Tape was used to first delineate the outline of the stripe, then filled in with more tape to protect the white paint. Measure the boundaries of the stripe from prominent locations like wings and cockpit windows, ensuring everything is symmetrical. Be cautious not to use the markings for the tops of the doors as a guide. Many aircraft (such as the Boeing narrow-bodies) have shorter doors on the right side compared to the left.

Double check all of the masks to ensure good adhesion to the model and that no gaps have been left to cause a bad day later. The stripe was painted Blue Angel Blue using the same glossy paint techniques. Be sure to make the first coat a light one so the paint does not pool around the edges of the masking tape, as this risks paint finding its way under the mask. Subsequent coats can be heavier and thinned accordingly as with the KLM build.

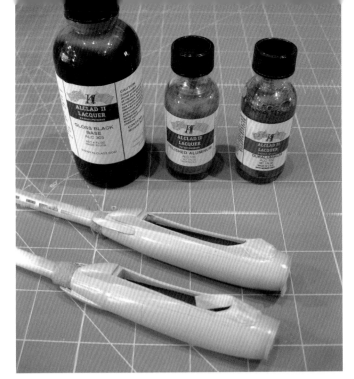

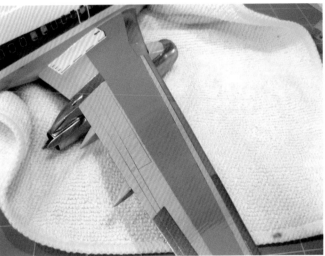

In my opinion, Alclad II paints are among the best bare metal finishes available, but they require care and a few different procedures to produce good results. The surfaces that will be painted in bare metal must be free from blemishes and sanded with a 600 grit (or finer) sandpaper prior to starting. After proper surface conditioning three to four *very* light coats of Alclad II Gloss Base Coat are applied. Alclad II is a lacquer, and if sprayed too heavily can damage the enamel-based paint beneath, so one must be careful. Afterward I allowed the base coat to dry overnight. It is absolutely imperative to not touch the Black Base Coat with your fingers prior to spraying metallic colors. Any fingerprints will show up on the final finish! Use dust-free latex gloves on your hands or clean rags if the model must be handled during the process. Once again easy does it, and the Alclad II must be applied in several *very* light coats. I used Polished Aluminum on the lower fuselage and the engine nacelles. Through the progression of light coats the surface will go from black, becoming more and more silver in appearance. As more and more coats are added the color will go from extremely shiny to a slightly more dull appearance. By using this tendency different panels can be picked out on the model for an additional coat or two. This produces the panelized effect many bare metal aircraft surfaces possess. Although Alclad II is one of the best in this regard, I still try not to use masking tape on these surfaces if I can avoid it, and if I have to, I minimize exposure as much as possible. Sticky notes are my favorite masking material for creating these panelized effects.

The decals were applied after being carefully cut out and soaked in lukewarm water. At this point the Authentic Airliner Decals 1/72 scale cabin window decals were added. Look closely, because these have left side and right side orientations, lest you have your passengers seated backward! I also used components of the very nice detail decal set from Nazca Decals on the wings, for static ports, and other small details. Any problem with your decals wrinkling or "silvering" can normally be cured with the use of Micro-Sol. On this model I wished to give the effect of fluid streaks on the wings, requiring multiple streaking applications of CreateFX to get the proper effect.

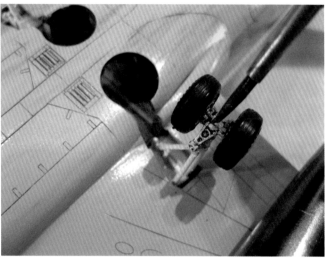

Due to the weight of this model I chose to use a metal landing gear set made for the BPK kit by G-Factor Models of California. I found these to be very well detailed, they fit perfectly without issues, and will create a sturdy support for the model. Parts are supplied for the main landing gear legs, nose gear, and nose gear drag strut (kit parts 11, 12, 7, and 1, respectively). These, once removed from the sprue with a small saw, were combined with the kit parts as directed with CA glue and airbrushed with Classic White prior to installation. The wheels were easily assembled (after the hubs and brake assemblies were painted Aircraft Grey) with the kit's rubber tires. After installation on the model an acrylic wash was applied and some cleanup done with a cotton swab. Lastly, the optional Unimproved Field Kit was painted, weathered, and installed to finish off the model.

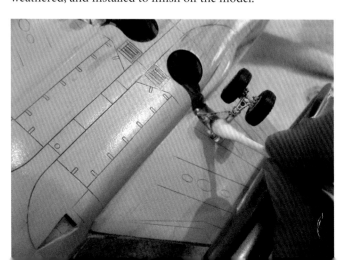

Conclusion

Modeling airliners like the Boeing 737 is a rewarding hobby and produces finished works that are interesting because there are many attractive paint schemes available and they provide modelers with some diversity in their collections. Airliners do require a few different techniques but are not necessarily more difficult than other models. The techniques I have described work well for me, but I learn new techniques from many available hobby periodicals and through websites like www.airlinercafe.com, where people share a wealth of knowledge on the subject. High gloss paints, bare metal surfaces, and extensive decal sets can be easily mastered with a bit of practice and patience, while many times the actual construction of airliner models is somewhat

simpler than comparable military models. Applying acrylic washes is something common in military aircraft modeling and is quite useful on airliners as well to make details really pop out and bring the model to life. The most important thing, in my opinion, is to make modeling fun and relaxing. Enjoy!

Disclaimer: Please note that this book is not sponsored, endorsed, nor otherwise affiliated with any of the companies whose products are represented herein. Most of the products in this book may be covered by various copyrights, trademarks, and logotypes. Their use herein is for identification purposes only. All rights are reserved by their respective owners. The information herein is derived from the author's independent research and experience.

GLOSSARY

Aeronautical Radio, Incorporated (ARINC): A primary provider of airborne voice and data link communication.

Aileron: Hinged surfaces attached to the trailing edges of each wing that work in opposition to each other to effect aircraft roll control.

Aircraft Communications Addressing and Reporting System (ACARS): An airborne "text type" communication tool that typically uses the aircraft's Control Display Units (CDUs) as an interface with aircraft pilots.

Air Data Computer (ADC): A computer that takes airspeed, altitude, and temperature data and digitally communicates with pilot instrumentation and various aircraft systems.

Alternating Current (AC): An electric current that reverses direction a certain number of times a second. Aircraft typically use 400 cycle AC, which reverses 400 times a second.

Automatic Dependent Surveillance (ADS): A surveillance system in which aircraft computers communicate flight and position data via data link to other users. Certain modes can allow the aircraft to uplink information as well.

Automatic Direction Finder (ADF): A low to medium frequency (190 Khz to 1750 Khz) instrument that displays relative bearing to the selected ground-based transmitter.

Autothrottles: An automatic thrust control system that can be engaged and commanded by the pilot.

Auxiliary Power Unit (APU): A small jet engine that can supply compressed air and electrical current to operate aircraft systems while the aircraft's engines are not operational. The APU can also be used as a backup in case of aircraft systems failures.

Bypass Ratio: The volume of air that bypasses a jet engine core compared to the volume that is involved with the combustion process in the engine core.

Cathode Ray Tube (CRT): A vacuum tube type display that produces an image when an electron beam strikes a phosphorescent surface, similar to some computer screens.

Center of Gravity (CG): A calculated balance point of an aircraft which can change depending on the loading and distribution of weight onboard.

Checkride: A qualification test for pilots which usually involves a knowledge test, and a simulator or aircraft flight evaluation.

Civil Aviation Authority (CAA): A European government entity responsible for overseeing aviation activities.

Cockpit Voice Recorder (CVR): An audio recorder which operates on multiple channels in an aircraft cockpit, and is used for incident investigation purposes. Normally, the CVR is powered any time normal electrical power is supplied to aircraft systems.

Computational Fluid Dynamics (CFD): A type of fluid dynamics that uses computerized numerical data and algorithms to solve fluid (air) flow problems.

Computer Aided Three-Dimensional Interactive Application (CATIA): A multi-platform computer aided design software developed by Avions Marcel Dassault.

Constant Speed Generator (CSD): A drive mechanism that rotates an electrical generator at constant RPM, regardless of the input drive speed.

Control Wheel Steering (CWS): A mode of the Boeing 737 autopilot that allows the pilot to control the autopilot in a basic attitude mode, making inputs to the system with the control yoke.

Cruciform Tail: An empennage design where the horizontal stabilizers are mounted to the vertical stabilizer at midsection, above the fuselage.

Cyanoacrylate Glue (CA Glue): A fast-acting adhesive used for household, medical, and hobby uses.

Deep Stall (also known as a "Locked-in Stall" or "Super Stall"): An aggravated aerodynamic stall where the turbulent airflow over the wings and rear-mounted engines blanks out an aircraft's elevators, making recovery difficult, if not impossible.

Dihedral: An upward angle of a wing from the root to the tip, providing stability in roll control.

Direct Current (DC): Electrical current which only flows in one direction.

Direct Law: A control law for fly-by-wire aircraft allowing the pilot more direct control of the aircraft's flight controls after a systems failure.

Drag: An aerodynamic force that resists an object's movement through a fluid (air).

Dutch Roll: An alternating rolling and yawing motion typical of swept wing and/or short coupled aircraft.

Effectivity Number: An alphanumeric code used internally within Boeing to identify a specific aircraft by its build specification. This convention started with the Boeing 727 Prototype, which had Effectivity Number E1.

Elevator: Flight control surfaces hinged to the trailing edges of the horizontal stabilizers used to effect pitch (nose up and down) control of an aircraft.

Engine Pressure Ratio (EPR): The pressure ratio between the exhaust nozzle and inlet of a jet engine that can be used to quantify engine thrust.

Extended-range Twin-engine Operational Performance Standards (ETOPS): A authorization that permits twin-engine jetliners to operate more that sixty minutes from a suitable alternate landing site.

Flap Asymmetry: A condition where the trailing edge flaps on a wing are not deployed to the same position as the other, creating a rolling and yawing moment.

Flap, Leading Edge "Krueger": A small flap that deploys forward from underneath the leading edge of the wing and is used to increase lift at low airspeeds.

Flap, Trailing Edge "Fowler": A type of trailing edge flap that slides rearward and down, increasing lift by expanding the effective wing area and increasing camber.

Flight Data Recorder (FDR): A device that records aircraft parameters for research and incident investigations. The FDR on the Boeing 737 is activated when either engine has an oil pressure indication or the aircraft is sensed to be in flight.

Flutter: An aerodynamic vibration that can cause structural damage and is most commonly experienced at very high airspeeds.

Fly-By-Wire Control System: A flight control system that uses either an analog or digital computer interface to replace traditional manual/mechanical aircraft control systems.

Four Dimensional Navigation (4D NAV): A concept where speed is controlled precisely to allow an aircraft to arrive over a certain point or navigational fix at a specified time. This feature is also sometimes referred to as Time Navigation or "T-NAV."

Full Authority Digital Engine Control (FADEC): A digital computer—sometimes known as an Electronic Engine Control (EEC)—and related equipment that have complete control over the operation of a turbine engine.

Fuselage: The main body of an aircraft used to carry passengers, cargo, and sometimes fuel.

Fuse Plug: A small plug that melts at very high temperatures, such as with extremely hot brake assemblies. When melted, the fuse plug allows a tire to deflate in a rapid but controlled manner, thus preventing the tire from exploding.

Future Air Navigation System (FANS): A new generation airspace system implementation consisting of elements of communication (data link), navigation (GPS, Inertial, and Ground Based), and Air Traffic Services surveillance.

Glideslope: A final approach descent path normally defined by a radio beam signal.

Head-Up Display (HUD) and Head-up Guidance System (HGS): A glass surface between the pilots' eyes and the windshield upon which flight instrument data is projected.

Horizontal Situation Indicator (HSI): An instrument that combines heading and VOR/Localizer/ILS into a single unit, typically below the Attitude Indicator.

Horizontal Stabilizer: An aerodynamic surface normally mounted horizontally on the rear portion of an aircraft creating aircraft stability in pitch (nose up and down).

Hydraulic System: A hydro-mechanical aircraft system commonly used to actuate primary and secondary flight controls, as well as landing gear systems.

Inertial Navigation System (IRS): A navigation system that uses a computer, motion sensors, and gyroscopic devices to calculate aircraft position, attitude, and speed without requirement for external inputs.

Inlet Vortice: A small tornado-like vortex that forms under the inlet of a jet engine while in operation.

Instrument Landing System (ILS): A navigation system used for landing consisting of radio beams for lateral and vertical navigation to the touchdown point on a runway.

Integrated Drive Generator (IDG): An electric generator and a constant speed drive (CSD) combined into a single unit.

Just In Time (JIT) Inventory System: An inventory system that has products arrive just prior to their scheduled use, thus limiting waste and inefficiency.

Kaizen: Japanese for "continuous improvement."

Krueger Flap: See Flap, Leading Edge "Krueger"

Lean Manufacturing: A manufacturing discipline where waste (time and resources) is eliminated using a systematic method.

Localizer: A radio beam that aligns an aircraft with the final approach course to a specific runway.

Mach Number: The ratio of an aircraft's velocity to the speed of sound. For example, Mach .79 would represent seventy-nine percent of the speed of sound.

Mach Trim: A system added to compensate for the pitching effects associated with flight at high Mach numbers.

Master Caution System: A system designed to warn pilots of non-normal conditions and situations.

Minimum Equipment List (MEL): A document approved by the administrator that allows flight with certain inoperative equipment.

Mmo: Maximum certified Mach number.

Mode Control Panel (MCP): An interface between the pilot and the aircraft's autopilots and flight directors allowing the selection of different modes of operation.

Muda: A Japanese word for "wastefulness."

Mura: A Japanese word meaning "lack of conformity" or "unevenness."

Muri: A Japanese word for "unreasonableness" or "excessiveness."

Non-Directional Beacon (NDB): A low to medium frequency (190 Khz to 1750 Khz) transmitter used for navigation in conjunction with an automatic direction finder (ADF).

P-Static: A static electricity buildup on an airframe due to the effects of precipitation.

Performance Improvement Package (PIP): An enhancement on the 737NG aircraft using aerodynamic and engine modifications to improve fuel burn and reduce drag.

Pitch: An up or down movement of the nose of an aircraft while in flight.

Pitot-Static System: An aircraft system providing airspeed and altitude information by sampling ram air pressure and static air pressure for use with cockpit instrumentation and onboard aircraft systems.

Powerplant: An aircraft engine used for the generation of thrust.

Precession (Gyro): A change in the orientation of the axis of a gyroscope, such as an aircraft heading indicator (directional gyro) over time. Gyros that are not slaved to a compass will slowly become inaccurate over long periods of time unless periodically corrected.

Primary Flight Display (PFD): A modern flight instrument arrangement that combines all major fight instruments into a single EFIS based display.

Rejected Takeoff (RTO): A maneuver in which a takeoff is terminated and the aircraft is brought to a complete stop on the runway.

Required Navigation Performance (RNP): A type of navigation that allows a three-dimensional aircraft path between points while ensuring adequate precision through positional crosschecks using external and internal sources.

Roll: The motion of the aircraft tilting from side to side, also known as "banking." Airplanes use roll control to make directional changes to the flight path.

Rudder: A control surface attached to the vertical stabilizer of an airplane that controls the "yaw" (or nose side-to-side motion) of the aircraft.

Runway Visual Range (RVR): Horizontal visibility along a specific runway expressed in feet or meters.

SITA: A company that specializes in communication capability for air transport aircraft.

Slat, Leading Edge: A high lift device that extends from the top of the leading edge of a wing and allows the aircraft to be operated at much slower airspeeds, typically for takeoff and landing.

Spoiler: A panel on the upper surface of a wing that, when deployed, "spoils" the airflow, thus reducing lift and increasing aerodynamic drag.

Stall (Aerodynamic): A condition where the angle between the chord line of a wing and the passing air (angle of attack) becomes excessive, resulting in a turbulent airflow pattern on the wing and an attendant loss of lift.

Stall Characteristic: A term that describes the handling tendencies of an aircraft during an aerodynamic stall.

Thrust: Jet engine power, normally measured in pounds-force or kilonewtons.

Thrust Reverser: A device that deflects jet engine thrust and/or fan air forward to aid in slowing an aircraft during landing or a rejected takeoff.

Time Control Navigation: See Four Dimensional Navigation

Transformer-Rectifier: An electrical component that converts Alternating Current (AC) into Direct Current (DC).

T-tail: A popular tail design employing a horizontal stabilizer mounted on the upper tip of the vertical stabilizer.

Turbine: The section of a jet engine that converts energy from exhaust gasses into rotational force to drive the engine's compressors, fan section, and accessory drives.

Turbofan Engine: A subset of jet engines in which some of the air pulled into the intake bypasses the engine's core and is used for thrust.

Type Certificate Data Sheet: A specification the FAA uses as a basis for the certification of an aircraft

Type Inspection Authorization (TIA): An authorization granted once an aircraft manufacturer has demonstrated an aircraft type's compliance with regulations, allowing progression to aircraft certification.

Unimproved Field Kit ("Gravel Kit"): A feature specific to the Boeing 737-200 that allowed operations from unimproved gravel runways, easily identifiable with the installation of a large nose gear deflector.

V1: A calculated takeoff performance speed sometimes referred to as "decision speed," it is a speed below which a takeoff can be safely rejected and above which it can be safely continued with an engine failure. This speed must be between Vmcg (minimum control speed on the ground with a critical engine failed) and Vbe (the maximum speed at which the aircraft can be stopped without exceeding brake energy limits).

Vbe: The maximum speed at which the aircraft can be stopped without exceeding brake energy limits.

Vd: Maximum design speed, which is well in excess of Vmo.

Vertical Bounce: A two-cycle-per-second oscillation in pitch common on some early Boeing 737 test aircraft.

Vertical Stabilizer: The vertical component of an aircraft's tail that stabilizes the aircraft in "yaw" (nose side-to-side) and incorporates the aircraft's rudder, hinged to the trailing edge of the surface.

Vmcg: Minimum directional control speed on the ground with a critical engine failed with the remaining engine(s) at full power.

Vmo: The maximum airspeed an aircraft is certified to be flown at during normal flight.

Vmu: The minimum airspeed at which an aircraft can lift off and is substantially less than normal takeoff speeds given the same conditions.

Vortex Dissipator: A device intended to discourage the formation of a tornado-like air current. The 737-200, with the Unimproved Field Kit, used high pressure bleed air discharged under the engine inlets to accomplish this.

Vortex Generator: A small aerodynamic vane used to energize the boundary layer of air on wings and stabilizers. On the Boeing 737-100 through 737-900, vortex generators are also used on the aft fuselage to prevent vertical bounce.

Vr: The airspeed at which the nose is raised during a normal takeoff.

Vs: Aerodynamic stall speed.

Yaw: A nose side-to-side motion of an aircraft.

BIBLIOGRAPHY

Books

Avrane, A., M. Gilland and J. Guillem. *SUD-EST Caravelle.* London, England: Jane's, 1981.

Barton, Charles. *Tex Johnston: Jet-Age Test Pilot.* Washington, DC: Smithsonian Books, 1991.

Boeing Aircraft Company. *Boeing Advanced 737-200 Program Review.* Seattle, Washington: Boeing, 1985.

Boeing Aircraft Company. *Boeing 727 Flight Manual.* Seattle, Washington: Boeing, 1982.

Boeing Aircraft Company. *Boeing 737-300/-400/-500 Maintenance Manual.* Seattle, Washington: Boeing, 1985.

Boeing Aircraft Company. *Boeing 737-300 Program Review.* Seattle, Washington: Boeing, March 1987.

Boeing Aircraft Company. *Executive Overview: 737-600/-700/-800/-900.* Seattle, Washington: Boeing, December 1998.

Boeing Aircraft Company. *Product Review: 737-300/-400/-500.* Seattle, Washington: Boeing, January, 1997.

Boone, Pat. *Management Reference Guide about the Boeing 737: Edition CL and NG.* Herk-De-Stad, Belgium: MCC bvba, 2012.

Brady, Chris. *The Boeing 737 Technical Guide.* United Kingdom: Tech Pilot Services, 2006-2015.

Canova. *The Cockpit Review: B737-200/-300.* Gilbert, Arizona: Canova Publications, 1998.

Cearley, George W. *Boeing 707 and 720.* Self published, 1993.

Cole, Linda. *Western Airlines Flight Times, Volume 17, Number 7.* Los Angeles, California: Western Airlines, 1970

Darling, Kev. *de Havilland Comet.* Marlborough, United Kingdom: Crowood Press, 2005.

Duffy, Paul and Andrei Kandalov. *Andrei Tupolev, The Man and His Aircraft.* Shrewsbury, United Kingdom: Air Life Publishing, 1996.

Francillon, Rene J. *Boeing 707: Pioneer Jetliner.* London, United Kingdom: MBI Publishing, 1999.

Freiburg, Kevin & Jackie. *Nuts! Southwest Airlines' Crazy Recipe of Business and personal Success.* Austin, Texas: Bard Press, 1996.

Gibbs, Rebecca. *Classic Airliner: The BAC One-Eleven.* Kent, United Kingdom: Kelsey Media, 2013.

Green & Swanborough. *The Illustrated Encyclopedia of the World's Aircraft.* London, United Kingdom: Salamander Books, 1978.

Hewson, Robert & Tim Laming. *Airliner Color Series: Airbus A320.* London, United Kingdom: MBI Publishing, 2000.

Hill, Malcolm L. *Boeing 737.* Marlborough, United Kingdom: Crowood Press, 2002.

Hoffman, Bryce, G. *American Icon: Alan Mulally and the Fight to Save the Ford Motor Company.* Danvers, Massachusetts: Crown Publishing, 2012.

Hunecke, Klaus. *Jet Engines: Fundamentals of Theory, Design and Operation.* London, United Kingdom: Motorbooks, 1997.

Jenkins, Maureen. *Boeing Frontiers Online, August 2002, Volume 1, Issue 4: Getting Lean.* Seattle, Washington: Boeing, 2002.

Kemp, Kenny. *Flight of the Titans- Boeing and Airbus, and the Future of Air Travel.* London, United Kingdom: Virgin Books, 2006

Kissel, Gary. *Poor Sailor's Airline: A History of Pacific Southwest Airlines.* McLean, Virginia: Paladwr Press, 2002.

Kommisarov, Domitriy. *Tupolev Tu-134: The USSR's Short-Range Jet Liner.* Midland, United Kingdom: Aerofax, 2004.

Minton, David S. *Boeing 737.* New York City, New York: TAB Books, 1990.

Muse, Lamar. *Southwest Passage.* Woodway, Texas: Eakin Press, 2002.

Nicholls, Mark. *The Airliner World Book of The Boeing 737.* Stamford, United Kingdom: Key Publishing, 2003.

Otis, Charles E. & Peter A. Vosbury. *Encyclopedia of Jet Aircraft and Engines.* Inverness, Colorado: Jeppesen Sanderson, 1991, 1997.

Pearcy, Arthur. *Airliner Color History Series: McDonnell Douglas MD-80 & MD-90*. London, United Kingdom: MBI Publishing, 1999.

Sharpe, Michael & Robbie Shaw. *Airliner Color History Series Boeing 737-100 and 200*. London, United Kingdom: MBI Publishing 2001.

Shaw, Robbie. *Airliner Color History: Boeing 737-300 to 800*. London, United Kingdom: MBI Publishing Company, 1999.

Shaw, Robbie. *Baby Boeings by Robbie Shaw*. Oxford, United Kingdom: Osprey Publishing, 1998.

Skinner, Stephen. *BAC One-Eleven: The Whole Story*. Stored, Gloucestershire, United Kingdom: The History Press, 2013.

Smith, P.R. *Air Portfilios: Boeing 737*. London, United Kingdom: Jane's, 1986.

Sutter, Joseph. *747: Creating the World's first Jumbo Jet and Other Adventures from a Life in Aviation*. Washington, DC: Smithsonian Books, 2006.

Taylor, Richard W. *Worldwide Operation of Twin-Jet Aircraft (Past, Present and Future)*. Seattle, Washington: Boeing, October 19, 1983.

Waddington, Terry. *Great Airliners Volume 4: Mc Donnell Douglas DC-9*. Miami, Florida: World Transport Press, 1998.

Wallace, Lane. *Airborne Trailblazer*. US Government Printing Office, 1994.

Wallick, Rebecca. *Growing Up Boeing*. Lynnwood, Washington: Maian Meadows Publishing, 2014.

Wegg, John. *Caravelle: The Complete Story*. Miami, Florida: Airways International, 2005.

Wright, Alan J. *Modern Civil Aircraft: 9 - Boeing 737*. London, United Kingdom: Ian Allan Publishing, 1991.

Websites

www.aircraft-engines.co.uk/cfm.html

www.airfleets.net

www.airforce-technology.com/projects/737aewc/

www.airlinercafe.com

www.airliners.net

www.airport-data-com

www.airwaysnews.com

www.austrailianaviation.com.au

www.b737.org.uk

www.boeing.mediaroom.com

www.cisl.ucar.edu, SCD Supercomputer Gallery, Control Data Corporation (CDC) 6600

www.collegeparkaviationmuseum.com/about_us/history/ radio_navigation_aids.html

www.DC-9.com, History Tab

www.gereports.com

www.kirtland.af.mil. This Week in History: First Automatic Aircraft Landing

www.planelogger.com

www.planespotters.com

www.rbogash.com

www.wikipedia.com

Unpublished Works

Imrich, Thomas. "All Weather Operations: History, Certification, Testing and the Future." Unpublished manuscript. Federal Naval Administration.

Steiner, Jack. "Jack Steiner Memoirs." Unpublished manuscript, 1964-1967. Boeing Archives.

Steiner, Jack. "The Boeing 737." Unpublished manuscript. Boeing Archives.

Published Articles, Essays, and Reports

Bachman, Justin, and Mary Schlangenstein. "Southwest is launch customer for Boeing 737 MAX but won't get the first delivery," *The Seattle Times,* January 27, 2017.

Fadden, Delmar; Thomas Lindberg; Peter Morton, and Richard Taylor. "Evolution of the 2-Person Crew Jet Transport Flight Deck." *IEEE First Hand.* (July 2014).

Jacobsen, Meyers. " 'Catch our Smile' A History of Pacific Southwest Airlines." *AAHS Journal* 45, No 3.

Le Moine, Michel. "Mercure, Air Inter's Fighter Jet." *Airways Magazine.* (November 2010).

Maxon, Terry. "Southwest Airlines goes big as it introduces a new airplane type," *Dallas News,* March 21, 2012.

McLucas, Dr. John; Fred J. Drinkwater III, and Lt. General Howard Leaf, USAF. *Report of the President's Task Force on Aircraft Crew Compliment,* US Government, 1981.

Maxwell, Cass. "Zero-Zero but Safe." *Popular Aviation Magazine.* (August 1940).

Sloan, Chris. *A Historical Look at Boeing's 737 Factory in Renton,* Airline Reporter, 2013.

Unknown. *Bureau of Standards Journal of Research* 11, July 1933.

Unknown. *Global Competitiveness of US Advanced-Technology Manufacturing Industries: Large Civil Aircraft,* US International Trade Commission Report (August 1993): 332-332.

Unknown, *Orders, Deliveries, Operators - Worldwide,* Airbus, December 31, 2016.

Unknown. "The First Autolanding." *Air and Space Magazine.* (August 2012).

Media and Video

First Flights: The Jet Age. The Museum of Flight, 1988.

INDEX